STORIES *of the* SOUTHERN SEA

Lawrence Winkler

Note for Librarians: A cataloguing record for this book is available from Library and Archives Canada at www.collectionscanada.ca/amicus/index-e.html

Cover image by Claire Elliot
Cover design by Jenny Engwer, First Choice Books

ISBN – 978-0-9947663-8-0

Printed in Canada  on recycled paper

FIRST CHOICE BOOKS

firstchoicebooks.ca
Victoria, BC

10 9 8 7 6 5 4 3 2 1

Stories of the Southern Sea

For David Green

Amnesia
The Southern Sea

'Ocean: A body of water occupying about two-thirds of a world
made for man- who has no gills.'

Ambrose Bierce

It lives in the hole where the moon used to be. And for most
of the worst part of the northern winter, over the last two
decades, so have we.

I started off to write an idyll, but that didn't work out. Robyn
and I remembered only the Southern Sea bliss that filled our
nets, oblivious to the centuries of salt water that had run
through them without sticking, like the lesson of the
patriarchal fish.

> 'There are these two young fish swimming along and they happen to
> meet an older fish swimming the other way, who nods at them and
> says "Morning, boys. How's the water?" And the two young fish
> swim on for a bit, and then eventually one of them looks over at the
> other and goes "What the hell is water?"'

Memory travels in the opposite direction of the water that got
us here, and the water that got us here was less than utopian.
The Pacific hadn't been very pacific at all. Instead of *Rascals in
Paradise* among the *Happy Isles of Oceania*, I found myself
shipwrecked on a catalogue of crime and calamity.

The Stories of the Southern Sea are the stories of migrations,
traders and whalers, headhunters and cannibals, blackbirders
and pirates, beach bums, and of misfits and missionaries and
mercenaries. The *primus inter pares* of misfit missionary
mercenaries had been its European discoverer. Vasco Núñez
de Balboa was a bankrupt Hispaniolan planter and pig farmer,
who stowed away in a barrel with his dog, *Leoncico*, on
Fernández de Enciso's expedition to what would eventually

become Cartegena, in what would eventually become Colombia. Balboa was discovered, and spared long enough, to suggest that the settlement be moved to found the new colony of Santa María la Antigua del Darién. He went on, through ambition and subterfuge, to become the governor of Veragua, and was known for, among other things, his intolerance of homosexuality. Balboa had fifty native men torn apart by his fighting dogs.

'The Great Nations of Europe had gathered on the shore
they'd conquered what was behind them and now they wanted more
so they looked to the mighty ocean and took to the Western sea
The great nations of Europe in the 16th century

Hide your wives and daughters, hide the groceries too
The great nations of Europe comin' through...

Balboa found the Pacific and on the trail one day
he met some friendly Indians whom he was told were gay
So...
he had them torn apart by dogs on religious grounds they say
the great nations of Europe were quite holy in their way...'
Randy Newman, *The Great Nations of Europe*

A true conquistador, Balboa attacked some tribes and befriended others, explored rivers and mountains and miasmic swamps, searching for treasure and slaves, and enlarging his territory. He collected a fortune in gold, from the ornaments worn by the native women, but he wanted more.

In the lands of *cacique* Comagre, he heard of more. Comagre's eldest son, Panquiaco, angered by the Spaniards' avarice, knocked over the scales they used to measure gold. 'If you are so hungry for gold that you leave your lands to cause strife in those of others, I shall show you a province where you can quell this hunger.' He told Balboa of a kingdom to the south, where people were so rich that they ate and drank from gold plates and goblets, but that he would need at least a thousand men to defeat the tribes living inland and those on the coast of 'the other sea.'

Balboa started his journey across the Isthmus of Panama on September 1, 1513, together with 190 Spaniards, a few native guides, and a pack of his dogs. For the next three weeks he would fight tribal battles and dense jungle. At noon on September 25th, he reached Pechito Parado, the summit of the mountain range along the Chucunaque River. Far away on the horizon he saw a shimmering and, four days later Balboa raised his hands, his sword in one and a standard with the image of the Virgin Mary in the other, walked knee-deep into it, and claimed possession of the new breakers and all adjoining lands, in the name of the Spanish sovereigns. He named the ocean *Mar del Sur*, the Southern Sea, since he had traveled south to reach it.

On January 19, 1514, Balboa arrived back in Santa María with a treasure in cotton goods, more than a thousand pounds of gold, and as much in pearls. Five years later, Balboa was arrested on trumped-up charges by another conquistador named Francisco Pizarro (but he's another story). He was placed on trial by his father-in-law, Pedro Arias Dávila, and beheaded in a clumsy effort requiring three axe strokes, on January 15, 1519. A year after Balboa's head went on display in Panama, Ferdinand Magellan renamed his Southern Sea the *Pacific Ocean* because of its calm waters. A year after that, a bamboo spear in the Philippines would discredit the choice of appellation. Balboa would have a lunar crater named after him; Magellan would have two. But the San Diego park named after Balboa would slowly evolve in flamboyant irony, to host the largest gay pride festival on the west coast of the New World.

The Southern Sea has been promising paradise and delivering dismemberment since Tahitian temptation gave Captain Sam Wallis and his Dolphin crew a bare-breasted welcome in 1767. The overactive Western imagination mutinied and ran off with Rousseau's pretty Noble Savages, until our gifts of whiskey and guns and venereal disease and Christianity caught up with the palm frond perfection in their blue lagoons. Melville and Stevenson and Somerset Maugham and Michener spun us the great yarns of this ocean. And now it's my turn, to spin you a tapestry of tales.

Two hundred years after Pandora's box discharged its tortured contents into the Pacific, the frangipanis that once adorned their ears have morphed into mobile phones. Tattoos have become tacky. Dancing is done in the clubs, rather than with them.

The romance of the Southern Sea runs as deep as its trenches, but after years away from and behind it, an old man's subtropical mind can become torpid. We develop an amnesia of the alluring, in the same way and for the same reason that untold numbers of us travelled to the Pacific in the first place- to forget.

This is what I still remember of the islands, now so far in space and time. It is not a travelogue or a travel guide. It is in no way exhaustive or complete. I haven't been to all the islands, not even some of the bigger ones you'd think I should have visited. You won't find any stories of Hawaii or

New Guinea or the Marquesas. I haven't so much written you
an inventory, as a book of saline psalms. *This is water.*
It is what it is.

5

> 'Right now I'm having amnesia and déjà vu at the same time.'
> Steven Wright

*　　*　　*

Castaways
Juan Fernández

'We have found a strange footprint on the shores of the unknown.'
Arthur Eddington

"Jamon y queso?" Asked the pilot, handing a sandwich back from his cockpit. He had five sandwiches. They were all ham and cheese.

"Gracias." I said, taking another for Robyn, impressed with the bloodstains of the maraschino cherries embedded in the white bread.

"De dónde vienes?" Asked one of the other three passengers sitting across from us, in the back of the old Cessna. *Where are you from.*

"Canadá." I said. "Y Ustedes?" *And you.*

"Somos españoles." Said another. *Spaniards.*

"Están muy lejos de España y Canadá, muchachos." The pilot said. And he was right. We were a long way from home.

The morning had started early, on the tarmac of Santiago's Aeropuerto Los Cerillos. An old Cessna 206 sat under the company's logo. 'Cuando pasa el tiempo no hay lugar demasiado.' *When time flies there's no place too far.*

"It might be too far." Said Robyn. "It's only got one engine." When the pilot arrived with the sandwiches, he made a quick circuit around the plane, and motioned for us to find seats.

"Vamos." He said, taking his own. An erupting cloud of blue smoke from the cowling filed the flight plan. "Tres horas. Seiscientos kilómetros. Tal vez." *Three hours. Six hundred kilometers. Maybe.*

The twice-weekly flight sometimes located the island, sometimes didn't, if the weather even allowed it to get that far. We climbed out across the frigid Humboldt Current, six thousand feet over the jagged spine of the Andes. It occurred to me that we were only the second generation to have seen clouds from above, as well as from below. If the droning engine noise hadn't made conversation futile, the white faces and knuckles of the Spaniards wouldn't have produced much anyway.

Two long hours after the maraschino cherries disappeared, the pilot pointed to a small white cotton bud gradually emerging from over the far horizon.

"Isla Más a Tierra." He shouted. *Closer to Land.* We broke through the cloud cover to an island divided precisely in half, a green Amazon out the leeward windows, and a barren golden rusted rugged rocky Atacama moonscape off our port side. I asked the pilot where the airstrip was.

"Justo debajo de nosotros." He said. *Right below us.* And he banked high and around for his only shot at the shallow bowl between the two extinct volcanoes. Sheer cliff faces soared a hundred feet straight up off the surf on either side of his attempt. He had a split second after the wheels touched the lunar surface to swing his wings in a tight semicircle, so we wouldn't go off the grim precipice. He'd done it before. We taxied past the wreck of a Piper Navajo that hadn't been quite as proficient, lying flat on its belly with its windows and doors blown out. The Spaniards crossed themselves in tandem with the pilot's own invocation. *Repent, for the kingdom of heaven has come near.* The silence that returned was deafening.

Robyn and I emerged to a red and white striped windsock, waving at us, horizontal against heaven.

"Estamos aquí." Said the pilot.

"He says we're here." Said one of the Spaniards. There was no debate. We had landed on the largest and only inhabited island of the Archipiélago Juan Fernández, but the airstrip was still almost two hours away from Cumberland Bay and the only village of San Juan Bautista, *John the Baptist.* He was supposed to have pointed the way to Jesus. We looked around for a finger to point us in the direction of Juan

Bautista. The pilot indicated the route we were to take to join them.

"Sigue el sonido de las focas." He said, waving goodbye. *Follow the sound of the seals.* We all hoisted our packs and began a long hot dusty walk down a track. We could hear it barking at the bottom.

Juan Fernández first discovered the archipelago on November 22, 1574, when he strayed on the way from Peru to Valparaíso. The boots of the pirates that first made landfall on Más a Tierra, were unable to find dirt, for the density of Juan Fernández seals underfoot. '*We were forced to kill them to set our feet on shore.*' The maritime fur trade fixed that problem so perfectly that they, like the aromatic *Santalum fernandezianum* trees, and the rebellious convicts in the later penal colony that were hunted down after their escape back to mainland Chile, were thought to have become extinct. The colony of two hundred seals that were rediscovered in the mid-20th century, had multiplied back to a thunderous welcoming party, on the rocks near the long ramshackle wooden jetty, at the bottom of the steep switchback trail. The small black pups, with their short ears and stubby flippers and hairy manes and bulbous noses, had no memory of the previous tribal genocide, and approached us with playful curiosity and yelping fish breath, despite their mothers' raucous warnings.

At uneven intervals, in the troughs between the churning foam swells on Bahía del Padre, we made out the shape of a determined small craft, heading towards us. One moment it was visible, the next submerged. The two crewmen carefully stayed away from crashing directly into the pier, and skillfully timing the rollers, for just the right moment for us to throw our packs, and then ourselves, into the hard bottom of their lobster boat. Once loaded, and deeper in the cauldron, they nudged us out between the two rock pincers of the cove entrance, on the hour-long trip around the massive jagged vertical cliffs of the northern coast, and the foamed chaos dancing at their feet.

Despite the absence of vital signs or vegetation, I could see why this fragile island would have been an ideal pirate hideout- there was fresh water in abundance from waterfalls and streams, seals for meat and lamp oil and clothing, an equitable climate, and no snakes or predators. It was far enough from the Spanish authorities, but close enough to the shipping lanes of their treasure-laden galleons, closer still to the wild goats they had released here.

"Ese era su cueva, allí." Said one of the lobstermen. *That was his cave, there.* And we rounded the last point from Puerto Inglés, into calmer water, and half-moon Cumberland Bay at the base of the three thousand foot flat-topped fine-misted volcanic peak that towered above it. Clinging precipitously to the tortuous jagged side of El Yangue Mountain, rising abruptly from the sea and almost lost in a sweep of eucalypts, guayabas, and chanta trees, appeared a cluster of wood and tin huts, crowding the narrow shore.

"San Juan Bautista." Said the lobsterman. "Mi casa." A few lobster boats nodded on their moorings. The rest of the town didn't look any more awake.

We landed outside time and space. The refugees had likely forgotten how and why they came to this frontier of the spirit. The few that roamed the street moved at the pace of the bread rising for them at the bakery. They looked at us indifferently, almost like we weren't really there, as we reached the rocky beachhead. The dirt roads were as deeply rutted as the faces of the lobstermen, and the only conveyances, other than the mail jeep, were the wheelbarrows. The few hundred inhabitants were neither rich nor poor. Their bungalows were weathered but tidy, with chimney pots and small yards and sparse gardens, and big leafy palm or fruit trees. There was a Catholic and Mormon and Evangelical church, as many shops of similar denominations, a primary school, and a red telephone box, the nerve centre and meeting place for young aspiring *escapados.* A big round rusted plate hung suspended below the hand painted red and white sign at the top of the two tall metal poles, in front of the town hall. *Emergencia.* I wondered what they would ever need it for. We were four hundred miles from the nearest medical care, and only way to get there had taken off hours ago.

She was waiting for us at the end of the pier. Dafne owned a small guesthouse at the eastern end of the village, over the water. Her wet suit said she was going diving. She told us she was going diving.

"Quieres una langosta para más tarde?" She asked. Did we want a lobster for later. Robyn's eyes lit up the answer. We both said goodbye to the Spaniards, and Dafne took us along the shore to our cabaña. It had a kitchen with a gas stove, and a very large pot. Our carton of Santa Rita 120 wine from Santiago took its place alongside a box of custard powder on the only shelf. We were good to go.

The three-foot packhorse that Dafne brought us back from her swim barely fit in the cannibal pot on the stove. It came out as red as the Milky Way came on white, outside. All the other colors were waiting in our dreams.

As remote as it seemed on any map of the Pacific, the island we awoke to was downtown Southern Sea history and myth and wonder. Robyn and I found the first reason for this in the village cemetery, on a brass plaque with an Iron Cross centre, and a verdigris border.

'In treuer Pflichterfüllung für das Deutsche Vaterland starben den
Heldentod: Ing. Asp. Lerche Ober- Matr. Hunger Heizer Reuter...
S.M.S. Dresden 14 Marz 1945'

In faithful performance of duty for the German Fatherland, died a hero. In 1915, the only German ship to escape the Battle of the Falkland Islands scuttled herself in Cumberland Bay, both a white flag and her war ensign flying in the wind. A third of her crew decided to stay in Chile after the war, and their descendents, and those of an original Swiss San Juan Bautista settler, constitute the predominant human invasive species. Above our heads, in the face of the overhanging cliff, were numerous large British cruiser shell holes, as well as the back of a solitary unexploded eight-incher, still in place.

We continued up a grassy slope, through glades of cypress, conifers and eucalyptus, into a tall lowland forest of unique white-flowered peppery canelos and orange-fruited myrtles. Ferns lined the steep mountain path, small at first, but growing taller and into giant Dicksonia and Thyrsopteris tree ferns, as our trail became steeper, our footing more difficult on the slippery volcanic rock. Our pace was unhurried, slowed further by the peace inside the upper montane rainforest. Robyn and I floated in an exotic landscape of luma, muchay and narajillo, pushing up from the dark, moist forest floor, seeking sunlight. We felt cleansed, decontaminated. There came a sudden loud raspy staccato Doppler drone, rising and falling in pitch, motoring by at the speed of sound, a bright red bumblebee on steroids.

"There are less than two hundred left in the world." I said. "And they're all here." It came around for another supersonic pass, five inches long, cinammon-red with slate gray wings, and an iridescent crown of emeralds and rubies and gold.

"He's beautiful." Robyn said. And he was. *Sephanoides fernandensis.* The Juan Fernández Firecrown, the world's largest hummingbird. The Spanish call them *picaflores*. Flower pokers.

"He's also doomed." I said. "They eat endangered cabbage tree nectar, and nest in myrtles that are disappearing because of habitat loss from human destruction, blackberry invasion, and rabbits and goats. Domestic and feral cats are taking the last of them." And the red bomber went by one last time.

> 'From scarlet to powdered gold
> to blazing yellow
> to the rare
> ashen emerald,

to the orange and black velvet
of your shimmering corselet
out to the tip
that like
an amber thorn begins you,
small, superlative being,
you are a miracle,
and you blaze.'

Pablo Neruda, Ode to the Hummingbird

Robyn and I climbed higher, into brushwood forest, past waterfalls, tumbling down the mountain. In heavy storms, they would take the surrounding rocks and trees back down the way we had come, in raging torrents. We emerged onto an exposed escarpment, rigid palms waving their ballerina arms above the audience of hanging myrtle. A golden mirror of ocean sheen hugged the wild coast, under cloud shadows traveling rapidly over the mountainous desolation far below. We could hear the boom of it hurtling into the land, several miles away. And the wind that funneled down into Cumberland Bay. It had had taken us an hour and a half to climb to the lookout. Beside us was the plaque we had come to see.

'In memory of Alexander Selkirk, Mariner, a native of Largo, in the county of Fife, Scotland, who lived on this island in complete solitude, for four years and four months. He was landed from the Cinque Ports galley, 96 tons, 16 guns, A.D. 1704, and was taken off in the Duke, privateer, 12th Feb, 1709. He died lieutenant of H.M.S. Weymouth, A.D. 1728, aged 47 years. This tablet is erected near Selkirk's Lookout, by Commodore Powell and the officers of H.M.S. Topaz, A.D.1868.'

"He did this every day, for over four years?" Robyn asked. "Never get out of the boat." I said. "Absolutely goddamn right. Unless you were goin' all the way."

*   *   *

He was a pirate, a hothead and a knuckle-dragger. He was also the archetype of what we have come to consider the essence of the castaway.

Born in 1676, Alexander was the seventh son of a prosperous tanner and cobbler, John Selcraig, from Lower Largo, a Fife fishing village, across the Firth of Forth from Edinburgh, then a bustling metropolis of thirty thousand people. The small Scottish town had a fifteen-foot wide main street, lined by ancient sandstone row houses, with orange pantiled roofs and crow-stepped gables. His mother, Euphan Mackie, shielded him from the discipline of his father, who believed that Alex was 'spoiled and wayward,' and had planned for him to join his shoemaking business. Her overprotection resulted in a simmering 'domestic strife and bickering,' that only reinforced the young man's innate quarrelsome and unruly dispostion.

On August 25, 1695, the church elders at the Largo Kirk recorded that 'Alexr Selchcraig, son to John Selchcraig' had been summoned to appear for his 'undecent carriage in ye church.' Two days later, the elders further noted that the nineteen year-old 'did not compear being gone away to ye sea: this bussiness is continued till his return.' Alexander had fled with a Scottish colonizing expedition to Panama, on the ill-fated Darien Disaster.

He didn't fare much better on his return. In 1701, when his brother, Andrew, made the mistake of laughing at him, after tricking him into drinking seawater out of a tin, Alex beat him with a wooden staff. This ignited a family row that resulted in a further assault on his father, his brother, John, and even John's wife, Margaret Bell. Once again he was 'compeared befor the pulpit and made acknowledgment of his sin... and was rebuked in face of the congregation for it, and promised amendment in the strength of the lord, and so was dismissed.' But Alex, 'a bit of a bastard, more respected in his absence than in his presence,' was fed up, and decided to join the English privateers being recruited against French and Spanish interests, a new opportunity derived from the War of the Spanish Succession.

The privateers of the time were as sadistically unsavory in reality, as portrayed in our literature and legends. The eighteenth century pirate, Edward Low, cut off his prisoners' lips and broiled them in front of them. Others employed the practice of 'woolding,' tightly twisting slender cords around the necks of their prisoners until their eyes burst from their sockets. The crew was just as dispensible, and their yellow fever scurvy-afflicted bodies were routinely dumped at sea. Pirate vessels stank of animals and excrement. Buccaneers captured in British colonies received no mercy. Their bodies were displayed in steel cages suspended at port entrances *'pour encourager les autres.'*

The pirate that young Alexander Selkirk found was one of history's most complex, and reluctant. He had been court-martialed for cruelty to a crewmember, after losing the British warship HMS Roebuck off the Australian coast. He was often drunk, and often let captured ships go free without looting them, a practice that infuriated his crew. Some thought him indecisive or incompetent, and he once narrowly escaped being eaten by his own men in the Pacific. But William Dampier was a gifted amateur naturalist and anthropologist, and had already circumnavigated the world three times, when Alexander signed up with him, and changed his last name to Selkirk. Dampier made him Master of the Galley under Captain Charles Pickering of the 120 ton Cinque Ports, while he commanded his own 320-ton flagship. The St. George was supplied for eight months of travel with two sets of sails, five anchors, 22 cannons, 100 small arms, 30 barrels of gunpowder and 120 men, five times more than it could comfortably accommodate- a morbid acknowledgment of how many would be lost to disease, battle and desertion. Both vessels were small by Royal Navy standards, and crewed by deperate men.

On April 30, 1703, the two ships embarked for the port of Kinsale, in Ireland. Dampier had a drunken violent argument with one of his officers, the first night they arrived. They left Kinsale on the 11th of September, and made Madeira two weeks later. When their original plan to attack the Spanish galleons returning from Buenos Aires fell through, Dampier decided to make for the Southern Sea by way of the Cape Verde Islands, and across the Atlantic and around Cape Horn.

By the end of October, the men were sick of dried peas, rock-hard sea biscuits, and salt meat. The occasional shark, dolphin, or weary bird was their only source of fresh food. They slept in wet clothes and mildewed bedding, perfect incubators for typhus, dysentery and cholera. By the time they had made the Brazilian coast, their remaining meat and grain was infested with roaches and rat droppings, the vitamin C deficiency had kicked in, and forty-eight men, including

Alex's Captain Pickering, had died of scurvy. His replacement, a 21 year-old upperclass lieutenant named Thomas Stradling, was so detested by the crew that continuous squabbling, and the constant threat of mutiny, became the onboard culture. The two ships had been separated rounding the Horn. Stradling holed up the Cinque Ports in Cumberland Bay, and Dampier caught up to him just in time to put down his crew's rebellion. Both ships continued up the Pacific coast as far as Mexico, capturing several Spanish ships en route. But by March of 1704, the two captains were in conflict, and Stradling had attacked Dampier as 'a drunk who marooned his officers, stole treasure, hid behind blankets and beds when it came time to fight, took bribes, boasted of impossible prizes and when there was plunder to hand, let it go.' In May, they decided to deliberately separate, and Stradling headed back south to Juan Fernández, to reprovision. The Cinque Ports was leaking so badly that the crew was pumping out water around the clock. Selkirk told Stradling that it was so riddled with worms that the masts and flooring were in danger of collapse. He began to argue with Stradling that the ship's unseaworthiness was a deathtrap, to no avail. In October, loaded with turnips and goats and crayfish, Stradling ordered him to prepare the ship to leave. Selkirk refused, indicating that he would rather be left on Más a Tierra. It was the most important decision of his life. Stradling granted his wish.

'He was put ashore from a leaky vessel, with the captain of which he had had an irreconcilable difference; and he chose rather to take his fate in this place, than in a crazy vessel, under a disagreeable commander. His portion were a sea-chest, his wearing clothes and bedding, a firelock, a pound of gunpowder, a large quantity of bullets, a flint and steel, a few pounds of tobacco, a hatchet, a knife, a kettle, a Bible, and other books of devotion, together with pieces that concerned navigation, and his mathematical instruments.'

Richard Steele, *The Englishman* 1711

No sooner had he waded into Cumberland Bay than Selkirk was overcome with fear and regret. He begged to be allowed back, but Stradling took great pleasure in refusing. Selkirk read his Bible, resigned to waiting for what he thought would be a few days, until another ship sailed by. He was wrong by four years and four months.

He found a cave on the beach, from which he barely moved for the first eighteen months. Frequent tree-snapping gales brought him to 'a state of terror and dejection.' He regretted the decision to abandon his ship and crewmates, shackled himself to the hope for rescue, and became ever more

> '...dejected, languid, and melancholy, scarce able to refrain from doing himself violence, till by degrees, by the force of reason, and frequent reading of the Scriptures, and turning his thoughts upon the study of navigation, after the space of eighteen months, he grew thoroughly reconciled to his condition.'

He initially survived on fish, which 'occasion'd a Looseness' in his bowels, and then turtle meat, 'till it grew disagreeable to his stomach, except in jellies.' Despite the fact that he was surrounded by ocean, he craved the inaccessible salt it contained. But he also had shellfish, and learned to boil the giant crayfish with his pepper berries, and managed to kill an occasional seal with his hatchet.

When his beach was invaded by hundreds of mating southern elephant seals, nineteen feet long and weighing up to two tons, their nocturnal wailing, and the approaching winter cold rain and howling winds funneled through the canyons, drove him to his senses, and inland.

In a grove of shade trees beside a stream on high ground, Selkirk built himself two huts out of pimento trees, with roofs of thatched grass. He constructed a crude bed, and covered it, and the huts' walls, with skins from the feral goats he shot.

When his gunpowder ran out, he learned how to run them down on foot.

The goat he landed on had cushioned his fall, and likely saved him from a broken back. Alex hamstrung some of the captives, and domesticated their kids, to provide him with milk and meat, with which he prepared 'a hearty goat broth with turnips, watercress and cabbage palm, seasoned with black pimento pepper.' Goatskins were sewn into garments, with a Cinque Ports nail he had fashioned into a makeshift needle. When his original ship's knife finally wore out, he forged new ones from iron barrel staves he had found on the beach. He cut his name into the trees.

The big fierce ships rats that had overrun the island tore at Selkirk's clothing and feet as he slept. His solution was to tame the feral cats that had arrived with them, into bed companion exterminators.

He exercised his mind and speech and spirit, by singing hymns and reading his daily bible devotions out loud.

'He was a better Christian while in this Solitude than ever he was before.' Without the vices of alcohol and tobacco, and salt and society, deep new truths revealed themselves through the cleansing simplicity of the demands of survival. As the volcanic terrain hardened his feet, his heart softened from its intimacy with his natural environment, running like the wind, from thug to Thoreau, blazing with the firecrowns.

But Captain Rogers wouldn't get to make that observation,

until he rescued Selkirk, and he wouldn't get to rescue Selkirk, until Alex had trekked to his lookout every day, almost sixteen hundred times. The first two ships that came to anchor in Cumberland Bay had been Spanish. The crew that spotted him, ended their pursuit with a collective urination beneath the tree he was hiding in, without detecting the additional heartbeat. Alex knew that, if he had been captured, he would have been enslaved into the South American gold mines. From that moment, he was careful with fires.

Selkirk's long-awaited salvation came on 2 February 1709, on the Duke, a pirate ship captained by Woodes Rogers, and piloted by his old commander, William Dampier.

> 'Immediately our Pinnace return'd from the shore, and brought abundance of Craw-fish, with a man Cloth'd in Goat-Skins, who look'd wilder than the first Owners of them.'

After so long without human company, Selkirk was incoherent with joy. 'So much forgot his Language for want of Use, that we could scarce understand him, for he seem'd to speak his words by halves.'

But they were all impressed with his physical vigour and agility, enough to bring down the two or three goats a day that restored the health of the expedition, and eliminated its scurvy. Rogers was more inspired by Selkirk's mental tranquility.

> 'One may see that solitude and retirement from the world is not such an insufferable state of life as most men imagine, especially when people are fairly called or thrown into it unavoidably, as this man was.'

As Selkirk's adamantine soles swelled in his new constraining footwear, his spirit was liberated with Dampier's story of how the Cinque Ports had indeed foundered off the coast of Colombia. Stradling and the half dozen survivors of his crew were taken to Lima, and left to rot in prison.

It would still take Selkirk almost three more years to arrive back in the Thames estuary. Rogers made him the navigator and second mate of the Duke, and then the commander of one of his prize ships, the Increase. In 1712, with his £800 share of treasure from all the Spanish galleons they had looted along the way, Alex traded his goatskins for elegant clothes of fine lace and gold, and surprised his family as they worshipped in the Largo Kirk. They had long before given him up for dead, and it wasn't long before their remorse had returned with his ghost.

Alexander wanted little to do with his relatives, preferring the cave-like shelter he built behind his father's house. He became a recluse, and resumed his drinking and fighting. A year after his grand reentrance, he was arrested for an assault on a Bristol shipwright. Four years later, he eloped to London with a sixteen year-old dairymaid, named Sophia Bruce. On a visit to Plymouth, he abandoned her to marry Frances Candis, a widowed innkeeper. In March of 1717, he left them both behind forever, to return to the sea as first mate of the HMS Weymouth, bound for Guinea and the Gold Coast, in search of pirates. A year later, he watched as a yellow fever outbreak on his warship began to destroy three or four men a day. On December 13, 1721, it destroyed Selkirk. 'North to northwest. Small Breeze and fair. Took 3 Englishmen out of a Dutch ship and at 8 pm. Alexander Selkirk . . . died.' As with the others, they threw his body overboard. He was 44 years old, and immortal. On New Year's Day of 1966, Chilean president Eduardo Frei renamed the smaller of the two main Juan Fernández Islands, Alejandro Selkirk Island. It had been called Más Afuera, *Further Away*. But it was the island that he marooned himself on, Más a Tierra, *Closer to Land*, the one that archeologists found his copper navigational dividers on thirty-nine years later, the one that Robyn and I had visited, that got the mythical name. Isla Robinson Crusoe.

'He had with him his clothes and bedding, with a firelock, some powder, bullets and tobacco, a hatchet, a knife, a kettle, a Bible, some practical pieces, and his mathematical instruments and books. He diverted and provided for himself as well as he could, but for the first eight months had to bear up against melancholy, and the terror of being left alone in such a desolate place. He built two huts with pimento trees, covered them with long grass, and lined them with the skins of goats, which he killed with his own gun as he wanted, so long as the powder lasted, which was but a pound; and that being almost spent he got fire by rubbing two sticks of pimento wood together upon his knee... After he had conquered his melancholy, he diverted himself sometimes with cutting his name on trees, and of the time of his being left, and continuance there. He was at first much pestered with cats and rats that bred in great numbers from some of each species which had got ashore from ships that put in there for wood and water. The rats gnawed his feet and clothes whilst asleep, which obliged him to cherish the cats with his goats' flesh, by which so many of them became so tame, that they would lie about in hundreds, and soon delivered him from the rats. He likewise tamed some kids; to divert himself, would now and then sing and dance with them and his cats; so that by the favor of providence, and the vigor of his youth, being now but thirty years old, he came, at last, to conquer all the inconveniences of his solitude, and to be very easy...When his clothes were worn out he made himself a coat and a cap of goat skins, which he stitched together with little thongs of the same, that he cut with his knife. He had no other needle but a nail; and when his knife was worn to the back he made others, as well as he could, of some iron hoops that were left ashore, which he beat thin and ground upon stones. Having some linen cloth by him, he sewed him some shirts with a nail and, stitched them with the worsted of his old stockings, which he pulled out on purpose. He had his last shirt on when we found him on the island.'

Capt. Woodes Rogers, *A Voyage Around the World*, London, 1712.

'I am now worth £800, but shall never be so happy, as when I was not worth a farthing.'

Alexander Selkirk

*   *   *

'At sea a fellow comes out. Salt water is like wine, in that respect.'
Herman Melville

It was the first story of the Southern Sea.

On 25 April 1719, just over a decade after Selkirk's rescue, and a year before his death off the African coast, an English merchant, political prisoner, and spy, published the first edition of his tale about a marooned sailor, surviving by the goatskin of his wits on a deserted Caribbean island. Daniel Defoe lived in an era when British booksellers, who carried the titles of controversial writers, were hung in public. But this book, *The Life and Strange Surprizing Adventures of Robinson Crusoe, of York, Mariner: Who lived Eight and Twenty Years, all alone in an uninhabited Island on the Coast of America, near the Mouth of the Great River of Oroonoque; Having been cast on Shore by Shipwreck, wherein all the Men perished but himself. With An Account how he was at last as strangely deliver'd by Pyrates,* created an eternal myth, a legend so real that, to this day, there are some Tobago islanders, who proudly proclaim one of the world's most famous fictional characters as an ancestor.

Robinson Crusoe was the first true English novel. Chock full of sailing ships and stormy seas and exotic desert islands, and muskets and wild boars and cannibals, it set the standard for every adventure story that followed.

Far more than exuberant action thriller, set in a faraway locale, *Robinson Crusoe* was the symbolic narrative of a lone man's ability to face the ultimate tests of nature, and emerge triumphant over hardship and adversity. Some felt that it was a Christian allegory for the development of civilization. James Joyce described Defoe's protagonist as 'the true prototype of the British colonist.' His enduring faith and steadfastness helped establish and promulgate the myth of colonial supremacy. Robert Louis Stevenson's assessment of the footprint scene as 'the most unforgettable in English literature,' confirmed Friday's rescue from his cannibal pursuers as the precedential paradigm of the White Man's

Burden. But those grandiose insights and claims still understated the larger significance of the legend that Defoe had created.

In 1731, a decade after Selkirk's death, and another before Defoe's, a German writer named Johann Gottfried Schnabel, in the preface of his work Die Insel Felsenburg, *The Island Stronghold*, coined a term that would become emblematic for the spawn of imitations that would define a renegade literary genre. *Robinsonade.*

In the classic robinsonade, the hero is suddenly isolated from the comforts of civilization, usually shipwrecked or marooned on a secluded island, often located in the Pacific, tropical, uninhabited and usually uncharted. He must improvise to become self-sufficient from the limited resources at hand. At its essence, the robinsonade is a Man versus Nature conflict, a solitary statement of survivalism.

The infinite number of potential storyline combinations and permutations, are tempered by thematic elements common to them all. There is always isolation, be it on a desert island, a virgin planet, a Lost World, or any other sufficiently remote wild wilderness. The principle characters are making a new beginning. There are encounters with natives, hostile or helpful, which leads to a commentary on the essence of society, and the construction of a new one, for better or worse, depending on the skill level of the castaway. A difficult ordeal, involving conflict, is required for character development, as typifies every hero quest. Elements of technological change and economic advancement, in the context of the assumed innate antagonism of nature, are important. The solitude had to lead back to society, or the ordeal would have no meaning. The natural world in which the castaway found himself could only take one of two forms, nice or nasty.

Thomas More had depicted nature as idyllic, and the Utopian robinsonades range from ingenious recreations of society's comforts, as in Swiss Family Robinson, to more questionably humorous forms, like Gilligan's Island. The two other iconic real-life desert island paradise robinsonades arrived on Pitcairn with the Bounty mutineers, and with New Zealander Tom Neale's *An Island to Oneself*, the autobiography of his sixteen years on Anchorage Island, in the Suwarrow atoll. Western literature, with its monotheistic estrangement from, and inherent antagonism to, the natural world, has many more Dystopian representations of robinsonades as less escapism than requiring escape. Defoe portrayed Crusoe's remote island as unforgiving and sparse, his Bible-reading, superior cultured, principle character managing to prevail in conflicts with heathens, and survive the elements, by virtue of his virtue.

> 'I am monarch of all I survey,
> My right there is none to dispute;
> From the centre all round to the sea,
> I am lord of the fowl and the brute.'
>
> William Cowper, *The Solitude of Alexander Selkirk*

Other wild wildernesses are hostile pits of savagery, and the castaways undergo feral regression, thematically best represented in Fielding's *Lord of the Flies*, Garland's *The Beach*, or a dozen other works of especially United States origin. The Americans are rather more utopian about the powers of human achievement, and definitely more dystopian about the friendliness of nature. They have a special affinity for post-apocalytic fantasy, in no small measure because they live so removed from Mother Earth, having historically used the U.S. Cavalry and the Army corps of engineers to move her out of the way of their pursuit of progress. The illusion of a secure existence off *The Road,* in a gated community theme park, is preferable to the reality of sharing their lives with the creepy crawlies, and an armed and paranoid populace. They can watch the latest episode of *Survivor* from their condo couch comfort, and leave the bugs to the *Starship Troopers*.

But even the beautifully seductive literary genre of the

robinsonade, and the salts it precipitated, sells the significance of *Robinson Crusoe* short of a bigger impact.

In his quest for survival, the robinsonade castaway not only becomes a perfect study about the man of nature, but the nature of man.

Before being complicated by more complex philosophers, Alexander Selkirk's biographer, Irish politician and *Spectator* founder, Richard Steele, had summarized its essential lesson. *This plain Man's Story is a memorable Example that he is happiest who confines his Wants to natural Necessities.*

This was a direct contradiction of the prevailing belief of the time that, without a strong central political authority to regulate the 'state of nature,' people would have a right, or license, to everything in the world, leading to a *bellum omnium contra omnes*, a 'war of all against all.'

The theory was the brainchild of a social contract theorist, Thomas Hobbes who, also born prematurely when his mother heard of the coming invasion of the Spanish Armada, had later remarked that she 'had given birth to twins: myself and fear.' During his formative writing years, the English Civil War of the time, grew his fear into a forest.

Hobbes had maintained, in the doctrine he outlined in his *Leviathan or The Matter, Forme and Power of a Common Wealth Ecclesiasticall and Civil*, that the nature of man of the man in nature is inherently evil, and must cede rights to government as the price of peace.

> 'In such condition, there is no place for industry; because the fruit thereof is uncertain: and consequently no culture of the earth; no navigation, nor use of the commodities that may be imported by sea; no commodious building; no instruments of moving, and removing, such things as require much force; no knowledge of the face of the earth; no account of time; no arts; no letters; no society; and which is worst of all, continual fear, and danger of violent death; and the life of man, solitary, poor, nasty, brutish, and short.'
>
> Chapter XII: Of the Natural Condition of Mankind As Concerning Their Felicity, and Misery, *Leviathan*

Hobbes left his last words, 'a great leap in the dark,' as a metaphoric legacy. The man that helped undo his influence, had an entirely different view of natural man.

In July of 1750, the Academy of Dijon established a prize competition for anyone who could answer the question, 'What is the origin of inequality among men, and is it authorized by natural law?' A Genevan romantic philosopher, Jean-Jacques Rousseau, submitted his *Discours sur l'origine et les fondements de l'inégalité parmi les homes,* 'Discourse on the Origin and Basis of Inequality Among Men,' in which he attempts to discredit Hobbes, for taking an overly cynical view of the species.

Rousseau's natural man possesses two essential benevolent innate characteristics- *'amour de soi meme'* love of self, and compassion for the suffering of others. These, he maintains, are the actual properties that have preserved us through time, not a constant fear of death, which we cannot really appreciate, because it moves out of the state of nature. Like other animals, man is concerned with 'food, a female, and sleep.' Rousseau's man is a 'savage,' self-sufficient loner, fast, strong, and capable of looking after himself. He only killed for his own self-preservation. The only qualities that distinguish him from the other natural creatures are our *'libre-arbitre'* free will, and our perfectability to develop more sophisticated survival tactics. Rousseau maintains that it is our interaction with those of our own species which transmutes his natural self-love into a state of *amour proper*, a corrupted love of self deriving from a dependency on the perceptions and favors of others. This results in competition, self-comparison with others, hatred, the urge to acquire power, and a decamping from our state of nature. The true evil that man is capable of, comes from the institution of property.

'The first man who, having fenced in a piece of land, said "This is mine," and found people naïve enough to believe him, that man was the true founder of civil society. From how many crimes, wars, and murders, from how many horrors and misfortunes might not any one have saved mankind, by pulling up the stakes, or filling up the ditch, and crying to his fellows: Beware of listening to this impostor; you are undone if you once forget that the fruits of the earth belong to us all, and the earth itself to nobody.'

Rousseau goes on to define the origin of society as the establishment, by convention, of a moral inequality characterized by enforced differences in power and wealth. He cynically asserts that civil society is anything but, a trick perpetrated by the powerful on the weak, a result of our having strayed from the true nature in man.

Unfortunately for Rousseau, the judges weren't buying it. The Académie des Sciences, Arts et Belles-Lettres de Dijon still exists, and still offers the prize.

Our original Juan Fernández castaway seems to have inspired Defoe's own fascinating adventure story, a template for an entire genre of literature, and an ongoing essential philosophical debate about the man of nature, and the nature of man. And still this is not his only accomplishment.

Selkirk's decision is an embodiement of all the myth and legend and allegory of life itself. We are all castaways, beautiful innocent natural savages marooned on our own islands of self-love, compassion, self-sufficiency, free will, and perfectibility. We are all awaiting rescue. Robinson Crusoe is not just the first story of the Southern Sea. He is the epic narrative of human experience, the heroic poem of our individual and collective existence. Everything we carry in our hearts followed his first footprint in the sand.

'But all I could make use of, was, All that was valuable. I had enough to
eat, and to supply my Wants, and, what was all the rest to me? If I kill'd
more Flesh than I could eat, the Dog must eat it, or the Vermin. If I
sow'd more Corn than I could eat, it must be spoil'd. The Trees that I
cut down, were lying to rot on the Ground. I could make no more use
of them than for Fewel; and that I had no Occasion for, but to dress
my Food.'

Daniel Defoe, Robinson Crusoe

*   *   *

'The shattered water made a misty din.
Great waves looked over others coming in,
And thought of doing something to the shore
That water never did to land before.'
Robert Frost, *Once By The Pacific*

On our last day on Isla Robinson Crusoe, Robyn and I met a plant biologist named Luis, in his conservancy greenhouse. He spoke eloquently about how, out of over two hundred native species of vascular plants, found nowhere else in the world, over seventy per cent were on the endangered list. A ray of sunlight landed on an enchanting small flower, stretching strange white petals, out of a small black pot.

"Es el ultimo." He said. *The last one.*

At the appointed time, we walked back past the town hall, beside the *Emergencia* rusted gong, suspended between its two tall metal poles, and timed an entry jump back into the open lobster boat that would take us back around the island to our return flight. As we bobbed along against the waves, one of the crew produced two large local crayfish, and two cardboard boxes for the return flight. These men had little, and we were humbled by their gift. Our old pilot greeted us as warmly, and told us how fortunate we were to have left with such a gesture. "Vamos." He said, motioning for us to find seats, and taking his own. The same erupting cloud of blue smoke from the cowling filed the flight plan. "Tres horas. Seiscientos kilómetros. Tal vez." *Three hours. Six hundred kilometers. Maybe.* The same maraschino cherries blood-stained the white bread of the ham and cheese that he handed over his shoulder on our rescue.

Our landing at Los Cerillos felt like Selkirk's return to Largo. Robyn and I arrived rich with stories and sea plunder, and decided to head for the coastal garden town of Viña del Mar, the same afternoon. We boarded the subway to begin our journey, precariously balancing our large boxes in our laps.

An elderly woman took the seat beside us, on the outside of our row. Our boxes jumped violently on our knees, as we left the station. She looked at us with a mixture of fear and suspicion.

"Langostas." I said. And the tension in her face relaxed.

An hour and a bit later, we were climbing the stairs to the lobby of a seaside hotel. The concierge greeted us, and I asked him to fetch me the chef. A sturdy white stained uniform emerged from the kitchen a few minutes later. I opened a crack in one the boxes to daylight, and asked him if he knew how to cook these *crustáceos*.

"Ciertamente, Señor." He said, with obvious admiration for our prizes. I told him we'd be down in an hour.

Robyn and I checked into our room and showered off the Southern Sea. Refreshed, we descended to the floor to ceiling glass harbour vista, in the busy restaurant. We were seated at a rare window table and, as few minutes later, a bottle of sauvignon blanc, and two giant red crayfish arrived with a flourish. The clamor of all conversations around us stopped dead. Diners from other tables began pointing in our direction. One group of Santiago businessmen next to us became insistent, and asked to see the chef. He arrived in the dining room, radiating a mischievous grin, as he approached the pinstriped executives. They demanded to know why he was refusing to provide them with the same delicacies that these Gringos were enjoying.

"Son los últimos. Náufragos." He said, shrugging his shoulders. *They're the last ones. Castaways.*

On February 27, 2010, a twelve year-old girl, named Martina Maturana, finally rang the rusted gong, suspended between its two tall metal poles, on Robinson Crusoe Island. A ten foot high tsunami came along right behind it, destroying most of San Juan Bautista, and killing eight of her neighbours outright, and causing eleven other to disappear. She had saved the rest with her quick actions, and compassion.

'To-day we love what to-morrow we hate; to-day we seek what to-morrow we shun; to-day we desire what to-morrow we fear.'
Daniel Defoe, Robinson Crusoe

*　　*　　*

'I was now landed, and safe on shore, and began to look up and thank God that my life was sav'd in a case wherein there was some minutes before scarce any room to hope. I believe it is impossible to express to the life what the extasies and transports of the soul are, when it is so sav'd, as I may say, out of the very grave…'
Daniel Defoe, Robinson Crusoe

Seven years after Rousseau submitted his Second Discourse, he published his neo-romantic novel *Julie ou la Nouvelle Héloïse*. Extolling a love for nature, and the '*mythe du bon sauvage*' hidden in its pages, its release was so popular, that it was rented by the hour in French bookshops. Rousseau's hero was modeled after George Anson, the English naval commander, who had been contracted by the South Seas Company in 1740, for a mission to disrupt or capture Spain's Pacific possessions. Poorly provisioned, and with impossible orders, his benefactors expected his expedition to live off the pillage of the sea, and the land. By the time he limped into Juan Fernández, at daybreak on the 9th of June of the following year, Anson had lost sight of his five other ships, having taking nine days, and the further loss of an additional eighty men, to even find the islands, because of the mistake in his navigation charts. The delay, however, may have save his life, as he arrived after the last Spanish ship had left. His crew

32

was too weak to lift the anchor, and took several weeks to recover their strength. Their improvement led to questions that eventually helped identify vitamin C deficiency as the cause of scurvy. Anson's later capture of the Acapulco galleon, *Nuestra Señora de Covadonga*, off the coast of the Philippines, made him a rich man. His circumnavigation of the globe laid the basis for subsequent scientific and survey expeditions by Captain Cook. Only 188 of his original 1854 sailors had survived the voyage. Anson's exploits were documented in the 1748 publication of *A Voyage Round the World*. He served as the prototype for Patrick Obrien's Aubrey-Maturin series, which in turn provided the inspiration for *Master and Commander: The Far Side of the World*. An incident on his round the world voyage was the subject of William Cowper's famous rhyme of this ancient mariner.

> 'They left their outcast mate behind,
> And scudded still before the wind...
> No poet wept him: but the page
> Of narrative sincere,
> That tells his name, his worth, his age,
> Is wet with Anson's tear.'

The poem was called *The Castaway*.

*　　*　　*

Tide Table
Chiloé

'I believe that every one was glad to say farewell to Chiloe; yet if we could forget the gloom and ceaseless rain of winter, Chiloe might pass for a charming island. There is also something very attractive in the simplicity and humble politeness of the poor inhabitants.'
Charles Darwin, *The Voyage of the Beagle*

Darwin had it wrong, of course. He was there in the summer. Which made it all the worse. Between the climate and the Spaniards, everything else had been beaten out of the poor inhabitants. What he got right, was the charm.

Robyn and I crossed the Chacao Channel, on the last day of the year. We always left our New Year's Eve celebrations to the 'Fates,' the three white-robed incarnations of Destiny, the spinner, measurer, and abhorred shearer of the thread of our lives. Chiloé would be no exception. Even if we wanted to party, there was nowhere, and no way, to make a reservation. We followed behind the logging truck on the concrete pier, filling the rest of the small space on the 'Adriana B.'

Our ferry crossing against the primordial strength of the Southern Sea, along the string of volcanoes crowned by Corcovado, had brought us to a desolation rich, as on Juan Fernandez, in lurid tales of English pirates, mutinies, castaways, and sadistic Spaniards. As with our Vancouver Island home, the desolation required grey skies and relentless rain, impenetrable blackish-green rainforests, a shy and diffident citizenry in knitted woolen clothing, and sonorous Indian placenames and quiet Indian canoes.

Inside all three archipelagos, there had been earth tremors and tsunamis, and shipwrecks and seafood survival.

But on Chiloé there was a distinct and dark mythology that the other two shorelines lacked. Seventy years behind Pablo Neruda, Robyn and I had come to find it. *Towards the Islands... nothing seemed to us far, everything could become entangled in any moment in the light that we produced.*

Beyond the ferry dock, there wasn't much left of Chacao, since the Spanish Governor of Chile, Carlos de Beranger, moved the original loyalist population, twenty miles further away from the upstart Chilean secessionist rebels. In 1768, he constructed a new settlement with the usual Hispanic architectural grandeur, and included a large Plaza de Armas, adjacent to the colossal Ahui fortress, impregnable, and bristling with lethal cannons and a string of land batteries, at the tip of the Lacuy peninsula. He named it after King Charles III, San Carlos de Chiloé, now Ancud. It would take almost sixty years for the Republicans to wrest it from the Spaniards, and only after two failed direct attacks, and a long siege. A hundred and seventy years on, we boarded a *Cruz del Sur* bus from another era, its vintage round rusted rooflines softened even further by the eternal dissolution of water and salt, washing over its curvature. As the driver plodded up his gearshift, the drizzle turned to downpour.

In the entire round the world *Voyage of the Beagle*, the only thing that Darwin had ever complained about, was the weather in Chiloé. *In winter the climate is detestable, and in summer it is only a little better.* But it was the rain and fog, and unique insularity, which had precisely fashioned its identity. The steep stony roads had been potholed by the water (like the original Huilliche *indigenes* had been pockmarked and decimated by the smallpox) tortuously and torturously winding to avoid the two lakes and the hundreds of creeks and bays that crisscrossed the island, and forced to detour and wander. Chiloé was the tenth proglottid segment of the Chilean tapeworm, its fertilised eggs connected to the rest of the world by a ship that came from Lima, once a year. Information didn't exist, food and accommodation was precarious and primitive, and nothing much had changed. But it was the subject of Darwin's only complaint that created one of the most beautiful places on the planet, a vast archipelago of iridescent mountainous island forests, fjords, a chain of active volcanoes, and broad beaches stretching south, to glaciers decending into the sea from the frozen continental shelf. The towns belonged to the Southern Sea, and the sea belonged to their tiny two-masted *lanchons*, and the whales and dolphins and sea lions and marine otters, and penguins, cormorants, and gulls they sailed among. In Huilliche, Chiloé meant 'place of seagulls.' They had hovered on the wind above us in the speckled late afternoon shadows of Chacao, but they would have already fled the darkness of our Ancud arrival, several hours later.

In the time between the climate and the Spaniards, Chiloé's first inhabitants had navigated the treacherous waters in their elongated narrow *dalcas*, essentially three planks, split off long alerce tree trunks with wedges, sewn together with bark fibre. *I doubt if six uglier little men ever got into a boat together.* They steered by the sun, a guidance system with obvious limitations, given the climate. The Huilliches ate fish and seafood, corn, and the special small potatoes that the region is noted for. They were two tribal subgroups, the thickly bearded Payos, and their tougher more feral Chonos cousins, living further south. *An Indian family, who had come to trade in a canoe from Caylen, bivouacked near us. They had no shelter during the rain. In the morning I asked a young Indian, who was wet to the skin, how he had passed the night. He seemed perfectly content, and answered, 'Muy bien, senor.'*

Darwin had been troubled by how these aboriginals were treated like slaves, by his Chilote companions. He made them presents of cigars and maté. *A lump of white sugar was divided between all present, and tasted with the greatest curiosity. The Indians ended all their complaints by saying, 'And it is only because we are poor Indians, and know nothing; but it was not so when we had a King.'*

It wasn't just the climate that had beaten the poor inhabitants into 'their simplicity and humble politeness.' In February of 1540, the explorer Alonso de Camargo, on his way to Peru, caught sight of the Chiloé coast. Thirteen years later, the Governor General of Chile, Pedro de Valdivia, sent Francisco de Ulloa, the man who helped Cortez subdue the Aztec capital Tenochtitlan with his naval power, across the Chacao Channel to formally discover the place, and meet the Chonos neighbours. In 1558, a soldier named Garcia Hurtado de Mendoza claimed it for the Spanish crown. As Viceroy of Peru, he later sponsored Álvaro de Mendaña y Neira's expedition to the Solomon Islands.

On the 12th of November, 1567, Captain Martín Ruiz de Gamboa hoisted the Spanish flag for the first time in what he called New Galicia, and founded the city of Santiago de Castro. An earthquake in 1575 brought a tidal wave, forerunning on the beaches.

What made the new outpost viable lived two thousand miles to the north, on the desert coast of Peru. The viceroyalty capital of Lima had no forests. Their next nearest source of timber was over the Andes, in Amazonas. Castro's initial success came to the attention of the Dutch. In 1600, two of their corsairs, captained by Baltazar de Cordes and Enrique Bower, and with the aid of the local Huilliches, attacked the colony, but without any lasting effect.

The lasting effect came eight years later with the Jesuits, evangelizing the archipelago in a summer 'circular mission.' They created a theocratic new world for the Hulliches- more than 150 wooden churches and large *encomienda* logging estates, trading Indian indentured labour for the gift of Catholic indoctrination. The native alerce planks were as renowned for their 'nobility,' elasticity, and lightness, as much as the Jesuits were not. They even came to be used as local currency, the *real de alerce*.

But the *encomenderos* of Chiloé were a brutal lot, more abusive then those on the mainland, where children were kidnapped and sent to work on the archipelago. One particularly bad actor was José de Andrade, who had tied an Indian named Martín Antucan to an apple tree, flogged his genitals with nettles, covered him in tar, and set him on fire. On February 10, 1712, the Huilliches attacked Castro in full revolt, burning buildings, killing Spanish nobles, and taking women and children hostage. The rebellion was crushed with any remaining future aspirations, inside of eight days. Jesuit intervention was required to finally stop the indiscriminate killing of Huilliches by the Spanish militia.

Marín de Velasco, the Royal Governor of Chiloé at the time, was suspended from his duties after the rebellion, but returned, with the approval of the King, in 1715, to make the situation even worse. It took another fifty years for the Jesuits to be expelled, and the Franciscans to take over the circular missions, and a further twenty to abolish the encomiendas. By then, Castro was comparatively and literally godforsaken, and barren and obscure. Many original colonists had migrated to more remote farms, returning only for festive days. New earthquakes further decreased the population, and the capital was moved to Ancud in 1788. Chiloé openly preferred the Spanish monarchy and actively resisted Chilean independence, condemning itself to further retributive isolation by Santiago. In 1826, eight years before Darwin's visit, the last Spanish stronghold in South America, they were annexed to the new republic of Chile. Except for the production of railroad ties for the continent, it became a backwater for French whalers, and forgotten.

It didn't look any more remembered when Robyn and I got off the bus in Ancud, late on New Year's Eve. Maybe it was the rain on the rusted tin roofs, or the scarcity of streetlights, in comparison the number of power lines. Fishing boats, painted in the same yellow oil, with blue and red trim, bobbed at anchor in Quetalmahue bay. The tide was in. There were hills. It was a little like San Francisco, if San Francisco had been rebuilt as an Antarctic whaling station, by a careless

German contractor, immediately after its earthquake.

The earthquake of 1960 had destroyed its glory. There was no historic architecture lining the Plaza de Armas to hint of former grandeur. The fort had been dynamited, its cannons damaged. Ancud's temporal power had been moved back to Castro, and its spiritual power flickered like its streetlights.

We hiked our packs down lanes of nostalgia, insularity, absurdity, and oblivion, until we found the small hotel we were seeking. There was less light in the lobby than there had been on the street. It took awhile for the *recepcion* buzzer button to bring him out of his cave. He didn't say much, nothing in fact. A registration form was politely guided across the counter.

"Feliz año Nuevo." I said, trying to be an ambassador. *Happy New Year.*

"Feliz...feliz." He replied. *Happy happy.* I asked him where the celebration was. He looked puzzled. I explained that it was New Years Eve, and there must be some kind of gala, somewhere.

"No lo creo." He said. *I don't believe so.* But his spiritual power flickered like the streetlights. We smiled an encouragement, turning up the voltage, lowering the resistance.

"Tal vez hay una cena en el Club de Pescadores." He said. *Maybe there's a dinner at the Fisherman's Club.* We asked for directions. He sighed, like we should have already known.

It was New Year's Eve. There wasn't anything else to do, so Robyn and I did the only thing possible. We went to the party.

*   *   *

So far, two hours before midnight, Robyn and I hadn't experienced a lot of fruitful furrow opening, or happy song singing. We had followed the desk clerk's directions down Calle Arturo Prat, and located the second house behind the big blue one, with the red and white entrance. Shabby was the only word.

There was a soft incandescence in the big windows above us, but nowhere near the amount of convivial noise we would have expected, if there had been a party going on. The stairwell to the second floor entrance was narrow and crooked and unlit. We knocked on the door at the top. A short dark man with bloodshot almond eyes opened a vertical crack of light.

"Si?" He asked. So we told him. It was New Year's Eve, and we had come from an island just like his, to help him celebrate. The door swung wide.

"Bienvenido." He said, inviting us in. Our first impression was of community. Crowded tables, full of brown fishing families, and half empty plates and bottles, were tightly spaced around the perimeter of the club. A buffet groaning board leaned against the only wall without windows. The room smelled of smoked fish and potatoes and pork, and wool and kerosene, and work and family. Our second impression was of poverty. The yellow illumination was meager, the mood and conversation muted, the music melancholic. Nothing, not even their emotions, would be wasted. They all motioned for Robyn and I to take a table, and pointed to the food. And so it began.

The meal had been started earlier in the day, in a five-foot deep hole in the ground. Stones from a bonfire were heated until red, placed in the bottom of the pit, covered with dirt and grass chunks, and then alternating layers of *nalca* Chilean rhubarb and wet sacks, and seafood and fish and meat and potatoes, and other splendid comestibles. The whole thing was covered with earth, until the smell of the smoke, mingling with the fog, announced that it was ready to disentomb. If Thor Heyerdahl had been serious about Polynesia having been colonized by South American cultures, he would have first connected the hot rocks of their umus and lovos and hangis to those of the curanto, rather than the cold ones they carved in a less similar fashion.

"Curanto." Said one of the fishermen sitting at the next table, puzzled at our sluggishness. We took our plates to the wall, piling them full of fish and *almejas* clams, *cholgas* ribbed mussels, *picorocos* giant barnacles, purple and rose-colored Chiloé potatoes, and the milcao bread they made from them, roast pig, and the crisp pork rind that was the only thing that hadn't come out of the ground. *Chicha de manzana* cider and Licor de oro, made with aguardiente firewater and whey and saffron and lemon peel, flowed over to our table from surrounding ones. Shy smiles and raised glasses returned our thanks. There was *kuchen* cake for dessert.

In the last hour before midnight, handkerchiefs came out, and, almost incongruously, the music brightened. Fishermen walked their women around the room, faced each other, waved their bandanas in the air, and began to dance. Like courting roosters and hens, never touching, they found intimacy through expressions in their faces and in their movement. The *cueca chilota*, with shorter steps, and louder, almost shouted, singing, was vital and agile and syncopated, until it suddenly finished, with the men kneeling on one knee, and their partner's shoe on the raised one. Robyn found a handkerchief, for the ones to follow. At midnight the kisses were salted, from the ocean, and from the sweat and tears of their lives, next and netted to it. Large white breakers of

Darwin's charm rippled through the hall. We left on a receding wave quietly. There were halos around the streetlamps outside.

Above us also, thirty-three years earlier, had been a pilot, in an airshow at the Ancud airport. He looked down to see a cloud of dust emerge from the earth, people running towards open spaces, and the sea in the Chacao channel recede so far, that Chiloé, for a brief moment, was reconnected to the mainland. But the gigantic wave that had formed recoiled, taking his heart along for the ride, and he watched powerless, as it returned to inundate and obliterate the city. The wooden *palofitos*, houses on stilts, were crushed or swept off their pilings, leaving long stretches of new beaches, and a patchwork of rooftops in the channel. The Colonization Find building uprooted and careened down the fjord, splitting open anything in the way, including the Pudeto Bridge. A van that braked to avoid hitting a woman, was swallowed by a yawning crevasse in the road, before the sea carried off all the other vehicles. The metal spire of the cathedral contorted in pain above the water. When the tsunami withdrew, it left fragments of blue crabs and oysters, fishes and seaweed embedded as a mosaic, in the few walls that remained upright. It left two thousand dead, a fifth of the population alive, not a few minutes earlier. It left the village of La Arena as a memory, and the entire island coast two meters lower, forever. Over two hundred aftershocks continued for a month, washing up corpses from the sea. The battered survivors, a few days after the earthquake, were laid low by an influenza epidemic, and an invasion of lice, like the typhoid that followed the smallpox, and required them to burn down their homes, in 1870.

Some Chilotes still believe in the old Huilliche myths, and blame *Coicoi-vilu*, the Serpent God of the Water, for the disaster. An eternal battle rages, between Coicoi-vilu and the Serpent God of the Earth, *Tentén-vilu*, for supremacy over the region. The battle between the protector of life on the land,

and the protector of life in the sea, are locked in eternal conflict, a mythical struggle responsible for the original creation of the archipelago.

Mankind is poised midway between the gods and the beasts.

'Ocean, if you were to give, a measure, a ferment, a fruit
of your gifts and destructions, into my hand,
I would choose your far-off repose, your contour of steel,
your vigilant spaces of air and darkness,
and the power of your white tongue,
that shatters and overthrows columns,
breaking them down to your proper purity.
Not the final breaker, heavy with brine,
that thunders onshore, and creates
the silence of sand, that encircles the world,
but the inner spaces of force,
the naked power of the waters,
the immoveable solitude, brimming with lives.
It is Time perhaps, or the vessel filled
with all motion, pure Oneness,
that death cannot touch, the visceral green
of consuming totality.
Only a salt kiss remains of the drowned arm,
that lifts a spray: a humid scent,
of the damp flower, is left,
from the bodies of men. Your energies
form, in a trickle that is not spent,
form, in retreat into silence...'

Pablo Neruda, *The Wide Ocean*

*   *   *

'Human brutes, like other beasts, find snares and poison
in the provision of life, and are allurred by their appetites
to their destruction.'

Jonathan Swift

On a sunny New Year's Day, Robyn and I were poised to head south. The eighty kilometers between Ancud and Castro had been connected by the railroad built in 1912, but this had been destroyed in the 1960 earthquake. It had only been two years before the quake, that the road had been completed. There had been a makeshift track in Darwin's time, but it had been hard won.

'I was told that several people had formerly lost their lives in attempting to cross the forest. The first to succeed was an Indian, who cut his way through the canes in eight days, and reached S. Carlos: he was rewarded by the Spanish government with a grant of land...'

His own journey to Castro been rather less agreeable than our own would be.

'The road itself is a curious affair; it consists in its whole length, with the exception of very few parts, of great logs of wood, which are either broad and laid longitudinally, or narrow and placed transversely. In summer the road is not very bad: but in winter, when the wood is rendered slippery from rain, travelling is exceedingly difficult. At that time of year, the ground on each side becomes a morass, and is often overflowed: hence it is necessary that the longitudinal logs should be fastened down by transverse poles, which are pegged on each side into the earth. These pegs render a fall from a horse dangerous; as the chance of alighting on one of them is not small. It is remarkable, however, how active custom has made the Chilotan horses. In crossing bad parts, where the logs had been displaced, they skipped from one to the other, almost with the quickness and certainty of a dog. On both hands the road is bordered by the lofty forest-trees, with their bases matted together by canes. When occasionally a long reach of this avenue could be beheld, it presented a curious scene of uniformity: the white line of logs, narrowing in perspective, became hidden by the gloomy forest, or terminated in a zigzag which ascended some steep hill.'

Robyn and I spent the first part of the morning between the rainbows, wandering what was left of the Ancud fortress, and buying empanadas for the trip. The Southern Cross bus was almost full, but we managed two aisle seats amidships. The clouds arrived as we departed, and gained on our attempts to outrun them. I was sitting beside a middle-aged man with a leather valise, and a face as square and as weathered as the alerce logs that Darwin had ridden over. *Every one on this road acts on the "hail fellow well met' fashion, and one may enjoy the privilege, so rare in South America, of travelling without firearms.* I introduced myself with an empanada.

"Miguel Ovideo Lagos." He said. Miguel was an Argentine writer, but he knew about the serpents of the sea and the earth, and all the other mythological creatures of the archipelago. He knew also of Bruce Chatwin, and *In Patagonia*, and his version of Chilote folklore.

"The Huilliches of Chiloé had a tradition of witchcraft peopled by demonic beings found nowhere else in the world. Chatwin described it like a mafia, or a Masonic conspiracy of movie monsters." He said.

'The Sect of the Brujeria exists for the purpose of hurting ordinary people. No one knows the exact whereabouts of its headquarters. But there are at least two branches of its Central Committee, one in Buenos Aires, the other in Santiago de Chile.'

"The Brujeria was much less organized, much more and much less supernatural, and much more terrifying." Outside our window, the mist had caught up with us. *The number of trees which were in full flower perfumed the air; yet even this could hardly dissipate the effect of the gloomy dampness of the forest. Moreover, the many dead trunks that stand like skeletons, never fail to give these primaeval woods a character of solemnity, absent in these of countries long civilized.* Miguel spread out the history.

In 1880, a most peculiar trial of a hundred warlock *brujos* was held in Ancud. They were charged with running a parallel alternative government to the one in Santiago, belonging to a select chosen *Mayoría*, part of a larger group they called *La Recta Provincia*, the Righteous Province. Their righteousness was called into question, however, by their more nefarious activities, which purported involved protection rackets, disposal of their enemies by poisoning, and the seemingly magical ability to inflict *sajaduras* 'profound slashes.' The most important warlock who testified in court was a 70 year-old farmer named Mateo Coñuecar. He spoke of the origin of the Mayoría in another conflict, between a Spanish explorer, José de Moraleda, and a legendary old Huilliche witch named Chillpila. In 1786, when Moraleda arrived in Chiloé, he decided to play the role of a warlock, to impress the natives. He was reported to have taken the form of several different animals. But Chillpila ran his ship aground on its side in the sand, and then, raised the tide and floated him free. Moraleda, in defeat and gratitude, presented Chillpila with a rare ancient leather-bound book, containing powerful incantations for the most arcane black magic. Chillpila brought it to a ravine near Quicavi, and the grass-covered doorway in the roof of a cave that belonged to a hierarchy of senior 'kings and viceroys.' She entered with a special 'alchemy key,' and brought *La Recta Provincia* its power. The cavern was over a hundred feet long, six hundred feet wide, and ten feet high. It was lined with torches and jugs burning human fat. In addition to the book of magic, the Mayoría had a *Challanco* crystal stone, or a bowl that, when filled with water, that continually surveyed and spied on all members of the sect.

The Guardian of the Cave was a grotesque monster of their making. Chatwin's description of the creation of this New World swamp thing was bone-chilling.

'When the Sect needs a new Invunche, the Council of the Cave orders a Member to steal a boy child from six months to a year old. The Deformer, a permanent resident of the Cave, starts work at once. He disjoints the arms and legs and the hands and feet. Then begins the delicate task of altering the position of the head. Day after day, and for hours at a stretch, he twists the head with a tourniquet until it has rotated through an angle of 180°, that is, until the child can look straight down the line of its own vertebrae. There remains one last operation, for which another specialist is needed. At full moon, the child is laid on a workbench, lashed down with its head covered in a bag. The specialist cuts a deep incision under the right shoulder blade. Into the hole he inserts the right arm and sews up the wound with thread taken from the neck of a ewe. When it has healed the Invunche is complete. During the process, the child is fed on human milk. After weaning, the diet is changed to young human flesh, followed by that of the adult male. When these are unobtainable, cat milk, kid and billygoat are taken as substitutes. Once installed as Guardian of the Cave, the Invunche is naked and sprouts long bristly hair. It never acquires human speech, yet, over the years, it does develop a working knowledge of the Committee's procedure and can instruct novices with harsh and guttural cries.'

What he didn't mention was even more macabre- that the necromancers kidnap a first-born infant before it is nine days old, that if the child has been baptized, the christening is razed off, or that the child is sometimes sold to the brujos by desperate parents; that his eyes are sewn closed, that his tongue is split in two, that the long bristly hair is grown by rubbing his skin daily with an ointment of *Huiripinda* and *Picochihuin* leaves; that the human flesh he eats is from newborn babies, and stolen from cemeteries; that when he shrieks horribly and pitifully from hunger, he is allowed to leave the cave to look for his own food; that he will only let in those who pronounce the required password from behind a certain tree, and only after they perform an *osculus nigrus* black kiss on his anus; that only the warlocks can see him, and non-members perceive only an inanimate object, and are left, numb and groggy, with no memory of the encounter *If he happens to be literate, he loses his hands and the ability to write*; that the invunche is extremely dangerous; and that, at a certain age of maturation, he is sacrificed, his own flesh rendered into a magical *charqui* jerky, to be distributed all over the island.

Miguel went on to tell me about the initiation rites of the

warlocks, and the six years of ordination ordeals, required of any successful candidate.

"The novice's diet consists of highly indigestible food." He explained. "During the coldest part of winter, he needs to bathe under a freezing waterfall in the Traiguén River for twelve or fifteen or forty nights, and then with the blood of an unchristened newborn baby, to wash away his own Christian baptism. He is allowed to eat a little toast only. He must carry out ambushes on lonely roads, spend a night lying on a cemetery tomb, catch a skull, without fumbling, from the crown of a tricorn hat, and sign his application form with the blood from his own veins. To demonstrate that he had destroyed all trace of sentimentality, he must kill the person closest to him, on a Tuesday or Thursday night, and then run three times around the island, calling to the Devil. And then he must make his Macuñ."

"His Macuñ?" I asked.

"Yes, his Macuñ." He said. "He must dig up a recently buried female Christian virgin, and flay the skin from her breast. After it is cured and dried, he would sew it into a 'thieves waistcoat,' a flying device that will light and guide his future nighttime expeditions. The soft white piercing light it gives off is either from the human grease remaining in the skin, or the hide's impregnation with phosphorescent Noctiluca scintillans *cauquiles*. Specific magic words are required for takeoff and landing. When he takes it off, it coils up into a small package. If he loses his Macuñ, it will return to him with the words, 'che, che,' and if any stranger dares touch it, the Macuñ will produce a ghostly yell which will scare the intruder to death.

When the novotiate has completed all these tasks, he is invited to appear before the Council of the Cave, thirteen warlocks presided over by their leader, the Buta. He is required to make contradictory vows, accepting the Devil, but promising to follow their 'moral code,' forbidding theft and rape. The ceremony concludes with a great feast on the roasted flesh of human babies, after which the new brujo is confined for a brief period, a lizard tied around his forehead with a bandana, from which is imparted the knowledge of how to transform himself into an animal, and how to open locked doors. The older warlocks then take him back in hand, to each him other important skills- how to use the big dark yellowish-green golden-maned Caballo Marino sea horses to reach the organization's ghost ship, how to send out a magical fluid which can influence thoughts dreams and transform minds and drive men mad, how to change the course of rivers, how to use sorcery to extract annual tribute from villagers 'to ensure they would have accidents in the night,' or their crops destroyed, or their sheep killed by sorcery from toads or special stones, how to inflict long scratches or incisions remotely, how to use the toxic power of plants to asphyxiate by *Llancazo* poisoning, and how to spread disease, particularly 'some new virus that will not respond to medical treatment.'"

"You mean like the AIDS virus that killed Bruce Chatwin?" I asked.

"Perhaps." Miguel said. "They teach him how to inflict mischief on a grand scale. And then they teach him how to fly. The new warlock followed a salt free diet, and was considered ready when one of his eyes began to water. Finally, with a tossing back of his poncho, he fully exposed his Macuñ, and with the word, 'arrehualhue,' an invocation to Satan to enable his flight, he was airborne. When he said 'Macuñ, arréame Diablo,' he descended gently."

"Was there any defense against this black magic mafia?" I asked.

"Some." Said Miguel. "Chilotes who hung an open pair of scissors in the shape of a cross in a doorway could cause these diabolical envoys crazy by causing them to stumble around blindly, without being able to leave the dwelling. If that's what you wanted. Better, if anyone saw a sorcerer in mid-flight, they could bring him down like a rock, by saying the Lord's Prayer backwards, or by carving a cross in the air or in the ground, with a knife. Gauchos, on the pampas in Argentina, still do this, to 'break' a storm, to avoid wind or hailstones."

"It doesn't seem like the average farmer or fisherman on Chiloé stood much of a chance." I said.

"No, not much at all." Miguel agreed. "The warlocks used adolescent girls as couriers. Stripped naked, they were forcibly fed a warm drink of wolf-oil and *natri* juice, so disgusting that it made them vomit up their own intestines at night. Their entrails were neatly folded away in a *ciruelillo* wooden box, which needed to be concealed. These *Voladeras* were now light enough to carry messages for the brujos, transforming into a long-legged bird known as a *bauda*, and flying off to fulfill their missions. Their caws were the most unpleasant sounds ever to fall on human ears. When the birds returned at daybreak, they sought out their bowels, swallowed them back down, and resumed human female form, like a reverse Prometheus, whose entrails were devoured by vultures and then regenerated by night. If the entrails were hidden or destroyed, La Voladora was doomed to be a bauda forever, indistinguishable from the other birds at sundown. Unable to tell them apart, Chiloé natives suspected each bird seeking food on the beaches, and loathed them all."

"Was that it?" I asked. Miguel just laughed.

"The warlocks used a brown owl-like bird, called a *Coo*, with big bright round red eyes, to bang on the windows of the sick at night, with their fluttering wings and gutteral chanting, and announce the imminent death of the occupant. They may have sent the jet-black Raiquén with him, its wings like two metal sheets banging together. If the Raiquén sings, the Indio dies. *Piruí-piruí-piruí.*

In the daytime they sent the dark gray *Mandao*, with burning eyes and black and red feet, to peck on the same windows, if the forthcoming death was to occur during daylight hours. Or they sent the *Deñ*, with its mocking eyes, to pick the next victim.

When the darkness fell out at sea, in the heart of the somber Chiloé channels, a low tide gathering fog might be a sign of its imminent appearance near the beaches. To a casual observer, it might appear as a floating log, going backwards or becoming invisible, if approached. If you were discovered, you might be left with a crooked mouth, your head twisted back, turned into a marine mammal, killed, or borne away by it. To see it beyond the fog, you needed to put a clod of earth in your mouth so they didn't smell your breath, and hide behind a *maqui* or *tique* tree. And then, and only then, might you get a glimpse of El Caleuche, the *shapeshifter* ghost ship of the brujos, laden with gold and music and light. Bright bone white, illuminated with countless numbers of glowing colored lights on her three spars, she emerges from under the water's surface, and can sail into the wind and through other craft effortlessly, a bodiless vision capable of astonishing speed. Her crewmembers all have one leg, on which they are forever hopping, the other being merely a vestigial stump, sticking out of their backs. They can turn into sea birds or sea lions or wolves or *cahuelche* dophins (whose appearance in front of a stilted house, was also an omen of impending death within). Their handshakes are cold. They are well dressed, and will kidnap any castaways, and harvest the drowned souls of wrecked sailors. Delerious mariners are sometimes found, singing songs of brujo blasphemy. But it is their endless singing and dancing that draws other vessels into a trap, a constant party of clanking chains and rich contraband, like the *Flying Dutchman* might have been, with more Huilliche blood in the veins of its company."

"How do you know all this, Miguel?" I asked. He told me he was writing a book. "The Chilean authorites went to considerable lengths to destroy the power of Chiloé's sorcerers. I wanted to find out why."

He went on to tell me about more myths of the island. The sea creature royal family of Huenchula, the beautiful daughter of a *Machi* Huilliche shaman, Huenchur, and a woodcutter, and the Millalobo who seduced her, part man, part fish, and part golden-furred sea lion. Their three children- La Sirena, the same singing temptress that enchanted Greek sailors to their shipwrecks; El Pincoy, the silver-skinned golden-haired seducer of unwary women, walking along the shore, just like his father; and La Pincoya, the daughter who determined the annual fecundity of the fish and seafood harvest, by how much she faced the ocean. *She was a mermaid who had lost her way. Not knowing tears, she did not weep tears. Not knowing clothes, she did not have clothes. She did not speak because she had no speech...Entering the river she was cleaned, shining like a white stone in the rain, and without looking back she swam again swam towards emptiness, swam towards death.*

"It seems like most Chilote myths were oceanic." I said. Miguel smiled.

"From the bottom of the sea to the floor of the forest, every act of life was governed by the brujos' witchcraft, and their magical creatures." He said. "The Millaoso is an enormous hybrid bear seal, covered in golden fur, that comes out of the sea for only a few weeks this time of year, to eat the wild strawberries that are its favorite food.

The Camahueto resembles a young calf, with a small golden horn, like a unicorn. It sleeps for twenty-five years in a swampy lagoon until, on a stormy night, it awakens and erupts from the earth with such power, and with such a desperate impulse to reach the sea, that it carves deep furrows through the surrounding woodland, knocking down trees, creating huge waves that will submerge any vessels floating nearby, and noisily destroying everything in its path. Any warlock that can lasso the Camahueto with a seaweed rope before he reaches the sea, and cuts off his horn, will tame him into a domestic ox. The horn can be cut into pieces to plant the next generation of Camaheutos, or scraped into shavings which, mixed with seawater and apple cider, becomes a potion to cure impotence.

The Carbuncos are the guardians of underground precious metal treasures, that take the form of tiny dogs surrounded by a greenish-red halo, or bivalve mollusks that send out sparks of firefly light, either of which can erupt from the ground in a flame, during the winter solstice. If lassoed, it will disappear, leaving buried treasure subterranean to its place of capture. Retrieving it, however, requires returning the next morning with an old widow, a black cat, and a new wooden shovel, digging until you reach a point where the black cat will disappear when thrown into the hole, and digging some more, until the cat reappears in the woman's arms. The black cat must be immediately thrown back into the hole, and digging resumed until it once more rematerializes in the widow's clasp. The process continues until the trove is found or the treasure hunter dies from inhaling the precious metal gas fumes released by the pursuit. In Chiloe, even when fortune knocks, it can still knock you dead. There's a sad catch to every toss of the coin.

The other dog legend is that of the beautiful shiny black Trehuaco, which lives in a den under a southern lake. At certain times of the year, infertile women will make a pilgrimage, to invoke his appearance on the shore, and help. The Trehuaco will impregnate them with a live human fetus, in exchange for a meal of another kidnapped child, brought in desperate trade. If she needs a baby-sitter, she only needs to find the Coñiponi, a small gray worm that lives in the stalks of potato plants. Fed a few drops of mother's milk, and placed under the newborn's pillow, the child becomes happily quiet, and will not cry.

"Gray potato worms, fed human milk, are babysitters?" I asked.

"And highly sought after." Said Miguel." Unlike the larger, nocturnal serpents of local folklore, all of which are to be avoided. The Peuchen is an ill-tempered ten-foot long flying snake with a loud whistle, covered in fungus and moss. Humans and sheep are usually paralyzed by its gaze, before having their blood sucked away in the night, like the vampire bat that likely inspired its creation. The Cuchivilu is a sea monster, half pig and half snake, with a voracious appetite for the fish and mollusks, inside the semicircular sea ranch fences of Chilote fishermen. Once it has left its cave in the ravine, and stealthily broken down the swampy beach enclosures to gorge on the hard work of the owners, no one can approach the pen, for the stink, the sterility, and the infective scabies it contains. The only way to remove the curse is with a magical ceremony called the *cheputo*, thrashing branches of laurel-smoked *mapucho* local tobacco around the perimeter. Only brujos can see the Cuchivili, and any ordinary person who hears it grunting will have a short life.

The most terrifying hybrid serpent, however, is the Basilisco, a cross between a rooster and a snake, that come from a small gray unfertilized egg. If undiscovered, it hatches as a worm, which slips away under a house. Within a few weeks it has grown into the monstrous basilisk of Greek myth, its soporific sounds of monotonous quiet crowing inducing a prolonged slumber of the inhabitants above, the software of sickness and decline. The Basilisco takes its nourishment from the saliva and soul of each sleeping victim, leaving them with an increasing dry cough, which dries and denervates, until death takes each consecutive member of the family. The only way to get rid of it, is to remove the egg immediately, and kill the rooster snake that laid it. If the eggshell is accidently broken, the house it was found under, must be burned to the ground. *Aliens.*

The final serpent fiend is the potato snake, the Vipoñi, feeding on the tender tubers of a Chilote farmer's crop, if he fails to pay the tribute that the brujos demand of him. Farmers have been known to contract the warlocks to harm neighbours by paying them to release potato snakes into their fields, or use the two terrifying black stones of Las Piriman, which also have the power to destroy crops, and kill sheep.

Perhaps the most terrifying local superstition, however, is the

Cuero. You know that, in Spanish, this simply means 'leather,' but in Chiloe, the huge bovine hide it refers to, lives in small dark lagoons. Around its edge are tentacles of sharp pincered claws, each of which ends in a pair of red eyes. In its center is a gigantic sucker, for absorbing the blood of its victims. When the tide moves in, the Cuero undulates towards its prey, enfolds it, and drags it to the sea bottom. Swimming in the sea is a potentially dangerous pastime in Chiloe. Once again, there is a magical defense. A Machi can lure it near the shore with the blue sweet round fruit that grows on the thick thorny bush of the calafate. As the Cuero wraps around it branches, the thorns penetrate, tearing it apart, and causing it to bleed to death.

In the clouds, live the Puyos, ugly bisexual incubuses, with two heads with twisted horns and three feet and grayish yellow fur. At night they ride the moonbeams down into the valleys to copulate. Any offspring that result are horribly deformed."

"There don't seem to be too many safe places in Chiloe." I said. "I wouldn't think it would be any more secure in the forests."

"True enough." Said Miguel. "But not as bad as on the sea or in the villages. The Trauco is a repugnant little forest gnome, with legs but no feet, who can fell any tree with his tiny stone hatchet. He also has the power of sexual irresistibility to young virgins, a convenient social forgiveness for any unwanted pregnancy in an imposed authoritarian Catholic culture. He is married to La Fiura, a short red-clad hag with a ravenous sexual appetite, capable of causing sciatica and paralyzing men with her foul breath. She is similar to the widow, La Viuda, a shadowy woman in black, with milky white feet, who appears in solitary places and seduces lonely men, before abandoning them."

"So, I don't understand, Miguel." I said. "Why is there such an abundance of evil superstitions on a quiet sparsely populated island?"

"Climate is only one of the factors that determines culture." He said. "Although the dense moody climate of Chiloe is more than enough of a fertile incubator for the receptive imagination, an equally important influence came in the form of the invasion of strict Catholic iconism into an animistic native society living a highly dependent symbiotic existence in a tough geography. The Huilliches created the Righteous Province as an affirmation of a continued aspiration to govern themselves, and as an alternative justice to the version that was being imposed on them by their Spanish conquerors. The remoteness of the authority of the repression created a partial vacuum, in which evolved the mythological instruments that could explain all their misfortunes."

"So, why did the Chilean authorities take thirty years to clamp down on the murderous *Mayoría* that terrorized the collective Chilote psyche?" I asked.

"The answer, like most power struggles, is political." Said Miguel. "The government was content to allow these deeply embedded superstitions to flourish, as long as they were only a distraction to their own increasing control. But, in 1880, Chile fell into crisis, in a brutal four-year War of the Pacific with Peru and Bolivia on one front, and the Argentinians reviving land claims along on their other border. The sorcerers had sheltered Chilean army deserters, and were resurrecting secessionist sentiments, an attempt to represent a legimate native government. It was simply easier to convict them of witchcraft, than treason."

The multicolored stilt houses reflected on the water, as we entered the rarified atmosphere of Castro.

"And now?" I asked.

"And now." He said. "And now the brooding mythological creatures of Chiloé are a world apart. They have been Disney-transformed and visually deformed. Their credibility has been corroded by what else Coicoi-vilu has carried in the salt air across the channel. La Pincoya, dancing in the seas, capriciously denying or providing fishermen with fish and shellfish, is no longer a goddess, but a watery Snow White. El Caleuche, sailing over or under the seas with the souls of mariners and fishermen, is now an amusing *Pirates of the Carribean* ghost ship. La Sirena can't compete with the constant supply of erotic signals on local television, and La Voladora sits idle, her arms folded.

Old chimeras have been replaced with Hollywood fantasies. The Costa Brava ferryman who carried the souls of the dead across the narrow channel separating the blackness of Lake Cucao from the other side of the Southern Sea to the afterlife, is shipwrecked by the tide table of history."

"But the people sleep better at night." I said.

"They sleep better at night."

'We were then in a dangerous, helpless situation, exposed daily to perils and death amongst savages and wild beasts, not a white man in the country but ourselves.'

Daniel Boone

*   *   *

We arrived in the mist between the stilts, held together with old moss and green algae. Under corregated sheets of rusting tin, the bright coloured shingled façades of the *palofitos* were losing a rearguard battle against the silver gray ether. The tide was out. You didn't need your tide tables, or your eyes open, to know that.

Just north of the nostalgia-laden port, was an odd collection of ancient trains, in the small Plazuela del Tren. The hostel we found had been painted a long time before the trains. We checked into a small room, separated from the others by thin wooden partitions. Any demonstration of high spirits would have rolled through the walls like one of the locomotives. The hot water had departed with the last caboose.

Robyn and I sat on the balcony with a pisco sour, looking out at the last failing rays of daylight on the palofitos lining the fjord. The curved bills of the black-faced ibises croaked out rasping *caws*, in the tree on the terrace below.

"Bandurrias." Said the pisco sour on my left. "Theristicus melanopis."

"I know." I said. I'd never seen a Franciscan priest gripping, and in the grip of, a big cocktail. But there he was.

"Father Antonio." He said, introducing himself. I told him I didn't know why he carried that title, since it was forbidden to be one.

"It's a metaphor." He said.

"Like everything else on this island." I said. Antonio was visiting from Santiago, but he had an impressive knowledge of history of the place. I told him about my own island, and Juan Fernandez, and the conversation turned to shipwrecks.

"The most fascinating one on Chiloé was Lord Byron's grandfather." He said.

"Really?" I asked.

"Cierto." He said. John Byron had sailed as a midshipman with George Anson in 1731, on his famous round the world voyage that had resulted in so much tragedy. He had been known as Foulweather Jack, a prophetic aponym, which anticipated the fate of his ship, ten years later. On May 14th, the HMS Wager foundered on a rock in the Guayaneca islands south of Chiloé. The survivors decided to split in two groups, the first to make its way back around the Horn to Rio de Janeiro, and Byron's, to sail north to meet the Spaniards. His adventures, published in 1768 as *The Loss of the Wager*, which later formed the basis of Patrick O'Brian's novel, *The Unknown Shore*. Initially, in order to survive the climate, hunger and the isolation and desolation, he lived with, and like, the Chono Indians, smearing grease on his body and wearing sealskins to keep warm. He was eventually captured, and taken to Castro, dirty, lice-ridden, and on the point of starvation. Incarcerated on a remote hill with two shipmate companions, a Jesuit priest finally came to visit him, trading a bottle of brandy, for the divulgence of the whereabouts, and subsequent theft, of their watches and rings.

"I'm a Franciscan." Said Father Antonio.

"Another metaphor." I said. "Transcending all levels of intellectual thought." Fairweather Jack was ultimately invited to spend some time on the rural property of a Chiloé society lady, but it didn't go well. When his host invited him to kiss their sacred Catholic stamps, his Protestant refusal coincided with a strong earthquake, and blame for the resultant divine wrath.

"His grandson would have kissed them." Said Antonio.

"His grandson would have kissed the invunche." I said. *Roll on, deep and dark blue ocean, roll. Ten thousand fleets sweep over thee in vain. Man marks the earth with ruin, but his control stops with the shore.*

The same earthquake that had destroyed Ancud on Sunday, May 22nd, 1960, hadn't been that much kinder to Castro. At then minutes to three in the afternoon, a radio message came in from Puerto Montt, two hundred kilometers away, that a violent earthquake was destroying the city, and it was quickly moving south, towards Chiloé. It tore into Castro ten minutes later, 9.5 on the Richter scale. It ploughed into the football match underway in the stadium, throwing the players to the ground, and the fans in the bleachers into the air, like it was shaking out a blanket. A brand new pier, and the Customs building next to it, collapsed. Dogs howled and flocks of birds flew loudly in random spirals.

The aftershocks were larger than some of the world's other major historical earthquakes. Hills caved in, burying entire families, and tsunamis charged five kilometers inland, sinking entire towns and forests in their own debris.

The hospital had been razed to the ground. Seven hundred homes were destroyed. Others had gaping wounds in the walls and inner rooms. Wood-fired ovens and braziers were overturned, starting so many terrible fires, that the city burned for three days and three nights, until the arrival of a fine mist.

The crosses in the San Juan cemetery that sank beneath the sea, will still today, depending on the tide table, sometimes emerge above the water line.

The Plaza de Armas in Castro became an outdoor bedroom and toilet and garbage dump and epidemic epicenter. The bust of General O'Higgens, Liberator of Chile, was decapitated, his head used for carrying water.

Three days later, there was still no mention of the 'Castrostrophe' in Santiago, as if the country had ended in Puerto Montt. The old historical insult caused by the island's refusal to seek independence from Spain was, once again, returned to its owners. It was just a barbarian Indian island of Huilliches and Chonos, and it would never again have a railway.

When the earthquake struck, the people of Castro looked towards the wooden church of San Francisco for their survival, and the lavender and canary-colored neo-Gothic church, steeple swaying crazy in the chaos, survived back.

After a breakfast of café, and bread with *queso* and *jamon* and *manjar*, Robyn and I crossed the Plaza de Armas to look inside. The first version had been built with the founding of the city by Martin Ruiz de Gamboa in 1567, but was destroyed and burnt down a number of times, until its currect resurrection in 1772. When the 220-ton Dutch privateer, Fidelidad, arrived with its pirates and flying colours, 18 cannons and bugle blaring, into Castro's beautiful fiord in April of 1600, its captain, Baltasar de Cordes, had already conspired with the local Huilliche chiefs, to take over the city. The Spanish envoy, Pedro de Villagoya, who boarded the ship to negotiate with the Dutch, initially succumbed to the personal charm of de Cordes, who had told him he was a Catholic. And then he and his other six officers had their throats cut. The pirates, supported by the Indians, began to massacre those city's inhabitants that had not taken refuge in the church. The women were spared for future carnal purposes or other forms of enslavement, but even the local priest was stoned and then decapitated. The plot was untilmately undermined by a brave military widow, Doña Inés Bazán, who placed nails in the holes where the lighted fuses were to be in the cannons, and by Captain Pérez de Vargas, who mobilized to retake the town, after the church had been razed by the pirates, and before he went on to hang over thirty traitorous Indian chiefs.

Darwin's observation that

> 'Although the inhabitants were so assiduous in setting fire to every part of the wood, yet I did not see a single fire which they had succeeded in making extensive...'

hadn't obviously influenced the major fire that destroyed it
again in 1771, although he was suffucuently impressed with
its reconstruction by the time he visited in the 1830s.

'The church, which stands in the middle, is entirely built of plank, and
has a picturesque and venerable appearance...'

Galvanized iron set in the roof set off the apertures of the
few stained glass windows. The interior woodwork was
stunningly beautiful. Walls, pillars, altars, carvings, and arches
were exquisitely composed, from larch, cypress, coigüe, raulí
and olivillo, and other native timber. The archangel Michael's
statue, with his sexy Moro kris sword, and gold and black-
striped ankle gaiters, was almost Florentine, but the Satan he
was standing on was all Chilote. Over his dark wooden skin
stretched an expression of native bewilderment. Behind the
Huilliche eyes and nose and lips, was an irregular row of large
sharpened, tobacco-stained teeth. Green horns burst blood
from his cheeks, and the whole apparition strangely flanked
by two vases of fresh cut roses. There were 150 Jesuit
churches in the archipelago, and Robyn and I were almost out
of time. Back outside was the Castro that Darwin had seen.

'a most forlorn and deserted place... the poverty of the place may be
conceived from the fact that one of our party was unable anywhere to
purchase either a pound of sugar or an ordinary knife. No individual
possessed either a watch or a clock; and an old man. Who was supposed
to have a good idea of time, was employed to strike the church bell by
guess...'

Past the cafes along Calle Blanco, and the masculinity of the
Port, we brought our eyes to adjust to the metal shed interior
of the Mercado Municipal. Among the women weavers and
purveyers of fish and seafood stews, was chaotic commotion.
The constant pouring of maté infusions intensified the
excitement of whispered scandal. *A Wool Cap I sent you for
winter...the channel current took her, like you love.* The PA system

was playing a corregated tin instrumental version of *Raindrops keep falling on my Head.* And so it was again, outside.

Robyn and I hiked our packs to the main bus terminal, at Sotomayer and Esmeralda. The ferry crossing was included in the price of our tickets. We passed the balcony of the poet, Mario Contreras Vega, overlooking O'Higgens street, on the way out of town. Over the railing he had placed an immense placard that read, 'No to the Chacao Bridge.' Even though the president of Chile is determined to join the mainland to Chiloé, and the project to build the longest span in South America has begun, and even though the billion-dollar project is designed for a lifespan of a hundred years, winds over 240 kilometers an hour, strong sea currents, and Richter magnitude 10 earthquakes, I don't think Mario Contreras Vega should lose any sleep. In the eternal struggle for supremacy between Coicoi-vilu and Tentén-vilu, the Serpent Gods of the Sea and the Earth, and all the mythology and massacre they have been witness to, my money's on the tide table of the Southern Sea.

'From the archipelago you have hair of larch fibres,
flesh that was realised by aeons of time,
veins that have known oceans of timber,
green blood dropped from the sky into memory.

No one can recapture my heart, lost
among so many roots, in the bitter cool
of the sun's rays multiplied by seething of waters:
there lives the shadow that does not depart with me.

So you rose out of the South like an islet,
crowned, populated, by plumage and timber,
and I sensed the fragrance of wandering woodland.

I found the dark honey I knew in the forest,
and touched at your hips the petals of shadow
that were born with me and that formed my soul.'
        Pablo Neruda, *Cien sonetos de amor*

Headhunting in Kansas
Sulawesi

'The Bugis are a high-spirited people: they will not bear ill-usage…They are fond of adventures, emigration, and capable of undertaking the most dangerous enterprises.'

Thomas Forrest, *A Voyage from Calcutta to the Mergui Archipelago*, 1792

Welcome to Kansas. That's what the sign said, anyway. And underneath the cigarette packet on the poster, was its Indonesian slogan, 'Langkah Pasti.' *Definite step.*

Robyn and I had taken a definite step onto the Silk Air flight that got us here, and then we took another one, getting off in Ujung Pandang. It wasn't called Ujung Pandang much before we got off the plane, and it wouldn't be Ujung Pandang after we left. The island we landed on was a large orchid, suspended in the Southern Sea by one of its twisted elongated sepals, draped over the equator like a necklace. Its original Portuguese name, Celebes, had been displaced by the rich Lake Matano deposits that retitled it Sulawesi. *Iron Island.* But when they pitched up in 1511, the Portuguese found a thriving cosmopolitan entrepôt where Arabs and Chinese and Indians and Siamese and Malays and Javanese came to trade their metal harware and textiles for gold, copper, pearls, camphor and spices- cloves, nutmeg, and mace, imported from the Spice Islands of Maluku. The Gowa and Tallo sultanates had become powerful enough to build a fortified sea wall along the coast, punctuated with a series of eleven fortresses.

The smell of clove Kretek cigarettes, and frying fish and chili sambal hit us, like the heat. If Toto had gotten off the plane, he would have been lunch before he cleared immigration. It definitely wasn't Kansas.

More like the Latinesia archipelagos of Juan Fernández and Chiloé, Sulawesi had iconic sailing ships and terrible earthquakes. And stilt houses and volcanoes. Its history had come out of pirates and castaways, resulting in the treaty that shaped its evolution.

ARTICLE 3

All rigging and tools, treasury, and every other articles without exception, which have been taken from the Honorable Company's ship Malvish (the Whale) cast away at Salyer, and from the Honorable Company's Yacht or Barge, the Lioness, cast away at the island Don Douange shall be restored to the Honorable Company. In that restoration however the eight iron guns, from the Whale, said by the above Maccasar power to have been paid for, shall remain in their possesson, if it be proved that the sum of 4,000 Spanish Dollars has been actually paid for them to the late Commisioner Gaamo, on belhalf of the Honorable Company.

R. Blok, *Appendix to Volume I. Treaty concluded in the year 1667, between the Dutch Admiral Cornelis Speelman and the King of Maccassar. Beknopte geschiedenis van het Makassaarsche Celebes en Onderhoorigheden,* 1817

The Dutch had negotiated this treaty with some of the most feared marauders and freebooters in the Pacific. Stories of their legendary ruthlessness found their way back to the homes of European sailors. Stories of the Bugis of Bone. Stories of the Bogeymen. *You thought it was a just a story... but it's real.*

The South Peninsula, separating the world's eleventh largest island from Borneo, is only one of four large narrow rugged mountainous, long forested natural barriers that dominated three major gulfs, and almost five thousand kilometers of coastline. No point on the Sulawesi orchid is more than ninety kilometers from the sea, and tribal connections between its petals had traditionally been more acccessible by boat, than overland. It was here, beside the verdant wet rice-growing plains along the western Strait of Makassar, that the fierce Buganese pirates boogied. They called themselves *Orang Laut*, People of the Sea. Around 2500 years BC, the Bugis began their southern migration from Taiwan down the Austronesian trail, like the Polynesians would do much later. But they weren't Polynesians.

In 1605 their animistic *Tolotang* beliefs were converted to Islam and fifty years later, at the end of a long civil war, they were scattered, in a diaspora that took them as far as Sumatra and the Malay Peninsula. They traded of the coasts of New Guinea and Australia, where they exchanged medicinal bark, and the skins of birds of paradise and mother of pearl, for knives and salt from the Yolŋu people, and other Melanesian tribal groups. They would sail the trades, and return laden with *trepand*, dried sea cucumber, before returning to Makassar on the dry season offshore winds.

By the time Joseph Conrad arrived on the 204-ton steamer *Vidar*, in 1887, hauling coal and resin from Borneo, Makassar was 'the prettiest and perhaps, cleanest looking of all the towns in the islands.' In *Lord Jim*, he wrote of 'a Bugis of Tondano only lately come to Patusan, and a relation of the man shot in the afternoon.' He wasn't as ebullient about the outskirts of town. 'They were a numerous and an unclean crowd, living in ruined bamboo houses, surrounded by neglected compounds...' Which is just about where Robyn and I came in.

The becak pedicab that sounded the loudest bell, got to take us through the clay dust yellow brick road, through the breeze and the beggars, and what had been the gateway to the Spice Islands. The Bugis that didn't live in pole houses, nine feet or more off the ground, with plank floors and walls, were in low concrete bungalows with corrugated tin roofs, radiating outward from the old Dutch fort.

The Quality Hotel we docked at, was still the Radisson, but wouldn't be, after we left. I negotiated a fifty per cent discount off their rack rate, without breaking any more of a sweat. We ate *Konro ribs*, and *Coto Makassar*, a stew of beef brain and tongue and intestine, mixed with nuts and spices, in the order it left the cow, with delicious glutinous Burasa coconut rice, washed down with an Anker Bir. In our *pisang epe* dreams, of pressed bananas and durian drowned in palm sugar sauce, the durian won.

The next morning we took a *pete-pete* minibus to Fort Rotterdam. The original fortress had been constructed out of clay by the Gowa sultan, I manrigau Daeng Bonto Karaeng Lakiung Tumpa'risi 'kallonna, in the shape of a turtle, as a metophor for the ability to live on land and sea. The Dutch were having none of it and, in 1667, ran him out town, and took over the trade in copra, rattan, pearls, Bêche-de-mer, sandalwood, and a famous oil made from bado nuts, which no European gentleman could groom his hair without. John Byron's grandson, the inestimable Lord, called it 'thine incomparable oil, Macassar.' The incomparability required the invention of the antimacassar, the small elaborately embroidered white crochet cloths used by the Victorians to cover the backs and arms of their chairs, to protect the upholstery from its oiliness.

The white stucco walls of the fort caught the early morning sun, and the steeply pitched roofs covered in russet tiles were definitely Dutch. It could have been Amsterdam or Capetown or Curaçao, but for the refuse and cockfights outside, and the 'Hello Misters' from the gangs of little urchins seeking *gula-gula* sweets. And the use the Japanese made of it as a prisoner of war camp in the war.

Not that the Dutch had treated the Bugis much better, after the Japanese left. A counter-insurgency expert named Ray 'The Turk' Westerling took only three months to eliminate local support for Republican aspirations, by eliminating local support. The 'Westerling Method' consisted of surrounding villages during the night, separating the men at daybreak, and summarily executing those he suspected of working for the independent movement. He may have been responsible for tens of thousands of deaths. His actions were not surprising, given how he had previously dealt with a gang leader in

North Sumatra. *We planted a stake in the middle of the village and on it we impaled the head of Terakan. Beneath it we nailed a polite warning to the members of his band that if they persisted in their evildoing, their heads would join his.'*

Robyn and I walked past the sea wall, followed by young boys who hadn't yet decided if they want to antagonize us, or try for candy.

"Hello, Misters!" They shouted.

"Apa Kareba?" I asked. *How are you.*

"Kareba melo!" They said. And we were friends.

The Paotere Harbour seemed deserted at first, but then we saw movement on the schooners, and a row of women sitting along the pier. Their caftans, white in the sun, and their faces, white with rice powder, were contrasted by the scarlet of their lips, stained from betel nut. They appeared like ghostly vampires, in a crude Kabuki play. One planted a splotch of orange saliva behind us as we passed. I interpreted it as an expression of territoriality. We stopped in front of a magnificent sleek ketch rig named Kota Bersetia. *Devoted City.* I'd seen these Bugis *pinisi* ships before, at the Ujang wharf in Surabaya. This one was two hundred tons, if she was an ounce, and the seven sails on her eighty-foot twin masts plied the Makassar Strait, one last majestic member of the world's last commercial sailing fleet.

Just after noon, we boarded a Litha bus to Sengkang, the epicenter of Bugi origins and culture. It hugged the coast for a few miles, through open countryside of grazing land and irrigated rice fields. A jagged range of limestone mountains, ten thousand feet high, rose to the east, and we turned towards them into the highlands, crossing and recrossing the Sadang River, until we left it behind, a brown line in the gorge below. It began to rain, swelling the streams that flowed into the light-shimmering rice terraces below. A man with his sarong flung over his right shoulder, smoking his *Kansas* in the middle of nowhere, waved as we passed.

At dusk we reached the shore of Lake Tempe, and the small

Bugis kingdom capital, buoyant bungalows on stilts. The last Buginese princess had lived in a cottage, now run by her nephew as the Apada Hotel. 'For its princely cockroaches.' Read one of its later reviews. Robyn and I were shown to our room by a handsome mature woman in sarong and blouse, her hair tied neatly in a bun.

"The feast is at seven." She said, bowing as she withdrew. And at seven we descended into a splendid courtyard, a royal refectory of dishes raised up on their lit burners. Flush-cheeked young women with red lipstick and long jet-black hair, in sarongs and sashes woven with silver and gold, and pearl necklaces, present us with flowers, as we sit crosslegged on the silk floor cushions. They serve us soup and goat meat and rice and vegetables, and fried crab in banana leaves and fresh grilled lake fish, and bir bintang. *Bugi board in a Bugi night.* Our descent next morning, down stairs floating into the lake, was rescued by a hardwood boat, with red, yellow, blue and white triangular string patterns on its curved prow. We passed under towering Cambodian palms, their own trunks submerged under the Tempe surface, past Chinese fishing nets, elaborately woven carpets draped over railings, reed houses on pilings with thatched roofs out of which protruded yellow flags high and crooked, flocks of flying foxes, and an old mosque suspended over the water, with a disintegrating cupola and short minaret. We visited silkworm factories, still marveling at how the Chinese first thought of using these ugly grubs to make such beautiful fabric, and we visited the looms, where the hand-weaving tradition continued. A Bugi family entertained us for the rest of the day, with stories of their recent history, and a remote epic. The *Sureq Galigo* is a Buganese legend, written between the 13th and 15th centuries, in a language that can now be read by no more than a hundred people. Its 300,000 verse lines outnumber the *Mahabharata* Indian heroic poem, commonly regarded as the longest in the world. It may never have been read in its entirety, so fragmented are the manuscripts that have survived the ravages of insects and humidity and decay and Islamist fundamentalism.

Once upon a time Sawerigading, the crown prince of Luwuq, visited his grandparent's grave in the Sunrise Kingdom. There he was told of an extremely beautiful girl in the forbidden area of the royal palace, who dressed up recklessly and spent all of her time bathing and talking to birds. When Sawerigading finally saw her, he felt his soul flew off him. But the girl he fell in love with turned out to be his own twin, We Tenriabeng.
Knowing he could not marry his own sister, Sawerigading took off from Luwuq, sublimating his desire by conquering the oceans of the world. News came from the North about I We Cudaiq, a Chinese princess prettier than We Tenriabeng herself. On the vast tapestry of waves to China, Sawerigading's fleet faced real human enemies, all conquered in seven large-scale oceanic battles. As morning broke over the Chinese Empire, the China Empress saw I La Welenreng, Sawerigading's main battleship, trying to reach the shore. Sawerigading had to find his way through a labyrinth to find I we Cudaiq, wrapped up like a giant butterfly cocoon with seven layers of Gods' silk. Her heart opened up neither by physical prowess nor material gifts, but by words: vast arrays of prose and poems composed by Sawerigading's mighty imagination, inspired by his wondrous journeys. But, it didn't work out and Sawerigading eventually left China, back slicing the waves, guarding and supporting his successors.

Or so the story goes, for six thousand pages. According to Bugis tradition, humanity is comprised of five distinctive genders— female makkunrai, male oroane, feminine male calabai, masculine female calalai, and finally, the bissu, a transvestite priest, possessor of spiritual knowledge. On the gigantic Bugi schooner of life, the love that Sawerigading had been actually seeking, may have been a Bugi man.

'Fear grows in darkness; if you think there's a bogeyman around, turn on the light.'
Dorothy Thompson

*   *   *

It was an eight-hour journey from the ochre world of the Bugis. Past the port town of Pare-Pare, our bus began a winding climb, through forested mountain passes patched together with gray cliff faces. The road levelled out onto a misty plateau, before crossing the verdant valley verge of Tanatoraja. We entered the world of the water buffalo, symbol of wealth in this life and the next, and the boys that rode them across the high country rice field dikes, greeted our arrival in Rantepao at dusk. Even the houses were shaped like their horns.

As was our immediate destination, the Hotel Indra Toraja. Robyn and I stowed our bags, and went down the road to the Mambo, for gado-gado and markisa juice, returning with the fog, to dreams in peanuts and passion fruit.

We awoke into a serenity of limestone and ebony groves and bamboo soaring sprays. The young formula one drivers outside the hotel had made excellent use of both of the latter in the construction of their racing vehicles, with intricate steering mechanisms at the top of long bamboo poles, and highly responsive multiple little ebony wheel assemblies on the bottom, more like B-70 bombers than Bugi Bugattis.

Their progenitors were believed to have migrated from what is now Vietnam, over three thousand years ago. Between their arrival in upland Sulawesi, and before the Dutch finally took an interest, the tribes the Bugis had referred to as the *To riaja*, People of the Highlands, were strong adherents of their own brand of animistic religion, the *Aluk To Dolo*, Way of the Ancestors. Some of it was pretty.

Their cosmos was divided into the upper world, the world of man, and the underworld. Heaven, covered with a saddle-shaped roof, had been married to earth, before the darkness, the separation, and finally, the light. Like a divorce lawyer would have promoted it. Animals lived in the underworld, a rectangular space enclosed by pillars, and a similar metaphorical minefield.

Mythical ancestors had descended from heaven down the same kind of floating stairs that had carried Robyn and I onto Lake Tempe. They were the connection to the Creator, *Puang Matua*. Other gods in the Torajan pantheon included the Goddess of Medicine, *Indo' Belo Tumbang*, the Goddess of Earthquakes, *Indo' Ongon-Ongon*, and the God of Death, *Lalondong*. The Torajans were big on death, and their language was intricately nuanced to express the subtleties of the sadness, longing, depression, grief, and mourning they experienced and, as we will see, shared around.

If death was mainly about funerals, life was all about agriculture, and *Pong Banggai di Rante*, the God of Earth. The earthly representative of both extremes was the *minaa* priest, responsible for how much beyond belief that Aluk controlled- law, habit, social life, ancestral rites, agricultural practice, and the imperative separation of death and life rituals, in the assumption that Torajan corpses could be spoiled by combining the two.

Not that there was much of a shared broad sense of identity, before the Dutch came up into their hills. Untouched by the outside world, the Aluk tribes functioned inside their autonomous highland villages, each with its own dialect, social hierarchy, and ritual practices. Interfamily relationships were codified by the exchange of buffalo and pigs on special occasions, and specified an individual's place in the social strata- who wrapped the corpses and prepared offerings, where a person could sit, who poured the palm wine, what piece of meat constituted one's share, what dish they could eat it on. The Torajans were matriarchical, and extremely class-conscious. Nobles lived in the large iconic buffalo horn-shaped *tongkonans*, commoners in bamboo shacks called *banua*, and slaves in small huts surrounding their owner's tongkonan. Slaves could buy their freedom, but their children still inherited slave status. Slaves were prohibited from wearing bronze or gold, carving their houses, or eating from the same dishes as their owners. Having sex with a free woman was punished by death.

The Dutch had ignored the Torajans for two whole centuries because access was difficult, they had little productive agricultural land and, behind well-defended walled hilltop fortresses, were serious slavers and headhunting warriors. What finally provoked the military colonial response was increasing Dutch concern about the spread of Islam in South Sulawesi, especially among the Bugis and Makassarese. In 1909 they drew a line around the Sa'dan area, and called it Tana Toraja, the 'Land of the Toraja.' They sent in the Reformed Missionary Alliance of the Dutch Reformed Church, to Christianize the Aluk tribes as a counterbalance. They angered the Torajans by abolishing slavery, by moving them to the valleys, and by taxing them severely. Despite, or because of, all the love, only about ten per cent of the Torajans had converted to Christianity. What got them the other ninety percent was the Darul Islam separatist attacks that forced them to finally ally with the Dutch for protection. In 1965 the Indonesian government recognized five religions. It took four more years for the Torajan *Aluk to Dolo* ancestral way to join the list.

"You should go to a funeral." Said the clerk at the desk next morning. "I will find you one." And she picked up the phone and began speaking to girlfriends in the same whiney lilt that sails on Malay lips, from Singapore to Mindanao.

"OK." I said, looking at Robyn. She looked back the same way.

"Go and have some breakfast, and some *Kopi Toraja* coffee." Said the clerk. "Then come back to see me." We went for breakfast and some *Kopi Toraja* coffee, across from a Bugi businessman. Something upset him about having to be here.

"The Toraja are infidels." He whispered. "Be careful not to attend any of their celebrations. They will slaughter pigs and serve you alcohol." We thanked him for his advice, and returned to reception.

"You must go by Kansas." Said the desk clerk. At least that's what we thought she said.

"You must go buy Kansas." She said, again. "Or a carton of Kreteks. Cigarettes."

"Cigarettes?" Robyn asked.

"Yes." She said. "As a gift to the bereaved family." So Robyn and I bought a carton of Kansas, and went to the funeral.

"Follow the smoke." She had said, when we asked how we would find it. *Follow the smoke*. But it wasn't from Kansas. It was from the food fires, inside the large *rante* compound. Robyn and I presented our carton of Kansas, and were quietly welcomed onto a grassy field of shelters, rice barns, and other ceremonial funeral structures by beautifully costumed young women with beaded antimacassars. I looked back to find our cigarettes already in circulation. The guest of honor was lying prone, wrapped in layers of cloth, atop the highest pavilion, supervising the preparations for his forthcoming long trip to *Puya*, the Land of Souls, from the treetops. One of his disciples instructed the proceedings through a microphone connected to the megaphone under his arm by a coiled serpent. A line of women in rose-peach dresses arrived and passed us, leading with the food bundles in their outstretched arms, crossing yet another in equally colorful garments, serving coffee and cakes, like competing teams of the half time show at the funerary Olympics. Our own contribution to the observance paled in comparison to the endless procession of gigantic trussed pigs, suspended from horizontal bamboo poles under their necks, steered by a man on each side that joined hundreds of others, left squealing and shitting in the muddy antechamber of their fate. There were scores water buffalo, tethered by the ropes through their noses, others wandering randomly and others yet, fighting, prodded on by the chile up their backsides.

Robyn and I entered a sea of conical hats. We joined

hundreds of sarongs, spread on the pavilion floors, or the ground, eating chunks of seared pork and vegetables and glutinous Burassa rice out of bamboo tubes, and drinking glasses of fermented *tuak*. Some were watching a *bulangan londong* cockfight, a sacred requirement to spill blood on the earth. Robyn knows how stimulus-averse I am to animal cruelty, and we quickly turned our eyes away. But away didn't work so well either.

Torajans think of the dead as being sick, and stuck in the living world, until their real demise is actuated by a *tomabalu* funeral specialist's dispatch of a buffalo. They believe that the deceased rides this buffalo to Puyo, and so it must be strong for the coming difficult journey over hundreds of mountains and valleys. They believe he will get there faster if he has many buffalo, although the biophysical logic of this is highly disputable. It didn't matter much to this man's tomabalu, who pulled the animal by the rope through his nose and, with a sharpened machete, quickly slashed the animal's throat. Young boys ran to catch the spurting blood in long bamboo tubes, which were then cooked as a sort of blood pudding over an open fire.

The butchering was done fast, the horns removed for the vertical collection attached to the pole on the front of the family house, and the buffalo roasted and eaten by the funeral guests. The boys who collected the blood clapped their hands and performed a bizarre cheerful Ma'dondan dance.

The number of animals slaughtered is proportional to the man's social status in life, and his age at death. At some funerals, up to a hundred have been immolated. Before the Dutch arrived, slaves or prisoners were also sacrificed, to provide servants in the afterlife. Inheritance goes proportionately to the child who slaughters the most buffalos. Sacrificed animals that had been given as 'gifts' by guests, are carefully noted as a debt to the lamented's family. I figured we were square.

Several buffalo carcasses, as well as their heads, were lined up on the field waiting for this owner. And then began the *Ma'badong*.

A company of men in black sarongs assembled in a ring, shoulder to shoulder, and began a slow circular dance and monotonous chanting. A reenactment of the cycle of life and the life story of the deceased brother, the Ma'badong would go on all night. This would be followed by other music and songs and poems and dances- the *Ma'randing* warrior dance would be done to praise the courage of the fallen one, with a large shield made from a buffalo skin, a helmet with a buffalo horn, and a sword. Elderly women in long feathered raiments would sing poems while dancing the *Ma'katia*. And the *Ma'akatia* would be danced to remind us all about the generosity and loyalty of our Torajan benefactor.

But Robyn and I left the ceremony. We took one last look at the shrouded pupa in the tall pavilion, and the beheaded water buffalo on the grassy knoll. It teemed down with rain. *Follow the smoke.*

We separated from Torajan death traditions next morning, and concentrated on some of their more life-affirming rituals, aware of how corpses are spoiled by combining the two. At least we thought we were being aware.

"You want to have Christmas dinner?" Asked our desk clerk. Yes, indeed, we replied, realizing that it was Christmas Eve. That would be fine.

"Better you have Christmas dinner at the Toraja Coralia." She said. So we thanked her, and booked in for that evening at the Coralia, on our way to the market. It was market day in Rantepao, with hundreds of huge pigs bound with green cords on green pallets side by side, rows of vendors with multicolored peppers, roosters, kreteks, green bananas, and long beans, more water buffalo with ropes through their noses, and firewood. When Robyn bought a finely made conical hat off the head of one of the elderly ladies in the clothing bazaar, I had the same shiver go up my spine as my purchase of an apron from a lady in Dali, many Chinese moons before. We drank Torajan coffee in glasses, and then I took her picture wearing her new headgear in a nearby bamboo grove, with shoots as wide as my arm.

The bemos near the market followed the universal general rule that the cheaper the fare, the more crowded and slower the ride. The boundary conditions for Robyn and I had been in a market in Nha Trang in the old Vietnam days, where two cents got us a ride to nowhere, all day long. The ten cents we paid in Rantepao got us almost nowhere in less than half the time.

Where we got to were some of the best examples of tongkonan architecture in Tanatoraja, immense thatch and woven bamboo houses with tremendous upswept high gabled buffalo horn roofs, facing north toward the home of the old gods, with a carved buffalo head talisman at the front. Large boulders loomed out of the mist at the base of each of the pilings. The long poles in front were nailed with a long column of water buffalo horns, arranged from the biggest at the bottom, to the smallest at the top.

The colors were Torajan colors of black death, yellow blessings from the gods, white purity, and red human life. The last also took the form of barefoot boys and their puppies playing on the thick tongkonan floor planks, or little ones peeking out of secret small window spaces above us, the tiny doors carved on the inside with roosters and an all-seeing eye.

Downhill on the right from this cluster of tongkonan, in another bamboo thicket, was a large tree with more small doors cut in it. Behind these doors, however, pegged shut, were the remains of children who died before their teeth had come in. The tree had absorbed these children and, when cut with a knife, it dripped white sap.

"Like milk." Robyn said.

"Like milk." I agreed.

We continued down the track past rice paddies and arching spumes of bamboo, into a forest across bamboo bridges. Half split bamboo canes, lain end to end within each other, brought water splashing into a bucket beside an isolated house a hundred metres further down the trail. We emerged at a crystal pool surrounded by limestone boulders and silence. Silent night. We made the bemo back to Rantepao in time for Christmas dinner.

"Today you go see Tau-Tau?" she asked, next morning. Robyn and I nodded our head affirmatively. Today was Tau-Tau day.

"See them now." She said. "Soon all gone." And she was right. The Tau-Tau were lifesized wooden effigies of noble takapua dead, sacred to living relatives who believed that they could bestow blessings and grant favors. Costing a year's wages to bring into being, Tau-Tau were also worth a year's wages to unscrupulous purveyors for the primitive art market, who stole more of the remaining figures every year, and caused many families to remove them into their homes.

The Makale bound bemo dropped us off at the Londa turnoff, and a two-kilometer stroll to the caves. Small boys were waiting with lanterns and entrepreneurial spirit. They were determined to give us our money's worth, and dragged us crawling through the claustrophobic warren of tight tunnels of skulls and long bones, spilling out of piled up coffins, some shaped like boats, intricately carved, and decayed. Sartorial sarong-garbed Tau-Tau statues guarded another part of the vault.

"Romeo and Juliet." Said one of the urchins, pushing the maxillary teeth of two of the skulls together for additional effect, and earning a ripple of nervous laughter from his other colleagues. They walked us back out along the checkerboard mud dikes of rice terraces to a waterworn limestone cliff face wall. Gazing out from a vertiginous height, was a row of weathered mannequins. One had his sarong flung over his right shoulder. Something protruded from his lower lip, even at a distance. *Welcome to Kansas.*

We paid the boys their rupias, and flagged down the same

Makale bemo, this time to disembark at the Lemo turnoff, for another two-kilometer trek to another sheer rock face. Big black butterflies with turquoise tails followed behind us. High above were two rectangular cut cave balconies with packed rows of effigies, eyes wide shut looking down, wooden hands with outstretched palms extended to receive offerings, and bestow blessings in return.

They were different carved heights and painted skin tones. One man wore a faded green shirt and jodhpurs. Another woman had a black dress and a red bandana. But there were common qualities to all the Tau-Tau. Their bags for traveling into the next world may have slung over their shoulders, but their clothes were tattered, and their expressions were emotionless, vacant. They looked tired.

They should have been, for the sights they had seen on their horizon. And the songs they had heard.

Kaloe' sambali' Manda'
Pentia' lambe'ko mai
Lakiperapi onimmu.

Parrots over there on the Manda'
Fly long and far on the way here
We're going to take up your song.

From the time a raid was planned, the expedition members were placed under a strict prohibition against eating foods made from palm or bamboo. The men commonly wore necklaces of octopus shells, which must be imbued with efficacy by a woman or no heads will be taken. The shells must still be dripping with seawater at the time of the rite. The Toraja equated the dripping seawater with the ejaculation of semen.

All warriors carried presents from a woman- a piece of cloth tied around the hilt of his sword, a penis-sized piece of wood, sucked during the raid, menstrual blood obtained by the man inserting his finger into a woman's vagina, and a tobacco quid taken from between a woman's breasts while she is sleeping. Sexual interest of any kind during the entire period of the raid was forbidden and would likely result in death. Without the presents, the warrior might not only obtain no heads, but also possibly die. Each man carried special rice prepared by a woman, alone in the middle of the night. The rice must be pure white and none of the grains should be broken. Any breach of protocol would abort the raid.

> *Malallengko toibirrin*
> *Tomatilampe bambana*
> *Lembum matil langkam borin.*

> Watch out you on the horizon
> You low on the foot of our land
> The blackened hawk is heading there.

The departure of the expedition was always at night
From an assault camp men crept into the enemy village and placed ash in a mortar there. They tried to get near enough to a sleeping member of the village to drop ash into their mouth. Under no circumstances was the head to be taken at this stage. The actual assault took the form of a general scrimmage, free of all ritual and rules, but one- it was absolutely forbidden to look at, let alone touch, the genitals of an enemy. This would bring misfortune.
No relative value is placed on male, female or children's heads, but if too large a number were taken, the surplus was simply thrown away into the bush, on the return journey. (If a warrior lost his own head in the course of a raid, his body was abandoned, and his soul became a dangerous wandering spirit luring other headhunters to the same end.)
The remaining heads on the return trip, carefully carried in the warriors' arms, were caressed, sung to, addressed and fed pre-chewed banana and other such foods. The warriors, prevented from re-entering their own village, because of their

contamination, were fed with ginger by a woman directly into their mouths, and showered with dry rice.

When the men were finally allowed back into the village, they were met by jealous and possessed women, who tried to steal or bite the heads.

Before they returned to their homes, the men were required to sit down with the women seated opposite them and sing various appropriate chants in antiphony, like Pacific Chorus frogs in the spring.

> *Sambanuami tobalu*
> *Satando'mi ana'bium*
> *Santanetemi u'bu'na.*

> One homestead the place of widows
> One hamlet the place of orphans
> One mountain the place of the graves.

During the festival which followed, the heads were referred to as 'Gifts from the Wurake,' a category of very high spirit, capable of ending a period of mourning. After 'The Feast of Bamboo Knives,' in which the villagers attacked and cut the remaining flesh off the head with bamboo knives, the skull of the dead was installed in a special building.

"They look tired." Said Robyn.

"They are." I said.

"And some are missing their heads." She said.

We had an early start in the morning.

"You leave today?" Asked the desk clerk. We nodded in the affirmative.

"You have fun in Tanatoraja?" She asked. We nodded a little less, to keep our heads on.

The name of the bus line ran the entire length of its fusilage. *Batutumonga.* We left the pristine cultivated valley of cassava and maize, wet rice terraces on the surrounding slopes, and climbed the cloud-covered eastern range of the central mountains. Our driver wove around the cloves and coffee drying in patches on the road, and Robyn and I opened our window to catch the sweet spicy scented alpine air, and views, and the most beautiful butterflies in Kansas.

TORADJA ALS KOPPENSNELLER (Z. W. SELEBES)

*   *   *

The Trans-Sulawesi Highway was a little like the Trans-Canada Highway. Not much, as it turned out. There were violent forces of chaos on the Trans-Sulawesi, just over the horizon. I swear I had no idea, or I would not have brought Robyn.

The first clue should have been the absence of foreign tourists on our Batutumonga express. The second should have been the absence of locals. There was Robyn and I, and a couple of official looking government types from Jakarata, sitting in the front of the big multicoloured Mercedes, making the ten-hour drive to Tentena, a town on the northern shore of Danau Poso. They weren't making any money from us.

Lake Poso is the third largest lake in Indonesia, over half a kilometer above sea level, and famous for its profusion of wild orchids, including a black one. Tentena was famous for two-meter long monstrous eels and, after ten hours inside the Batutumonga Express, we were ready for a feed of several centimeters. We entered the small town on the Poso River, both sides of which were connected by a blue and yellow bridge. Blue and yellow horizontal stripes decorated large vertical flags outside each household, and blue and yellow and red outriggers lined the sandy lakeshore. It was a blue and yellow kind of lakeside resort town.

There were V-shaped eeltraps, and where there were eeltraps, we reasoned, there were eels. Robyn and I checked into the Hotel Intim Danau Poso, and went to the Lotus restaurant. They were eelated to see us, and served up eelongated eels by hurricane lamp.

On returning to the Intim, we asked the owner what time the bus left for Poso next morning. He looked like we had just hit him with a shovel.

"No bus." He said, extending out his palms, like a tired Tau-Tau.

"No bus?" Robyn said. "So how do we get to Poso?" Now he looked even more tired.

"No bus. No bemos. No fly. No go Poso." He said. Robyn and I tried to understand the concept of how it was not possible to get from one place to the next. His wife emerged from behind the curtain.

"Maybe one way, but not stop in Poso." She said.

"Where then?" I asked.

"Palu." She said. "You must go all the way to Palu." My head, still on my shoulders, was beginning to hurt. We could get to Poso, but couldn't stop in Poso, and had to go all the way to the west coast town of Palu, another 220 kilometers.

"How do we get to Palu?" I asked.

"Toyota." She said. I nodded. She picked up the phone. Ten minutes later a young man with a ponytail and flipflops, and a packet of Kansas, appeared in the dimly lit reception. He didn't look Indonesian; he looked Cheyenne. He was with two other flip-flops, a thick tough Chinese wearing a blue and white baseball cap, with a fish-in-mouth raptor emblem on it, and a thin dark younger one, with a single eyebrow. It was Boxing Day, and I heard the bell for the first round. These kind gentlemen would drive us to Palu. It would take all day. We would pay for the trip, and their trip back.

"How much?" I asked.

"Sixty dollars." Said Cheyenne. And I thought the eels in this town were slippery.

"Forty." I said.

"Fifty." He said. "Very dangerous." Cheyenne's accomplices shifted ever so slightly on their flip-flops.

"OK." I said. Whatever. I should have offered them more. Spectacular stars and meteors painted the black out of the dark sky that night, and shimmered on the lake.

The black Land Cruiser was waiting outside the Intim at daybreak. Cheyenne was clearly anxious to begin. His associates sat in the front beside him, and Robyn and I piled into the back seat. We had arranged to stop at the Salopa waterfalls, a diversion that would take valuable time, but we didn't want to miss it. There were white sandy beaches and butterflies, and then a long walk through rice fields and winding lanes, to a crystal clear series of pools, cascades, and falls, in a beautifully serene and unspoilt forest. We had paradise to ourselves.

Cheyenne turned the Toyota north, towards Poso. There were far too frequent roadblocks, and conversations with paramilitary officers checking documents, that seemed longer than necessary, for a simple chartered vehicle hire.

As we passed through one small town, there was a kind of street commotion we hadn't seen before. Shirtless men, wide-eyed with anger, carried machetes in threatening poses, and shouted even more incoherently than they should have been, if we could have understood the language. Some appeared to be drunk. The smell of fear and blood and diesel was in the air. Cheyenne put his right foot down. I looked back to see a dark ridge of mountains, towering palm trees, and burning houses. Two bamboo tubes of sweet glutinous Burassa black rice came over the front seat, from the flip-flop friends.

"Very dangerous." Said Cheyenne. He was driving us through the opening salvos of the Poso War, and Robyn and I had no idea what that even was. We knew about Muslim-Christian violence in the Moluccas, but not what had just roared into flames behind and ahead of us, on the Trans-Sulawesi. Tentena was *red zone* Christian; down on the coast was the enemy. The *white zone* Muslims controlled coastal Poso town and much of the lowlands. The substrate for the conflict began, as in Tanatoraja, when the Dutch established colonial control of Tentena's Pamona headhunters in 1892, and offered them free lifetime membership in the Central Sulawesi Christian Church. But this also opened the door to nearby coastal settlement by Muslim fishermen from other parts of Sulawesi. After independence, the Indonesian government compounded the problem by transmigrating Balinese Hindus, and granting tracts of local farmland to Muslims from Java. The demographic tectonic plates began to grind against each other in the corrupt competition for local administrative control and employment, with the Muslims outflanking the Christians for all the choice positions. The flashpoint ignited by an argument about Christian youths drinking alcohol near the mosque in Poso. And Robyn and I hadn't even got there yet.

The Christian retaliation would come behind us, five months later. A group that claimed to be defending its ancestral home, would launch itself in Tentena. They called themselves the Black Bats, because 'the black bats move at night, black is the color of war, and bat soup is a local delicacy.' Dressed in black masks and capes, they terrorized Muslim cocoa and coconut plantations, kidnapped and executed hundreds of young Muslim boys, and left their bodies in local rivers and creeks. Many were missing their heads. Poso's Muslims would not eat fish for months.

The two sides fought with spears and bows and arrows, and homemade guns welded together from bits of spare piping, deadly to a range of over 250 feet. Paramilitary police weighed in on the Muslim side, with more automatic weapons. Over 1,000 people were killed in the violence, riots, and ethnic cleansing. And they were only warming up. In August of 2001, a branch of the *Laskar Jihad* 'Warriors of Jihad' declared open warfare, and dispatched fighters to Poso, equipped with AK-47s, grenade and rocket launchers, bulldozers and tanker trucks. The resultant scorched-earth campaign destroyed dozens of Christian villages, and pushed fifty thousand refugees into Tentena. In a supreme contest of eelimination, they would become a vigilante mini-state fortress, hemmed in by Muslims from the north, and from the south.

But this was still 1999, and Cheyenne and his two flip-flop friends were still high on Kansas in the front seat, guiding two foolish foreigners, through a war zone they hadn't even realized existed, to a refuge they didn't even know they needed.

Our Land Cruiser, the color of war, passed through the life-affirming montane forest of Lore Lindu National Park, containing birds that laugh like people, others that lay their single egg in hot sand, pigs that look like hippos, the largest snake in the world, and midget buffalo. I asked Cheyenne whether there was a chance of seeing any of these creatures.

"We may see one, or we may see God." He said. "The odds are about the same." The reason for that presented itself in the form of illegal new settlements we drove through, squatters clearing large patches of forest for agriculture. The National Forest was being destroyed by the National Migrants from Java and Bali. We stopped to admire the Balinese Aging Jagad Raya temple complex in Toini village, seven years before it would be pipebombed by Muslim terrorists. It seemed that Hindus would have the same chance as the other creatures of Lore Lindu, of seeing God.

Even though we had transmigrated the Poso War, we still had 170 kilometers of Trans-Sulawesi highway before we would arrive in Palu. Cheyenne and his flip-flop friends chain-smoked Kansas, and jabbered away in Bahasa, while Robyn and I watched the unpaved mountain roads getting narrower, and more precipitous. Just when we thought it couldn't get more treacherous, the violent forces of chaos returned once more, to prove us wrong. As Cheyenne negotiated a particularly tight turn around the track, cut out of where the mountain once was, the road disappeared. We stopped in disbelief. It hadn't actually disappeared, but it had appeared that it was buried beneath a landslide. No ordinary landslide, it was more like and tropical soil avalanche, come to reclaim the profile it had been born with. No one was going anywhere. We weren't going forward, and Robyn and I were determined that there was no way we were going back. Cheyenne and his flip-flop friends squatted on the edge of the universe, smoking their way through the rest of Kansas. Robyn and I kept an eye out for rare creatures, or God. We waited on our side of the mountain road, for all of three hours, before we heard the sound of deliverance. What finally broke through the earthen wall with a mighty roar, made us pinch ourselves, and rub our eyes. A brand new bright yellow D9 Caterpillar bulldozer, Kansas hanging from the operator's lower lip, tore through the topography like the US Corps of Army Engineers. It took another hour before anything like a roadbed was deemed safe enough for us to pass, but when it was, we did, and the last roadblock was behind us.

The eelation we all felt, as the black Toyota pulled into Palu, was eelectric. It was like driving down the Champs-Élysées in Paris, if Paris had been in the middle of a drought, and bombed by the CIA. Cheyenne motioned to us in the rear view mirror.

"Golden?" He asked. That sounded good to both of us, and we nodded in unison. A few minutes later, down Jalan Raden Saleh, we pulled up outside the Hotel Palu Golden. There were no words.

We paid Cheyenne and shook hands, and wished them well, on their road back to the Poso War. Inside the magnificence of the Palu Golden, none of what we had experienced was on any radar screen. We were checked into one of fifty-five of their three-star rooms, with quiet refinement, and invited to dine in their Ebony restaurant before it closed at ten. We had *koktel udang* prawn cocktails and Guinness, before returning to our room. There was a stick man sign in the bathroom. Penggunaan kloset yang benar perawatan. *Use proper toilet care.* I wondered about some of the clientele.

Robyn and I awoke to the sun's diffused dawn glow on the two swimming pools below, and Palu Bay and the mountains beyond. And the dilemna we had avoided all night. Where do we go from here? How the hell do we get there? And how long would that take? It was still a thousand kilometers from where we were, to our other area of interest in Manado. We needed to fly, if we could, and soon.

Robyn and I tripped over each other, down the open marble staircase to reception, to find out. Our desk clerk made several telephone calls. Yes, there were flights to Manado, but only once a week. Yes, it appeared it was today. Yes, there were seats left, but only two. On Robyn's ticket, she was identified as 'Robun.' No one cared.

The Merpati plane was an old Spanish Casa C-212, which had been put together by Dirgantara Indonesia, *Indonesian Aerospace*. I had never seen those two words nailed together before and, looking at the thing, had to agree that the original Spanish name, *house*, not only more than described its appearance, but its probable aerodynamic properties as well. And we were not to be disappointed for, despite the fact that our only way out of this part of Kansas was in this flying garage, it soared exactly like the box it was. The first hundred kilometers wasn't terrible, but when we flew into the mountain ranges of North Sulawesi, we almost flew into the mountain ranges of North Sulawesi. It probably didn't help that that plane was full, and that no one had weighed the luggage. It probably didn't help that we had entered a patch of particularly inclement weather and heavy turbulence. But it definitely didn't help that the lone pilot was making an effort to meet and greet the two foreign passengers, who had chosen to grace his route that very day. He lit up a cigarette in the aisle, while his aircraft played handball with the sky outside. He wanted to know all about us. I wanted to know who was flying the house.

"Autopilot." He said proudly, blowing Kansas from between his yellow teeth. We entered the tornado in the Wizard of Oz, when he excused himself for 'something important.' To our relief, he headed back to the cockpit, and we slowly, very slowly, found level flight.

Things didn't go much better on the ground, after Robyn and I left Central Sulawesi. In 2003, 'unknown masked gunmen' killed thirteen Christian villagers in Poso District. Two years later, Palu suffered both a 6.2 Richter scale earthquake, and a Muslim nail bomb at a market stall selling pork to Christian Minihasa for New Year's eve celebrations, killing eight people and wounding another 53. The same year someone killed another 22 Christians with a bomb in Tentena's public market, and Islamic militants in Poso beheaded three Christian schoolgirls.

The message found next to one of the heads was fairly clear.

A life for a life. A head for a head.

*   *   *

> 'The little town of Menado is one of the prettiest in the East...To the west and south the country is mountainous, with groups of fine volcanic peaks 6,000 or 7,000 feet high, forming grand and picturesque backgrounds to the landscape.'
>
> Alfred Russell Wallace, 1859

What Darwin had been to Chiloé, Wallace was to Sulawesi. It was the line on either side of this orchid of the Southern Sea, that separated the species of Asia from those of Australia, and made Sulawesi, as a distinct biogeographical entity containing marsupials and mammals, part of what is known as *Wallacea.* It was the finish line of the theory of evolution, which Wallace had actually crossed first.

Robyn and I could see Manado Bay in the distance, as our Merpati flying house made its final approach. Volcanic cones rose out of the Celebes Sea from great submerged monsters, and puffs of cloud hovered over the surface of the water like steam from their nostrils.

We thanked the pilot for his hospitality, and marveled at his longevity, once we were safely on the tarmac of Sam Ratulangi. We passed Sam's statue on the way into town, six giant clay garden gnomes in gray cubscout uniforms. The musical creole of Manado Malay greeted our exit from the bemo, with numerous borrowed words, like those for horses and chairs and enticing women and bad men, from their Portuguese and Spanish and Dutch *Stranger Kings* history. But there were also Chinese shops and Kung Fu movie houses, and ice cream banana splits at the News Café on Jalan Sam Ratulangi. It was a lively place.

Robyn and I had been spoiled by our night at the Palu Golden, and our search for truth took a degenerate detour towards beauty. We checked into the old colonial feel of the Hotel Minihasa, and checked out its tiny infinity pool, with the plump juicy cloud-covered volcano hanging on the water's edge. In Minihasa, there was one church for every hundred meters of road. We dropped into a few hundred meters worth, and then stopped by the red and kaleidoscopic colors of the three hundred year old Ban Hin Kiong Chinese temple, whose pamphlet description excused the fact that 'there is not much to buy in this complex because it is basically a house of worship.' We ate more koktel udan, and smoked fish *tinutuan*, a rice porridge containing corn, greens and chilies, at the Dolpin Donut restaurant.

The next day we pushed it further, and traveled twenty miles down the southwest coast, to Tangawangko Bay, and the Tasik Ria. *Where comfort is paramount*. It was two days before New Years, and the entire resort was empty. We got our choice of cobalt blue-tiled roofed Chinese bungalows, with white pillars, and a view of palm-filled gardens and expansive pool, and dined on delicious Tasik Ria fried chicken with chilies and kecap manis, in the Bunaken coffee shop. For the New Year's Eve that would welcome in a new millennium, we flagged down a bemo back into the city, and checked into the Novotel Manado. A Minihasan orchestra of wooden marimbas was playing in the lobby. There were 'Happy Third Millenium' cards, with a picture of the solar system, on our pillows and, later, under the door, as if in answer to the Y2K paranoia of the age, a friendly note from the manager. 'To prevent any problems at midnight we will stop the operation of all elevators at the main lobby between 23:50 to 00:10.' The fireworks display outside was more of a threat. It should have incinerated the entire city.

On the last night of the Twentieth century, Robyn and I ate at the Rumah Mkan 'Bahari.' We had heard that Minihasa food could be all 'bat, cat, and rat,' not to mention *rintek wuuk* dog, so we stuck to the *rica-rica* spicy fish and *dabu-dabu* sambal beef, with *sayur bunga* sautéed papaya flower buds.

On New Years Day, Robyn and I took a boat across Manado Bay, to Palau Bunaken, an eight square kilometer island of jungle known for its marine biodiversity. It had seven times more genera of coral than Hawaii, seven of the eight species of the planet's giant clams, and seventy per cent of all the known fish species of the Indo-Western Pacific, including over thirty-three species of butterfly fish, and graduate schools of groupers, wrasses, gobies, and damsels. I paddled mine in an outrigger along the eastern coast, until we found a small beach. Robyn was content to check into one of the small bungalows, but I had heard that the accommodation was better on the other side of the island.

"I'll go check it out." I said, and left her with half the water. There was a scarcity of fresh water on Bunaken, and drinking water had to be imported from Manado.

"How long will you be?" Asked Robyn.

"Not long." I said. "It doesn't look that big on the map." Unless you got lost.

I started up the bushtrail to what I thought would be the most direct route to the other coast. The path grew steep and started to meander through the tropical forest, as the heat of the day began to penetrate the canopy. The streams of perspiration were the only streams on the island, and threatened to outpace my water supply. I trudged on and off the path, in the direction I thought should be due west, but I couldn't see the sun above the green maze and, even if I could have, it was midday. Two and a half hours later, heat prostrated and parched with thirst, I finally punched a hole in the jungle, and onto the western coast. I almost collapsed onto the first two Bunakenese boys that I encountered, and they quickly revived me with water and reassurance. I explained that Robyn was still around the island on the eastern shore, and asked if there was a way we could rescue her from what, by now, must be a similar degree of dehydration. One of the boys disappeared down the mangroves. Not five minutes later he was back at the wheel of a deafening noise. It looked like a World War II American PT boat, and it was, except for the lack of torpedos, and the fact that it had been constructed of local hardwoods. But it had the same shape and displacement hull, and two seventy-horse Johnson outboards on the stern. It flew like a Sulawesi horeshoe bat out of hell, and we were around the northern tip of the island in no time. I pointed to the beach that Robyn should be waiting on, and they cracked open the outboards to warpspeed. I crawled onto the large curved bow, and stood up with my arms crossed, for added effect. As we roared into the shore, I saw Robyn emerge from the tree she had sought shade under, and I straightened my profile and pose, like MacArthur would have, if this had been the Philippines. I caught the first terms of endearment from my rescued damsel, just as the boys shut down the Johnsons.

"Where the hell have you been?" She demanded. I wasn't so much offended, as startled, by what I thought was the rather inappropriate ingratitude that had been demonstrated, considering the lengths I had gone, to ensure her salvation. She piled onto the PT boat, and the boys roared us back around the island, to a small homestay, which was also ultimately deemed to be anything but an improvement on what I had initially paddled our outrigger to.

"Mangroves?" She said. "You brought us to mangroves?" There was nothing for it, but to admit the truth of her observation. The mangroves were fairly obviously there. We got the last room in the crowded homestay, next to the noisy lounge where the divers drank at night. And then the mosquitoes arrived, just to make it all perfect.

Our trip back across the bay next morning continued south and inland to the rusted tin roofs, donkey drays, and tarp-covered market stalls of Tonohon. We climbed to the caldera and sulfur smell of the Mahawu volcano, and its crater lake, before continuing on to the *waruga* stone sarcophagi of Sawangan. Gnarled frangipani trees contributed to the eeriness of the place. Ancient Minihasa, wearing huge copper necklaces and bracelets, were buried otherwise naked in a fetal position, squatting atop a china plate, inside stone graves shaped like a house. The rooflike lids were carved with scenes depicting the life inside the hollowed-out rectangular base. There were almost 150 of them, the oldest dating back to 900 AD. The Dutch outlawed the practice in the early 1800s, because of outbreaks of cholera and tuberculosis, long before they were able to outlaw the practice of Minihasa headhunting. The Minihasans were as fierce as the Bugis and Torajans. Ceremonial *Foso* feasts celebrated successful hunts with accomplished headhunters in their exclusive red garments, dancing their Kabasaran war dances. The novelist Thomas Mayne Reid, who was a drinking mate of Edgar Allen Poe, admired Lord Byron, and was admired back by Robert Louis Stevenson, Vladamir Nabakov, Teddy Roosevelt, and Conan Doyle, not only wrote *The Castaways*, about a party shipwreck in the Celebes Sea, but also *The Headless Horseman*.

"Headlessness seems to be another common theme in the Southern Sea." Said Robyn. It was not too far wrong.

"Even San Juan Bautista, on Isla Robinson Crusoe, was named after St. John the Baptist, whose head was presented on a silver platter to Salome, at her request, as a reward for the dance she had performed for King Herod."

We spent the night at a losmen on Lake Tondano, inside four walls of floor to ceiling carmine curtains, chunky faux French Provençal furniture, and tall vases full of pink plastic flowers. But the bamboo lakeside restaurant that supplied our lunch, from pens containing the huge carp we pulled up with nets, was a delicious fresh fish feast of gastronomic grandeur. Along the shoreline north were fisherman pulling up their oen Chinese fishing nets, and a manufacturer of prefab rare hardwood houses, that looked so much like alien crabs, I expected them to begin moving sideways with us, along the road.

The final stop of our Northern Sulawesi excursion south of Manado, was to the Tongkoko National Park, thirty kilometers from Bitung. We entered a forest of tremendous trees, buttressed with protruding fins like rocket ships, strangler figs, spiraled vines, and subdued light. We were so surrounded by crested black macaques, at one point, that I seriously feared for our safety. Twenty-five of them, baring their long eyeteeth and grimacing, moved in random patterns around us. One female turned to show us her red bottom, not a highlight of our journey, in any sense.

What Robyn and I had really come to see, was a tiny extremely shy nocturnal primate with soft velvety fur, and unusual anatomy. Only ten centimeters long, their hind limbs are twice this length, due to the elongation of their tarsus bones, from which they get their name. Each of their enormous eyes is as large as their brain, and their fingers are extremely extended, with their third finger as long as their upper arm. In light of how fast we are driving them to extinction, it didn't seem like an inappropriate adaptation. We hired a guide to take us back in with flashlights, in the middle of the night. After scrambling around for what seemed like hours, one illuminating beam caught a small gremlin above us on a branch. It was a tarsier, with a baby, jumping at insects. She was magnificent. We spent the night in the ranger's accommodation. The locals, including the women, were drunk on beer.

But in the early morning there were swooping hornbills, with large eyelashes. On an island where more than 60 percent of its mammals and more than one third of its birds are found nowhere else on the planet, Sulawesi has lost more than eighty per cent of her forests, from logging, agriculture, and mining. The animals themselves are disappearing because of habitat loss, hunting for bush meat and the exotic pet market, disease introduced by domestic animals, and the lack of any truly organized conservation measures. The Sulawesi and Knobbed hornbills are some of the most endangered, declining at a rate of forty percent over three generations.

"How does he hold his bill up?" Asked Robyn. His red comb and blue beard and yellow bill made one more pass throught the canopy.

"His first two vertebrae are fused together, and his neck muscles are very powerful." I said. "It may confer some slight protection against the headhunters."

We walked to the beach and rested under the huge mimosas. I made a big heart on the black sand with two dozen of its white and red-fringed flowers. On the way back through the ranger's village, we came across a local marching ensemble made up of elaborately plumbed facsimiles of euphoniums, tubas, trombones, and some that had no comparators. They were made of bamboo. Just before the bemo back to Manado arrived, we were visited by a slow large marsupial Sulawesi bear cuscus, which seemed to have come to remind us of Alfred Russell Wallace. Or to plead for help.

We had three more days left in Kansas. Before we left Manado, I had made some inquiries. There was a place off the coast on an island called Pulau Gangga, which had a resort owned by some businessmen from Northern Italy. It was apparently empty and in trouble, but still open, and we negotiated a favorable discount. A heavy plank boat picked us up late morning and, with Robyn sitting on the anchor in the very bow, holding onto her Torajan conical hat, we plied the Celebes Sea, through pods of dolphins and square sailed outriggers, to the white beach and coconut palms of the last resort. We were greeted by Surat, who took on the role of man Friday. He showed us to a luxurious bungalow, and welcomed us every morning with fresh papaya and a Peter Lorre flourish.

"Enchoy you Brakefasst." He would say. And we would. We spent three wonderful days on Pulau Gangga, eating pasta in squid ink in the Coconut Bar, collecting rare shells and red coral that had washed up on the shore, and playing along the waterline with the kids and dogs in the village on the next beach over. And then it was.

Surat gave us two coconuts to take on the plank boat journey back to Manado. They were carved. In the shape of heads.

*   *   *

Reece's Place
Fiji

'Oh, East is East, and West is West, and never the twain shall meet...'
Rudyard Kipling, *The Ballad of East and West*

The big Fijian island of Viti Levu is divided by more than its central mountain range, and West is East, and East is South. Robyn and I found out about the West is East part, during a two-week Fiji diversion, on our way to begin a new life in New Zealand. We landed at Nadi's airport at the same time we would always land at Nadi's airport- in the heaviest frangipani-laden tropical torpor of a Southern Sea predawn. We carried our packs and lethargy onto the tarmac, and into the dimly-lit incandescence of the shabby open terminal. We were greeted by massive moths on mustard walls, and massive black men, with massive black brillo hair. A deep resonant noise came out of the blue shirt and white triangle-hemmed *sulu* skirt, who took our passports.

"Bula." He said, stamping them with such force that the imprint, but for the fixed date, might have been good for a few more arrivals. Colorful posters were tacked on the walls, warning of AIDS and elephantiasis. Outside, the insect swarms around the streetlights grew smaller with the increasing crimson of the horizon, and the flame trees that burst into the day, along the curb. Robyn and I had landed on the Cannibal Isles. All we needed now, were cannibals. Instead, a thin dark moustache pulled his car alongside, and rolled down his window, like he was using his last ounce of energy. A flock of mynas, black heads on chocolate brown bodies, squawked and foraged around us.

"Nadi town?" Asked the Indian taxi driver. *West is East.* We negotiated a price that converged on correct, when his head bobbled, and piled in the back. He drove out of the airport slowly.

"First time to Fiji?" He said. But he didn't really care.

I was reminded of what James Mitchener had written. *"It is almost impossible to like the Indians of Fiji. They are suspicious, vengeful, whining, unassimilated, provocative aliens in a land where they have lived for more than seventy years. They hate everything: black natives, white Englishmen, brown Polynesians and friendly Americans. They will not marry with Fijians, who they despise. They avoid English ways, which they abhor. They cannot be depended on to support necessary government policies. Above all, they are surly and unpleasant. It is possible for a traveler to spend a week in Fiji without ever seeing an Indian smile."* I wasn't convinced that any of this was true and, if it was, I had some understanding of why.

The tragedy of Fiji's Indians began in 1879, with the arrival of the *Leonidas*, a Mayflower of misery, bringing 463 indentured workers from Calcutta to the sugarcane plantations beyond the port of Levuka. It was the predecessor of other labor transport ships that would land another sixty thousand over the next 37 years. Indentured Hindus and Moslems from Madras and Calcutta were herded down into the lower decks of these coolie ships. The women were often victims of sexual predation by the European crew. Condemned to eat, sleep, and sit amid their own waste, many did not survive the long brutal 'middle passage.' Their dead bodies were unceremoniously thrown overboard. Every one of them had signed agreements, which they knew as 'girmits,' requiring them to live in the squalid shacks and work in the cane fields for five years, before their bond would be repaid, until the planter paid their passage home. It seldom happened. Their descendents were called 'girmityas,' like the one driving our taxi.

"The Polynesians brought black rats, and the British planters brought us, and the mongoose to kill the rats in the cane fields." He said. "But the mongoose is awake during the day, and the rats are awake during nighttime. They never meet."

Just like the Indians and the Fijians. I asked how everyone was getting along.

"The situation is dormant." He said, like he was describing a volcano. The Prime Minister at the time was Major-General Sitiveni Ligamamada Rabuka, OBE, MSD, OStJ, otherwise know as Colonel Steve Rambo. Rambo had previously staged two military coups the year before we arrived, and was on record as wanting to 'send the Indians home,' even the ones that had been born in Fiji. The Indians considered the Fijians 'jungalis,' poor backward hillbillies occupying the southern coasts and mountains, and the capital of Suva. *East is South.* Mitchener liked the Fijians as much as he disliked the Indians. *It is doubtful if anyone but an Indian can dislike Fijians. They are immense Negros modified by Polynesian blood. They wear their hair frizzled straight out from the head...They are one of the happiest peoples on earth and laugh constantly.*

In some peculiar Disney fashion, the unintended admixture of Fijians and Indians worked for us, tempering happy, sleepy and dopey Melanesian dysfunction, with an Indian dose of bashful, grumpy and stealthy Indian efficiency.

Our taxi turned off onto a dusty side road lined with multicolored Bougainvillea, yellow orchids, red hibiscus, bananas, palms and papayas, and pulled up in front of a white trellised façade. There was a hand painted sign above the entrance. *Nadi Sunseekers.*

"It is the most economical hostel in town." Said our driver. We paid him, and entered to a hospitable reception, scoring the only double room in a ramshackle rabbit warren of dorm beds. I locked the door with our own padlock, and Robyn and I headed back down the lane, across the Nadi River Bridge, and down the single market street of double-storied pastel houses, demarcated by external air conditioners, like rows of double-six dominoes. The shops sold clothing and jewelry and too many duty-free tchotchkes and trinkets, heavy on the trinkets. The largest emporium of artifacts and handicrafts and souvenirs was Jack's of Fiji. Robyn and I entered the air-con, to look at jack shit. Inside were brash Australians, sizing up the Kava *tanoas* for salad bowels, and the hardwood cannibal weaponry for serving implements. I picked up an *iculanibokola* replica, the multipronged fork that had been used by attendants, for feeding chiefs considered too holy to touch their own food. I seemed to have touched off a homing signal, and was immediately surrounded by several Indian floor staff.

"Fork." Said the tall one who had closed the gap the fastest. "For eating."

"For eating people." I said. Head bobbles all round.

"You are needing one perhaps?" Another asked.

"Perhaps." I said, picking my teeth with a fingernail, and watching them all back away.

Robyn and I continued along the street towards the main market. Many Indian shops looked old and shabby, with prominently displayed 'close-out' signs, for the purpose of emigration rather than expansion. We stopped in at the Sunflower Airlines office, to book our flight to Kandavu for the next morning. *The Airline with a Heart.* The market was in Technicolor, with yellow bananas and lemons and breadfruit and jackfruit, mauve eggplant and big pink yams, red chilis, green mangos and watermelon and cabbages, ash-grey manioc, tall tied pink and green taro, and bright orange pineapples. Large Fijian women with frizzled black hair, in their garish Mother Hubbard dresses, sat on plastic tarps around the outside of the stalls. There was the smell of flowers and fish and dust and frying oil. We walked under a sign, reassured. *Poisonous fish prohibited for sale.* The stringy earth color we were seeking, was sold only by Indians, for consumption only by Fijians. We needed it for our arrival in Kandavu. In one of the most interior stalls, we found trays of the long curled roots of *Piper methysticum*, the 'intoxicating pepper' of the Southern Sea.

"You are wanting Yaqona?" asked the stall proprietor, pointing to his collection of kava. "Very powerful." We had been told to buy powerful, so this was the guy. He told us the price. I flinched.

"Gratitude is expensive." He said, not appearing like he had much to be thankful for himself. The cost of four year-old roots had apparently doubled in the previous three years. I paid him.

Down the southern road was the blue and pink and lime pastel Sri Siva Subramaniya temple, aspiring to emulate the Dravidian skyscrapers of Southern India. But the concrete contract had obviously gone to the lowest bidder, and the tropical mildew was making inroads, like it had with Paul Theroux's *namba*, in the same Fijian humidity. *The situation is dormant.*

Back at the market, we boarded a bus to Lautoka, for the evening firewalking. Just north of Nadi, we passed Raymond Burr's Garden of the Sleeping Giant, four thousand acres that he and his paramour, Robert Benevides, bought in 1965, to house his orchid collection from Sea God Nurseries. I remembered his emergence from the closet, and the scandal created at the time for a Canadian actor, playing the role of a brilliant legal mind with impeccable integrity, to have so deceived his fan base. *When you pick someone to lie to Mrs. Granger, never choose your doctor or lawyer. In both cases they can be fatal...In any country but this, they would have let him in.*

We made the 24 kilometers to Sugar City in record Indian bus driver time. Lautoka had the largest crushing mill in the Southern hemisphere, but the sugar produced, like its girmitya producers, was brown, not white. Bligh had charted the coast while making his epic lifeboat voyage to Timor after the mutiny, in 1789. Not much had changed, except for the Japanese honeymooners that had also arrived for the firewalking ceremony. Robyn and I recognized the Australian salad bowl seekers from Jack's. The social anthropologists who pretended to understand the purpose of these types of activities define a notion of *collective effervescence*, in which a common arousal results in a feeling of togetherness and assimilation. They quote data that purportedly demonstrates the synchronization of heart rates of the firewalkers and nonperforming spectators. This is presumed to be the physiological basis for an alignment of an aroused emotional state, which strengthens group dynamics and forges a common identity. I looked around at the social dynamics between the Indian owners, the Fijian dancers, and the tourists, and rather than finding any evidence of collective effervescence, I saw a bunch of tourists that seemed anxious to see some feet burnt. The dancers were Sawaus from the island of Beqa, and would be walking on stones that were white hot, from the bonfire that had been lit hours earlier. In the old days, the participants had to abstain from women and coconuts for two weeks before the ceremony, or the gods that had given them the gift to walk unharmed on these stones, would withdraw their protection. The guy with the girl on his arm, slurping his green coconut water through a straw, seemed blithely unaware of the injunction. Just after sunset, he defiantly pounded his way across the rocks, and emerged unscathed. I knew this was a phenomenon of simple thermodynamics. The 'mind over matter' was 'matter over matter,' quickly. The amount of time the foot is in contact with the ground was not enough to induce a burn, and the stones were not good conductors of heat. The square root of the product of thermal conductivity, density, and specific heat capacity is called *thermal effusivity*, and explains how much heat energy the body absorbs or releases in a certain amount of time per unit area, when its surface is at a certain temperature. It was the *Leidenfrost effect* from the insulating vapor barrier under the dancer's wet feet that protected him, not his deal with the gods.

But you have to keep moving, or the thermal conductivity will catch up with you. The twenty managers of the Kentucky Fried Chicken outlets in Australia, who confidently jumped into the firewalking team-building exercise three years after they were buying salad bowls in Fiji, were treated somewhat differently, for severe burns.

The collective effervescence also didn't bubble up the fact that Iron Age Indians had been firewalking on coals since 1200 BC, when the current Fijians were still living an aboriginal existence on Taiwan. We all left the party after the situation was dormant, burning with togetherness and assimilation.

*　　*　　*

'It is easy enough to define what the Commonwealth is not. Indeed this is quite a popular pastime.'

Elizabeth II

Each bay, its own wind. Robyn and I were back out at Nausori airport in the early afternoon next day. We had eaten lunch at Poon's 'Fully licensed wine and dine,' and had acquired the same taxi driver that had brought us the nine kilometers, a day earlier. We checked in at the Sunflower Airlines *Airline with a Heart* desk, and were directed out onto the tarmac in the blazing sun, to wait for our pilot, beside the eight-seater matchbox toy Britten-Norman Islander. I asked the frizzy Fijian lady behind the counter if the flight was full.

"Only you two and the pilot." She had said. As the sun began a descent past our 2:30 Flight 2S44 departure time, I wondered if there was only going to be the two of us when, loping out of the hanger, came a skinny white guy, tucking in his white shirt, and swearing a blue streak.

"G'day." He said, unapologetically. "Bloody baboons. They could have bloody told me. Where are youse two from?"

105

"I'm from Canada." I said. "And my wife is from New Zealand."

"Yeah, well I'm from Australia." He said. Not that there was much doubt.

"I guess we're just one big happy Commonwealth family." I said, trying to soften the edges.

"Don't give me that shit, mate." He said. "I've got no time for that bitch."

The Airline with a Heart. He went on to tell us that he was a 'solid republican.' I was hoping he was as solid a pilot.

"Hop in." He said, like we were going for a spin. He pointed to Robyn. "You can sit up front with me." He took off like a republican. I leaned over and asked him how he ended up flying for a small airline in Fiji.

"A man's gotta eat." He said, veering off to the right. A few minutes later,

Robyn let out a giggle.

"Hey, hon." She said. "I'm flying the plane." I looked over the seat again, to find her clutching her wheel, and the Aussie looking out the window.

"Give it back." I said. "Please." It wasn't but a few minutes later that the forested wasp-shaped form of Kandavu hove into view, and the pilot made his descent. I guess that's what you could have called it, except for the fact that it was more like an abrupt nosedive, ten thousand feet straight down. He pulled out at the very last minute, hitting the muddy ground like he was landing an Aussie Rules football.

Out of the Britten-Norman, I put on my straw hat, and lit up my pipe. I looked up to find a tall striking older Fijian man, with a straw hat and a pipe.

"Humphrey." He said. "Humphrey Bogart Reece. But you can call me Reece." His handshake finished with the sweep of a large index finger.

"My boat is down that hill." He said, pointing beyond the far end of the landing strip. "It will take us to Galoa Island later, but first we need to go to the village. Did you bring the yaqona?" I pulled the paper bag full of roots out of our daypack. He opened it and took a deep breath.

"Powerful." He said. We got it right.

Past the volleyball net and the top-hinged shuttered open windows of the whitewashed school building, Reece and Robyn and I walked for several minutes out of Vunisea, to a small building, and a warm welcoming *sevusevu* ceremony from some *mataqali* village elders in sulus. We joined the large circle, already seated on woven rectangular pandanus mats, layered on the floor. They inquired after our health, and where we were from. We told them.

"Commonweath." Murmered around the circle. *God save the Queen.*

With a nod from Reece, Robyn pulled the bag of roots out of the daypack, to expressions and mutterings of obvious admiration. Reece place the bundle in front of oldest one with the thickest glasses. He clapped his hands three times.

"Chief." Reece whispered.

"Vinaka." Said the deputy seated next to him. *Thank you.* And the Chief made a speech in Fijian, there was chanting, and then the herald clapped three more times when the monologue was finished.

"Tell them the purpose of your visit." I had this one covered. Under no circumstances were we to consider this a material exchange. We had come to pay our respect to the village and its traditions. We were bringing, not taking. There was a slight vertical nodding of heads, definitely not side to side. The conversation shifted for good into Fijian and, except for the odd recognition of our names, Robyn and I were lost in the honorifics.

"You are now members of the village." Said Reece. We sat a little taller on our mats.

A large old dark wooden tanoa appeared, without the salad greens. Its attached *magimagi* coconut fiber cord, adorned with cowrie shells, was extended out towards us.

"Grog bowl." Said Reece. Three men closed in behind him,

one to mix the yaqona, and two to serve. An ancient polished sperm whale tooth *tabua* was placed on the mat in front of him.

"Qai vakarau lose Saka Na Yaqona vaka Turaga." Said the mixer. *I will mix the Yaqona for the Chief with respect.*

Upright and cross-legged, he pounded the kava quickly in a large stone with a small log, blended it with cold rainwater, and strained it through hibiscus fibers. In the old days, the yanqona roots would have been chewed by young girls and spat into the tanoa, for better extraction of its active ingredients, but the missionaries, who had brought the Fijians Mother Hubbards and the word of God, took away their saliva and their joy, in exchange.

The mixer filled a coconut shell *bilo* with the murky liquid, lifted it high, and poured it back into the tanoa, so the Chief's herald could see its opacity.

"Wai." He said. *Too strong.* More rainwater was added. Another stream careened through the air. I could sense the saliva, coming into mouths around me.

"Wai donu." Said the herald. *Just right.* And the mixer circled the tanoa with his arms.

"Qai darama saka tu na Yaqona Vakaturaga." He said. *The chiefs yaqona is ready to drink with respect.* He clapped his hands three times, and carefully took the Chief's own full bilo to him. Cupping his hands, and clapping deep and dignified, the Chief took his first drink, as everyone clapped in slow cadence.

"Maca." Said the herald, after the Chief had finished with a single flourish. *Empty.* Everyone clapped three times. Then it was the herald's turn.

"Maca." He said, again. Everyone in the circle clapped twice. The herald touched either side of the tanoa.

"Taki vakavo Na Yaqona vaka Turaga." *Now all may drink of the chiefs Yaqona.* And he clapped twice.

Everyone else would drink from the same coconut cup as the

herald had used. The bilo came around the circle clockwise, with much clapping and ceremony. It got to Robyn, and left with a grimace. By the time it got to me, it had left a trail of stories being told in Fijian. I looked down into the bowl. It looked and smelled like muddy water but, draining it in one long swallow, it tasted like muddy water, with a little pungent peppery wintergreen sawdust thrown in. I clapped three times, and then the novocaine hit. My lips and tongue were frozen for the next ten minutes. It was passed to the single toothed smile to my left.

"Fiji Bitter. " He said. As a physician, I had read about this stuff. Sun-dried kava root is about fifteen per cent active kavalactones, water-insoluble compounds destroyed by heat, and producing a mild cheerful sedation, relaxed muscles, analgesia, talkativeness, and vivid dreams, through GABA neurotransmitters which increase dopamine and noradrenalin in the brain. The mechanistic theories always sound more scientific than they really are. What kava is definitely associated with, is liver damage, puffy faces, scaly yellow skin rashes, addiction, and lazy days. But in a culture where the principle preoccupation used to be cannibalism, kava was an excellent way to relieve short-term anxiety, and a peace pipe between quarrelling groups. Given a choice of conflict resolution methodologies between the collective effervescence of firewalking, or kava, kava wins, hands down. The hands were down to indicate that the tanoa was empty, and another bowl of grog was mixed, and made the rounds. After it passed me the second time, I realized that my legs didn't work. This was a potential life-threatening situation, as I was aware of the fact that kava ceremonies could continue on late into the next day. Earlier, I had received another warning from Reece.

"You may be asked to say a few words." He had said. "We call it *talanoa*, shooting the breeze." The breeze was about to become a gunshot fatality. I noticed the Chief waving his arm towards me.

"He wants to know about your travels." Reece said. And I couldn't move my legs, and my mouth wouldn't work either. "But I told him we must go to our boat, before it gets too dark." I managed to exhale, and told Humphrey Bogart Reece what his namesake had said. *The problem with the world is that everybody is a few drinks behind.*

Robyn and I thanked our hosts, swayed on our legs in gratitude, and followed Reece back through the village, and down to the long handmade hardwood skiff on the mud beach at the bottom of the hill. It was painted white and yellow, with red gunnels, and took but a single heave from our Fijian host, to launch us into Namalata Bay. The last of the daylight was almost gone, but we could see the northern tip of Galoa Island from our departure point, and it took but a few minutes to make the high-tide crossing. A hurricane lamp, suspended in the darkness on the other shore, nodded up and down, like the heads on our village hosts. Hovering just above it was Mona, Reece's wife, a delightful charming Bacall for our Bogart. She welcomed us with happy Fijian enthusiasm, and brought us directly into the low ceiling of her kitchen, where we had the first of many home-cooked dinners of fried fish and casseroles, yams and potatoes, and pasta, rice and taro.

Reece's Place was basic. There was no hot water, no telephone, no cold beer, no obvious maintenance, and electricity from a generator too expensive to run, except for the hour Mona needed it to prepare dinner each evening. Flat-wicked kerosene lamps provided light, and ambience. Our thatch *bure*, in a coconut grove under a large laden breadfruit tree, was decorated around its base with a continuous line of giant porcelain clam shells. The absence of mongooses on Galoa had ensured a ready supply of skinks inside our room, and a continually changing panoply of large moving head-height spider webs outside the square apertures that passed for windows. It was wonderful.

We awoke to clouds of noisy collared lories, kaleidoscopic

flurries of purple parrot heads and bums, green necks and wings, red undercarriages and yellow beaks, all of them high-pitched shrieking that we were missing the best part of the day. We emerged to a profusion of birds that existed nowhere else in Fiji, or on earth- Kandavu Honeyeaters, Kandavu Fantails, Crimson Shining-Parrots, Velvet Whistling Doves, Scarlet Robins, Fan-tailed Cuckoos, Fiji Bush-Warblers, Fiji Shrikebills, Golden Whistlers, Polynesian Trillers, and Vanikoro Flycatchers, all of them found only on the Kandavu archipeligo. And this didn't include the Collared Kingfishers, Pacific Swallows, Black-throated Shrikebills, and dozens of other birds, which were endemic to other parts of Fiji as well. Kandavu, in fact, was a destination for birders, divers, and nobody else, except us.

Mona had rung the big metal triangle, announcing her breakfast of *babakau* Fijian fried bread, fresh pawpaw and pineapple, watermelon and bananas, and lemon leaf tea, but Robyn and I had a gauntlet to run, before we would reach her kitchen. The gauntlet was real and metaphorical. Hundreds of loaded coconut trees were swaying in the breeze above us, like there was already kava inside their shells.

The coconut tree was originally from here in Melanesia, and had been named by the Portuguese, after their word for 'head,' from the size and the three small eyes. *Coco*. Across thousands of kilometers of the Southern Sea, adrift for as long as six months, a light and buoyant and highly water resistant coconut, beaching on some new shore, will put down roots from two of these eyes, and send a shoot up into the warm sunlight, from the third. Within six years it will have become a fruit-bearer, with a lifespan of a hundred years. Its first metaphor, that of the ultimate vehicle for self-sufficiency, is echoed in its Sanskrit name, 'kalpa vriksha.' *Tree of life*. The Fijians, and other islanders, pressed it for oil, scraped it for cream, and used it as fire fuel. Its husks were used as *coir* for ropes and mats, and *sennit* for twine. The trunk of the tree was used in construction, and the palm leaves were employed as roof thatch, and woven into baskets. Sap was fermented into palm wine and toddy, and the juice from the leaf stems made into palm sugar. There is only one species, found in a vast area all over the world, usually from 30° north of the equator to 30° south, but as far away as Norway. It is the most abundant single food tree in existence, contributing as much as forty percent of national income in some Pacific Island nations. It is a metaphor for their Diaspora. In New Zealand, successful Island migrants are still know as 'coconuts.' It is a metaphor for salvation. It was here in Fiji, during World War II, that the liquid inside young coconuts was discovered as a substitute for blood plasma.

It is a symbol for wealth. Beginning in the 18th century, Europeans suffering a shortage of dairy fats in their home countries, and with the comparative expense of harvesting whale oil, discovered the preciousness of coconut oil, and the dried *copra* flesh, its extraction left behind. It takes about six thousand full-grown coconuts to produce a ton of copra, with sixty million tons a year now produced in over eighty countries for the production of soap and shampoo and detergent and cosmetics and cooking oil and glues and epoxies and lacquers, the Europeans efficiently exchanged this new source of wealth for disease and territorial and religious and cultural and genetic bloodline colonization. Which is the fourth metaphor. Exploitation.

The presence of coconuts in a landscape always seemed to connote a 'backwardness' that required civilization. The 'millionaire's salad' of shredded coconut heart palm, required the death of the tree for its extraction, like the sacrifice of souls for Christ, or whole islands for atomic research.

But the Big Kahuna metaphor for the coconut tree, the one that did most of the damage, was that of Paradise. The seductive image of pristine, palm-fringed beaches was the one essential element on any exotic tropical brochure, capable of transforming white pasty lives of quiet desperation into real naked hedonistic freedom. The coconut was the icon of the castaway. To tourists, it was their ticket to a culture of 'friendly' natives. The coconut clashed with any concept of cannibalism, and encroached on reality.

The final metaphor encroached on our own heads, eighty feet above our circuitous path to Mona's kitchen. The only revenge for the coconut, and the Southern Sea cultures that the Europeans exploited for it, for all the economic dependency and nuclear testing and social unrest and domestic violence and high unemployment and Japanese whalers and disease, is gravity. The only justice meted out for the intrusive cultural consumption of cocktails in half-coconut shells by the pool, and the conversion of cannibals into quaint local happy natives dancing in grass skirts, is a two kilogram coconut falling at eighty kilometers an hour with a contact force of a metric ton, or more. About 150 people are killed every year by falling coconuts, fifteen times the statistical likelihood of death by shark attack. Traumatic coconut head injuries account for 2.5% of hospital admissions, in areas with plantations. Many travel insurance companies now include coverage for injuries caused by falling coconuts, and many tropical resorts, to avoid costly lawsuits, now remove all the fruit from coconut palms, or replace them with other trees. Indian government officials ordered coconuts removed from the trees at Mumbai's Gandhi museum for President Obama's visit, not that it would have likely made any difference to the intelligence of his foreign policy. How ironic, that the most poignant romantic symbol of the fertile Southern Sea paradise, requires emasculation, for the safety of the seeker of Shangri-la. The shoreline of Waikiki is now graced by eunuchs.

Not so on the way to Mona's breakfast shack, however. The 'thud' of hard falling coconuts would shake the ground, and wake us at night.

Robyn and I spent three barefoot days at Reece's Place, exploring the rock pools down at the beach, snorkeling on the Great Astrolabe Reef, named after French commander Dumont d'Urvilles shipwreck, in 1827. We watched green turtles during the day, and spooked ourselves silly, in the midst of the crunchy movements of the gigantic coconut crabs, at night. We thrived on Mona's casseroles, with views of the rugged forests and volcanic mountainous terrain of Kandavu, just across the bay. We could just barely make out the eight hundred meter high top of Mount Ndelainambukelevu, on the southernmost tip, on the clearest day. One day we went across, to boat down a river, and swim under a waterfall. On our return, Reece and I played guitar and smoked our pipes, full of *Amphora* and philosophy. I was curious about how a Fijian would get such a name, but he didn't really know. When the captain of the HMS Pearl, James Goodenough, the man responsible for the annexation of Fiji to the British crown, visited Naitisiri province in 1874, he stopped for a night with a Mr. Reece.

> 'The ground and labourers in good order. He has a horseshoe
> of 1100 acres, cultivates 270, and says that a man should look
> after three acres. He has a little cane in the ground, like every
> one else. It takes from thirteen to fifteen months to be made fit
> for crushing. Had an excellent dinner of turtle-soup and pie, and
> tea with milk... The officers slept in the cotton-house, the men
> chiefly in the boats, a few of us in Mr. Reece's house. Mosquitoes
> all night through. I don't think I slept fifteen minutes together; a
> horse kept on moving all night, and I kept an end of my sheet in
> my hand, and flicked at the mosquitoes constantly. I think that
> every one was glad when the bugle sounded to rouse out at 4 a.m.,
> and all jumped up and dressed.'

The day we left, the sky opened up, and the water came down in torrents. Life is like this: sometimes sun, sometimes rain.

'Better sleep with a sober cannibal than a drunken Christian.'
Herman Melville

115

*   *   *

Three hours from Nadi, down the only road on the island, three hours from Monoriki, where Tom Hanks and Wilson the Volleyball were filmed in *Cast Away*, was the history of real castaway, and the de facto capital of Oceania.

Robyn and I crossed over naked muscular sugarcane hills and the Sigatoka River, along the southern Queen's Road mangroves, tidal mud beaches and fringing reef, the hotel glut of the Coral Coast, to the busy peninsular harbor of Suva.

Paul Theroux, who 'needed happiness to write well,' was less than charitable. (Suva) *reminds me of an aunt of mine who drank too much, delightful, prone to stumble, clothes a little askew, and always a strap of her slip showing... the sort of place you could buy a screwdriver or teapot or roll of tape, but never a pair of shoes or clothes you liked.* His description of the city as 'seedy,' may have sprouted from the fungus on his namba. We found it charming, an old colonial blend of Melanesian melatonin and missionary monotony. The sun radiated down on the steep steps of the South Seas Private Hotel. Robyn and I sat on the veranda, watching lawn bowls and a rugby game, in the green of Albert Park below us. It was my birthday, and the Fiji bitter wasn't. We had just returned from the Fiji museum, in the Thurston botanical gardens. Implements of the country's history were displayed in static cases behind glass, in a deliberate civilizing effort to sanitize the savagery, but you could still smell the air inside.

The story, like many in the Southern Sea, began with a real castaway, actually three shipwrecks and two castaways. In 1798, the first ship arrived in Port Jackson, Australia.

'The Argo, an American schooner, arrived from the Isle of France, having on board a cargo of salt provisions, French brandy, and other articles on speculation; which, as usual in this country, found a ready sale, much more to the advantage of the owners than the colonists.'

Two years later, on her way from China back to Sydney, the Argo was wrecked on Bukatatanoa reef, east of Lakeba. Aside from the crew, which managed to reach Tonga before all but two were killed, the Argo left three surviving legacies, which changed the archipelago forever.

The first was a dysenteric epidemic that tore through Fiji's virgin immune system. No one knows what 'the wasting sickness,' *Na lila balavu,* was (it may have been cholera), but it ravages devastated native communities so badly, the remnants were left to weak to bury their dead. It was accompanied by other gifts of civilization- measles, tuberculosis, syphilis, gonorrhea, and rum and muskets.

The two Argo survivors were rescued in 1802.

One of them, Oliver Slater, had spent the two years after the wreck near Bua Bay, where he discovered prodigious numbers of sandalwood trees. The news of this, on his arrival in China, led to an explosion of sandalwood exploitation on Vanua Levu. Four years after Slater's rescue, a second ship's disaster occurred, again in Tonga, on Lefooga, in the Ha'apai Group. The crew of the tall privateer warship Port au Prince, almost 500 tonnes, armed with 24 long nine and twelve pounders and 8 twelve-pound carronades, were massacred, and the ship burnt to the waterline. There was but one survivor, Charlie Savage, who was to become 'the most notorious beachcomber in the South Seas.' His luck didn't change much, when he was rescued a year later by the third ship, the *Eliza,* a 135 ton American sandalwood trading brig out of Providence, Rhode Island, on its way from Sydney to Fiji. In June of 1808, it was wrecked on Mocea reef, off Nairai Island. Savage was equal to the promise of his surname. Fluent in Tongan and Fijian, and violent to the point that even large Fijian warriors were wary of him, Charlie salvaged a large number of muskets from the wreckage of the Eliza, demonstrated their potential to the great *Vunivalu* Bau Island chieftain, Ratu Naulivou, and with the powerful combination of circumstance, personality, and technology, launched the terrible carnage of the Fijian Wars. Lacking any of the cultural inhibitions of the Bauian leaders (like not immediately attacking enemy chieftains at the beginning of battle), he brought a lethality never seen before in the islands. His 'victims were so numerous that the townspeople piled up the bodies and sheltered behind them; and the stream beside the village ran red.' Charlie took credit for the victories, and numerous wives and a share in the sandalwood trade, in more physical remuneration. Drawn by tales of wealth, unscrupulous seamen from other ships loading sandalwood, deserted or obtained discharge, bought muskets and ammunition, and joined Charlie's growing band of mercenaries at Bau. Within two of three years there were twenty reckless, cruel, pampered profligates, living the morality of the poultry yard.

But Charlie Savage only lasted five more years. In 1813, he briefly joined Captain Robson's Calcutta sandalwood trading ship, *Hunter*, and went ashore on Wailea, to destroy a number of local canoes. They walked into an ambush. According to the account of the third mate, Peter Dillon, several thousand natives chased the crew up what was to become known as Dillon's Rock, and laid siege. Charlie suggested they break and run, but was overruled by Dillon. Several Wailean chiefs climbed the hill, to offer friendship and peace, and Savage, 'accompanied by a Chinaman,' went down to parlay. When Dillon refused his instruction to come down, and another sailor tried to escape, the Wailea took out their frustrations on Charlie, drowning him in a well, and baking him with his companion, as 'long pig'. His bones were later made into sail needles. When Olle Strandberg visited some of the smaller islands in 1950, he found local Fijians still singing traditional songs about their most famous castaway.

> 'Charlie Savage with the purple beard
> Was eaten by men from Vilear.
> His hands and his feet gave them strength.

His fat women were driven up into the hills,
Charlie Savage with the purple beard
Fed a hundred warriors with his flesh.'

Dillon, for his part, seized the priest who eventually came to negotiate, thrusting loaded musket muzzles into his back and ears, and marching him through the thwarted throng of screaming warriors, back to the Hunter. He later returned to the Wailea, 'assisting them to destroy their enemies, who were cut up, baked, and eaten in his presence.' Charlie Savage died the same year as the sandalwood trade. By 1840, the US Exploring Expedition had trouble finding even a few specimens for their collections. Every stick of the wood had blood on it. As the trees declined, the natives had become more hostile, wreaking their vengeance for outrages committed by one ship on the crew of the next. Traders were murdered for their metal implements, and eaten for their protein. It had been said of Savage that he shot certain Fijians, discovered in the act of eating human flesh, but the culture of cannibal cuisine was too pervasive to give this much credence.

Despite the fact that two-thirds of ethnic Fijians are Methodists, the highest proportion of the population of any nation, and that the exhibits at the Fiji museum had been made more presentable by this influence, the missionary movement in Fiji had initially been more about meat than Methodism.

The last documented act of cannibalism had occurred in Nabutautau, in 1867. The Reverend Thomas Baker, a Methodist missionary from Sussex, mistakenly broke a tabu by attempting to retrieve a comb from the Chief's head, and ended up as the final feast. Other ministers witnessed horrific acts of cannibalism. In 1844, Reverend Thomas Williams witnessed the recapture of a Lakeba chief's wife, who had run away in the middle of the night. Her arms were chopped off and cooked. That evening, the chief made her sit across from his dining table and watch him consume her arms in horror.

> 'Cannibalism among this people is one of their institutions; it is interwoven in the elements of society; it forms one of their pursuits, and is regarded by the mass as a refinement.'
> Reverend Thomas Williams

Two years later, Reverend John Watsford witnessed a regular display of slaughter on Bau, in a terraced arena, around which were sited raised stone seats for onlookers.

> 'In this space was a huge 'braining stone,' which was used thus: two strong natives seized the victim, each taking hold of an arm and leg, and, lifting him from the ground, they ran with him head foremost – at their utmost speed against the stones – bashing out his brains.'

The Bau chief told Watsford that he did not like the taste of the flesh of white people, even when most delicately cooked, any more than he liked the flesh of the people of the Carpenter Tribe, both of which he considered tough and tasteless.

Fijians now regard those pre-Methodist times as *Na gauna ni tevoro*, the 'Time of the Devil.' Their original adoption of the act was an adaptation to the rigors of long voyages at sea. When they arrived in Fiji about 500 BC, they took on the customs of the Polynesians that had preceded them a thousand years earlier, including the constant warfare and cannibalism. The reputation of feasting Fijian ferocity deterred European ships from sailing anywhere near *Cannibal Isles*, and contributed to its isolation for decades longer than other archipelagos in the Southern Sea.

Sacrifices were an integral part of conquest and commemoration. Ceremonial occasions required stacks of piled-up freshly killed corpses, and 'Eat me!' was the proper ritual greeting of a commoner to a chief. No important business began without the slaying of one or two human beings as a fitting inauguration. For every chief's canoe made, a man was slain for the laying of its keel, a fresh man was killed for every new added timber added, others were crushed to death, as rollers at its launching, and yet more were killed at the first taking down of the mast. Other men were slaughtered to wash its deck in blood, and furnish the feast of requisite human flesh. New buildings were consecrated by burying live adult prisoners in holes dug for the support posts, so the spirit of the ritually sacrificed would invoke the gods to help support the structure. Captured enemy children were hung by their feet from the rigging of the victors' canoes. The ultimate humiliation to an enemy, however, was to eat their flesh. Victims were bound ready for the ovens, as unharmed as possible, lest any of their blood should be lost. The more impatient gourmands, unable to wait until the ovens were sufficiently heated, pulled the ears off the poor wretches and ate them raw, sliced off fingers and tongues, or chopped out large muscle groups to cook more quickly, while the sufferers, kept alive, watched in agony. Skulls were used as drinking bowls, and sexual organs were hung from trees as trophies of victory in battle.

William Speiden, the purser on the 1840 US Exploring Expedition, wrote from ringside.

'The men doomed to death were made to dig a hole in the earth for the purpose of making a native oven, and were then required to cut firewood to roast their own bodies. They were then directed to go and wash, and afterwards to make a cup of a banana-leaf. This, from opening a vein in each man, was soon filled with blood. This blood was then drunk, in the presence of the sufferers, by the Kamba people. Sern, the Bau chief, then had their arms and legs cut off, cooked and eaten, some of the flesh being presented to them. He then ordered a fishhook to be put into their tongues, which were then drawn out as far as possible before being cut off. These were roasted and eaten, to the taunts of 'We are eating your tongues!' As life in the victims was still not extinct, an incision was made in the side of each man, and his bowels taken out. This soon terminated their sufferings in this world. One man actually stood by my side and ate the very eyes out of a roasted skull he had, saying, 'Venaca, venaca,' that is, very good.'

He also described how a whole tribe had been condemned to be eaten to extinction by the Namosi people, as a punishment for some misdeed. This was achieved over a period of years, with one household eaten each year.

The most famous Guinness book world record holder for 'most prolific cannibal' was a chief named Udre Udre, who recorded his human consumption by making a placing a rock on a cairn he had created, for each one eaten. The final count was 872 stones. Over a hundred had been white men.

Because a *bokola* feast was constipating, human flesh was always eaten with three kinds of vegetables, the leaves of *malawaci* and *tudauo* leaves, *boro dino* cannibal tomatoes, and *taro*, stuffed into the victims' cavities.

The *iculanibokola* forks behind the glass cases of the Fiji Museum were more elaborate and elegant and less embarrassed than their Methodist descriptions. Our search for cannibals in the Cannibal Isles seemed to have been hermetically sealed. Robyn and I wandered down to the market for dinner.

The land for the original town of Suva had been extorted from King Cakobau by the Americans, for looting that had taken place, after a cannon exploded at the house of the US consul. The Australian Polynesia Company bought out the Americans, with the intent of turning it into a cotton plantation. Cakobau ceded the whole country to the British. *Commonwealth*. In 1953 the Richter 6.5 Suva earthquake had triggered a reef platform collapse and a submarine landslide tsunami that killed eight people, two in Kandavu.

Southeast trades moisturized the evening mountains behind us, and the sinusoidal centipedes of shops, squirming down to the sea. It was my birthday, and the market stall we chose was full of big Fijian families of big Fijians, gorging on favorite dishes. One of them was *palusami*, a casserole of taro leaves and coconut milk and onions and cannibal tomatoes, and Spam. It was delicious. There was a rumor about the popularity of Spam that must have brought a combination of smiles and shivers to the Hormel executives back in Austin, Minnesota. The smiles had come from the market saturation they have enjoyed in the Southern Sea, since it invaded with American GI stomachs in World War II. For almost the same reason, it now forms the basis for wedding gift boxes in Seoul, since the Korean War. But the popularity of the mystery meat in the Pacific was more attributable to the shivers. It seems that pork is not the only 'other white meat.' Spam tastes like long pig, and the Fijians were passionate about the stuff. I shared this insight carefully with the immense Fijian rugby player at the next table, tucking into his Fiji Bitter and his Spam palusami.

"I think this one used to be a clown." He said.

"A clown?" I asked.

"Yeah." He said. "Tastes funny."

'Strange to see how a good dinner and feasting reconciles everybody.'
Samuel Pepys

Isa lei, na noqu rarawa
Ni ko sana vodo e na mataka.
Bau nanuma, na nodatou lasa,
Mai Suva nanuma tikoga.

Isa Lei, the purple shadows falling,
Sad the morrow will dawn upon my sorrow.
Oh! Forget not, when you are far away,
Precious moments beside Suva Bay.

*   *   *

The Most Beautiful Beach in the World
Vanuatu

The Southern Sea rooster outside our window saluted his survival of another sunrise in the local creole. *Yufala i mas wekap!.. Yufala i mas wekap!*

I rolled out of bed and dressed quietly, so as not to disturb Robyn. We had come a long way to get here, and it hadn't been completely effortless.

"Its early." She said. "Where are you going?"

"I'll go get us some breakfast." I said, and slipped out the door.

The island of Efate had arrived late the previous afternoon, as a smudge of jungle green on turquoise. Below us, Port Vila appeared like it had been dropped disorderly from our Air Pacific wingtips, all its bungalows and shops and Quonset huts sliding downhill in chaos, toward the deep harbor. Random erupting splashes of carmine, *Delonix regia* flame trees, put their rusted tin roofs to shame. Coconut palms streamed along the shoreline, just beyond the meandering main street consumed by the small shacks at its vanishing point.

We landed at Bauer Field, named for Harold Bauer, an American WWII flying ace, who had shot down eleven Japanese planes, and was killed in Guadalcanal. *Plen i foldaon.* There was speculation as to what would happen to his brass plaque, with the signing of Japanese-Vanuatu joint venture to improve the airport.

Outside the terminal waved the country's flag, a patchwork of floating red for the blood of its boars and men, bottom green for its verdant forests, a black triangle containing a boar's tusk and two leaves of the local *namele* fern, and a bright yellow Y-shaped fimbriation, lighting the Gospel through the archipelago. Captain Cook had already lost the plot when he named it the New Hebrides, in 1774. There is nothing about Vanuatu, not the climate, the geography, nor the culture, which could possibly have reminded him of the dreary flat shivering barren moors of those northern Scottish Islands. But then the Presbyterian missionaries arrived and converted a third of the population, lighting the Gospel through the archipelago, and ensuring the local hotel employees would never know the sin of tipping tourists. In 1906, the French and British agreed to share sovereignty over the island group. I use to collect postage stamps from the *New Hebrides Condominium*, which had nothing to do with the form of accommodation we were seeking, and didn't encounter.

The first lodging we arrived at had apparently escaped the light of the Gospel fimbriations. A sordid scene of pre-Presbyterian carnage had broken out in front of the hotel, warring clans of drunken Melanesian males, poisoned but not yet paralyzed, fighting with shouts and sticks, and worse on the way, a patchwork of floating red for the blood of its boars and men. The reggae that was pumping itself out of the bar, turbocharged the tribal testosterone mob of black faces and red eyes, trying to focus on who was in the taxi.

"I think we'll look for somewhere else." Said Robyn. Gazing out at the display of New Hebrides Pandemonium, I recognized it as a lost cause. By the time we found a small hotel in the center of town, it was too late for anything but sleep.

But the crack of dawn had brought new hope and, while Robyn slumbered, I set out on a missionary quest of my own. For Vila had been the capital of the Anglo-French Condominium, and where there had been the French, there would be the quintessential Gallic item of *petit dejeuner* indulgence. Here, in this most black backwater of colonial seclusion, somewhere, someone would be baking croissants.

I emerged into the moist sweet early morning air of smoke-dried copra coconut kernels, and tropical mud. Huge spider webs joined the power lines to anything they could, their fat owners hanging arachnid languid, in the center of each radiation. Grass grew unevenly along the road. Everything else needed a new coat of paint. There were a few big Melanesian women with frizzled hair and Mother Hubbard dresses, carrying primary color triangular segmented umbrellas, and men in singlets, heading half-asleep towards parked pickups and vans.

The dead calm shifted almost imperceptibly, and I caught a faint but unmistakable whiff of my quarry. *Butter.* It was butter. I could already hear them suffering, layers of crusty crackling crumbs outside a soft honeycomb. *Le feuilletage.* I turned the corner in the street, and there it was. Pacific Paris paydirt. I entered the boulangerie, and pressed my nose up to the glass counter. Inside, still warm, were my captive cannibal croissants.

"Bonjour." I sang. "Je voudrais acheter quatre croissants s'il vous plaît." I was going to buy four.

"Moning." Said the voice behind the counter. "Hamas yu wan?" And there, of course, was the epiphany. For not only did the bakery employee not speak French, it seemed more than reasonable that I should be able to communicate with him in something that sounded vaguely like English. Which, of course, it was, but not really. Bislama, his native tongue, was high, as they say, on the morphosyntax. Even its name had come from pseudo-French 'Beach-la-Mar,' or bêche de mer, the dried sea cucumbers that formed one of the foundations of 19th century regional economic activity. It was also called 'Sandalwood English,' for the second most important trading activity. But the language itself, its English vocabulary and Oceanic grammar, was born of slavery. Beginning in the 1870's, almost half the adult male population of the New Hebrides, and several other Pacific islands, were kidnapped in 'blackbirding' raids, to work the plantations of Queensland, Fiji, and the guano island off the coast of Peru. Hundreds of thousands of these slaves needed a *lingua franca*, and the pidgin that evolved from these tragic circumstances, became the basis of Bislama communication among the 113 different languages on the Vanuatu archipelago, when those indentured laborers that survived, finally returned home. Verbs do not conjugate and pronouns do not decline.

"Yu pem fo?" Asked the bakery clerk.

"Mi pem fo." I said. The aroma dragged me back to the hotel, and woke Robyn from her sleep.

"Where did you ever find those?" She asked.

"Jes laki." I said, shattering shards of croissant all over the bed. And after that, I noticed Bislama all around us.

It was posted as a warning in our bathroom.

> Hotel ia y kat septic tang system mo toilet pepa blong iusum. Yu no mas sakem strong pepa i go long toilet, iusem toilet pepa nomo. Plis yu iusum plastik bin we i stap long bathrum mo sakem of strong pepa or ol narafala pepa i go long hem. Plis mi nitim co-operesen blong yu long notis ia.
>
> Thank yu.

It was the language of the Bible in the top drawer of our bedside table.

> Tufala i stap yet long Betlehem, nao i kam kasem stret taem blong Meri i bonem pikinini. Nao hem i bonem fasbon pikinin blong hem we hem i boe. Hem i kavremap gud long kaliko, nao i putum hem i slip long wan bokis we oltaim ol man ol i stap putum gras long hem, blong ol anamol ol i kakae. Tufala i mekem olsem, from we long hotel, i no gat ples blong tufala i stap.

It was the language of the Home loan pamphlet, in the ANZ bank we changed our money in.

> ANZ 'Yumi hapi!' Yumi Hapi Land Lon...Fes Step Blong Yu Gat
> Yumi Hapi Hom Lukaotem Vanuatu ANZ bank
> Yumi Hapi Land Lon

Hemi fes step blong yu blong save get wan haos blong yu.
*Yu lukim wan pis land long Vila o Luganville we yu laikem blong gat?
*Yu gat permanen wok we yu risivim salari long hem?
*Yu gat cash deposit?
*Yu save pem lon ova long 5 yia i go kasem 10 yia?
*Sipos yu talem 'Yes' long ol kwestin ia, kam mo toktok wetem ANZ...
*From mifala I tink se mifala I save helpem yu blong drim blong yui kam
        tru.
*ANZ's special lon interes ret hemi lo blong helpem ol Ni-Vanuatu blong
        oli save pem wan land blong olgeta.
*ANZ bambae I no jajem eni bank fis long lon blong yu.
*ANZ's flexibal repelmen tems hemi mekem i mo isi long yu.
*ANZ bambae i ademap legal mo transfea fi (go kasem 30,000 Vatu) long
        lon blong yu.
*ANZ's enginia bambae i jekemap graon blong yu blong mekem sua se
        hemi gud blong mekem haos long hem (smol fi bambae I apiae).
Yumi Hapi Land Lon
I Mekem Drim Blong Yu I Kam Tru.

Judging by all the white smiles on black faces, and the lineup for home loans in the ANZ bank, there must have been a lot of *drim blong yu i kam tru* happening. The Happy Planet Index, published by Friends of the Earth International, estimated the Ni-Vanuatu to be some of the happiest, most ecologically efficient, and longest living people in the world, not that urban squatter migration, and alcohol-related morbidity, and the sign outside the central covered market wasn't somewhat disconcerting.

Lukaot Long Sik
AIDS/SIDA
No slip olbaot- yu save kasem sik!
Tinkbaot se yu gat wan laef nomo
Yu mas karem kondom!

The words in Bislama for 'I love you' were actually *mi ded long yu*, but overall, life in Vanuatu was still a *nambawan lafet*, an excellent party. The language was as playful as its native speakers. A child was a *pikinini*, Jesus Christ was *pikinini blong God*, a helicopter was *mixmaster blong Jesus Christ*, and Prince Charles was *nambawan pikinini blong Missus Kwin*.

Petrol was *bensin blong truck* and wine was *bensin blong man*. A saw was *pulem i kam, pushem i go, wood i fall down*. A woman's brassiere was called a *titi basket*. But the most fun lived in the names of the musical instruments. A piano was a *black fala box we i gat black teeth, hemi gat white teeth yu faetem hard i sing-out*, and a Violin was a *wan smol bokis blong white man, all i scratchem beli i singout gudfala*. And you could improvise, and they would understand you.

Robyn and I improvised our way through the covered market, admiring the colorful taro and yams and pineapples and pawpaws and mangos and plantains, and eating the *aelan kaekae* coconut crème fish and stodgy *lap lap*, in the stalls of the frizzy haired Mother Hubbards who made it so delicious. We visited the shop where they bought their muumuus. A notice in the window warned of consequences.

Lukaot
Stil Long Stoa
Hemi wan trabol.
Bae mifala I singaot Polis sapos
yu stil
no mata hamas yia
yu kat.
NO STIL

Robyn and I had arrived between a major cyclone and a major earthquake, but we had come for a purpose. North of Efate, in the northern part of the largest island in the archipelago, was a remote landmark with the reputation of the most beautiful beach in the world. We had already booked a flight for the following day to Espiritu Santo, and our jet lag was fading. It was World Police and Fire Games Fundraising night at the Le Legon Resort, and Robyn and I had tickets for the 'Dinner Dance Custom Dancing Show,' with a pig roast, and a great Vanuatu string band of guitars and ukeleles and slit gongs and rattles. Their rendition of *Goodnight Irene* was *nambawan*.

*   *   *

'I wish I could tell you about the South Pacific. The way it actually was. The endless ocean. The infinite specks of coral we called islands. Coconut palms nodding gracefully toward the ocean. Reefs upon which waves broke into spray, and inner lagoons, lovely beyond description. I wish I could tell you about the sweating jungle, the full moon rising behind volcanoes, and the waiting. The waiting. The timeless, repetitive waiting.'

James A. Michener, Tales of the South Pacific

Utopia means elsewhere. There is no island named Bali Ha'i. It does not exist in space and time. It was invented by Michener, inspired by the forested volcanic peak of Ambae, which filled the view of his Pacific tour station in Vanuatu. More than anything else, more than castaways and pirates and earthquakes and headhunters and cannibals, more than any Anglo-French desert island fantasy, the essential American story of the Southern Sea required a Bali Ha'i, a romantic, oriental, exotic, tropical Shangri-la, flavored with the innocent nostalgia of good-natured good guys demonstrating good-natured tolerance, and having good-natured fun. *For other nations, utopia is a blessed past never to be recovered; for Americans it is just beyond the horizon.*

Mr. Michener's 'shucks and golly' may have leaked some elements of film noir uncertainty, tragedy, and even death, in his recording the heroic adventures of the good-natured good guys, but his buddies, unlike European interlopers like Stevenson and Gauguin, always won through in the end. There was none of this condominium leasehold intervention stuff. The paradise of the American Pacific was freehold. Bali Ha'i belonged to the visionaries who took it. *Your own special hopes, Your own special dreams, Bloom on the hillside And shine in the streams. If you try, You'll find me Where the sky Meets the sea; 'Here am I, Your special island! Come to me, Come to me!* Wherever you

131

go, there you are. It was chromatic and unattainable, and ludicrous.

The same Americans who had taken Michener's Southern Sea mythology home stateside from Vanuatu, had abandoned planeloads of the stuff behind them, when they departed.

The natives, for their part, had only one question. *Where is John Frum?* It wasn't a Bislama question about a man's origins. It was a mantra about a god's current location. During the Second World War, the New Hebrides Pandemonium was fueled by three hundred thousand American troops, and the unimaginably overwhelming amount of supplies they had brought with them. In the haste and wealth of their departure, they left a massive enormity of 'cargo,' some thousands of tons of equipment and machinery dumped into the sea at Million Dollar Point on Espiritu Santo alone, and a new messianic religion. John was a pilot *frum* America. The word in the jungle was that he had been a Negro US serviceman. There would have been nothing more seductive to the Melanesian mind and Southern Sea soul of a poor black Ni-Vanuatu, long oppressed by the evil triumvirate of planters, traders and missionaries, than the idea of a black man bringing material wealth from the sky. Melatonin mojo, and the Jesus Christ, flying the *mixmaster blong Jesus Christ*, was one of theirs. His appearance was heralded as the dawn of a new age, and a directive to reject all aspects of European colonial society- Christianity, Western education, money, tithing, and work on the copra plantations, and return to the old animist beliefs. Such a return to traditional *kastom*, was the ticket to the expulsion of all white people, including their prudish meddling missionaries, and access to the material wealth and prosperity that they enjoyed. The John Frum Cargo Cult was born- divine deliverance and industrial goods, from Melanesian magic.

His disciples set to work clearing symbolic landing strips, and erecting their own control towers, strung with rope and bamboo aerials. They carved wooden air-traffic controllers, wearing wooden radio headsets with bamboo antennae. Villagers stood on their runways for weeks on end, waving the landing signals they had once seen landing cargo-carrying planes from the now empty sky. They constructed other towers connected by tin cans and wires, so John Frum could *toktok* to his people. Piers were built to attract ships that would come laden with the objects of their material desire- lorries and iceboxes and concrete houses and televisions and radios and boats and watches and Coca-cola and Spam and rice and tolls and tobacco and medicine and machines for making electric light. And freedom.

The Stars and Stripes was run up flagpoles, and the Red Cross emblem seen on wartime ambulances became the symbol of resurgent religiosity. Adherents were buried in cemeteries with little red crosses, surrounded by white picket fences. *John Frum- He will come.* One of the reasons that something like a cargo cult took hold in Vanuatu and not elsewhere in the Southern Sea may relate to how the Ni-Vanuatu got to the place, in the first place. Melanesians always emerged locally from the land, unlike the Polynesians, who arrived from long sea voyages. Wherever you go, there you are. It got even more bizarre with the branch cult formed by the Yaohnanen tribe, which advocated the belief that Prince Philip, the Duke of Edinburgh, was the divine pale-skinned son of a mountain spirit, and brother of John Frum, himself.

In 1941, John Frum's followers threw away their property in a frenzy of spending, left the missionary churches, villages, schools, and plantations, and migrated inland to immerse themselves in traditional rituals. The colonial authorities tried to suppress the movement, by arresting and exiling cult leaders. In 1957, a militia was mobilized, faces painted in ritual colors, clad in white t-shirts stenciled with the letters 'T-A USA,' *Tanna Army USA*, began to march in the annual mid-February John Frum Day parades. What had begun as a religious awakening, became an avatar of political change, but not the one you would expect. In the 1970's the John Frum adherents opposed independence, out of concern that a centralized government would favor modernity and Christianity. They have their own political party, with parliamentary representation. A map of the world that does not include Utopia leaves out the one place that men are truly seeking. The natives of Espiritu Santo were waiting for home delivery.

The sign behind the *Air Melanisie* check-in counter said 'Cargo In.' Robyn and I were invited to weigh ourselves on the scale underneath it, before we were issued tickets. *Pasenja yu save holem wanfala handbag nomo. We i no bitem. 5kg. max.* The Mother Hubbard agent pointed us toward the Britten-Norman Islander on the tarmac, through the 'Cargo Out' door. Minutes later, we took off towards the most beautiful beach in the world. *Most people live on a lonely island, Lost in the middle of a foggy sea. Most people long for another island, One where they know they would like to be. Bali Ha'i May call you, Any night, Any day. In your heart You'll hear it call you: 'Come away, Come away.'*

The Santo-Pekoa airfield on Espiritu Santo had been built for the squadrons of B-17 flying fortresses in the US Pacific bomber command. Our pilot touched down as though he was landing one, playing chicken with how many inches could be shaved off the end of the runway. Robyn and I quickly found the main street of Luganville (it was difficult to miss- not only was it almost the only one but it was very wide, the result of an American base commander who insisted that four trucks could be driven in a row, along the road), and room number 5, at the Unity Park Motel. We sat for a while on a handmade chaise-lounge under the palapa, surrounded by dogs wet from the rain and powdered from the sand, eating the biggest sweetest brightest orange pineapple in the world. The sun came back on, prodding a search for lunch, and a table next to local planter in the Little Saigon café. Emile shared his soy sauce, and we shared the story of our quest for the world's most beautiful beach, and Michener's Bali Ha'i boosting of the offshore island as paradise.

The first European had named *La Austrialia del Espíritu Santo* in 1606, believing that he had discovered the great southern continent. The Portuguese explorer, Pedro Fernández de Quirós, was working for the Spaniards, to discover gold and spread the word of Christianity, in that order. But Quirós had failed charm school, and his Callao crew from Peru was unimpressed with his enforcement of daily prayers, and the prohibition of gambling and swearing, almost to the point of mutiny. He and his men were initially welcomed warmly on the Banks island of Gaua, but the haircut and shave he forcibly gifted to the chief, quickly swept them back into their ships. From the island of Tikopia, he eventually came to Utopia, having left his navigation 'to the will of God.' *Over the vast Pacific with white wake at their sterns, The ships of Quiros on their great concerns Ride in upon the present from the past!*

His landing place on the shores of Big Bay he named *New Jerusalem*, and the river emptying into it, the *Jordan*. He again gave a demonstration of charisma for his new adopted flock of jealously separate tribes, who had come out to greet him in their canoes, bows drawn. *Savages made rush attack upon us. Ten of these we soon laid dead, black, ugly men, their nostrils pierced with bone.* He provided a 'whiff of arquebus shot,' killed a chief, shot a few pigs, kidnapped a few boys, and plundered food, without offering any payment. Exalted on the vapors of illusion, he dedicated his New Jerusalem to 'the faith and welfare, material but first of all moral, of the natives.' The natives wanted their boys back, and offered pigs. The phantasmagoric maniacal religious grip on Quirós took possession of the land, as far as the Pole, in the names of the Trinity, Jesus, St Francis, John of God, and King Philip III. Within a day of his arrival, he had constructed a church of boughs and plantains, with a cross of local orangewood. He celebrated that same Pentecost Day with music and dancing and feasting and fireworks and such extraordinary zeal, that his startled new congregation retreated further in fear, into the bush. The marble that Quirós had chosen to wall in his New Jerusalem and build a greater cathedral than Rome's St Peter's was actually coral, thrust up in a previous volcanic eruption. Quirós bestowed thirty-four ministerial titles for his new municipal government, including magistrates, justices of the peace, a chief constable, a treasurer, a storekeeper, a minister of war and a registrar of mines. He founded a new Order of Chivalry, the *Knights of the Holy Ghost*. Even his aged priest waxed satirical about the 'marvelous diversity of knights-negro-knights and Indian-knights and knights who were knight-knights.' Whatever was gripping Quirós, it was becoming clear that his own grip on reality, and his command, was deteriorating. The crew wanted out of Utopia.

'... you would give us so much gold and silver that we could not carry it, and the pearls should be measured by hatfuls... We have found only the black devils withpoisoned arrows; what has become of the riches?.. all your affairs are imaginary and have gone off in the wind.'

After fifty-four days of native hostility and internal disputes and malaria and poisoned fish, both of Quirós' ships left New Jerusalem, in opposite directions. It was a hundred years before Bougainville came through, and then Cook eight years later, and our old sandalwood trader friend Peter Dillon fifty years after that, who began the rush of immigrants that culminated with the French planter, sitting on the other side of our soy sauce. I asked Emile what kind of plantation he had.

"It used to be cotton, but when international prices collapsed, it was switched to coffee, then cocoa, then bananas." He said. "And after my inheritance, I changed to coconuts and cattle." I asked him if he'd been north, to see Champagne Beach, the most beautiful beach in the world.

"Mais, bien sûr." He said. "It is near my plantation."

"And is it Utopia?" I asked. He pouted and grimaced backward, the way the French do, when they're thinking forward.

"The problem with Utopia begins when people arrive." He said.

*　　*　　*

'Live in the sunshine, swim the sea, drink the wild air.'
Ralph Waldo Emerson

There were only three roads that had escaped from Luganville. One followed the south coast for just over twenty miles, ending in the village of Tasiriki. Another penetrated slightly inland, northwest to where Quirós had landed in Big Bay. And the third, the one Robyn and I couldn't see, for the Utopia of singlets and Mother Hubbards, and frizzy hair and humidity, inside our *fulap* minibus, ran right up the east coast road to paradise.

We had almost exhausted our oxygen supply by the time we were extruded from our confinement, past the blue holes, near Hog Harbour. The sun was blinding and the forest magnificent. Rainbow lorikeets and fruit doves flew overhead. A kingfisher's laugh, and two black faces greeted us with smiles, at the end of the white coral drive. Rozario and Olima

137

worked for the owner of the bungalows. An outrigger canoe rested on the soft talc beach, balanced between a cobalt sky and a turquoise sea. There were no other guests. Robyn and I stowed our packs, and the box of bad Aussie Shiraz transported from Luganville, in our bungalow, and stretched out in the shade of a nearby palm. Rozario's smile approached, with a question.

"Ia naet bae yutufala wantem kaekae?" He asked. *What you want eat tonight*. Robyn and I thought about it. A flying fox flapped overhead. We had heard about *civet de rousette*, and made inquiry.

"Yutfala wantem flaengfokis?" He asked. We nodded, a little tentatively.

"OK." He said. "Yutufala wantem kava fastaem?" We nodded, a little more tentatively. We had heard about the local kava, too. Vanuatu was the original home of kava, and reputed to be the strongest in the Southern Sea. It was usually consumed in local kava klubhouses called *nakamals*, signaled by a glass lantern at the entrance, and the glassy eyes and waxy candles and expressions inside. Santo's kava potency came from two factors. First, it was prepared by chewing the roots, producing finer particles in the paste that is spat into and as the final brew. The second source of potency came from the concentration of kavalactone dihydromethysticin in Vanuatu kava. It came from the potency, period. Some varieties were known as *tudei* kava, because their psychoactive effects would last for two days.

"OK." He said again, checking his list. "Yutufala wanten kava wetem flaengfokis." Robyn and I briefly considered the animal and vegetable constituents of our dinner, shrugged, and nodded. It wasn't clear what the precise wine match was for large bats, but I thought the box of Aussie Shiraz could probably handle it.

A few minutes later we saw Rozario and Olima walk by our bungalow with what appeared to be a loaded 12-gauge shotgun. Robyn threw me a stare. I tossed it back. Not long after that a low-pitched Bislama K*a*B*lama* echoed off to our right, followed by a black punctuation mark spiraling down out of a tree. The sky grew black-brown with pandemonium long enough for all but one more Bislama K*a*B*lama* victim, to scatter like the rings in a pond. Two sets of white teeth went by, as they walked back beside our bungalow, proudly holding up dinner.

"Flaengfokis." Said Olima, smiling.

As the sun began its decline towards the horizon on dusk, Rozario called us to a picnic table near the open kitchen. The mosquitoes were ferocious. We set our *waen bokis* beside the hurricane lantern, and received two half coconut shells, filled with dishwater. We recognized the potion, and its characteristic nose, from our Fiji Bitter experience with Reece on Kandavu, but this would be different.

"Palarasul kava." Said Olima. "Vanuatu Bitter." I recognized the name as one of the *tudei* varieties. I noticed both him and Rozario standing back, like it was flammable. "Nambawan." He added. Robyn and I threw it back like we had before on Fiji, just before what happened next, happened next. Just after we heard Rozario and Olima swallow their sharp gasps, the mosquitoes disappeared, the ones that could. And then the sun went down, not like we had ever seen it set before, but throwing rose petals and white chrysanthemums and green lighting bolts. It was all very quiet and kaleidoscopic, and the clouds layered out luminous, like they'd been poured into a lava lamp. The sky exploded into a tsunami of novocaine, paralyzing everything from our noses down. The only thing we could feel was our saliva. What arrived next, under our dribble, didn't help at all. On my plate, it looked like someone had dismembered a large bat, and tried to reassemble it with yams and taro and island cabbage. It was never going to fly again. We managed to find Rozario and Olima's teeth in the darkness.

"Bon appétit." They said, or something like that in Bislama. It was the kind of encouragement that would have been more than rude to have ignored, so we managed to get enough of our fingers working, to tackle the bat. There were far too many textures. Most meat can be compared, even remotely, to chicken, except for the black chewy stuff on our plate that night. The small broken bones were an invitation to painfully choking to death, especially since we were barely able to swallow, or chew without confusing our food with our frozen tongues. The stretchy rubber skin of the gossamer wings of the thing was a bit like fruit leather, without the fruit. I spat a small metallic *ping* onto my plate, and heard it ricochet off. "Watch for buckshot." I said.

Rozario and Olima had poured Robyn and I a glass of our box Shiraz, the consumption of which, absolutely, in combination with the pre-dinner kava cocktail, brought us as far from Utopia as we would ever be in our lives. On the way back to our bungalow, I looked back to see our hosts smiling, clearly confused about the difference between being contented and being crippled.

Our first impression of the sunrise was relief that we had likely survived the battering. The second was the realization that, on this day, Robyn and I would finally get to see the most beautiful beach in the world. Champagne Beach was three kilometers through the jungle, down a parallel two parallel white sand tracks the width of a jeep wheelbase. Rozario and Olima fed us a quick *dring ti* of mangoes and local *kofi*, and we set off through the forest.

What greeted our final approach were two rough hand-painted signs. The first was understandable.

ANY TRUCK GO TO CHAMPAGNE BEACH ENTRENS FEE
200 VT.

SIGN
MR OBED TOTO

The second was a bit of overkill.

NO 2 NOTICE
TO PEOPLE STAYING LONIC BUNGALOW BEFORE USING
CHAMPAGNE BEACH 200 VT PER PERSON.
SIGN
MR OBED TOTO
TRUE BLOOD CUSDOM OWNER
CHAMPAGNE BEACH

Robyn and I put our 400 Vatu into the honesty box, and turned the corner. In front of the high jungle clad slopes and the swaying coconut palms of the plantation, was a broad crescent of blinding fine white sand, tinged with pink, dotted with shade trees, angled into the clear aquamarine and turquoise of the coral-fringed lagoon. A fine effervescent fizz, from gas escaping from the sea floor volcanic rocks below, lifted the picturesque view of Elephant Island off the shoreline, swimming in bubbly. *Champagne.*
"You reckon this is it?" I asked Robyn.
"Oh, yeah." She said. We spent the day. Of course, Emile had been right. *The problem with Utopia begins when people arrive.* We had heard nightmares about cruise ships chock full of Australians, that invaded Utopia on certain days. But this not only wasn't one of them, the only thing we ended up sharing Champagne Beach with towards the end of the day, was a small herd of cows that seemed to belong to the coconut plantation. It was just like the pamphlet at the ANZ bank said it might be, even without the 'Yumi Hapi Land Lon.'
I Mekem Drim Blong Yu I Kam Tru.

'In every outthrust headland, in every curving beach, in every grain of
sand there is the story of the earth.'

Rachel Carson

*   *   *

141

*   *   *

The rain had washed off the first morning of the tudei kava, by the time that Rozario had organized a truck for us to get back to Port Vila. We wanted to visit some of the smaller inland villages on the way, but both the Jordan and the Saranata rivers were in full flood, and there was no guarantee that we would be ably to get across.

Our driver managed to get us to a few more remote settlements, before the washed out roads and wide torrents blocked any chance of our continuing further. Despite the obstacles and the downpour, or perhaps because of it, it was all magically surreal. The bloodshot eyes of naked pikininis, and older Ni-Vanatu, clad in not much more than grass belts covering their loins, greeted us from smoking fires and clusters of thatched huts, under huge dripping banyans and strangler figs and trees buttressed with large serpentine rocket fins. Streaks of mud splatter rose on their legs. Pigs and chickens wandered, under columns of pig skulls, with large rounded tusks, near narrow plots of taro. Our driver exchanged stick tobacco, for smiles of black pegs.

"Kastom village." He said. And we could imagine the first interface of cannibal and trader, the first abandoning the inedible corpse of the latter, because of his canvas shoes. And the missionaries who brought their equally dead ideas, and the tinned corned beef that tasted like their carcasses.

The downpour was unrelenting.

"That's why they call it rainforest." Robyn reminded me. The muddy track south took us to Fanafo, the home village of Jimmy Stevens, an Old Testament rebel with a Moses beard, who almost changed the course of Vanuatu independence, and set off a series of events that culminated in the Coconut

War. Jimmy was the head of the Nagriamel movement, supported by French landowners, the French government (secretly), and the Phoenix Foundation, a staunch anticommunist American business cabal that wanted to establish a libertarian tax haven in the New Hebrides. In 1980, Jimmy and his men, armed with bows and arrows, rocks, and slings, destroyed two bridges, took over Santo-Pekoa airport, and declared the independence of Espiritu Santo as the new state of 'Vemerana.' The Prime Minister elect of what was supposed to be the new state of Vanuatu, a shrewd Presbyterian Minister named Father Walter Lini, arranged for Papua New Guinea to send troops to Santo. The war lasted twelve weeks, and ended when Jimmy's son was shot dead, trying to run a PNG roadblock in his vehicle. Jimmy went to prison for eleven years, and the new state of Vanuatu became a tax haven anyway.

The sun pushed away the clouds as we made it back into Port Vila. It was our final night in the Pandemonium, and Robyn and I had decided on a similar kind of Gallic splurge that brought us croissants on our arrival. We walked to the highest hilltop restaurant in town, and watched the slow disappearance of a coconut crab, under our noses and across from a brilliant red cloud sunset against the coconut trees that had sustained him, prior to this idyllic evening.

We were leaving more than a little bit of paradise here in Vanuatu. But it was also a little bit of a paradise lost, a lost cause, and a lost utopia.

Five years after we left the turquoise behind us, Tropical Cyclone Zuman would smash into Espiritu Santo, destroying over a hundred buildings, more than half of the major crops of the region, and flattening the entire town of Port Orly. A year later, an earthquake and tsunami left thousands homeless on the island of Pentecost. Their relief consisted of fifty tarpaulins. In 2002 the same thing happened in Port Vila, and another of Richter magnitude 7.2, struck the capital in 2007.

A more poignant irony of paradise lost would hit Ambae, Michener's Bali Ha'i, in 2005, when its beautiful Manaro volcano erupted, displacing half of its ten thousand inhabitants, and requiring the evacuation of two hospitals. Manaro is regarded as one of the world's top ten most dangerous volcanoes, with the potential for catastrophic explosion, and the generation of lethal tsunamis within this archipelago.

The big problem with Utopia, however, as our planter friend Emile well knew, 'begins when people arrive.' Vanuatu's population is also exploding, placing unsustainable pressure on local resources for farming, grazing, hunting and fishing. Deforestation, leading to soil erosion and landslides, is inexorable, literally fuelled by logging and slash-and burn agriculture, and the creation of more coconut plantations and cattle ranches. Freshwater is becoming scarce, as upland watersheds are destroyed. Issues of waste disposal and air pollution are now affecting the *yumi hapi pipol*. But even these fault lines are as threatening as the real gift we brought the Ni-Vanuatu. The increasing gap between wealthy expat business owning land lease holders and rural families locked into self-reliant subsistence has resulted in urban migration and youth employment and the breakdown of traditional *kastom* mores, a consequent increase in crime and alcohol and drug abuse and resentment, and the one thing that makes Utopia and Drim Blong Yu I Kam Tru impossible. *Dissatisfaction.*

> 'Happy talk, keep talkin' happy talk,
> Talk about things you'd like to do.
> You got to have a dream,
> If you don't have a dream
> How you gonna have a dream come true?'
> Oscar Hammerstein, *South Pacific*

*   *   *

The Prow of the Canoe
Solomons

'There is no gainsaying that the Solomons are a hard-bitten bunch of islands. On the other hand, there are worse places in the world. But to the new chum who has no constitutional understanding of men and life in the rough, the Solomons may indeed prove terrible.'

Jack London, *The Terrible Solomons*

There was only one place in the world that had both headhunting and cannibalism, and that's where we were going. *The Happy Isles*. My dreamtime images of the Solomons were all in living color- sparkling tropical lagoons containing the blackest blonde-haired people in the world, proudly paddling their tall-prowed war canoes, in a desperate race to rescue crews of engine oil and salt water saturated American sailors from the next terrible shark attack, or another Jap strafing run. They were Henderson Field and Guadalcanal and thatched huts on stilts, and the castaway of the Southern Sea voted most likely to succeed. As a young boy, I remember assembling and painting the torpedo tubes and curves, on my styrene model of John F. Kennedy's PT-109, and guiding it through the maze of volcanic *British Solomon Islands* in my stamp collection. But the archipelago of almost a thousand atolls of orchids and butterflies would be as elusive as it was seductive.

There was no way I could find to get there. All the flights were indirect and booked up, and the only response I had received from the numerous travel consultants on the other end of the phone, was stony silence, followed by more questions than I had.

"Where?" One said.

"Why?" Said another. But I was only interested in the How

and, after a long painful search, the solution presented itself in the form of a small agency in San Francisco, which had taken their name from one of Mitchener's books about the South Pacific. I made the call.

"Rascals in Paradise." She answered. "How may I help?" Maryles listened carefully to our plan and our plight, and took control.

"You need to send me all these things immediately." She said. "There is no time to lose." I told her where I thought I wanted to visit, but she was having none of it.

"You need to go to Uepi." She said. I looked it up on my thousand-island map. In the Western Province of the Solomons, in the largest lagoon in the world, was a tiny dot only six hundred meters wide, dropping off two kilometers into New Georgia Sound, four major battles in which had seen some of the fiercest fighting of the war. 'The Slot' ended in Iron Bottom Sound, where fifty ships of the allied navies and the Tokyo Express had been sunk, an expanse of water so sacred, that strict silence is still observed by any vessel passing through.

Ten days later, the phone rang again.

"There are six bungalows on the island." Maryles said. "I got you the last one." We had flight tickets, and a destination.

It was all bright white and dark green and turquoise from the air. From the Bougainville Strait north to Tikopia, granular streaks of coral reef shorelines radiated around and out from a thousand miles of exquisite islets, under the cotton fluff below. The view was painfully beautiful. We began our descent over an increasing density of scattered lighter green fields and tin roof reflections and a network of earth colored roads. A flotilla of large rusted cargo vessels lingered offshore. Our final approach into Honiara was as fast as any other landing gear that had ever touched down on Guadalcanal, and just as pregnant with hope and anticipation. Two immense carved brown hardwood masks, inlaid with nautilus and covered in dust, followed our slow progress through immigration, inside the terminal. Heavily armed Australian and Pacific island police patrolled the lawlessness and ethnic tension and between the resident Guadalcanal Revolutionary Army and the settler Malaita Eagle Force. Their arm patches were embroidered with a dove, and the name of their operation. *Helpem Fren.* Debate raged as to whether the Solomons had been a state poorly constructed, or one that had failed.

Robyn and I loaded our packs on a trolley tormented by the same question, its only two revolving wheels becoming paralyzed by mud and gravel, on the way to the domestic terminal. We hiked by the Mother Hubbard *muumuus* and kaleidoscopic umbrellas of an impromptu market, under the red and purple floral genitalia of the banana trees hanging behind them. Crimson betel nut stains splattered the path to our connecting flight, like hospital passageway markers to a trauma ward. Robyn and I passed a billboard that had been erected by the Ministry of Health.

Stop the (7) Killer diseases
Hepatitis B- Tuberculosis- Diphtheria- Polio-
Whooping cough-Tetanus- Measles
Get immunised and enjoy life!

Of course there was no vaccine for the other killer diseases of the Solomons- malaria, dengue, chikununya, filiariasis, Ross River and Murray Valley fevers, and leptospirosis, poisonous spiders and sea snakes, headhunting and cannibalism, and boarding the Britten-Norman Island Islander, waiting on the tarmac. It was painted like the flag, with the five white stars of the main island groups in the surrounding blue of the ocean on the tail, and the green of the land and gold of the sun on the undercarriage.

What Maryles hadn't emphasized was that our destination in the Marovo lagoon had been one of the epicenters of headhunting activity in the archipelago. It was a five hundred year old tradition, revving along in top gear when the first European to visit, Álvaro de Mendaña de Neira, following Incan legends of gold-laden islands 600 leagues to the west, arrived from Peru in 1568. The fleet of welcoming canoes that came out to meet and greet, presented him with cooked pieces of a quarter of boy garnished with taro leaves. Mendaña did eventually discover gold in the interior rivers of Guadalcanal, still mined today, and named the islands after the mythical African king. When some of the locals were murdered by one of his more sadistic deputies, they massacred nine of his men in reprisal. Mendaña torched every village he could reach, and left the islands in ashes. Longitudinally challenged, he had also mapped them 700 leagues off their real position, and no one else would find the place for two hundred years.

Headhunting in the Solomons had initially evolved, culturally and purposefully, like in Sulawesi, as a superstitious imperative of spiritual protection and physical and metaphysical dominance. Expeditions were undertaken only after the *hiama* ritual specialists had received approval from tribal ancestors, and participating warriors abstemious and purified. Potential victims were metaphorically converted into 'wild fish' or other animals before their slaughter, and similarities between bonito fishing and headhunting ceremonies extended to their related shrines.

Up to fifty warriors, in up to five canoes almost fifty feet long, were recruited for long-distance raids, to kill powerful rivals, or to destroy entire hostile groups. The beauty and grace of their ocean-going *tomakos* astounded early European visitors to the archipelago. They were constructed from hand-hewn planks attacked by cane ties, lashed onto ornate internal spreading ribs, and sealed with *tita* nut putty. Both the sky-high vertical prow and stern posts were richly inset with mother of pearl and *bleu ovalum*, each surmounted by a pair of spirit figures, looking out, and after the welfare of the canoe and its crew, in all four directions. No two were decorated in the same way.

The most remarkable sculpture was the *nguzunguzu*, a carved dog-human hybrid figurehead with protruding jaws, painted black and ornamented with inlaid nautilus shell, with either a skull or a dove in its paws, depending on the ill or goodwill of the mission. It was mounted near the waterline on the prow, so that it dipped in and out of the water, picking up spiritual momentum, and guarding against hostile water spirits.

Heads were taken for the *va-peza* launching of a war canoe, and carried on its maiden voyage, to prevent any *tamu garata* malediction. Others were needed for the inauguration of a new communal house, to commemorate the death of a chief, or to release widows from confinement. Headhunting raids also captured children for work and purification sacrifices, and young women for labor, ritualized sex and marriage.

Some of the earliest accounts of such activity were recorded in the 1840s exploits of the sandalwood trader, Andrew Cheyne, who reported the large numbers of heads taken in these raids, 93 from one attack alone. The situation calmed considerably over the next ten years, during a period known as the 'Great Peace,' but headhunting would explode into another far more evil dimension, accelerated in scope, frequency and ferocity, with the destabilizing arrival of more Europeans, with iron axes and other metal tools, and shell ornaments to trade. Human heads suddenly went from icons of religious reverence, to currency.

Local rivalries that had traditionally driven neighborhood brushfire conflicts within the Marovo lagoon, expanded into distant political warfare, as far as Guadalcanal and Isabel. Pressure intensified on every coastal chief to amass large amounts of *nibaka* war-chest shell money, in order to finance increasingly competitive mercenary expeditions, in an arms race of heads, and slaves and human protein, and children for sacrifice. The southern coast became so depopulated and terrorized that remaining natives were reduced to building and find shelter in tree forts. The supply of 'currency' became scarce, commodity prices inflated, and headhunting raids increased to meet demand.

Bad enough that white traffickers had provided the metallic material means for the headhunting wars to escalate, it was far worse that trading ships were directly involved in the taking and buying and selling of human heads. In 1868, a Scottish sailor from Stromness became a latter day shipwrecked castaway Robinson Crusoe mascot of the offshore 'salt-water people,' escaping the malaria-infested jungles of Malaita. Lost to Arcadia and Orcadia, John Renton had become a white headhunter of the 'bush people' cannibals who inhabited the main island, until he was rescued eight years later by a blackbirding ship, involved in this new kidnapping form of trade, in the Solomon arena of death and deprivation. He eventually landed in the New Hebrides, where he lost his own head. The Queenslander 'snatch-snatch boats' whose cargo didn't end up on some remote Peruvian guano island, found themselves working for a new class of white settler, owners of vast independent plantations of rubber, vanilla, sisal, or cocoa.

Perhaps the most pernicious white headhunters arrived in the mid- 19th century. Approximately a hundred missionaries, Anglicans, S.S.E.M., Methodists, Catholics and Seventh Day Adventists, came to steal the souls of *these multitudes of little brown folk... the wild creatures of the woodland.*

The most famous was an Anglican priest named John Coleridge Patteson, son of the niece of the poet Samuel Taylor Coleridge, author of *The Rime of the Ancient Mariner.* The albatross around his grand-nephew's neck was an appointment as the first Bishop of Melanesia, a servant of God for the inhabitants of hundreds of hostile islands, scattered over an area of almost two thousand miles of ocean. He tried to be fun, and went barefoot. Patteson was the founder of the Melanesian Mission on Norfolk Island. On each one of his new spiritual possessions, he swam ashore, emerging from the surf wearing only a top hat, bringing presents for his people. On one of them, finally, in Santa Cruz, he was done in with poisoned arrows, and eaten. Some claimed that it was some form of blackbirder's revenge, for his antislavery activities. Whatever the reason, blackbirding and headhunting and cannibalism were outlawed because of him, and the Solomons became a British protectorate in 1894. The Solomons was governed by a Gilbert and Sullivan hierarchy of clumsy colonial caricatures, who formed as inept an administration as could be found in any other tropical outpost of Empire. Their miniature fantasy world of isolation, infirmity, and intense humid heat was held together by ritual, whisky, and quinine. It was all very *pukka*. When Jack London visited the islands in 1908, cruising the Southern Sea on his boat, the Snark, he wrote of both the Melanesians and their masters.

'It is true that fever and dysentery are perpetually on the walk-about, that loathsome skin diseases abound, that the air is saturated with a poison that bites into every pore, cut, or abrasion and plants malignant ulcers, and that many strong men who escape dying there return as wrecks to their own countries. It is also true that the natives of the Solomons are a wild lot, with a hearty appetite for human flesh and a fad for collecting human heads. Their highest instinct of sportsmanship is to catch a man with his back turned and to smite him a cunning blow with a tomahawk that severs the spinal column at the base of the brain. Heads are a medium of exchange, and white heads are extremely valuable. Very often a dozen villages make a jack-pot, which they fatten moon by moon, against the time when some brave warrior presents a white man's head, fresh and gory, and claims the pot... and yet there are white men who have lived in the Solomons a score of years and who feel homesick when they go away from them. A man needs only to be careful—and lucky—to live a long time in the Solomons; but he must also be of the right sort. He must have the hallmark of the inevitable white man stamped upon his soul. He must be inevitable. He must have a certain grand carelessness of odds, a certain colossal self-satisfaction, and a racial egotism that convinces him that one white is better than a thousand niggers every day in the week, and that on Sunday he is able to clean out two thousand niggers. For such are the things that have made the white man inevitable. Oh, and one other thing- the white man who wishes to be inevitable, must not merely despise the lesser breeds and think a lot of himself; he must also fail to be too long on imagination. He must not understand too well the instincts, customs, and mental processes of the blacks, the yellows, and the browns; for it is not in such fashion that the white race has tramped its royal road around the world.'

Unfortunately for the inevitable white man, his royal road was about to be tramped back, by the mental processes of the yellows. Over a span of two hundred days in 1942, some of the most desperate and ferocious fighting in history, took place in the Battle of Guadalcanal. Beneath our Britten Norman Islander, on the steep flanks of Bloody Ridge and the dark forested mountainous interior, over 3600 Americans were killed or wounded. Of more than 36,000 Japanese soldiers that had fought on Guadalcanal, some 26,000 were killed, 9,000 died of malaria or battle fatigue, and only a thousand were captured. Still scattered among the taro patches and banana leaves below, were the boots and bones and guns and grenades and helmets and heroism where they had fallen.

We landed at the southernmost tip of New Georgia, on an airstrip that had been carved out of the jungle by the Americans in just ten days. *Welcome to Seghe.* The vertical blue and white stripes of the shack on the side of the runway had been painted to identify it as the terminal. The blue and white checkerboard shack that stood beside it had been painted to identify it as the police station. No one was home at either one. But there was no shortage of older Mother Hubbards and shirtless pikininis, porters lifting cargo onto their heads, the blackest people in the world, some with the blondest hair, motioning for Robyn and I to follow them down the hill to their canoes.

But no graceful hand-hewn *tomako* masterpieces, with inlaid skyscraper prows and sterns, waited there on the shore. Instead, we had two long aluminum dugouts, each equipped with a Johnson 40 outboard. We were hardly seated, before it sped off into the Marovo lagoon, throwing choppy swells of salt chuck in painful large plumes at our faces. We were soaking wet and bruised within minutes, and there was still another twelve kilometers to travel, at the speed of iron bottom sound.

Finally, when our waterboarding wake subsided, we came to blue and white curved sign at the end of the pier, on a curved emerald island of coconut palms. *Welcome to Uepi Island.* The rows of white teeth were dazzling.

*   *   *

'If I were a king the worst punishment I could inflict on my enemies would be to banish them to the Solomons... On second thought, king or no king, I don't think I'd have the heart to do it.'
Jack London, *The Cruise of the Snark*

Jill was at the Jetty. She didn't seem to care much about the blacktip sharks, swarming around our canoes, as we carefully extricated ourselves. The description from Maryles had been accurate. *Sites close to the Resort are highly populated with marine life and always exciting.*

Giant porcelain clam shells, filled with red hibiscus and ginger flowers and white spider orchids and rainwater and suffused alabaster light, received us onto a small tropical island of meandering paths through cultivated gardens, butterflies and flowers, the rainforest behind, and six thatched bungalows stretched out along the sandy beach of the calm lagoon. It was the only place I had ever been, where the all the borders of the trails were lined with orchids. A postcard would have spontaneously combusted. It was stunning.

The tranquility was fractured by a torrent of abuse in sharp Australian, for the porter who had contaminated Jill's dock with a fresh orange splash of betel nut. She welcomed the rest of us, taking special care to make us feel at home. We sat in the open dining room, and met the other guests from our canoes, for the first time. No one had said a word on the way over, so mesmerized by the magic of the motion, and the scenery, and the spray. A quiet middle-aged British couple had come for the diving. No one who had came this far out in space was here for anything other than the diving. Except for the tall man with receding grey curls, large hands, and big round eyeglass lenses wrapped in faux turtle shell frames. He spoke with a Midwestern accent, but it had obviously been tempered by his Brussels address, and intellect. What Kevin didn't know about Melanesian art and ethnography, or Southern African cultural pieces, or double bass playing, or any one of a number of other eclectic disciplines, would require you to abandon the rest of the sentence. His gentility and knowledge and passion for his purpose here was magically infectious, and I soon found myself developing my own enthusiastic appreciation for the elemental aesthetic subtleties of our surroundings. He had arrived with his English wife, Anna, and their young son, Max, who would celebrate a young birthday in the Marovo lagoon, as any son of such a man should. Jill's husband, Grant, appeared to round off our welcome, and Robyn and I were shown to our bungalow, and carefully abandoned to our own, and surrounding, nature.

Like the complexion of any other island in the Southern Sea, Uepi was not a paradise without some minor blemishes. Blackish green and gold-speckled *Varanus indicus* mangrove monitor lizards, four feet long and as big as basset hounds, protruded their long purple tongues and serrated teeth into the open door of our bungalow, until we closed it. I watched one dislocate its jaw one morning, to swallow a rat the size of a rabbit, when I went out to fetch our breakfast off the veranda. The Japanese had introduced them into the Marshalls during WWII, to get rid of the rats. They did such an initially admirable job, they ran out of rats and started in on the local chicken coops. When the Americans arrived they introduced the poisonous cane toad to get rid of the monitors. As the lizards died off, the rats came back with a vengeance, with the end result that the Marshalls now have an infestation of both rats and cane toads. A similar introduction of cane toads into Palau, resulted in the demise of the monitors, and an explosion of beetles that damaged the coconuts. But there were no cane toads on Uepi, and the monitors thrived on the leftover scraps from the resort, when they ran out of rats. You had to get up pretty early in the morning, to beat them to your breakfast tray, delivered under a talisman of tin foil by three lovely black ladies, in flowered *lava lavas* and t-shirts.

The coconuts were healthy as well, and waited stealthily for unsuspecting guests to wander haplessly underneath, before deliberately releasing their lethal cargo. Sometimes they had no choice, when the daily cyclonic squalls blew in and juggled them through the torrential turbulence. There were large spiders, in every available area between the boughs, *Gasteracanthan* spiny spiked orange-red monsters and Golden orb spinners, web silk as strong as Kevlar, and used by both the spiders and the local boys to catch fish. There weren't enough of them, and no amount of repellent on earth, to make a dent in the biting flies and midges and mosquitoes that greeted us at dusk. But so did the musky post-coital smell of ripe and rotting papayas and tropical compost, and the black and white silhouette of curving coconut palms and pandanus huts, before it went sepia, and the colors kicked in.

Orange smoke and purple cloud sunsets would follow us to the dining room, after I encountered Kevin down at the shore, to admire the clear lagoon and mountainous island backdrop beyond. The Soltai No 3, a rust bucket oil-streaked trawler, held together with iron oxide and humidity, rumbled metallically past, like a Solomonian Heart of Darkness version of the *El Caleuche* ghost ship of Chiloe. He asked if Robyn and I wanted to join him next morning, on a tour of the lagoon in a quest for experience and artifacts. I formed a mental image of a *nguzunguzu*, mounted near the waterline on the prow, so that it dipping in and out of the water, picking up spiritual momentum, and guarding against hostile spirits, with each stroke of twenty paddles.

"Headhunting." I said. Kevin nodded, and we went for mud crab. Before the moon began its ascent over the lagoon, the stars had already lit up the night sky.

They were feeding the sharks off the welcome landing next morning. I asked one of the bucket boys where we could go for a swim.

"Here." He said. "But later." Kevin and Robyn and I motored off into the deep aquamarine and turquoise Venetian glass of the lagoon, between arches and spumes of salt spray, fanning high above the gunnels behind us. Mountains loomed on the horizon, and islets of white sand circumferences and green interiors danced out of our way, until one of them didn't.

Sago palm leaf huts with double-sloped roofs, rising off stilts on coral foundations, with square thatched shutters held ajar by sticks, faced the lagoon to catch the air. Among patches of taro and yam and cassava, hard won from ancient Melanesian rainforest, giant trees ran all the way up the slopes, in exchange for the children of the village running all the way down. Coconut trees waved to us from the top of the island above the church. Three girls in identical purple clothing, hoisted the paddles of their canoe in greeting, and another thirteen villagers went by with the same enthusiasm, crammed into a vessel half that size, but blessed with antique two-stroke propulsion.

As the shoreline approached, I looked down into water so clear, it appeared like we were hanging in space, and I gripped the gunnels tight, until the vertigo gave way to more shallow marvels. The range and diversity of the corals were astonishing- staghorns, huge rust-colored tabletops, spikes radiations of *acropora*, crusted spheres of fuschia and green, and rippled brains, on the prow of the canoe. A flashball of blazing yellow fish discharged through another group of metallic blue lightning, both pausing briefly beside us, to consider what had just happened. Out of the corner of my eye, I caught a similar stampeding chaos of dark children on land, dancing limbs and blond and black hair, laughing and shouting and rampaging down the beach, pale soles shooting sprays of white sand in every direction.

Between a jagged cut in the worlds largest tropical aquarium, we glided onto the grinding crunch of sand, and looked up to rows of little black feet, white toes underneath, greeting us on the dock. Kevin wiped the salt from his glasses.

"It's amazing how the blackest children can have lemon cotton candy for hair." Said Robyn.

"They have more melatonin than anyone else in the world." I said. "But about ten percent of them have this strange TYRP1 gene which gives them blond hair. It's completely indigenous, and nothing to do with any European contact." A very young girl with flaxen frizz, sat under a nearby tree, holding a snot-nosed baby wearing a single sock. Both were chewing sugarcane. A quintet of older boys, led by one with obvious Chinese ancestors, guided us along village paths lined with thatched huts, up the hill to the church. The lines of laundry were as colorful as the flowers. One particularly long string of suspended singlets was as bright white as the teeth of their owners. We passed a fresh raised bed with black soil, lined with coral rocks and coconut wood, and decorated with bouquets of bird of paradise, ginger, and orchids.

"Dead." Said the small Chinese boy.

"Dead." We agreed. The boys pointed out a small wooden shed, painted with English letters. *Neuclear Power Station four stroke power and intake.*

"Generator." Said the small Chinese boy.

"Generator." We agreed. At the top of the hill small pikinini with buck teeth and checkered shorts played his ukulele for Robyn. She played it back to him, to his surprise and delight. Our guides took us into the church, and leapt onto the benches lining tables covered with mauve plastic tablecloths and matching plastic flower bouquets. Kevin found a bass guitar, and a groove. When he found the conch and its high note, the rest of the village children appeared. One young girl, wearing pink jodhpurs and carrying a red flower as big as she was, stole Robyn's heart. Her younger brother stood naked on a vast expanse of sage green moss, almost Florentine in the Michaelangelic majesty of his pose.

We walked along other paths, of other lives. A small puppy was busy eating the last dried strands of sinew, deep inside and out of an overturned turtle shell that dwarfed his shadow. The old woman sitting cross-legged on her dirt floor, sewed leaves into a wall panel between her pendulous breasts, punctuated by grim-faced puffs on her pipe, between stitches. Kevin's networking, by now, had unearthed several finds, some of them literally. He peered with intent through his thick goggles, a kultural Keplermaniac, studying the surfaces of heavenly objects. We looked with him, but failed to see the nuances that a lifetime of passion and brilliance could discern. He carefully considered a blackened model of a skull house, and a volcanic stone mortar cut in half by the strong shadows of the afternoon sun, before rejecting them both as less worthy. Then, the chief arrived, all skinny with an oil-stained red t-shirt and sunglasses, and something more special. It was a black head, inlaid with nautilus, holding a dove underneath.

"The village nguzunguzu." Kevin said. "Not that old, but a lovely piece of folk art." He said it would be a good start to a collection and, if I was interested, he would help bargain for me. I looked at Robyn. She was quiet. I nodded. The bargaining began and ended quickly, for more than I thought I would pay. But Kevin reassured me that the price was fair, and going to a good cause, and there was no going back. We returned to our canoe, suspended in air on the lagoon, and waved all the way back to Uepi.

Grant joined us for dinner that evening, and provided his own insights on running a resort in Marovo lagoon, the bizarre corrupt politics of the Solomons, and how Japanese logging companies had been barging in white vinyl-sided plastic houses to give to local chiefs, in exchange for entire rainforests.

"The trade in timber is brisk." He said. When Kevin asked about wild pig, Grant told us that he would be sending out several men and dogs the next day, on a hunt. I indicated that I would appreciate an opportunity to accompany them.

"It's a young man's sport." He said. And that was that.

The next morning, after beating the monitors to breakfast, Robyn and I decided to find the beach side of Uepi. The trail began at the sign just beyond the last bungalow, and the last incident light. *Forest.* The arrow underneath seemed a bit superfluous.

We soon found ourselves in near darkness, under a large canopy of unpronounceable hardwoods, although I recognized the walking palms and rocket fin roots of buttressed figs. Their bark patterns were fantastic and varied, from horizontal lines to splotches to gnarly convolutions, some streaked with powdered termite tunnels, calligraphically reducing the forest, and the houses made from it, to dust. There were orchids and fungi, and ant plants, strangely formed spiked greenish grey hedgehogs, with leaves growing out of their noses, dangling from some of the trees. In exchange for a safe home in small purple high-rise rooms in the sky, some species of ants act as undertakers, making nocturnal forays to the forest floor, returning with the carcasses of other insects, and dropping them into other spaces to rot. Mushrooms growing inside the ant plants, release nutrients that nourish the internal rootlets of the epiphytes. The ants get a home, the plants get their daily bread, and the mushrooms get another generation. It's a three way symbiotic win, soon to disappear with the last white plastic house delivered to the last black chief.

But until then, Robyn and I felt at home in the forest, watching golden whistlers and olive green white-eyes and honeyeaters in the canopy. A raucous commotion broke out above us, in a flock of emerald male *eclectus* parrots, red flashing under their wings, as they flew among their blue and crimson female partners. A bird-wing butterfly the size of my hand flew random tremors in the high branches, in a search for nectar. The beach, and snorkeling on the other coral shelf on side of the island was in the clearest water in the world, with lionfish and white and black banded sea snakes, far too many sharks, and totally magical.

The sunset turned the bottle of chardonnay more golden. Robyn wore a blue dress, and a frangipani behind her ear. It was Christmas Eve, and the turkey came with stuffing, and the stuffing came with more stories from Grant.

I went diving with the British couple next day, while Robyn lazed in the hammock. Before my faulty regulator ran me out of air, fifty feet down, I had been enraptured by all the reef jewelry but, again, especially the sharks. The islanders believed that their dead ancestors live in their sharks; the same could be said of the descendents of American sailors, whose ancestors had been taken before they were rescued. But still, in the Solomons, there were still more people killed by pigs than sharks.

Kevin's son Max's birthday cake that night was adorned with seven candles surrounded by an orchid and frangipani heart, and guitar accompaniment.

We left Uepi next morning. I could sense the nguzunguzu in our pack, wanting release onto the prow and into the water, but Robyn and I were picking up enough spray and spiritual momentum, for the three of us. We arrived at the Seghe airfield early enough to work up a thirst, sitting beside the fat women with the umbrella. Her two pikininis climbed into the trees to get us green coconuts, after they had tired of tormenting the huge ground boa they had found lying in the grass behind us. It was so hot even the green skinks were slow enough to catch. When the old twin otter with completely bald tires finally landed, we were more than ready for airborne. The biggest sign in the cabin didn't have much to do with safety. *It is forbidden to remove life jackets from this aircraft.* But we couldn't see much of it, for the fumes. Every so often the smoke would clear, and we could see the hundreds of turquoise gems below us, in The Slot.

Just a little over a year after we left Uepi, a major 8.0 Richter magnitude earthquake struck the Solomons, causing forty-four aftershocks, the death of 52 people, the loss of thousands of homes, and a thirty foot tsunami. It was mounted near the waterline on the prow, picking up momentum, and leaving many once pristine coral reefs exposed on newly formed beaches.

*   *   *

It was born in war and sustained on violence. The airport we returned to had been wrestled from the murderous Battle of Henderson Field, just a grenade's throw from the other extremes of the Guadalcanal campaign. It was an appropriate description. The big boom box in the back of our station wagon taxi announced our arrival, past the storefronts of *Xtreme Meats* and *Xtreme Haircuts*, on the way to our hotel. Cannibals and headhunters. We were grateful for the big red air freshener, dangling from the mirror.

The name of the capital sounded so musical and mellifluous, that one could be forgiven for thinking it was anything but a Southern Sea idyll. But Honiara, christened either from Álvaro de Mendaña's hometown, Wadi el Ganar, or derived from *Nagho ni ara*, 'Place of the East Wind,' in one of the Guadalcanal languages, was no palm tree paradise. What had been a small village, not fifty years earlier, not only was one of the few places not liberated by all it had sacrificed during World War II, it had continued to paddle itself through a sequence of cyclones, and into other turbulent backwater vortices of political unrest and ethnic bloodshed and rioting. Fighting between the Malaitans and Guadalcanal natives resulted in a coup attempt less than five years before Robyn and I appeared, the murder of two New Zealand diplomats and several others, and the consequent need for Australian military and police intervention, just to restore order.

Our rap-thumping boombox bounced in and out of betel-stained potholes through blocks of tumbletown decay, past the wildest looking people on the planet. They looked fierce, feral, ferocious, with chaotic hair on top, immense bare feet on the bottom, and tattoos and trauma and torn threads, in the middle. They were dirt floor poor, but in their own world, between the fighting and drinking, there were still large remnants of small village kindness.

"Yu orait?" They would ask. And mean it.

Our boombox pulled up at the big *Welkam* sign, at the wideopen entrance of the King Solomon Hotel. The *Leaf Haus* thatched foyer ceiling foyer was supported by beautifully carved poles, and Robyn and I with welkam drinks, and the reassurance of a 24 hour reception and security desk and our location, directly across from the Police station and the Australian Consulate. The logo was equally reassuring. *Home away from Home.*

It wasn't quite like home. The mosquitoes from the tiny pool were fierce, feral, and ferocious. The security guards doubled as bellboys. Every nook and cranny was occupied by larger than life-size painted kitsch concrete fantasy figures- Donald Duck by the pool, and then an angelfish, a clownfish, a mermaid and an orchid, each more garish than the other. Breakfast would be flyblown and inedible, and the instant coffee was an archeological dig of fused ancient bricks. The wooden funicular, fastened to the hillside, that was supposed to take us to our room, didn't. The lock on our door had seen too many surgical interventions, the nonfunctional air conditioner was as loud as a lawnmower, and in place of a toilet seat or toilet paper, the toilet had a sign. *Gud wata toelet helt.* Another notice on the bathroom mirror advised against drinking the water.

But the water outside was Iron Bottom Sound, containing sixty ships and thirty thousand dead sailors, and we were doing just fine. The *Bamboo Hut* downstairs did a mean poison in buerre blanc and crayfish Mornay, with tomatoes carved in the shape of roses.

I shook hand of the security guard, far too thin for his uniform. He wore a banana colored shirt and brown tie, banana striped brown pants, and brown and yellow striped Aussie bush hat. He could barely see out from under the size of it. Robyn and I left for the market, and made the mistake of walking along the sound. *Showtime.* Was a sign on a nearby movie theatre marquis. The show hadn't changed much in half a century. The shoreline was all damp shadows- people defecating near the waterline, dead bloated pigs washed up on the beach, mosquitoes, and rubbish and untreated sewage. Sitting at anchor was the thick blue paint and rust of the Hamakyo Maru and Arrow Endeavour, spawn of the wreckage beneath them.

As we approached the market, pijin billboards advertised soda, *Hem nao diringi coca Cola Distaem*, and cigarettes. *Simoka save spoelem lang bilong iu- Gafman helt woning.* There should have been government health warning at the central market entrance, to give a wide berth to the scary muscle-bound monster with the wild frizz hair and beard framed face carved out of briarwood, the one wearing the open snakeskin shirt with the bright pink towel around his neck, the one who glared. We moved away quickly, to patches of red yams and green plantains, little piles of *ngali* nuts and crab claws, and mountains of watermelons. The women waved cloth whisks, keeping the flies off the fish, and the absolute need to be there, keeping the smiles off the women. But the depression and oppression of the market soon lifted, as we arrived on the market streets of Chinatown.

Here were quiet lanes of small shops, their frontier facades painted with amateur renditions of the goods for sale within. There was hardware and electronic goods and items of clothing in primary colors, and the names were almost enchanting.

Happy Day Shop... Beautiful Shop... New World... Red Sun shop... Abundant Life- fresh meat and Christian books... H.Q. Shop... Six Plus Exterprises... Baby Blue Store... Chase Wholesale... Ox and Palm... John Tom & Sons, exporters and buyers of wet and dry cocoa... Bridal Corner... Please Babe give me a chance... Buyers of: bech de mer & shark fin... Oriental Cuisine-licensed to retail fermented and spirituous liquor for consumption on the premises with meals.

Something not quite tame, not the same as wild, hung on the air here. Anything you needed for fine Guadalcanal living was available- aluminum cookware and kerosene lamps, spam and corned beef, dried shark fin and tinned lychees, and laundry soap and plastic buckets. Robyn and I stopped into an air-conditioned teahouse, near Lydia's Christian Academy (*Thank you and God bless us*), for the air-conditioning.

The Japanese shop across the street was offering to buy endangered dolphin teeth or giant clams or turtle shell. The harshness of what Admiral Halsey ordered painted on the rocks above Tulaghi harbour seemed to echo in the heat. *Kill... Kill... Kill, Kill More Japs.*

But it was the Chinese that were about to lose everything. Four months after Robyn and I left Honiara, the Chinatown we had found so beguiling was razed to the ground. The commercial heart of Honiara was reduced to rubble and ashes. The newly elected Prime Minister, Snyder Rini, had been accused of using bribes from Chinese businessmen to buy votes from members of Parliament. Two days of rioting displaced a thousand Chinese residents, who lost everything, and were housed in Honiara's main police station until China sent in chartered aircraft to safely evacuate them from the Happy Isles. Jack London, for all his punch-drunk racist views about the 'yellow peril,' may have provided them a warning about the echo in the heat... *to the new chum who has no constitutional understanding of men and life in the rough, the Solomons may indeed prove terrible.*

"I was just telling Mr. Arkwright that there are no antidotes for native poisons.'
'Except gin.' said Brown.'

Jack London, *The Terrible Solomons*

*   *   *

Alice in Wonderland
New Caledonia

'Begin at the beginning," the King said, very gravely, "and go on till you come to the end: then stop.'

Lewis Carroll, Alice in Wonderland

To get to where Alice was, you needed to get beyond Monique, and to get beyond Monique, you needed to get to Sylvanna. To get to Sylvanna, you needed to get through Rose. To get to Rose, you needed to get through Immigration, and to get through Immigration, you needed to get your pack off the slowest carousel in the world.

I had been to New Caledonia twenty years earlier. The landing formalities at Tontouta airport were still on daylight wasting time, which gave me an hour to pick out a few bottles of Côtes du Rhône in the tuck shop, while Robyn guarded our place in line, waiting out the lone dyslexic marine, protecting the frontier from the sudden attempted incursion of all these airline passengers. Customs would eventually take on a whole different meaning.

We were still over fifty kilometers from Noumea, but our hotel ride would have been parked just outside the terminal. If he would have been, but he wasn't. Robyn and I approached the taxi driver, a hundred meters away, and inquired as to the fare. *Why, sometimes I've believed as many as six impossible things before breakfast.* He could see the defeat in our eyes, but René was going to turn out to be a better ambassador than a businessman, and asked for the name of our hotel. We told him. *Le Lagon.*

He punched in the number and handed me his cell. My initial halting French became more fluent fast, when the desk clerk informed me that we didn't have a reservation. I asked him to check again. Nope. I asked him to check the date of the reservation confirmation email I had in my hand. Oops. He told us to take the taxi, and he would take care of René. Meanwhile, we had been joined by Monika, a molecular biologist from Dunedin via the Balkans who, for the week off over Christmas, had closed her eyes and launched an index finger at a map of the Southern Sea. As it began to rain, she piled in the van with Robyn and I, and René launched us towards the capital city of the country, located on the slopes and valleys of the southwestern Grande Terre peninsula.

We had arrived the day before Christmas, and René was concerned that we would find ourselves without provisions, during the three-day closure of shops and restaurants that would accompany the holiday. He took us to a supermarket, and waiting while we stocked up on essentials. This was not an easy task. The raw oysters and foie gras and hundreds of French cheeses and wines that lined the shelves in this most remote of Gallic outposts did not seem to appear on the radar of my most Kiwi of New Zealand wives. I was forced to whittle down my list of dire needs to survival rations, although I did manage to enlist a generous lump of *Reblochon* and a *pâté de campagne* in the upcoming battle for space in our bar fridge.

It was pouring buckets back outside, and would continue to do so over the next two days. We arrived at Le Lagon, and bade a fond farewell to René, once we were sure he had been adequately remunerated.

The countenance behind the counter was a Kanak countess. Rose was a big Melanesian girl with a red and white Santa cap, and a radiant smile. She stored our baggage, but told us it would still be a few hours before our rooms would be ready. Robyn and I arranged to meet Monika later, and went out in the downpour to see the neighbourhood, before it would all shut down. We scurried from shelters to overhangs, lining the shops along Promenade Roger Laroque, absorbing the contrasting shops of ethnographic Kanak objets d'art and colorful tribal murals, and the loud amusement park abominations of giant fiberglass giraffes and elephant heads and pineapples and strawberries and gigantic ice cream cones protruding out from their Anse Vata beach storefronts. The place that had Entrecasteaux had originally written of as inhabited by the 'anthropophagous,' *avid for human flesh and do not hide it*, had evolved through a convict penitentiary and leper colony, a cowboy settler town that Robert Louis Stevenson, during his visit in 1890, described as 'built from vermouth cases,' into a Jerry Lewis Mickey Mouse Riviera of pizza places and burger joints and nightclubs. Robyn and I picked a burger joint. The French still made the best French fries.

Back at the hotel, Le Lagon was preparing to, as they had noted in their brochure, 'welcome you as if you were a famous travel writer.' Rose handed over the keys and another admission that she, and many of her coworkers, would someday like to emigrate to Australia. How odd, I thought, to want to trade your own culture for none.

Noumea was believed to have meant 'sunrise' in one Kanak language, but you couldn't see very much of it next morning. Still, out of our window, on Route de l'Anse Vata, was a riot of butter yellow flowered alamanda, crimson, fuschia and champagne bougainvillea, Cook pines, cyclads and palms. Rose pointed out our Christmas presents under the tree, in the lobby. Robyn and I walked past an edifice, with a huge Buddha and Jersey cow on the roof, and took a bus down to the market. It let us off at the Hotel de Ville, and a holy day of empty streets. An old lorry, painted as a powder blue tidal wave, was parked in front of a harbour, filled with expensive yachts. One was named 'Harmony,' as in *harmony offshore bank accounts would you need to afford it.*

We knew we were home when we smelled the fish, and saw the Mother Hubbard dresses inside the entrance. Every stall was adorned with golden tinsel and Christmas decorations. *Aux produits fermiers.* The shell jewelry at *Boutique Exotique* was exotic. An old bald tattooed Frenchman, adorned with many earings and a Rolex, was sitting at the central café, nursing his café and an ashtray full of *Gitanes*. Thickset Kanak women in blue *muumuus*, sat outside, frowning. We walked back, via the only open patisserie, Docteur Mob, and the Cathedral, with a statue of Joan of Arc outside. Five inebriated young Kanaks on our bus home, had to rescue their sixth, from coma, and an entire day of his life on the bus.

The sun presented its credentials by early afternoon, and Robyn and I took the crowded boat taxi across to Isle aux Canards, intending to sunbathe and recreate. Unfortunately, every square centimeter was not only more densely populated and less appealing than what we had left, extortionate hands were outstretched, even if you only wanted to simply sit on the sharp stone and coral beach. I loved the beach carvings of the wild pigs, and drew parallels with the Parisiens that were monopolizing the beach chairs. Robyn and I returned early, to find Monika in the Le Lagon lobby, rethinking her choice of Christmas venue, unsure, as we were becoming, of whether or not the expense of getting here, would result in anything memorable enough to justify our presence. But then we told her of 341100NC, the little white Chevy whatever that Robyn and I had rented for the next two days. We asked if she wanted to come with us next morning, to drive around the most southern part of the Island. She signed on immediately. I told her she was crazy. Otherwise, it would have violated the rules of informed consent.

> "But I don't want to go among mad people,' Alice remarked.
> 'Oh, you can't help that,' said the Cat: 'we're all mad here. I'm mad.
> You're mad.'
> 'How do you know I'm mad?' Said Alice.
> 'You must be," said the Cat, or you wouldn't have come here."
> Lewis Carroll, *Alice in Wonderland*

*   *   *

The owner of the car rental shack was late to arrive next morning, but he seemed more preoccupied that his little white micro might be washed away in some river torrent than any possibility of our being injured. I asked him about insurance.

"Pourquoi?" He asked. In a land of an uncivil war between cannibals and colonial cowboys, it was only reasonable to answer a question like that with another. Monika slid into the back seat, Robyn took the wheel, and I poured over the map of Noumea, in an effort to navigate a way out, towards the eastern coast. Rose had told me.

"Si vous suivez les baies, vous trouverez le chemin." She had said. *If you follow the bays, you'll find the way.* The bays carved the coast into a thousand views of the sea, and we must have seen each of them, and the supermarché at Mont-Dore, three times, before I figured out the right road. We headed fifty kilometers inland, along the red roads mined out of the green hills, for the *Parc Territorial de la Rivière Bleue*, to hike the forest trails of kauri and araucaria, a miniature version of the Norfolk pine that Robyn and I would later find, in all its endemic splendor on that island, and a definitely more delicate Provençal version of its more remote giant monkey puzzle relatives, soaring up out of the southern forests of Chile. We crossed a stream to an old telephone box. Its door was off its hinges and the handpiece had been manhandled off its connection to the outside world. I pretended to make a call, to Robyn and Monika's amusement, but the gates were closed anyway. The only remnant of the outside world arrived in the form of a day operator of an escorted mountain bike tour, with the keys to the locks, and an offer to include us for too much money and too much time.

New Caledonia had the richest biodiversity in the world, per square kilometer, the product of Grande Terre's central mountain range. Not only botanical species but entire genera, and even families, are unique to the island, and survive nowhere else. The archipelago is home to the Kagu, which although flightless, can use its wings to climb branches, and another bird, likely the smartest in the world. The New Caledonia crow can make sophisticated hooked tools out of twigs and leaves, and has been shown to pass on individual innovations to others of its species. It will place nuts in the path of oncoming cars, and then wait with human pedestrians at traffic signals, until a green light shows them it is safe to retrieve their shelled treasures. Monika and Robyn and I stopped at another nature reserve that we thought would provide an opportunity to hike in a local forest, but the Kanak women caretaker wanted CFA payment upfront and, when we hesitated, her very angry partner emerged from around the corner with his own hooked machete, to make the point. Our craving to commune with the local flora, was completely discouraged by the local fauna, and our white micro beat a hasty retreat backwards.

We passed Netcha where the white moss bubbled out of the ground, like fimbriated sponges on a coral reef, and arrived at the wide expanse of Iguazoidal waterfalls at La Chute de la Madelaine, with more exotic plants, some with red berries, other with white flowers. And the white flowers became the White River joining the Blue River to form the broad Lac de Yaté, Mont Pouédihi and Ouénarou in the background, on the downhill curving road to the eastern beaches of the town of the same name. Just beyond the copper roof and whitewashed and powder blue walls of the simple village church, we spread ourselves over low tide rocks, gorging on pizza bread and croissants and paté and apples, and watching a local fisherman throw his net in successive spirals along the surf. White on blue.

We turned south on the Rue Touaourou, held up briefly by a landslide that an excavator made quick work of, to one of the most beautiful waterfalls on the planet, for a swim, to a spooky Japanese iron mine, where I picked the most perfectly ripe giant feral papaya, through the torrential deep whitewater washouts of what passed for concrete bridge spans in these parts, and on to the quintessential remnant of penal colonialism on Grande Terre.

A single sloop sailed across the shimmering blue invagination of the Baie de Prony, far below the vivid orange rust dirt and green mine-scarred scrub switchback vertigo we navigated in our now less than white micro. Fifteen minutes of motion sickness landed us at sea level, and in a place like nothing like we had imagined.

Prony had been named after Captain Jean Joseph de Brun's steamship, which surveyed the bay in 1854. The village was founded as a logging venture by Captain Hippolyte Sebert in 1867, the same year the guillotine arrived in New Caledonia, three years after the the *Iphigenia*, the first of 75 convoys, bringing 20,000 convicts, arrived in the new penal colony of New Caledonia. For common 'straw hat' criminals, political prisoners from the 1871 Paris Commune uprising, or Algerian Arab rebels, it was a four-month voyage around the Cape of Good Hope from France. Those that survived were sent to the 'slaughterhouse' dungeons of Camp Brun, the Ducos peninsula, Île des Pins, or Prony. They suffered beatings and beheadings and isolation and homesickness, and many, especially the artists and poets and others of a more sensitive disposition, committed suicide. At night the convicts were locked up inside the prison, and during the day they cut down trees, and dragged the massive trunks to the bay, where coastal steamers transported them to Noumea. When the supply of lumber ran out in 1907, the village was evacuated, and went to ruin. In 1953, it was bought by a mining company, which supplied three million tones of iron and cobalt and chromium ore to an Australian concern, one convict colony to another. Then, in 1968, it was deserted again, and fell silent. Which is how we found it.

Silent and deserted it was, windows shuttered closed, but not abandoned. The cluster of old mining huts had been lovingly transformed into holiday shacks, corrugated tin façades painted to look like stone, with a jumping marlin and a squirrel on one, and a likeness of Popeye smoking his pipe on another. A model of de Brun's *Prony* steamship was proudly and prominently positioned along the path. The real stone buildings and iron bars, built by convicts, had become their own ironic prisoners, strangled inside the roots of magnificent giant banyan trees, *revanche* for the beheadings inflicted on their forest relatives, and the deportees forced to cut them down. There were flowers and gigantic philodendrons everywhere. So incongruously peaceful and tranquil at first, we followed a path to a grotto of captioned drawings of the evil that had occurred, imprisoned in their own protective frames.

The *courbaril* was a box not big enough to stand up or lie down in, the *crapaudine*, a rope tying arms and legs together over a tree branch, like the splayed chicken it was named for. Monika became queasy. We left in a hurry.

Back at the top of the Chemin du Prony, we climbed along beside banks of windmills, and to a lookout where our eye level clouds, played puppet shadows on the valley forest and red earth far below. Another set of hills took us to a wide river, an even richer vermilion than the surrounding soil. It smashed into the blue ocean like a ketchup milkshake.

"That has to be coming from somewhere." Said Robyn, shifting down to take us over the next hill. And somewhere rose to fill the entire horizon in front of us, a towering starship colossus of steel and lights and skyscraping smokestacks and arc sprays of furnace fire, the largest helter skelter smelter in the Southern Sea, and maybe the world. It robbed our oxygen, as we drove by. No one spoke.

Its not like there wasn't a history of big in New Caledonia. *Ducula goliath* is the largest species of pigeon, *Rhacodactylus leachianus*, the largest gecko, and *Phoboscincus bocourti* is the largest skink in the world. Its not as if life in New Caledonia can't survive in the toxic metalliferous soils- native flora like the *maquis minier* had been thriving in dirt that would poison any foreign plant species. But this plant was, like me, Canadian and, in a world that warned you not to take any wooden nickels, in New Caledonia at least, the French got the wood, the Canucks got the nickel, and the Kanaks got taken.

Back in Noumea, in exchange for half the feral papaya, Monika thanked us for the day, and sprung for a round of mango gelati. It was wonderful, but it tasted imaginary, like the day, almost too much refinement for the authentic experience that Robyn and I thought we might have found in Wonderland.

We needn't have worried. For the next day, we were going down the rabbit hole. The next day, we were going to meet Alice.

'They're making a ton of money, and no one is getting a nickel.'
Rueben Blades

*   *   *

*   *   *

'If you don't know where you are going any road can take you there'
Lewis Carroll, *Alice in Wonderland*

The rainbow over the *cédez-le-passage* sign on our way
northwest next morning, was already too far down the road
to challenge. Rose had tried to dissuade us, and then thought

better of it. We were already too far down the road to challenge.

"Why do you want to go to Hienghène?" She had asked. I told her it was about as far as we could get in a day, before having to turn around the next morning to come back. This tiny sliver on a map of the Southern Sea was 350 kilometers long.

"That ees why they called it Grande Terre." She said. But it wasn't the distance that had her concerned, and it wasn't something we were going to find out about, until we got there. Over the rainbow, I mentioned to Robyn that we should make an effort to visit one of the local Kanak tribes, and pointed to our map.

"Lets try that one." I said. And we turned off the main road into the mountains towards Tribu Ouan Tom. We drove for several kilometers, until six crudely constructed crosses protruding above white stone rectangles, under an immense mango tree, suggested we were close. The tribu was deserted, and eerily so. Dogs barked. We stopped in front of the tiny peach painted stucco church with its powder blue tin roof, and an effigy of Saint Somebody, encased to the same sort of frame we had seen in Prony, housed above the front door and just below the concrete cross on top. The flagpole bore the two official flags of the *entente* that had followed *Les Evenements*, the events of widespread chaos that tortured the country for two years during my last visit, until the defining climax that had occurred in the location we didn't know we were heading to yet. The first was the vertical red white and blue of the French tricolour. The second flag was the standard of the Kanak and Socialist National Liberation Front (FLNKS), with its horizontal blue, red, and green stripes, symbolizing sky and ocean, Kanak blood, and sacred soil, a yellow disc representing the sun, and the black Kanak flèche faîtière rooftop spear in the center, signifying the chief's ancestor, his voice, and the protection from evil spirits afforded by projecting spikes. For all the pain it carried, it definitely flew in the sun with more jazz than the tricolour.

We made it to La Foa by lunchtime. The tall wooden totems in the sculpture garden were Marley Melanesian, full of humor and gravity and the same time. Robyn ordered us two *croque-monsieurs* under the baseball hat ceiling of the Buna Hotel, where the leaders of the Vichy French governors had been crunch-mistered themselves, imprisoned before their deportation in WWII. We ate them on the patio, among the wafting *Gitanes* smoke and cellphone banter of the local French settler Caldoches.

A little further up the road, we came to the New Zealand War Cemetary in Bourail, paper bark peeling off the trees in great weeping sheaths outside, and giant hibiscus and bright orange flowered trees lining the serpertine rows of two hundred squat headstones in the well manicured lawn of remembrance inside. Forty thousand American soldiers under Admiral Halsey were stationed in New Caledonia during the war. They, and the New Zealanders buried under this grass, had been headed for the Battle of the Coral Sea. It was quiet.

"Long way from home." Said Robyn.

"Didn't stand much of a chance." I said, calculating their ages, and mine.

But it was in the museum at Koné where the Kiwi innocents revealed their innocence. Old bottles of Lemon Paeroa sat beside old radios, with an old smiling stuffed Kiwi bird mascot sitting up against the glass case.

"Long way from home." Said Robyn.

The French contribution to the exhibit was a boulangerie and crèmerie out the back, and the old guillotine upstairs. The poster caption tried to justify its use. *Up until the mid 18th century, nobles were beheaded, highwaymen were put on a wheel in a public place, regicides and state criminals were quartered, counterfeiters were boiled alive, heretics were burnt, and thieves were hung.*

In the cellar were the decapitated heads of two oxen, still yoked together. Robyn pointed back into the room above, and made a slicing motion with her hand. After the 18th

century, in New Caledonia apparently, oxen were guillotined.
The road carved inland and up from there, on its way to the
rainforest of the east coast. There were massive mimosas with
pandemics of pink flowers, hubcap toadstools along the
winding route. We climbed into mountain coolness and pines,
under brooding clouds, past thatched Kanak tribal rondavel
cases, all with conical roofs, some with *flèches faîtières*, some
with television aerials, some with both. Perhaps the new flag
should have an aerial, I thought. We drove off the road into a
village of palms and 'big box' *cases*, waving at the feasting
Bopope Melanesians, obviously puzzled at the alacrity of our
almost simultaneous extrance and exit.

The sun returned with extreme heat, and the view of a
beautiful Koné-Tiwaka river, that would have made an ideal
swimming hole, if it hadn't been proscribed by the 'first
occupant' clans.

"It's taboo." I said. But Robyn had already pulled over and,
not a minute later, was striding down to the rocks and
bamboo plumes, and deep green and whitewater pools of the
confiance. It turned out so painless, we went in a second time,
just as we thought we were leaving.

A little further along, at a panoramic outlook of river we had
just bathed in, I discovered a local custom in the Cook pines
along the ravine.

"Come here." I said. "I'll show you something."

"What have you got?" She asked.

"A New Caledonian money tree." I said.

"Naw." She said.

"Streuth." I said, reaching into the branches where I had
found the coins. "Produces two kinds. Your ten franc money,
and your hundred franc money."

"Is this bad luck if you take it?" She asked

"Dunno." I said. "We'll find out."

It was actually good luck, and got us a bag of mangos at a
road-side stall, and one of the old Kanaks chasing after us, to
return coins he felt we had been cheated into initially paying.

We hit the east coast like the tropical paradise it was. White sand beaches and coconut palms and fringing reef, it was all there. But so were the hamlets of concrete churches and terraced graves beside the roadway, some simple piles of volcanic rocks or wooden crosses, others cement slabs, and others raised and tiled like your bathroom. As we approached Hienghène, the coastline became a World Heritage site. A thousand birds flew spirals overhead. Sharp outcroppings of steep fractured karst limestone cliffs and pinnacles, like I had seen in Halong Bay in Vietnam or the Stone Forest in China loomed like gigantic black alien castles, against the aquamarine of the marine aqua lagoon. The most famous formation was called *Le Poulet*, because it looked like a brooding hen. Another was called *Le Sphinx*, but not so much. We drove up to a lookout called, appropriately enough, Point de Vue, and watched the sun beginning to melt tangerine, on the late afternoon. I was planning to surprise Robyn with a stay in Club Med, but the sign swung across the dirt road entrance said either closed or *complet*, it didn't really matter. So we drove back between the Linderalique cliffs, into town, and nearly missed it.

In the local Fwa dialect, Hienghène means 'Crying in Walking,' as the history of the town would well justify. It began with the unholy trinity influx of missionaries, sandalwood traders, and coffee planters in the 1843. Eleven years later the first New Caledonian governor, Tardy de Montravel stripped Grand Chief Bwarhat of his title, and banished him to Tahiti. The French army burned his villages, displaced the inhabitants, and allocated more land to the plantation owners, who brought in indentured Javanese, to work their plantations. Bwarhat's grandson committed suicide after an aborted rebellion that took the lives of four settlers in 1917. And then what happened in 1984 happened in 1984, causing all the French and Indonesians to leave, but Robyn and I didn't know that yet.

What we did know was that Hienghène was an entirely Kanak

town that contrasted starkly with the Orwellian French investment that had rebuilt it after independence. We passed a Kanak driver in a half-ton, doing wheelies in the dirt tracks on the near side of the river. The light was well over the yardarm, when we crossed to the other side. The French investment consisted of a luxurious new marina with no boats, a local mall of small closed shops, and a tourist information center, open. We thought, *thankfully*. Inside, however, was more crying in walking, but there was also Syvanna. We had come through Immigration, and Rose, to Syvanna. She was, like Rose, a *beeg* Kanak woman, a Grande Terre of her own, with a *beeg* voice and, *thankfully*, a *beeg* heart. We inquired after accommodation.

"Tous sont complets." She said. Matter of fact. I asked if there was anything at all.

"Tribu." She said. "Une tribu." She was already tapping her purple nail polish on the buttons of her mobile phone.

"Allo. Monique?" She asked. And then went on to explain how she had these silly *étrangers*, who didn't know it was between Christmas and New Years and had rocked up on closing time and, well, was there anything she could do.

"Très bien, merci." She said, and hung up. Sylvanna looked at us, and shook her head.

"Tendo." She said.

"Tendo?" I asked.

"Oui." She agreed. "Tendo." And she made a rough drawing of what turned out to be a map of the interior jungle of the island, and put an 'x' where the paper ended.

"Tendo." She said. I asked how far.

"Vingt-quatre kilometers." She said. I looked at Robyn. I looked at the sun, or what was left of it.

"Demandez Monique." She shouted after us, as we ran for the white micro.

What Sylvanna hadn't told us was when the road would run out. She needn't have bothered. It ran out, right out of town. We found ourselves clinging to the tight winding gravel of a riverine precipice, on our way to who knew where, at dusk. The rainforest grew up alongside us, and the streams and white noise our little car had to ford through became deeper and wider, and faster. I got out and forded the concrete spans barefoot, to allow the *leetle* hope we had to ride higher. A large wooden cross stood on the opposite side of the scariest one.

"Well, I hope she's going to put chocolates on our pillow." I said. A chestnut horse with a white mane appeared in the forest beside us. *Unicorn.* But my, wasn't it a wonderland. Glimpses of the Hienghéne River below occasionally flashed through the bush, like irregular Ming mirrors. Two old Kanak men sat contemplatively, across from a wide waterfall.

We passed what appeared be a huge twisted pile of rags, appearing like almost an accident, which we were told it was, but it wasn't. There was a small basalt plaque, with a flèche faîtière etched on the bottom. *Fils de Kanaky... Souviens toi.* Sons of Kanaky... Remember you. We passed through the small village of Tiendanite, the tribu of FLNK leader Jean-Marie Tjibaou, assassinated in 1989 by another Kanak, for making too many concessions to the French. The French now revere him as a wise leader, who wanted to preserve the Kanak culture by peaceful means; and the Kanaks see him as the father of an independent nation.

At sundown, all we can see is no end to the track in front of us. *Oh my ears and whiskers, how late it's getting.* Two adolescent Kanak girls, appear out of nowhere.

"Monique?" I ask. They turn to take us, and we enter a bucolic huddle of thatched *cases*, surrounded by gardens of cassava and taro. Melon-sized hibiscus blooms droop from winding vines.

"Monique?" I asked, again.

"Oui." She said. But we were not destined to stay with Monique. Monique was *complets*. She already had a couple from France, and could accommodate no more. *Curiouser and curiouser.* She told the girls where to take us.

"Alice." She said. And we went to Alice. We went, via a local hunter and his dogs, shouldering the rifle that had brought down the wild pig he was returning with, eviscerated and hanging off his horse, rib bones facing outwards, grinning in victory.

Louis Carroll might not have recognized Alice, but I did. By her smile. It was so real, sitting above her blue *CFC Froid Climatisation* t-shirt, and whitest teeth, and paisley dress, and earings, and big hands, and blue and white flip-flops. Alice was the realist thing on the planet. I was in immediate love. The *case* she showed us to, among the flowerpot and palms, as our bedroom that evening, was a bit daunting at first. You had to duck your head to enter. It had seen its fair share of hearth fires inside, to the point where the smoked bamboo poles converged at the center of the universe, high above our thatched conical ceiling. There were yellow flowers, with white wingnut ears, just outside.

Alice explained that, we slept in her *case*, but the bathroom was in a separate building down on the river, and we would have dinner in a third hut, only ten minutes down the river from our mattress. Tendo was turning out to be an ecumenical form of hospitality.

I made a confession to Alice, paired to a request. I told her that I had brought one of my bottles of Côtes du Rhône from Noumea, and asked if she had a corkscrew, and would like a glass. She said yes, and no. *The Mad Hatter: "Would you like some wine?" Alice: "Yes..." The Mad Hatter: "We haven't any and you're too young."*

It was pitch black by the time Robyn and I had braved the giant geckos in the dark river shower by headlamp, and returned to Alice for directions to dinner. Our path was lit with more hope than light, navigating the wetness of the grass. The shack at the bottom of the hill was festively decorated, rough-hewn wooden posts wrapped in the colours of the FLNKS flag, a green and white floral banner over the table, and curled ribbons dangling from the rafters. Tall glass mugs held vertical paper napkins, near jugs of fruit juice, covered in aluminum foil, on the red and white paper tablecloth. A row of six entrée trays, white rice, *chien chaud* hot dogs, fried plantain and purple taro, chicken, wild pork, and cut mangoes, had been laid out before us. Across from the Morton salt and fern centerpiece, sat a French couple which, having arrived in Hienghène with the notion that they would be staying at a Club Med, were still caught in the headlights of their Kanak village homestay transmutation.

And then the chef emerged from the dim light of the dirt floor kitchen, to complete the visuals, a French Melanesian hybrid version of Peter Tosh- drooping grey Rasta dreadlock tam and chin-beard, iridescent blue athletic shorts with white strings dangling out the front, and grey shirt open to gaunt ribs and abs, he stood with his spatula, seemingly astonished at his own culinary accomplishments, and our applause of his efforts.

After our pleasant remote repast, Robyn and I returned to our *case*, to find that, in the meantime, Alice had turned a flashlight on, outside the open square, in the wall above our mattress. The insect swarms it had attracted, forced us under our sheets, until the heat forced us back out, until the cycle could be repeated, throughout the night.

Alice had French pressed local coffee and tropical fruit ready next morning, and a sad reluctance to see us go so soon. Robyn and I felt the same, but we had a long drive ahead, all the way back to Noumea. She asked if we had seen the accident site, on the way here the previous day. I told her we had, and asked what kind of accident it was.

"Dix frères." She said. "Une tragédie." *Ten brothers.* I asked if it was ten brothers from one family.

"Oui." She said. "Dix frères d'une même famille." *Yes.*

We passed it again, on our way out through the winding watery washouts. It looked different to us the second time, not like a roadside memorial to a traffic mishap, but more significant. It was only many years later that we learned the truth about the huge twisted pile of rags, the burned-out remains of the car, and the nature of the accident that killed the brothers and sons from one family.

On 5 December 1984, ten unarmed FLNKS Kanaks from Tiendanite had been returning from a political meeting, when they were ambushed and shot and set alight by local Caldoches. The brothers that Alice referred to were her *Ti-Va-Ouere*, Brothers of the Earth. In retaliation for the Hienghéne Massacre, outraged Kanaks set fires to the houses of, and chased out, most of the French settlers and other immigrants, and engaged in a boycott of the referendum on independence. The magistrate reviewing the case determined that the perpetrators had acted in 'self-defense,' and none of the self-confessed French killers have ever been prosecuted for the crime. *"Either it brings tears to their eyes, or else —"*

"Or else what?" said Alice, for the Knight had made a sudden pause.
"Or else it doesn't, you know."

Robyn and I passed through Hienghéne but, instead of heading immediately south, took a northern detour to see the *Bac de la Ouaieme*, the last surviving river ferry in the country. The bridle path masquerading as a road to get there, was breathtaking, with soaring sheer scarps rippling into palm and fern-sewn emerald peaks, veined by waterfalls, on one side, and plunging precipices to the wave-pounding ocean, and scattered columns of black rock throwing salt veils across our white micro, on the other. This was the inflection point, on which our journey to Wonderland turned.

We drove by white churches with brick colored conical spires and full front yard cemeteries, past rusted rivet bridges, and through small villages with bizarre carvings. A small town on another river offered the promise of lunch in a Caldoche café, but the vibe was all wrong, and we paid far too much for an old baguette and a piece of cheese in our escape from the only shop. Returning along the bays into Noumea was like driving into Monaco. Rose welcomed us back to *Le Lagon*, with her *beeg* Melanesian smile, and no small apparent relief.

Robyn and I spent the next two days filling in the gaps that had been closed over Christmas. We visited the surrealistic Jean-Marie Tjibaou Cultural Centre on the Tinu Peninsula, a monumental architectural interpretation of Kanak building traditions. It was described for us as 'a perfected masterpiece and a deeply impressive, earth-bound example of a new interpretation of modernism,' and it was certainly all that, and more. But it was also all that, and less. The architect was from Italy, the iroko wood from Africa, the prefabrication from France, and the castings from foreign aluminum and not local nickel or chrome. For us, the scale of the stadium dwarfed the exhibits and, instead of an endearing intimacy with Kanak cultural life, it produced an amphitheatrical bombast of laminated confusion.

Similarly, the forty-foot carved Mwâ Ka totem pole downtown, designed as a symbolic burying of past suffering related to French colonization, was surrounded by a metal fence, padlocked shut.

I took Robyn out to *La Chaumière* in the Latin Quarter one night, and *Le Roof,* out on the ocean boardwalk in Anse Vata, on our last. Dolphins and stingrays streaked along beside our table. I splurged for a bottle of Bordeaux. The Metro transplanted sommelier fresh off the boat from Paris tried to give me an inferior vintage, and seemed surprised that I caught him on it.

But not as surprised as he was going to be, if he decided to stay and live his life in New Caledonia. That morning I had been to the supermarché in Le Mont-Dore, and waited in the wine aisles for Robyn to finish some last minute shopping. Three colossal black Kanak men, in full cannibal regalia, going to or from I know not where, paused in front of the high end Bordeaux shelf beside me. One pointed to the very expensive bottle behind the glass.

"Pas une mauvaise année." He said. "Mais pas comme le '61."

Not a bad vintage, but not like the '61.

And there it was, I thought. In less than two hundred years, some of the fiercest Melanesians in the Southern Sea, were coming through some of the most vicious forms of colonization and exploitation, with some of the richest mineral wealth on the planet about to fall into their laps, from kava crude to claret cosmopolitan. Payback was coming to Wonderland, speaking French, and turning dirt into paydirt, and both into romance.

'Everything's got a moral, if only you can find it.'
Lewis Carroll, *Alice in Wonderland*

*   *   *

'It was the Law of the Sea, they said. Civilization ends at the waterline. Beyond that, we all enter the food chain, and not always right at the top.'

Hunter S. Thompson

Like most things run by Americans, I was expecting some inherent contradiction. He told me it was the only way to get there. I had to ask the agent a second time.

"The sole airline that flies to one of the most remote archipelagos of some of the smallest islands in the Pacific, among the last habitable areas on earth to be occupied by human beings, is called Continental?"

"Go figure." He said. Chris was a different sort of travel agent; that only became gradually apparent. I called him in Seattle about visiting the former Trust Territory of the Pacific Islands.

"The best way to find out if you can trust somebody is to trust them." He said. "Didn't work." The commission guy was quoting me *Hemingway*. I asked about the Compact of Free Association that had been signed with the US in 1982.

"None are more hopelessly enslaved than those who falsely believe they are free." He said. *Goethe*. Chris explained that Continental operated a twice-weekly schedule through Guam, to all the islands that Robyn and I wanted to visit- Palau, Yap, Pohnpei, and Kosrae. We hadn't expected the free detour to the Marshall Islands, also hopelessly enslaved.

"The plane's undercarriage is coated with Teflon, so it can operate on coral runways." He said.

"Cunning leads to knavery." I said. *Ovid*.

On the outward leg, I remember being impressed by the floor-to-ceiling aquarium in some shop pretending to be a rainforest, inside SeaTac airport. Waiting for me, in the waters surrounding the rock islands of the Southern Sea, 'floor-to-ceiling' was preparing a whole new multidimensional storyboard.

I had booked the cheapest place to stay for our late arrival the first night, some lime green motel named after the initials of the owner. I hadn't told Robyn that I had arranged for us to stay at the best place for the rest of our time, and that certainly hadn't been free.

The inherent contradiction continued outside the terminal. Cars were ambidextrous, with steering wheels on either side of the vehicle. Speedometers were in *km/h*, but the few speed limit signs were in *mph*. There were no traffic lights, very few stop signs, no street names and therefore, no street signs. Our taxi driver had to refuel at the only gas station in the 'Rainbow's End' country, on the half hour drive into Koror. The sign under the Shell logo was prescient. *We Fix Flats Change Oil Cold Beer Betel Nuts Ice.*

Robyn and I checked into our initial initialed inn, and went down the dark road, to the only eatery open this late, in the middle of the biggest ocean on Earth. Over eleven thousand kilometers from LA, we had two orders of burritos in the Rock Island Café. It was all very Continental.

Santa waved to us from one of the thatched roofs along Main Street next morning. His reindeer seemed to be having some difficulty getting the sleigh airborne in the torpid heat. The big guy in the t-shirt and sunglasses, outside the white clapboard and air conditioner wainscoting of the National Congress building, was only a little faster at raising the flag on the nation's flagpole. It was a big yellow dot on a powder blue background, a symbolism that I had thought rather obvious. But I was wrong. The blue actually signified the 'transition from foreign domination to self-government,' and the golden disc represented the full moon, which the Palauans consider the best time for 'human activity.' Some Tokyo International Relations professor named Futaranosuke Nogoshi indicated that the moon motif was there to pay homage to the rising sun on the Japanese flag, as 'a symbol of amity between Palau and Japan.' One of the other sons of the rising sun, who later became a president of Palau, reacted with no small irony. *That's one way of putting it.*

The full moon shone out from the 'o' in the green Palau Shop sign, closed in the early side-streaked sunrise, its painted white-striped orange clownfish still inert, above the blue anemones on its whitewashed exterior. Inherent contradiction was prominently displayed, further along Main Street. Next to the government billboard, *Aim for a healthy weight... a Guide for Pacific Islanders*, with a cartoon of a fat Palauan woman in a red and white hibiscus muumuu, shooting the rivets out of the scale she was standing on, was the American second amendment response. *Low Carb Lunch Buffet... All You Can Eat!*

A jumble of iron and wooden houses and shops, built in Japanese or American style, took us through Koror's Urban Oceania, to the Belau Museum reconstructed wood and thatch *bai*, or traditional men's club, that had formed the social and political epicenter of Palauan life. Robyn and I would visit many more of these tall diamond shaped barn-like single status structures, large expanses of wood broken only by two fireplaces, their eight interior beams and exterior gables held together by seamless joints.

The three priorities that had driven the male cultures of the colonial invaders, were the same preoccupations as the boys of Belau had - Nietzsche, Marx and Freud. In Palau it was warfare, a strange form of currency, *udoud*, consisting of high-fired clay and glass bead necklaces, and sex. The women were exploited or concubine complicit in a network of *omengol* clubhouse prostitution, and the number of *bai* in a village, their rank within the community, and the hierarchy of seating inside was a measure of the Micronesian man.

The carved wooden figurehead over the entrance to the *Bai ra Ngesechal* was a naked woman, legs spread wide.

Clubhouse decorative elements were painted in shades of white, black, red, and bright yellow, made by mixing line, soot and ochre with parinarium nut oil. Two kinds of ornamentation trimmed the timber. The first were symbols of roosters, spiders and clams, *udoud* currency, the frigate birds credited with bringing *udoud* to Palau, and a god with earrings containing the currency, and Mingidabrutkoel, the deity who had taught Palauan women natural childbirth.

But it was the pictographic art mnemonics, and the legends they were painted to recall, that fascinated. The fables themselves were the usual standard creation myths, morality plays, and stories of unrequited love- there was a mythical giant named Uab, who had created the archipelago, another named Melechotech-a-chau, with an unbelievably large penis, and my favorite, the *Legend of the Turtle of Ngmelis.*

A pair of young lovers first met on Ngmelis Island on a moonless night, on the nesting beach of a hawksbill turtle. In the morning, the sun revealed that the woman's grass skirt was missing. She made a makeshift garment, and agreed to meet her paramour on the island again, in two weeks time. When they returned, a noise disturbed them. The hawksbill that had come ashore, to lay her eggs in the sand, had the woman's missing grass skirt, wrapped around the its legs. In the darkness of their original tryst, the woman had mistaken the turtle's back for a rock.

It was all about the legends. Like everywhere else in the world, legends died hard, survived truth, made reality, and became the template for human behavior. Like everywhere else in the Southern Sea, the most important story of first contact involved a shipwreck, and a castaway. In 1783 an English naval captain of the British East India Company, Henry Wilson, returning from Macau by the 'Eastern Passage,' to avoid the southwest monsoon during the Fourth Anglo-Dutch War, strayed too far east, and ran his *Antelope* up on Ulong reef. He spent three months rebuilding his ship. One of his crew knew Malay, and was able to befriend a local ruler, Ibedul, and helped Wilson settle an ongoing regional conflict, with the assistance of a ship's cannon. Wilson took Ibedul's son, Prince Lee Boo, back to England with him, as a *Noble Savage* ambassador. After only a few months Lee Boo died from smallpox, but not before creating tremendous trading interest in Palau's trepang, coconut oil, and turtle shell, in exchange for smallpox, influenza and leprosy. Robyn and I passed the statue of Captain Wilson, covered in Christmas lights, the replacement legend illuminating subsequent contact.

The 'Black Islands' had been settled two thousand years before the birth of the man who had inspired the lights, by Negritos from either the Philippines or Indonesia. A fascinating character named O'Keefe brought Yapese to Palau to quarry their own stone money, until the Pope granted foreign governance to Spain in 1885. The Spanish were known for a peculiar form of suffocating water torture called *toca*, after the strip of linen introduced into the victim's mouth which, together with the iron prong *bostezo* used to keep it open, was favored because it produced no marks on the body.

In 1899, following its defeat in the Spanish-American war, Spain sold Palau to Germany. The Germans started a police force of two, with a fellow named Winkler (no relation) as the station supervisor, for the purpose of coercing the local chiefs into establishing coconut plantations. Winkler waged an all out war on the custom of *bai* clubhouse concubinage, fining the Palauans who resisted in their own currency, or sentencing them to work on the newly begun canal in Ngarchelong. The Germans had their own form of water torture called *Schwedentrunk*, or the Swedish Drink, which had evolved during the Thirty Years' War, and used to force peasants to hand over food or, ironically, to extort sex from women.

After WWI, Germany gave Palau to Japan, under the Treaty of Versailles. The Japanese, in the next war, developed their own version of the 'water cure,' but in between the conflicts, introduce Buddhism and Shinto, island causeways, airports and seaplane ramps and commercial air service, public schools, agricultural stations, phosphate and bauxite mining, and one more legend. A year before Walt Disney created the storyboard in the US, a Japanese art teacher named Hisakatsu Hijikata introduced the idea of taking the high beam *bai* beam traditional legends, and creating separate, individual storyboards, as a unique artistic expression of local folklore. The story of storyboards, began with ironwood and finished by painting it with either different colors, or in black and brown shoe polish, allowing it to shine in the true shade retention of the wood.

Robyn and I never got to see the storyboards for sale in the local prison, and the ones in the shop we passed were too expensive for us to purchase, if we were going to be able to also 'stay at the best place for the rest of our time.' In front of The Professional Spiritual Counseling Office, in the same building and right beside the Office of Substance Abuse Programs, I hailed a taxi to take us to the 'best place.' We pulled into 64 acres of lush landscaping, and were escorted into an expansive lobby for a welcome drink, and a tropical garden room with rattan furniture, tile floors, a ceiling fan, and private *lanai* veranda that was upgraded to an ocean view for the fun of it. We watched the staff feed the resident pool stingrays and green turtles, and snorkeled off the thousand feet of beautiful white sand beach. There were lionfish and giant clams and an orchid collection in the greenhouse that was magnificent.

"Ungilbung." Said the resident gardener. *Pretty flower.*

"Ungilbung." We agreed. The sunsets across the coconut palms and blue ocean and white expanse of sand outside our window, were nonpareil.

We signed on for the 'boat tour' next morning, and it was destined to become a legend of its own, beginning with the graffiti on the cabin's canopy. *Peace and love are useful.*

Our captain piloted through all the colors of the Rock

Islands, the clearest sky-reflected azure blue and turquoise lagoon blue and aquamarine blue and the most opaque blue powder blue of the white bottom talc we spread on each other's bodies, the whitest coral sand beaches and linen clouds, and the jungle palm green and lichen mimosa green of whatever could squeeze its roots into the sharp grey crevices of the sheer limestone cliffs and rock mushrooms in between. Robyn and I snorkeled and posed for photos in front of a natural bridge arch, and swam into underwater caverns, holding our breath until we ran out of water, and into echoes, and ozone.

The highlight of the day came in the Southern Lagoon between Koror and Peleliu, the site of the landing of the US First Marine and the 81st Infantry Divisions in 1944, at a cost of almost two thousand American lives, and six times as many Japanese. Our own landing on uninhabited Eil Malk island was peaceful, except for the belligerence of the rocks and protruding roots, on the uphill trail to the lake.

The isolated lake on Eil Malk was different to any other lake that Robyn and I had ever swum in. It was a seawater lake, twelve thousand years old, surrounded by rock walls and trees, and stratified into two layers. The bottom layer, below fifteen meters, had no oxygen, and no life, except for a dense population of purple photosynthetic bacteria at the boundary. The reason there was no life below this, however, has nothing to do with the lack of oxygen. It has to do with the toxicity. Any diver dropping into this layer would die from the eight-fold lethal concentration of hydrogen sulfide that would be immediately absorbed through his skin. It wasn't what couldn't live below the purple bacteria that was its highlight, of course, but what did live above it.

Robyn and I put on mask and snorkel, and waded into a world of pulsating suspended rubber, bouncing bells of buoyancy, millions of muscular medusa of *Matigias papua etpisoni*, the daily horizontal migration of Golden jellyfish.

During the night, the jellyfish reside in the Western Basin of the lake, making repeated vertical excursions between the surface and the purple bacteria, to acquire nutrients for their symbiotic algae. Then, always rotating counterclockwise to provide even solar exposure, on sunrise they follow the sun to the eastern basin, and then back again in the afternoon, as the sun falls back towards the west. The east to west migration is modified to some degree by their need to avoid shadows, and the jellyfish-eating anemones that are waiting for them to drift within range. There is another species of jellyfish that also lives in the lake. The Moon, like its golden brother, also doesn't have powerful enough *nematocyte* stinging cells to cause anything but a little electric buzz around your mouth, but it doesn't migrate, and wasn't decimated in the El Niño die-off, that had occurred six years earlier. There was definitely no shortage of either species when Robyn and I were there, so densely packed at one point, that Robyn's claustrophobia won out over the sheer fun of swimming in pool of tennis balls.

We returned for an evening out with two couples from our tour, to a Japanese sashimi repast. We spoke of local legends, and one in particular, about a dugong, inspired by a mural we had passed, on the way.

Once there lived an old man and his wife. One day the wife went to her taro patch while her husband remained at home. While she was away, the old man was turned into a nut tree by an evil spirit and, when she returned, he was gone. She called out for him but could get no answer and she knew something strange must have happened. She then called out the names of all the plants nearby hoping for a response, the lemon tree, the banana tree, the pineapple plants, and the breadfruit tree, but she got no response. For a while she sat down to rest and then remembered that she had not called out to the nut tree. She shouted so loudly at the nut tree that a branch bent over, and blood dripped from it. One day she felt a stirring in her womb and delivered a beautiful baby girl. The girl grew up very obedient but asked about her father. Her mother told her that she must never eat the nuts from the nearby tree. Years later, however, while her mother was working in the taro patch, the girl picked some, and was just about to eat them, when her mother reappeared. She put the nuts in her mouth and ran towards the sea. Her mother followed her daughter, begging her not to swallow. The daughter ran into the sea, and was turned into a dugong, and disappeared. The girl had the nuts in her mouth but had not swallowed, when she was turned into the dugong. There is still a bulge in the jaws of the dugong, where the nuts are.

Big plastic Santas guarded the radial tire gardens and Christmas tree lights of a house of kitsch, on the way into town next morning. It was going to be Christmas Eve, and Robyn and I braved the immense suspended fiberglass nautilus in the mall, past the *Chinese Herbalist Doctor Acupuncture Massage* sign over the New Koror Hotel, also advertising *Taiwanese snacks*, to arrange our celebration with Maria, offering a whole suckling pig, with crackling and cassava, taro, and yam, and San Miguel beer, at her restaurant that evening. Robyn wore a white orchid tiara, and I wore my Hawaiian shirt. It was legendary.

*　　*　　*

'Not everything that dives into the water is a mermaid.'
Russian Proverb

Thirty kilometers northwest of Koror the speedboat veered off course, so hard and so fast that most of us on the starboard bench were almost thrown out. The tanks had tried to escape their wooden frames.

"Change of plan." She said. "Conditions are better at the Corner right now, although it may be a bit of a challenge for you." *Sweet.*

Today was about to alter more than my direction. The surface chop was mixed with white, and the winds were whipping a meringue. I had spent many evenings in the dark cold winter of Vancouver Island, preparing.

"If we're going to Micronesia," I said. "I guess I'd better learn how to dive." Robyn agreed, although she herself wouldn't sign on, because of claustrophobic memories of life-threatening asthmatic attacks, as a young girl in New Zealand. I sought succor in the deep haloclines of the telephone directory. There was only one local company offering an Open Water PADI course for beginners. *Where the World learns to Dive.*

"Sundown Diving." He answered. They could have chosen a different name. Ed was the boss and owner, and quickly convinced me I had rung the right place.

"There are three evening sessions of class and pool time, and then a weekend of ocean diving." He said. "And then you'll be set for Palau." I asked him if that was all there was.

"You can swim, right?" He asked back. I told him how I liked to do it for fun, but I wasn't particularly keen to do it not to die. And then I remembered what Bob Marley had said. *Well, me don't swim too tough so me don't go in the water too deep.* And that was all about to veer off course.

The classes and subject material were provided in small gulps, by two young seal pups, swimming in more testosterone than seawater. Their first act was to cull the more attractive young female students off from the rest of the pod, establishing a Greek alphabetical hierarchical colony of descent. Teaching methods came straight out of the *Animal Farm* School of Dive Instruction. *Oxygen is overrated. Chlorine is my perfume. The water is your friend.* But I still managed to learn about breathing and buoyancy, terminology and timing, and equalization and equipment- about BCD's and regs and first stages and second stages and gauges and octos and masks and snorkels and fins and weight belts and releases and tanks and acronyms-acronyms for getting into troubled waters, *S-O-R-T-E-D*, and getting back out, *S-T-A-K-E-D*.

At the indoor pool, entombed in the black rubber body-armor of the absurd, I crawled like an awkward alien insect down the ladder, beginning at the top and working my way to the bottom, counting and checking off boxes, until I didn't have to. And then, for a moment, I felt a sensation of utter tranquility, and peace with the pressure and penetrating fluorescent light, timing my bubbles with my heartbeat, until one of the seal pups interrupted my trance, with further instructions for survival. I decided I was going to like this. At night, in between classes, I would fall into sleep, breathing as I descended, conserving air, refining my rhythm, emptying my mind.

The final written exam was a cakewalk. I finished before any of the others, and got a perfect score.

"I've seen this before." Said the seal pup that marked it, except you could tell that he hadn't.

The open water weekend part of the course occurred on a shallow bay called Fin Beach, in a park named Neck Point, and in Tyee Cove. It was cold and cumbersome, and the visibility allowed for silt and the odd rock. But I had now dived to 60 feet, and accumulated a total bottom time of 149 minutes.

"Congratulations." Said one of the seal pups. "You're now an open water diver." But, like Buffet had said (Warren, not Jimmy), its only when the tide goes out do you discover who's been swimming naked.

And so, three months later, I found myself having signed up for the Advanced Open Water Diver course, off course with my English instructor, Jacky, to 'a bit of a challenge.' There would be no words, but I will try.

The speedboat driver's t-shirt said some of it. *Life's a Beach and then you dive.* I had heard about The Blue Corner. Most dive magazines rated it as the single best dive in the world. Over an hour and almost fifty kilometers later, the speedboat driver eased off the throttle. The rollers returned, and the rest of the already advanced open water divers jumped for their equipment.

"Its too rough over there." Jacky said. "We'll have to go down through the Blue Holes." She didn't tell me it was recommended for those with a cave diver rating. Sometimes God calms the storm. At other times, he calms the sailor. And sometimes he makes us swim.

"When you get to the bottom of the hole, just put in your reef hook, and wait for me." She said. I had never seen a reef hook.

"I thought you were coming with me." I said. She told me she would meet me at the bottom.

I was in the tropics, no wetsuit, going through what I could remember of the routine. Slide the BCD over your neck, tighten the strap at just the right height, screw the reg yoke into place, hook up the inflator, turn on the gas, gauge pointed to the bottom of the boat.

The hoses stiffen as the unit inflates. Alive. Breathing through the primary and octopus, the asthmatic regulator wheeze tastes like latex. Spit in your mask, if you can. Remember the story of Shaka Zulu, who used to ask a row of warriors to spit, to see who was lying. Fear shuts off the parasympathetic part of your autonomic nervous system, the 'Fight or Flight' reflex refusing to allow saliva to get involved. I get just enough to coat the glass. Swish it in the sea, drained, and tightened around your head. Mask on, snorkel inserted between the straps. Sling your weight belt, add a couple for the good tuna sashimi you've had far too much of, low on your hips, like the gunslinger you are. Put your reg in your mouth, bend to strap on your fins, too much tuna sashimi again, tuck the octo into its holder. One with the unit, you sit down on the gunnel, salute the skipper, and lean back. *Live in the sunshine, swim the sea, drink the wild air.*

There is nothing to tell you when the ocean will begin, except the soft recoil of deceleration, far too slow to turn back now. The water tastes like blood, and it should, for we come from it, and your bubbles escape while they still can. You can feel your pulse through your temples inside your mask as you right yourself. The sea doesn't know how old you are. You purge your mask, tighten you waist and shoulder straps, and vent air from your vest. You find neutral buoyancy. Signal-orientation-regulator-time-equalization-deflate, and you are *S-O-R-T-E-D*, and you descend, into the Blue Hole, and the first person, singular.

I drift over to where the vertical hole begins, traveling with the current. The coral falls away as I pass over the ledge. I go down, into the silence. I go down, kicking, barely using my legs, almost hovering, to slow my fall. Atomic oxygen spins my head around in the clear blue light. Depth robs color on descent. Clear blue becomes bluer, and then greener, and then, past the soft corals and *Tubastraea* decorating the walls, fade to black. It's a hundred feet down to the side entrance to the Blue Corner, and I have never been that deep before. Fear is only as deep as the mind allows. There is a cave entrance at 85 feet that leads into the 'Temple of Doom.' People have perished. I keep going until, finally, to my left, appears a round dark blue patch of light, which leads to the Blue Corner. I ready my reef hook, and swim through to the other side. The current is strong, and difficult to kick against. *The man who is swimming against the stream knows the strength of it.* After 150 feet, it reverses, and I place my hook. Suspended six feet off the coral, I look up in disbelief. Circling around me slowly, in a continuous gigantic cylindrical wall, are thousands of chevron barracuda, glass eyes focused on me. I was floating in a revolving weightless circus ride of horizontal and vertical black and silver stripes, and the optical effects were mesmerizing. And when they finally broke ranks, the rest of Neptune's kingdom was waiting. Sharks of every description, White Tips and Black Tips and Grey Reef sharks and Great Hammerheads, cruised and darted and weaved on the high definition depth. A manta flapped by, and then an Eagle ray, mixed with immense schools of Jacks and Black

Snapper, Redtooth Triggerfish, Pyramid Butterfly fish, and solitary green turtles and giant groupers and my favorite, the big lipped electric turquoise Napoleon Wrasse. I could hear the grinding of the Humphead Parrotfish's teeth, feeding on the coral. And the coral was magnificent, consisting of giant Gorgonian sea fans and hard cabbage and swaying soft purple corals and all the small colorful fish on the planet. A tap on my shoulder turned out to be Jacky who, true to her word, had found me. She unhooked me from the reef, and we careened along the sheer coral cliff at current speed, marveling at the rest of the living treasure, until our gauges began to groan in pain. I didn't want to leave, but there wasn't an option. I had been so excited to be there that my air was gone, and I hadn't noticed, because the needle on my gauge was stuck at 50 barr. My next to final breath was all aluminum. Luckily, my final one was on Jacky's octopus, which had made it to me in three seconds flat, after I signaled that I was out. We began the process for getting back out together, signal-time-arms up and look-kick-exhale-done, *S-T-A-K-E-D*. Our inflated safety sausage attracted the boat. Its ladder reintroduced me to gravity, and mammalian life forms. "That was your drift dive." Jacky said. But I couldn't speak. Drifting occurs in the sea, in the snow and the soul. Mine was complete.

Over the next three days, I made four more dives, but nothing would ever come close to the house at Blue Corner.

I did a multilevel dive at Ngedbus Coral Gardens, a hundred kilometers in the other direction. There were many deep canyons and crevices, horizontal and vertical, cut through the slope, with large coral heads providing shelter to batfish and stingrays and cuttlefish, Blue Ribbon Eels and Snake Eels and Crocodile Eels, and Scorpion fish and Lionfish. My advanced navigation dive was through the channel that the Germans had blasted and dredged during the first Winkler's impact, to carry guano for export to Europe. My navigation was mostly through the maze of trevally and snappers and jacks, and mantas and schooling sharks, one standing vertical at a 'cleaning station,' while butterfly fish and cleaning wrasse provided his spa service. The sandy bottom was an urban hub of Gobies and Mantis shrimp, and hundreds of comical garden eels, popping up in curious colonies, like marine meerkats, wondering what I needed to navigate for. The current picked up and flew us over patches of lettuce coral and giant clams.

The spookiest dive was on the *Helmet* wreck, a ship of unknown provenance, with its bow lower than its stern. We dropped down the mooring line to the twisted rusting guardrail around the aft deck gun platform, and the mangled gun barrel pointing to port. The depth charge release boxes on each side still contained their lethal cargo. The starboard side had been torn open by whatever had sunk it, revealing the ship's ribs, and strewn explosive charges. Stacks of corrosion-cemented helmets were stuck to the port upper deck, between piles of rifles and ammunition, and gasmasks, staring out from the sediment. Jacky took me through the inner passageways, leading to several small rooms and a catwalk above the engine room. I got my regulator caught on a jutting piece of sharp metal, and imagined what it might have been like, had it cut my air hose. We left the silt I had kicked up carefully, so we could see our way out, past radial engines and brass lanterns, gradually being extinguished themselves, by the staghorn and brain coral growing around them.

"Congratulations." Said Jacky. "You're now an advanced open water diver." But I didn't feel advanced. I had seen and survived the 'floor-to-ceiling' multidimensional storyboard of the Blue Corner of Palau. This was more than two of my medical colleagues had seen and survived. The first, a pathologist from my home town in Northwestern Ontario, who had turned me on to the joys of medicine, died on the bottom in the Bahamas; the second, an internist like myself from the same Vancouver Island community, died on the bottom, not far from where I had entered the ocean as a diver for my first underwater experience. The world was getting to be such a dangerous place, a man should consider himself lucky to get out of it alive.

*　　*　　*

*　　*　　*

While I had been hanging off my reef hook, Robyn had been hanging around the Palau Pacific Resort. Back with my advanced certification, we rented a cherry red 4X4, and crossed the causeway, heading for the mountains of Babeldeob. Dogs and chickens gave way to west coast mangroves, colorful *bais*, skyhigh jungle with towering philodendrons and other vines, lining silent paths to magnificent waterfalls and wonderful pools to swim and cool down in. Rainbow's End, at the top of the island, was the mysterious site of Badralchau, a two thousand year old scattered collection of 39 stone monuments with carved faces, and no known history. The monoliths were smaller and coarser than those of Easter Island. The largest weighed only five tons. The difference was, the material was imported. From a long weigh away.

Robyn and I were still a long way away, as the sun began its descent behind the mountain rainforest on our east coast return leg to Koror. The roads were challenging, the beaches lovely, and the pink paint and green roof and Santa on the house we passed were also imported, but more recently. As were the rusted out Japanese tanks and antiaircraft guns, and the shells casings underneath the blast holes in the concrete walls of the Airai State Public Work building, with the new Mitsubishi van inside.

The most important storyboard epic of Palau was its creation myth. And its fate. According to legend, Rainbow's End was once a single large landmass, on which lived a very unusual man named Uab. When he arrived as a child, Uab didn't play with the other children, but was simply preoccupied with eating and sleeping. He would eat even more than the adults, and soon became enormous. *Aim for a healthy weight...a Guide for Pacific Islanders*. As he continued to grow, he began to consume all the food of his neighbors and his community. People began to starve, just to keep up with his demands. *Low Carb Lunch Buffet... All You Can Eat!*

They held a secret meeting, and decided to burn the giant, by building a large fire around him. When Uab fell, he kicked Peleliu away from Angaur, and his partially submerged body became the other islands of Palau. His legs became Koror, his stomach formed Ngiwal, rich in foodcrops, his head rested as Ngerchelong, whose people are now known for their intelligence, and his penis became Aimeliik, the place with the wettest weather.

The storyboard of Uab is also not an unfitting metaphor for how the US Continental has exploited Palau, legs spread wide. The Americans were not without their own history of waterboarding, from the 'hydropathic torture' of New York's Sing Sing prison in the mid 1800s, to the 'water cure' used by Teddy Roosevelt's troops in the Philippines after the Spanish-American War of 1898, to the 'third degree interrogation' by US police before the 1940s, and to the Vietnam war. More recently, prisoners at Guantanamo were introduced to the practice and, most recently, some of those same prisoners were introduced to Palau. In 2009 the Obama administration paid 200 million dollars to bring 17 Chinese Moslem Uighurs to Rainbow's End, about 12 million bucks per head. The Chinese government wasn't happy, and pulled out all its development aid and investment. The local Palauans weren't happy, because the Uighurs don't fit in. And now, the Uighurs aren't happy, because they feel like they belong nowhere, and the Palauan government, having seen the money run out, isn't happy. The one Uighur that escaped to Turkey from Palau is happy. The rest are shipwrecked castaways on the proverbial Pacific 'American Lake.' The Compact of Free Association with the United States apparently doesn't extend to respecting Palau's 'Nuclear Free' constitution, or resisting the compulsion to bombard the population (and that of the Federated States of Micronesia) with military recruiters, having readjusted the economy to make this the only viable option for unemployed young men. The movie *Hell in the Pacific* was filmed on the Rock Islands here. Palau was the site for the reality television program Survivor. Walt Disney's storyboard continued with the investments of his son Roy, in the gated 'secret garden' Miami development of 'Palau at Sunset.' Uab continues to eat the people of Palau out of house and home. When the legends die, the dreams end; there is no more greatness.

'for whatever we lose (like a you or a me)
it's always ourselves we find in the sea'
e.e.cummings, *maggie and milly and molly and may*

*   *   *

Big Money
Yap

'Only Rai gathered in the old way has any value.'
Captain David O'Keefe, *His Majesty O'Keefe*, 1954

If the sign on the refuse bin in the airport was any indication, we had arrived deeper into the red spectrum of Rainbow's End. *Do not spit betel nut chew into this garbage can.* It was surrounded by splotches of what the Yapese called *langad*, the preparation of areca nut and lime, that went into a betel leaf, into their mouths, and into the obvious orange respect they had for rules.

Our driver didn't say a word during the entire trip to Colonia, more because of shyness that the fact that his mouth was full of betel nut. Robyn and I had arrived late in the afternoon, on a flyspeck of an island less than forty square miles, with almost as many lights twinkling in the equatorial dusky distance. The darkness had chased away the last betel-colored rays of the sun from Chamorro Bay, as the car pulled up to the first of three places we would stay on Yap. Across a wooden suspension bridge, we were greeted by roosters and barking dogs, a caged fruit bat in the thatched lobby, and a warm San Miguel beer. The old man in the white T-shirt that had handed it to us, with the key to our tree house, told us that the restaurant would close early, and we should hurry if we wanted any selection of food. The place had advertised itself as an ecolodge, and the ecology was indeed lodged in every crevice. At the top of a series of suspended pathways on a steep tropical rainforested hillside, was a traditional *faluw* hut on stilts, and an open lanai where we could sit and enjoy the sunsets. Inside we found beautiful *haku* lei on our pillows, made with fern fronds and red bottle brush and orchids. But there was also mold in the mattress, geckos on the hardwood walls, and mosquitoes outside the net for them to munch on. The no-see-ums down at the restaurant were the only sign of life for the first half hour, before a dead half chicken that had likely begun his journey to us as a half dead chicken, shuffled in on two plates counterbalanced with taro. Menus were obviously not on the menu. Robyn and I looked longingly at the luxury of Trader Ridge across the bay- we would be there in just a few days, if we survived the ecology on this side of the water.

Our Continental breakfast next morning had undoubtedly been named after the airline, rather than the continent. We walked into town, but it was closed. Under a large thatched cover, hanging between two pillars, was a ladder of boards connected by chains, on which were written the names of all the shops of the co-operative mall, maybe more than all the shops of the co-operative mall- *FSM Customs-FSM Finance-Les Video Rental-Diving Seagull-Ganir Restaurant- Bank of the FSM-Micro Tech Services- Moylans Insurance- Community Ayum Service Credit Union- FSM Tax and Revenue- FSM Public Defender- MR & Tee Drug Store.* A Stop sign stuck out the side of one of the poles. Across the street were three big letters made from rocks set into a grassy knoll. *Yap.* I wondered why they needed reminding.

The outside of the Office of the Public Defender was a charming amateur hand-painted undersea blue mural of coral and grasses and reef fish, with a big white jellyfish lurking on the closed window. All the other white and powder blue buildings were shut. The palms were still. We walked past the Mnuw, an old brown and blue Pinisi schooner from Sulawesi, reminiscent of our Bugi-men days, *Headhunting in Kansas*, to the hospital. *Alert...Please do not spit in any area except for waste basket, or 'tafenedow.' Even better bring your own spit or waste can!!! Keep our hospital clean.* There was a new wasp nest in the old air raid siren.

But the siren would have blown it apart eight months before we got there. On April 9th, Typhoon Sudal slammed smack into Yap. The strongest in fifty years, with winds of over 226 km/hour for over four hours, it produced 22 foot-high waves along the coast, dropped eight inches of rain, sunk ships, damaged the coral reefs, flattened trees and destroyed 90% of the structures on the island. The hospital, airport, most government facilities, and the water, power and communications systems were either badly damaged, or destroyed.

The intrusion of salt water destroyed almost all of the food crops on the island. Following the typhoon's passage, about 1,000 people, an eighth of the population, were left homeless, and another 500 were forced into shelters. The Yapese were still recovering from the effects of Typhoon Lupit, the year before. It may have partly explained why their betel boluses were missing the trashcan at the airport.

But there was another natural catastrophe that had occurred just as we were flying into Yap, which was about to affect our day. It was waiting in the form of a telex from my sister-in-law, back at the ecolodge. *Call your father.* My heart jumped into my throat. What could it mean? And where could I make an international long distance call, on one of the most remote islands in the Southern Sea, after the worst typhoon in fifty years.

"You'll have to go to the Telecom dish." Said T-shirt.

"Where's that?" I asked.

"At the top of that hill." He said, pointing to the sky. Of course, I thought, that's where it would be. It was 32 degrees. The sun was overhead. We started across the causeway and up the hill. The views of the inlets and bays on the way were beautiful, with wide expanses of silver shimmering off the ocean below, but I was drenched by the time we made the connection to the connection. The official inside the telecommunications office was wonderfully accommodating, and handed me the receiver, even before I had finished thanking him for his efforts. It rang the ring of Northwestern Ontario on the other end of the line, half a world away.

"Hello." My father answered.

"This better be good." I said. "I'm paying big money for this call." He paused for a brief moment, until the voice recognition software kicked in.

"Stay out of the water!" He shouted.

"What?" I said, not getting this at all.

"Stay out of the water!!" He repeated, even more desperate.

"Why?" I asked, confused.

"People are dying all over Asia!" He shouted.

"What?" I asked.

"People are dying all over Asia!!" He said again.

"We're not in Asia." I said. And then, there came a long pause.

"Oh." He said. It became apparent to me that, while my father had always kept up well with news and current events, and knew of the Boxing day Indian Ocean earthquake and tsunami which had killed almost a quarter of a million people in over 14 countries, his knowledge of geography was still a bit on the challenged side.

"You said you were going to Indonesia." He said.

"I said we were going to Micronesia." I said.

"Where the hell is that?" He asked. I told him that it was time for a map, and that I loved him very much. When I hung up, Robyn asked me what was wrong.

"He got his natural disasters mixed up." I said. And we started back down the hill.

A shaded path provided a welcome detour on our descent through lush forests and gardens. We came out at the bakery. Its exterior was lavishly painted in murals of Yapese legends. One in particular, the Legend of the Lizard-Man of Dugor, seemed to dominate.

In the village of Dugor, lived a lizard who could turn himself into a man. As a man he was very handsome, and every young woman on Yap was attracted to him. Unfortunately, however, any woman who went with him to his cave was never seen again. Their families never found out what had happened to them. After a time, and the disappearance of several young women, the villagers began to suspect that there was something not quite right about this handsome young man. One day, the lizard-man met another beautiful young lady, who promptly fell in love with him. He thought he would enjoy her company for a while before eating her, and took her to his cave. When she became hungry, he brought her foul smelling frogs and crabs and other dead creatures. Terrified, she remembered the stories she had been hearing about a suspected lizard-man, and ran away home as fast as she could. The young woman told her parents about the horrible experience, and the father thought of a way to deal with the lizard-man, and discover his identity. He waited for him to come looking for his daughter, and when he arrived, the father asked the lizard-man to climb a tree and get him a coconut. Anxious to please the old man, lizard-man climbed the tree. But as he came down the tree with the coconut, he gave away his identity, descending headfirst. The father was prepared, with a pole with a loop at the end, and at just at the right moment he slipped the loop over the head of the lizard-man and pulled it tight, strangling him. The lizard-man fell to the ground, dead, and reverted to his true form as a lizard.

Robyn and I read and obeyed the warning on the entrance. *Do not drink beer inside the bakery...Thank you.* We walked past a large hardwood carving of a maiden with generous naked breasts. She had a red and white Santa cap on her head. The air conditioning had cooled my ardor, and Robyn had already ordered two coconut tarts, and a Japanese bottle of water from the beer fridge. *A valid drinking permit is required to purchase any alcoholic beverage!* I think I was less astounded by the fact that you needed a valid drinking permit to buy a beer, than by the fact that the drinking water was imported from Japan, and wondered where the drinking permits were imported from. The bakery seemed to be the hangout for the local teenager girls who, between sips of their colas, seemed to be waiting for their own lizard-man to arrive. One of them drove up to the entrance as Robyn and I were leaving, slicked-back hair, sunshades, and a four digit license plate on the rusted bumper of his Japanese Corolla. *Yap State... Island of Stone Money.*
The next morning, Robyn and I walked along the southern shore, to find some. Hibiscus grew wild along the roadside,

humungous flowers as big as your head, sharing the traffic with bird of paradise and a hundred other inflorescences. Here was stone money, large heavy wheels of it, leaning up against rock walls and coconut trees and lining paths, like it was waiting for a ride. And we rubbed it for luck and posed for pictures on it, and we must not have given it a second thought, because of the flagstone path that took us up into the tropical garden and mimosas and big leaf taro above it, and eventually to a truck box painted with a Japanese zero undercarriage, in flight overhead, and back to the I.L.P. restaurant that night, where we offered to pay in stone money.

*　　*　　*

'It's all about the money.'
Joe Jackson

'Money just draws flies.'
Mahalia Jackson

The big money had been drawing flies long before the castaway arrived. There were five kinds of traditional currency strewn about the island. There was New Guinea shell money called *Yar*, which was still used to buy oneself a bride.
The local stone stuff was small and either about a foot wide, *Reng*, or up to two feet, *Mmbul*, from the municipality of Aalipebinaw. The fourth was *Gaw*, long, up to ten feet in length, and imported from an island called Ganat near Pohnpei, our next port of call. The most valuable stone

216

money on Yap was also of foreign provenance, but had transmuted from coinage to cult. On a tropical paradise where 'all food, drink and clothing were readily available, so there was no barter and no debt,' life was still a game, and money was how the Yapese kept score. High value transactions were given higher value through the material and materiel and medium of the transaction, transactions conducted with five-ton rocks that had been towed on rafts behind wind-powered canoes, almost five hundred kilometers across the open ocean. It is reasonable to deduce that the Yapese that had done this, and the purposes for which it was done, were nuts.

The Palau stone from which they quarried their *Ray* or *Rai* or *Fe'* or *Fei*, was a special sort of translucent limestone that glistened in the light, called aragonite, the same stone that the Spanish King Ferdinand, husband of Queen Isabella, and his daughter Catherine of Aragon, first wife of Henry VIII, were named after. The Yapese had only shell tools, to make their large twelve-foot wide calcite donuts, thicker toward the middle, beginning around 1400 AD. It took twenty men to carry one, on a pole slung through the hole bored through its center.

Their value, kept high because of the hazards and difficulty involved in obtaining them, was measured by a complex formula that included their size, age, quality, and the number of lives lost in bringing them to Yap. The money supply was fixed and shiny, like gold had been, in other parts of the world that the Yapese had yet to be illuminated about.

Once on Yap, the *Rai* were used for land title transfers, the tattoo masters, in marriage gifts, or as compensation for damages suffered by an aggrieved party. Despite the widespread use of US currency for everyday transactions today, stone money is still mandatory for more traditional or ceremonial functions, despite the fact that it no longer physically moves around. The islanders know who owns every one of the 6800 pieces, and can trace that ownership through centuries of trade. It isn't even necessary for the stone to have reached Yap to be still considered valuable. There are stories of some gigantic *Rai* that remain the valuable property of the chief that had sponsored its carving, even though it was in several hundred feet of water, after the canoes transporting them had been lost at sea.

Robyn and I walked along the coast south of Chamorro Bay, beyond a green corrugated tin house with a purple door and roof, to a beach with stone money and a solitary palm that survived the hurricane winds of Typhoon Sudal. The sun beat down on us, and the place where another typhoon had dumped the castaway into the history of Yap, 130 years earlier.

David O'Keefe had been born in Ireland in 1823, and was driven by the potato famine to the US as an unskilled laborer at the age of fifteen. He ended up in Savannah, Georgia in 1854, and went to work on the railroad, and then at sea, until he became captain of his own ship, the Anna Sims, moored in Darien. He ran the Union blockade of the Confederacy, during the American Civil War. When a member of his crew assaulted him with a metal bar, O'Keefe shot him in the forehead. After eight months in prison, in 1869 he was acquitted on the grounds of self-defense, and married a Savannah teenager named Catherine Masters. Less than a year later, frustrated and reduced to running day excursions for picnickers, O'Keefe knocked a second crewmember into the Savannah River, and fled. He signed on to the steamer, Belvedere, and escaped to Liverpool, reappearing briefly in Hong Kong long enough to send his wife a bank draft for $167, along with a brief note promising to be home by Christmas. He never made it.

O'Keefe was hired by the Celebes South Sea Trading Company and, on a dangerous mission to the Hermit Islands in search of bêche-de-mer, lost most of his men to fever. When his boss was killed by an ax blow to the head on Palau, O'Keefe was fired, and he retreated down the trade winds headfirst, beaching up on the spot in front of us in 1871. A local Yapese named Fanaway nursed him back to health, and O'Keefe experienced two successive epiphanies, that turned him from an ordinary Southern Sea trader, into one of the greatest merchants in the Pacific. The first came in the Freewill Islands, of the north coast of New Guinea, when he concluded a treaty with the Sultan of Ternate granting him the exclusive rights to harvest coconuts on the isthmus of Mapia, in exchange for an annual tribute of fifty dollars. Less than ten years later, the little sandspit was producing over four hundred thousand pounds of copra annually, allowing O'Keefe to establish a network of other trading stations, recruit European agents to the waterfronts of Singapore and Hong Kong, and expand his fleet with the addition of the *Seabird* in 1876, the *Wrecker* in 1877, the *Queen* in 1878 and the *Lilla* in 1880.

But it was the second epiphany that would truly make his fortune. In 1874 O'Keefe realized the real value of the big money on Yap, for which the islanders would work like demons. By eight years later he had 400 Yapese, nearly ten percent of the population, quarrying Rai on Palau- with iron tools- and transporting them back to Yap on his ship, the *Catherine* (of aragonite). He paid them in their own stone money, for sea cucumbers and more copra, and, despite the inflation it produced, allowed O'Keefe to build his trading company into a private enterprise worth almost ten million dollars.

He continued to send money back to Catherine in Savannah, the last draft drawn arriving in 1936. But his letters gradually became less frequent, and less affectionate, ending initially from 'Your loving husband,' through 'Good bye, yours truly,' and finally ending with a final ending of 'Yours as you deserve.' In 1954, Burt Lancaster was cast as the forgettable Hollywood version of *His Majesty O'Keefe*, but the real big money Irishman was far more interesting, and complicated. He introduced the Yapese to alcohol and firearms, and himself to three wives and several mistresses. His first wife was Charlotte Terry, the daughter of an island woman and an ex-convict that O'Keefe had employed to manage his affairs on Mapia; his second wife was, scandalously, Charlotte's aunt; and his third wife was named Dolibu, a Pacific islander sorceress from Nauru, who bore him several children.

By the early 1880s, His Majesty had built himself a red brick home on Tarang, an island in the middle of Yap's harbor. He filled it with a large library of books, a piano, valuable antiques, and sterling silver utensils. He flew his own flag over Tarang, the letters OK in black, on a white background.

But it wasn't OK, of course. The man who had made Yap the greatest entrepôt in the Southern Sea, with thirty sailing ships a year and a large steamer every eight weeks in its harbor, had also made enemies. He was "at war with all the other whites of the Island, all of whom thoroughly detest him." Leaf lice pests were brought to the island in trading cargoes, and devastated copra production to less than a hundred tons a year. The island was hit by two more massive typhoons. And the Germans were muscling in on the action. When O'Keefe had finally had enough, in 1901, it was another typhoon, like the one that had first shipwrecked him on Yap thirty years earlier, that caught his schooner *Santa Cruz*, and drowned him and his two eldest sons, on their way to Savannah, and mythology.

With O'Keefe dead and the Germans thoroughly entrenched, things began to go badly for the Yapese.

The new rulers conscripted the islanders to modify their ancient footpaths to accommodate wheeled vehicles, and dig a canal across the archipelago. When the Yapese proved unwilling, the Germans painted black crosses on the most valuable *Rai* in the disobedient villages, a symbolic takeover of ownership, to be reclaimed only by in provision of the labor being withheld. The modern financial management was more barbaric than the megalithic culture it was fused with. Even worse, the Germans forbade the Yapese from travelling more than 200 miles from their island, solving the problem of inflation by cutting off supply, and price-fixing the largest money in the world. The one good thing the Germans brought was an end to the highly complex caste seven tiered ranking system that existed among Yap villages, based on violent warfare and inter-village intrigues. Lower ranked villages were required to pay tribute, and prohibited from harvesting and eating more desirable seafood.

Robyn and I moved out of our first accommodation to what would become our favorite, a great family run place further into Chamorro Bay, with a view of the water, and the coconut palm forested hills on the other side. The ESA had opened in the 1970s, but was as good as new. We arranged our books and Honey Crunch cereal and Japanese bottled water on our table looked down from our balcony onto another, full of wrapped Christmas presents for the staff party that evening. The only thing the ESA didn't have was a corkscrew, so Robyn and I walked back to the Pathway's bar, to open our bottle of Jacob's Creek chardonnay for the evening festivities. There was an old *State of Yap* jeep, filled to the roof with garbage, along the roadway. It was surrounded by splotches of betel nut chew.

And the Spanish had begat the Germans, who begat the Japanese. In 1914 Japan brought rice and infrastructure, and a law allowing Japanese men to marry Yapese women, but not vice versa. The vice continued with the expulsion of all foreign companies and Japanese control over all business, the importation of Chamorros from Saipan to work the phosphate mines with the locals, and the conversion of Colonia into a small Japanese town, the Nipponese and other foreigners outnumbering the Yapese inhabitants. In 1942 they began drafting the islanders into the Japanese military. Luckily, the Americans bypassed Yap, in their 'island-hopping strategy' of WWII; Unluckily, they bombed it instead. I posed inside the rusted cockpit of one of the wrecked zeros on the airfield, a good six feet behind where its bent propeller had landed. The sun grew merciless, descending headfirst onto the elaborate floral hearts and crosses, dominating a group of freshly dug graves.

We hiked off into the forest, along one of the betel palm flagstone paths 'improved' by the Germans, to an abandoned village on a raised platform, fenced with a *malal* bank of big money stone discs. Coconut palms of different ages, grew randomly, out of the middle of the dais. Immense wheels stood on edge, like upright Flintstone circular saw blades, surrounded by more organic chickens and taro and yams, and bananas and breadfruit, and papayas and pineapple, and tobacco. I could hear the syncopation of the stick dance and the standing dance, in the stillness of the space. And I thought of how the great ancient navigators had migrated from New Guinea, the Solomon Islands, the Malay Peninsula, and the Indonesian Archipelago to their new home of *Wa'ab*, and how some Spaniard had misinterpreted what a native had misinterpreted, when he asked the name of the land, as was told the name of the canoe paddle the native had thought he was pointing to.

"Yap." I said.

"Yep." Agreed Robyn.

And then Richard appeared out of nowhere, with his goatee and original heavily soiled white T-shirt and far too baggy shorts. Richard was from Oregon, and had come decades ago, because even Oregon was too far from the land and the sea. He lived alone with his solar cell connection to the outside world, just enough to remind him of the sanity he had chosen, instead. He was glad to see us, which you could see upset him, because of his choice had been totally pure, he should not have been so glad. He told us of the five kinds of big money on Yap, and the five main kinds of magicians. Oh, there were magicians for the usual ailments of society and individuals, those with a talent for sickness and epidemics and revenge and affairs of the heart, but these magicians were very expensive and not the five main types, although they used the same eggs and coconut fronds and crabs and bones and plants and small stones, in their magic. But mainly there was *Trur*, who brought luck in fishing, *Plaw*, who brought success in navigation, *Yaw*, who brought victory in war, and *Dafngoch*, who could increase the population. And finally, who not only brought rain during drought, but could also control typhoons by keeping them away from the islands, or getting rid of them when they came. The material he used was stone, turning it in different ways, to cause rain to come or typhoons to leave. I told Richard that, in my estimation, or all the magicians, it was *Ganiniy*, who was the underachiever.

Robyn and I rented a car next day, a silver sedan that was fabricated in a place that was totally alien to where we would drive it. Yap was only ten miles long and seven miles wide, and it didn't take long. The shores were lined with mangrove swamps, and all the villages were located near the shore, in coconut groves. We found thatched *bai*, with black octopus and sharks on white planks, on leaning yolk yellow pilings, among gigantic red hibiscus, a church with a Yapese Jesus, and Yapese kids swimming together, like nothing had begat anything, and nothing had come headfirst down any trees. But the only thing that was important, was the magnificent Honey Crunch magical chardonnay full moon that Robyn and I sat and marveled at, on our balcony overlooking Chamorro Bay, after midnight, on a flyspeck in Southern Sea.

*   *   *

*   *   *

'With regard to the character of these people, little can be said in their favour. They are exceedingly treacherous, and should an opportunity offer, would not hesitate to cut off any vessel which might visit the island. Foreign finery however is a great temptation to savages and excites their covetous disposition to attempt obtaining by force, what their indolent habits prevents them from procuring by a fair and honest traffic. The dress of the males, if such it may be called, is slovenly in the extreme.'
Andrew Cheyne, *A Description of Islands in the Western Pacific Ocean,* 1852

Most of the treachery, from where Robyn and I were quartered, had actually come from the covetous disposition of the visitors. When Andrew Cheyne arrived in Yap, for two months in the 1840s, he brought a disasterous sea cucumber enterprise, and an influenza epidemic that killed fifty people in the Tomil district. He barely escaped from Chief Leok's plan to kill him in reprisal.
When Robyn and I walked up to Trader Ridge, that

224

magnificent looking South Seas Inn that was in our view and on our horizon across Chamorro Bay, since the first day, indolent habits were still making fair and honest traffic difficult. But it was the habits of the New York owners, gathered behind the desk with their fax machine and calculators, which gave offense. We just wanted to know if it was possible to drop our things off early on the day of our reservation, because I had arranged a dive booking with *Beyond the Reef* for early the next morning. Apparently, it wasn't, and we had committed some unspeakable sin for even climbing the hill to inquire. The Japanese had begat the Americans, and there were flies. Money's a horrid thing to follow, but a charming thing to meet. Except when you meet it coming down headfirst.

The dive in Mills Channel was brilliant. My buddy was a chubby brown bald Oriental-looking Marlon Brando with a chin beard, who was so involved with his betel nut chew that it accompanied him underwater. I could track him from the occasional orange streak that appeared in his bubbles. *If you want something from an audience, you give blood to their fantasies. It's the ultimate hustle.* Chubby took me right to the manta coral cleaning stations, and back to my first encounter with them, snorkeling off Bora Bora, when the sky overhead went dark. There were Buffalo fish, and a lone Yap money stone, at the bottom. *Liquid Assets.*

Robyn met me back at Trader Ridge, on time to check in, where one of the New Yorkers tried to tone down the treachery, and turn up the charm. She smiled like the Yap crocodile fish I had just see below the surface. One of the staff, betel chew in cheek, showed us to out room. It was calm and well appointed with tropical hardwood furnishings, and a ceiling fan. I read more of what Andrew Cheyne had written of Yap, a century and a half earlier.

'When Magellan arrived there on 6th March 1521, he named the group 'Islands of the Lateen Sails,' but on further acquaintance with the people he changed the name to 'Ladrones' (the Islands of Thieves). The betel-nut tree is cultivated with the greatest care at this island. It is a beautiful slender palm; and grows amongst the coconut trees, which it resembles in appearance. The nuts are pulled before they are ripe, and are chewed, with the usual condiments - lime and Aromatic leaves - by both sexes. These people like all savages are exceedingly superstitious, one of which is their mode of procuring a light for their cigars. I have often wondered when sitting in their houses - where they generally have good fires - at seeing both men and women labouring away to procure a light by the friction of two sticks, and they were sitting close to the fire at the time. On enquiring their reason for this unnecessary labour, their reply was, that were they to light their cigars from the fire, some calamity would be sure to happen.'

Robyn hung out at the pool while I splurged for a cigar at the bar. No sticks were involved. My money went up in smoke, into a ring that hung in the air, like a large *Rai* stone wheel. Later we descended to examine the double-hulled voyaging canoe down the hill, assembled from planks and rope and painted orange and black, lying silent under thatch and in the shadow of some of the most renowned navigators in the Pacific. In the supermarket were cats and rolls of Christmas wrapping paper, against a backdrop wall of colorful canned goods, mostly spam and corned beef and other dead remnants of fair and honest traffic. We spent our final evening in a sushi restaurant, against a local fish chart that went on forever. And then it was over, and we found ourselves back at the sign on the refuse bin in the airport. *Do not spit betel nut chew into this garbage can.* It was still surrounded by splotches orange respect. Five years after we left Yap, Trader Ridge went into escrow, and the New Yorkers went home.

> Capt. David O'Keefe: Where did I go wrong, old man?
>
> Fatumak, Medicine Man: The whale that swallows the dolphin chokes and dies, but the whale who lives without greed is the king of the sea.
>
> His Majesty O'Keefe, 1954

For the Yapese, however, the treachery of fair and honest traffic is about to get much worse. American aid currently accounts for seventy per cent of public spending, and Washington has put its Micronesian allies on notice that it will end all subsidies by 2023. Enter the Deputy Assistant Secretary for the US Interior Department's Office of Insular Affairs, David Cohen, and a speech he made in 2007. *Christianity was alien to the Pacific until the 19th Century. Today, it is a fundamental part of most Pacific cultures.*

To help smooth the way, Mr. Cohen, now a lawyer in LA, was one of 'several American consultants' hired by a very wealthy Chinese developer to 'help assess community support' for a megaproject proposal for Yap. He was flown to meet him in China on the developer's private plane.

"I played an advisory role rather than an advocacy role." He said. And I believe him. For what treachery could a nice Jewish boy get up to, with his deep insight into the fundamental part that Christianity played in the colonization of the Pacific, as a Los Angeles lawyer, on the private jet of a Chinese developer?

The answer lies in the identity of the Chinese developer. Deng Hong is also a master of the public private partnership. The son of an Air Force Officer, Deng spent eight years in the military, sold clothes in a Beijing market, became and importer-exporter to San Francisco, married an American girl, and returned home to earn almost a billion dollars, building convention centers, and resorts for Beijing's burgeoning Bourgeoisie, on government land. His company, Exhibition and Travel Group, ETG, built *Jiuzhai Paradise* in the Jiuzhaigou nature reserve, and the Intercontinental Hotel in the Tibetan capital of Lhasa. I'm not sure they consulted the giant pandas, or the Tibetans. His Panda Travel agency boasts of arranging a million international trips a year for Chinese tourists.

Deng's proposed billion dollar development on Yap involves the construction of 10 luxury hotels, a 4000-room casino and golf resort, a convention center, and the expansion of Yap's airport to allow it to handle jets large enough to fly directly to Yap from Mainland China, just over three hours from Shanghai. *Choosing Yap was simple, said Yang Gang, the island's local ETG representative. "The location is close to China." he said, sitting in his Yap apartment, lit by a bare light bulb, a Spam can overflowing with cigarette butts on the kitchen table.*

And the Americans beget the Chinese invasion of imported workers, doubling the island's population, dividing Yap into a 'tourist area' and a 'native town community' of apartments for the displaced residents. Ancestral villages would disappear. *"I don't know why they think we will take their land." Said Yang Gang, ticking off the benefits that the project would bring to residents. "We can't take over. We aren't Japanese soldiers. We do all business legally, with permits. We never force anyone to lease land. It's all based on free will."*

But wait. It appears that Deng Hong has been arrested by Chinese Communist Party anti-corruption officials, for improprieties linked to some of his land deals. *But Mr. Yang is still signing land leases and pointed to a recent visit by the Chinese ambassador to Micronesia as a signal of support. "The project is going forward smoothly." He said in an email.*

Robyn and I boarded our Continental flight to Pohnpei. She wore a tiara of orange orchids, and posed for a photo under the bilingual Airline Ticketing sign. I hadn't noticed the second language at the time. It was Mandarin.

The people of Yap have a long history of making big money the hard way. But the real big money, is coming down the tree, head first.

'The price we have to pay for money is sometimes liberty.'
Robert Louis Stevenson

*　　*　　*

Pepper, Palisades and Pearls
Pohnpei

'Epithets, like pepper, Give zest to what you write; And, if you strew
them sparely, They whet the appetite: But if you lay them on too
thick,
You spoil the matter quite.'

Lewis Carroll

If the color of Yap had been money, the color of Pohnpei
was black. The pepper was black, the palisades were black,
and the pearls were black. Darker still was the intrigue that
swirled around them, in one of the rainiest places on the
planet. And the center of the intrigue was The Village people.

'Together we will go our way, together we will leave some day.
Together your hand in my hand, together we will make the plans.
Together we will fly so high, together tell our friends goodbye.
Together we will start life new, together this is what we'll do.'

No, not Village People, the gay fantasy disco variety, The
Village people, the owners of The Village, the treetop eco-
resort that Robyn and I had booked into. Eight years before
Go West was released, as a single in 1979, Bob and Patti
already had, as a young couple with four children. From
Southern California, they pulled up stakes and went further
west, leasing a steep-sided spit of land pointing out into the
lagoon, and building the largest thatched structure in
Micronesia. Bob had been an industrial designer, and retaught
the locals how to do thatching, from what he had learned
while living in Honduras. He imported mahogany from the
Philippines for the floor of the Long House, and then,
between the breadfruit and banana trees, built twenty more
cottages.

Robyn and I were driven across the Deketik causeway, through the capital of Kolonia (blacker than the Colonia we had left on Yap), past a burnt out Japanese tank with the wrong sort of camouflage for where, and probably why, it was destroyed, another twenty minutes east to The Village. Up the stairs of the mangrove poles and expansive thatch was a bar called the Tattooed Irishman and beyond that, the restaurant, both open to spectacular views across the reef, the smaller islands that dotted the lagoon and, on the distant horizon, the profile of Sokeh's Rock. Patti welcomed us with two cold coconuts and straws, and we took them out along a walkway that led to a thatched gazebo overlooking their tropical paradise. Sea breezes blew gently through the palms, and the space we were perched on. It was a damn fine coconut. We were shown to our cottage. Under the mosquito net was a waterbed. You can take the boy out of California. I hoped the floor would hold,

But small cracks began to appear in the Garden of Eden around dinnertime. Patti's friendliness had disappeared, and she snapped at me for trying to compliment her on what she and Bob had accomplished, with time and thatch. I didn't know then, about how it was all unraveling around them, and I wouldn't for another ten years. The food was adequate for where we landed, but quesadillas were not what I had expected for a New Year's Eve dinner. The huge spiders above us in the rusting ceiling fans were also a novelty. I should have learned from the ecoexperience on Yap, but The Village would take that several notches higher. Two young boys uncorked the bottle of Tokay we had brought to celebrate the New Year, and poured it to the brim of our glasses. The path back to our shack was unilluminated, but I had my headlamp. The absence of water pressure in the shower was more than adequately supplemented by the mosquitos, and the rats. In 1991 the US government bestowed Bob and Patti with the first eco-tourism award, for constructing a hotel 'in tune with nature, with a low impact on the environment and the culture.' We slept somewhere between the howling of the dogs and the crowing of the roosters.

"Paradise." Robyn whispered, into my twilight sleep.

"Paradise is exactly like where you are right now." I said. "Only much better."

She ordered a platter of Pohnpei hotcakes for breakfast next morning. It came with a maraschino cherry on top, like the ham and cheese sandwiches, on our flight to Juan Fernández. Outside the veranda, the rain was hosing down, trying to reach its annual quota of 300 inches in a single monsoon. Robyn and I did the only thing we could do on a New Year's Day, in a torrential deluge, on a remote island in the Southern Sea. We rented a car.

It arrived as a silver Mitsubishi sedan, with windows so severely tinted, I wasn't sure how we would navigate in the downpour. It was an endemic problem, as we were to discover. Everywhere we drove was littered with dead cars- eviscerated cars, cars upended on their side and braced up at strange angles with bamboo poles, perhaps to allow access to their innards, for most were missing parts, and all were missing their tires, for whatever reason. We sunk into potholes that should have drowned us, but thankfully the sun came out, before we reached the 300 inches.

It got positively wonderfull at Kepirohi Falls, a seventy-foot cascade a fifteen-minute hike from the far end of the village of Sapwehrek. We swam deliciously in the bottom pools, paradise regained, until a freak gust of wind blew half the cataract through my Fuji camera. Maybe it was some form of retribution for what the Japanese had done to the Pohnpeians during the war, but all my photos would henceforth look like the burnt out camouflage tank we had passed in getting here.

Robyn and I stopped to visit the Catholic church in Awak village, with a simple but moving interior, backlit by open blockwork in the shape of two crosses. The exterior could have been Balinese, if rusted corregated tin had been the construction material of choice in Bali.

We continued on to the southern part of the island, where the dark intrigue began, with a softspoken Japanese farmer. Mr. Sei owned a cafeteria in Kolonia, but he also had the only remaining operating pepper plantation and processing facility. Only five of his hundred acres were planted in Indonesian and Sri Lankan pepper, on eight-foot *balabala* fern support posts. Among the long strings of green beaded pepper vines, were magnificent orchids, acting as coalmine canaries, like roses do for grapes, in Burgundy.

To hear the way that Bob and Patti would tell it, the pepper business in Pohnpei was nearly dead, when they formed the AHPW Corporation, to produce black pepper and buttons, in 1985. No one had apparently told Mr. Sei that it was nearly dead, and no one can really explain what a black pepper enterprise has to do with manufacturing buttons from trochus shells. But that was what Bob and Patti did, when they borrowed more than $620,000 from the Federated States of Micronesia Development Bank. Bob and Patti assumed that the loan was made to their corporation. The bank assumed they were lending to Bob and Patti.

The following year a moratorium was placed on harvesting trochus shells, because of concerns about sustainability. The buttons went bye-bye, and all the button factory machinery that Bob and Patti had imported, went the way of the cars with the overly tinted windows. The year after that, in response to complaints by pepper farmers that Bob and Patti were being too fussy in purchasing only high quality pepper, the State of Pohnpei got into the pepper processing business, and put Bob and Patti out of it, in 1998. When the bank called in their loan, for which they now learned they were personally responsible, paradise found became paradise lost.

A year before Robyn and I met The Village people, Bob and Patti filed a lawsuit, Civil Action 1999-053, against the governments of Pohnpei and the Federated States of Micronesia, alleging that *'In buying pepper from Pohnpei's pepper farmers at a price greater than market price, Pohnpei prevented competition in the manufacture of a commodity, in this case processed pepper,'* they had essentially driven AHPW into bankruptcy. The lawsuit also alleged that the State of Pohnpei had failed to hold the annual trochus harvest, even though AHPW had been repeatedly assured that there would be one, and that sixty metric tons would be available. Bob and Patti asked for $225,448 in damages. The FSM Supreme Court, to their intial delight, not only found in their favor, but tripled the amount of the damages to $676,344, which would have been enough to pay back the bank loan. When the State of Pohnpei appealed to vacate the trebling of damages, the Court not only refused, but also awarded Bob and Patti an additional $37,422, under the *theory of detrimental reliance*, for the loss of their button business. Time and thatch, however, unravel at different rates. The two bills that the Governor submitted to the Pohnpei State Legislature to pay Bob and Patti, failed to pass, even though there were sufficient funds to do so. While the State of Pohnpei was getting its head around having to pay damages to Bob and Patti, the FSM Development Bank was wasting no time in calling in its loan. It could have explained Patti's black mood, and why she might have thought I was pushing her buttons.

> 'Together we will love the beach, together we will learn and teach.
> Together change our pace of life, together we will work and strive.
> I love you, I know you love me; I want you happy and carefree.
> So that's why I have no protest when you say you want to go west.'

Our Pohnpei circumnavigation turned north, and the high volcanic cone formation *of Pwusehn Malek*, in Palikir. The local legend relates a story of the defeated ruler of the Saudeleur dynasty, who changed himself into a giant rooster, to fly to Nan Madol, leaving an enormous pile of his droppings. At the foot of Chickenshit Mountain, Robyn and I met a group of inebriated women, celebrating New Year's Day, all flipflops and Santa hats, carrying green plantains, and banging their bottles and big square tin cans with sticks, and laughter. We posed in front of an old panel van, with so much vegetation growing so fast out of its cockpit, we made a mental note to close our tinted windows, later. Kolonia was empty, but the signs were still there- *Do not spit betel juice on the premises. Pigs for sale 50 lbs to 75 lbs Call and ask for Welson Nedlic... Must be sold during Xmas.* Back in The Village's retaurant that evening, I had the chicken salad. The disparity between the price and food quality had risen in direct proportion to the size of the pepper mill. It was gigantic, and I had an awful black feeling that Patti and Bob had known exactly where we had been.

'I may not know much, but I know the difference between chicken shit and chicken salad.'

Lyndon Johnson

*   *   *

They had been constructed from long prismatic columns of hexagonal black basalt almost 20 feet in length, piled log-cabin style, some sixty feet high, forming 92 artificial islands over an area of 200 acres. Robyn was barely visible in the deluge, held captive in the kayak next to mine, navigating the mangroves, and the palisades between them.

Two days before, we had found the poverty of Pohnpei, in the Kirinese carvers of Porakied, transplanted by the Japanese in 1919 from Kapingamaranga atoll, 35 inches above sea level and 740 kilometers south of their old new village of thatch and corrugated iron. Hanging banana bunches and full rain barrels, rigged from commercial food containers, projected off rooftops, and car wrecks rusted languidly under the coconut palms in the front yards. On the day of our visit, their settlement, like their origins, was mostly water. The concrete graves in the cemetery glistened silver in the rain, and even their connected crosses were of cement, a *cementery*, the only color coming from scattered bouquets of plastic flowers extruded from more temperate climates. We bought a handmade turtle carving, flippers woven from light natural coconut and darker pandanus fibers, from an old Kapingamarangan lady, whose smile betrayed how much more her people had lost than gained, in the move onto higher ground. She was still perhaps more fortunate than the other Pohnepeian immigrants from Pingelap, Oliver Sack's *Island of the Colorblind*. My camera, meanwhile, was afflicated with the opposite problem, and was adding colors not found in nature, to the washed out pig roast celebration, congregating in a clearing back towards the center of Kolonia. Japanese flatbed trucks arrived on masse, each with monster pigs, legs already tied around the poles that four men would

235

be needed to huff and puff them down from, into the waiting firesmoke. Other smolderings hung around mirrored sunglasses, from cigarettes on lower lips, as breadfruit and yams suspended on similar staves, were portaged bouncing, towards plastic tarps and waiting knives. Perhaps it might have been more festive, if there had been fewer Japanese and American ghosts in the vaporised psychedelic images on my memory card.

Robyn and I passed into the main part of town, and the signage that announced its urbanity. *Welcome to Good Luck Bingo*. Said one. *Site Bingo $500 cashpot. Good Luck*. On Pohnpei, apparently, luck was easier to come by than justice. Outside the *Dollar-Up-Enterprises* shop, *Growing with Pohnpei*, and the *Island Soda Headquarters*, a big yellow smiley face, surrounded by pennants and Chinese lanterns, tried to provide both. *Please try and park straight...so everyone can have a parking place*. An Israeli flag, lurking behind a large Santa Claus decal, carrying a bagful of toys, seemed to promise neither. And another sign, *STD's: The Quiet Epidemic Gonorrhea Syphilis Hepatitis B HIV/AIDS etc.* offered a hybrid of the good and the bad. I wondered what the *etcetera* was.

Robyn and I posed for photos on the wrong camouflage of the old Japanese tank, and under the arch of the Spanish wall fort remnant, near the Pohnpei Ladies Club, halfway between Honolulu and Manila. A flame tree posed more brightly near the clocktower. A philodendron was making a nest in the cab of another dead truck, near the spot that we picked up our ride, hitchhiking back to The Village. The views of the lush bay behind us, from our open truckbed, were idyllic, and left the heat and humidity with our exhaust, until we stopped.

The next day, Robyn and I climbed up Sokeh's Ridge. We were warned at the bottom. *Danger- Steep road. Hazardous for both motor vehicle and pedestrian traffic Travel at your own risk!!* The hike was arduous in the midday heat, but the panorama of Kolonia harbor from the top, and the ocean expanse beyond, was just that breathtaking. There were nesting tropicbirds and fruit bats on the way up, WWII Japanese antiaircraft battery, pillboxes and tunnels at the top, and strange bracket fungus, like cuneiform commas, on the way down. Robyn and I continued by coconut-oil coiffed women in an open boat among the sailboats mooring below, giant hibiscus, and an old guy with a backwards New York baseball cap, jeans, and miraculously white T-shirt, barbequeing chicken in an open kettle on the street. It was brilliant. *I may not know much...* We returned to The Village to collect shells and snorkel, and to float asleep on the waterbed later, until the mosquitoes found the hole in our net, before dawn.

> 'Once upon a time, a man named Sapkini built a large canoe. He knew that the sky is a roof that touches the sea at its edges. His people, sailing in their fine canoe to the place where the sky meets the sea, would find land there. On the way, they met an octopus who showed them a shallow reef in the ocean. The people brought rocks and stones from faraway lands to make the reef higher. But the waves broke up the stones. So they planted mangrove trees to protect the island. But the ocean was still too close.
> So they built a fringing reef around the island. Two women brought soil and the island grew larger. On its top the people built a shrine to the spirits and named their new land- *Pohn-Pei*, Upon-the-Altar.'

Upon the altar of too many soft consonants of Mandolenihmw district, were the palisades on the other side of dawn, where the sky met the sea, beyond the kayaks that had come off our hour-long speedboat trip to the southeast coast of the island. Robyn and I had been dropped onto the mangrove-covered coral shore flats in a torrential downpour. Even with the protection of our ponchos, it was going to be an elemental day. We definitely had the place to ourselves, wherever it was. The rain and the wind, washing over the thick green jungle and slate grey ocean chop beyond, made the unadorned black architecture even more intimidating.

It had originally been called Soun Nan-leng, the 'Reef of Heaven.' But we were paddling the Venice of the Pacific, named for the 'spaces between' the canals that crisscrossed *Nan Madol*.

"Rubble." Said Robyn, summing up every megalithic ruin on the planet. Instead of an enlightening verifiable historical record to marvel at, rubble was always buried into even deeper confusion, by voluminous academic speculation. The rubble expert, so as not to appear ignorant, in the absense of knowledge and meaning, would describe and invent and publish what he thinks he should be seeing.

According to legend, Nan Madol had been founded by two brothers, Olisihpa and Olosohpa, twin sorcerers from the mythical Western Katau. They had arrived in a slightly larger canoe than ours, seeking to build an altar and religious community, focused on the adoration of the sea, and dedicated to the god of soft consonant agriculture, Nahnisohn Sahpw. On their third attempt, the brothers levitated huge stones with the aid of a flying dragon. After Olisipha had died of old age, Olosohpa became the first Saudeleur, the first ruler of the Dipwilap Deleur dynasty. From about 1200 AD, over the next five hundred years, the clan chronicle emerged from legend to lineage with each subsequent saudeleur.

A few were benign rulers. Inenen Mwehi established an aristocracy, and Raipwenlang was a skilled magician. Others were cruel. Raipwenlake used his magic to locate the fattest Pohnpeians, and ate them. Another, Ketiparelong, is remembered for his gluttonous wife who was fed her own father's liver by suffering commoners at a banquet. Perhaps that worst was Sakon Mwehi, who taxed his people ruthlessly, requiring frequent tributes of seafood and breadfruit during *rak*, the season of plenty, and yams, taro, and fermented breadfruit during *isol*, the season of scarcity. Over time, the initial seasonal demand became much more demanding of labour and material, leaving a wake of starving slaves in the tidal canals. Each time that public dissatisfaction broke to assassination, another Saudeleur simply rose in place of the last.

The Saudeleur derived his legitimacy from the central cult of the Thunder God, Nahn Sapwe, who used the sakeu ceremony, the kava of Fiji and Vanuatu, as an elaborate affirmation of dominance and dedication. Sakau was first made through magic, also by two brothers, Widen-ngar and Luhk. Widen-ngar was the ghost of thunder, and Luhk, the ghost of the underground. Luhk had hurt his foot on the way to the Pohnpei, and his injured skin was pounded into small pieces and, using hibusicus bark, squeezed out the liquid, using Widen-ngar's kneecap to catch it.

The meat of the 'Life-Giving' Turtles and the 'Watchmen of the Land' dogs was reserved especially for the Saudeleur. He controlled potential rivals by requiring them to live in Nan Madol, rather than their home districts, in the same way that Louis XIV controlled his nobles at Versailles. He controlled his population with the food and water supply, which needed to come across in boats from the mainland.

All of Nan Madol, itself, in fact, had to have come over from the mainland. Prisms of black basalt were dislodged from their main island quarries by building large fires at their bases, and cooling them suddenly with sea water, to cause them to fracture. The stones were manoeuvred onto rafts, floated within the fringing reef across to the building site and, with inclined planes of coconut palm trunks and strong hibiscus fiber rope, slid into orthogonal islets of headers and stretchers, and filled with local coral. Pole and thatch structures were erected on top of the platforms, residences and meeting houses for all the black intrigue that would follow. For a people that had no pulleys, no levers and no metal, the 750,000 metric tons of black rocks moved into place at Nan Madol, averaging almost two thousand tons a year for four centuries, represented a much larger per capita effort than had taken place during the construction of the Egyptian pyramids.

In 1628, the last Saudeleur was overthrown by an outsider

named Isohkelekel, who divided Pohnpei into the multiple *nahnmwarki* chiefdoms that still endure. Hidden weapons had suddenly appeared.

Robyn and I kayaked down the Nan Modol main street, the central waterway separating Life and Death. To the southwest was Madol Pah, the lower town administrative sector where royal dwellings and ceremonial areas had been located. We pulled up onto the high-walled complex islet of Pahankadira, the residence of the Saudeleur, a basalt battleship almost three footballs fields in area, the 'place of announcement,' surrounded by prismatic palisades over sixteen feet high. A bathing pool had been excavated inside. On the islet of Idehd was the place where turtle entrails had been offered to the sacred eel, kept in a sacred tunnel-like channel, constructed of carefully cut coral laid between basaltic prisms. We passed a row of sakau pounding stones, where two conch shells trumpets had been excavated. Nearby was Durong, where clams had been cultivated. The largest walls rose almost sixty feet high, on the south corner of Pahnwi.

It began to teem down, as we paddled towards the 58 islets northwest mortuary sector of Madol Powe, the upper town where the priests lived, and the tombs. Some islets served a special purpose- food preparation, canoe construction on Dapahu, and coconut oil preparation, for anointing the dead, on Peinering, the most beautifully proportioned islet on Nan Madol. Students of Western architecture familiar with the Golden Section of 1:1.618, would hear the arias of stacked prismatic basalt headers tilting markedly upward, projecting beyond the exterior wall faces to form a crafted cornice of some of the most sensitive skilled masonry in the world. The sun came out.

The crowning achievement of Nan Madol was the elaborate royal mortuary of Nandauwas, a 25-foot massive sea-walled palisade surrounding a central moss-encrusted tomb enclosure within the main courtyard. One of the cornerstones weighs 50 tons. Here were entombed the Saudeleurs, before being buried elsewhere. Powerfully conceived, sensitively sited, and skillfully executed, we approached it by kayak from the open lagoon, and moved along the jungle-covered islets on both sides of the canal, ascending steps that led to the interior courts, enclosures, and tombs. The breaking waves were deafening. Here were found adzes, circular heads, bracelets, needles, breast pendants, necklaces, pearl-shell fishhook shanks, and other valuable shell artifacts. Even a gold crucifix and silver-handled dirk were found by visiting ships' captains between 1834 and 1840, suggesting possible Spanish contact before the 1820s.

Robyn and I arrived on a beach with hermit crabs and button shells, and returned for dinner out in a café under thatch along the river, tortured by a cute young girl with two red orchids in her hair. The food arrived under aluminum foil, from the main island.

'Go west, life is peaceful there.
Go west, lots of open air.
Go west to begin life new.
Go west, this is what we'll do.
Go west, sun in wintertime.
Go west, we will do just fine.
Go west where the skies are blue.
Go west, this and more we'll do.'
The Village People, *Go West*

*   *   *

S.W. SHOULDER OF INNER LINE OF WALL ENCLOSING THE KING'S VAULT

NANIF AND LEWIS KEHOE IN FOREGROUND

*　　*　　*

Black clouds swirled over the remaining intrigue on Pohnpei. In 1886, the Spaniards, as part of their claim to the Caroline Islands, as part of the Manila-based Spanish East Indies, founded Santiago de la Ascensión, in a place that the Pohnpeians had known as Mesenieng, the *Face of the Wind*. The Germans had renamed it Kolonia.

Robyn and I visited the Pohnpei Visitors Bureau, admiring the old thatched buildings and the soft curves and consonants of Miss Madolenihmw, *18127 miles from Berlin*, according to the signpost outside. It hadn't made any difference to the German colonial administration how far they were from Berlin. They had brought all their ideas, and toys. One of their ideas was to force the Ponhpeians to labor 15 days a year on public works projects. One day in October of 1910, a young man from Sokeh Island refused the instructions of his overseer, and was flogged for his transgression. The following morning, all the Sokehs refused further labor, and returned to their island. The District commissioner, Gustav Boeder, with his assistant Rudolf Brauckmann and two translators, was rowed to Sokeh by six Mortlock island boatmen, to 'reason' with the laborers. Riflefire rang out from a concealed position, and only the two translators and one oarsman escaped. It took two months for the news to reach the Colonial Office in Berlin. A month after that, the light cruisers *SMS Emden* and *SMS Nürnberg*, joining the gunboat *SMS Cormoran* and the survey ship *Planet*, fired their main batteries on the rebel fortification on Sokeh's ridge, and then launched an assault team of sailors and Melanesian police up the mountain. The rebels gave as good as they got, but couldn't hold out, and surrendered on February 22, 1911. Two days later, fifteen of them were executed by firing squad, and the 426 remaining souls of Sokeh's tribe were banished to

Palau.

The Styrofoam crosses in the storefront window, behind all the left footed shoes on display, were decorated with colored ribbons, and bouquets of artificial flowers, that flowed into the patterns of the material shop next door. We passed the Touch 'N Go Windward Mart, and a handpainted poster of a pregnant woman, smoking. *Simoke sika karehda serihkan ipwidi paun tikitik.*

The burned out ruin of the State Department of Education, with the Japanese *Kanji* script below, had stopped smoking after the American delivery of 118 tons of bombs, 600 incendiaries and their own naval artillery bombardment had destroyed Kolonia during WWII. A newer sign underneath the ruin, was buckled and soiled. *Pohnpei Sarawi Our Home Our Pride.*

Another, at the library posted its 'standing rules.' *Keep quiet at all time The following are not allowed: No food, pets, smoking, betel-nuts and fighting.*

The Japanese had brought thousands of Okinawans to Pohnpei, during their occupation. Visitors to Kolonia in the 1930s reported that they had been able to walk the length of Namiki Street under shopkeepers' canopies without getting wet in the rain. The Americans had bombed out the canopies, and Robyn and I enjoyed no such protection. We were drenched by the time we found Joy's Restaurant, and a table for one of Joy's black and red lacquer tray tuna sashimi lunches. Two men with dark faces and white teeth joined us, after Joy had made a phone call, after we had seen the brochure on her counter. They were Polynesians from Nukuoro atoll, a remote island 450 kilometers southwest of Pohnpei, with 300 residents, no airstrip, a sea charter connection that called only every few months, and cost ten thousand dollars per visit. George had been the Chief Magistrate for Nukuoro. He pulled out a case of what he had brought, each one nestled in a little round plastic box with a white foam bed. They were charcoal, with iridescent hues in blues and greens and violets. They were gorgeous.

George's cooperative had seven employees who harvested about 6000 black pearls a year, enough to find enough round ones to make a single necklace.

"It takes eighteen months to produce a pearl." Said George. "We have to bring in a 'seeding technician' from Tahiti to seed them, and that costs about three dollars an oyster." In the photo, George held up his brochure, his assistant held up the traveler's cheques, and Robyn held up her new pearls. She was the pretty one with the jewels. A thing of Joy is a beauty forever.

A quarter of a century earlier, Laurie Anderson, the experimental performance artist and wife of Lou Reed, had arrived in Pohnpei to work on her new album, *The Ugly one with the Jewels*. It got very ugly, and the joy ran out, as she eventually related in her track, *Word of Mouth*.

'In 1980, as part of a project called Word of Mouth, I was invited, along with a living other artists, to go to Panape, a tiny island in the middle of the Pacific. The idea was that we'd sit around talking for a few days and that the conversations would be made into a talking record.

The first night we were all really jet-lagged but as soon as we sat down the organizers set up all these mikes and switched on thousand white light bulbs. And we tried our best to seem as intelligent as possible. Television had just come to Panape a week before we arrived and there was a strong excitement around the island as people crowded around the few sets. Then the day after we arrived, in a bizarre replay of the first TV show ever broadcast to Panape, prisoners escaped from a jail, broke into the radio station and murdered the DJ. Then they went off on a rampage through the jungle, armed with lawnmower blades. In all, four people were murdered in cold blood. Detectives, flown in from Guam to investigate, swarmed everywhere. At night we stayed around in our cottages, listening out into the jungle.

Finally the local chief decided to hold a ceremony for the murder victims. The artist Marina Brownovich and I went, as representatives of our group to film it. The ceremony was held in a large thatched lean-to and most of the ceremony involved cooking beans in pits and brewing a dark drink from roots. The smell was overwhelming. Dogs careened around barking. And everybody seemed to be having a fairly good time... as funerals go.

After a few hours Marina and I were presented to the chief, who was sitting on a raised platform above the pits. We'd been told we couldn't turn our backs on the chief at any time or ever be higher than he was. So we scrambled up onto the platform with our film equipment and sort of duck-waddled up backwards to the chief. As a present I brought one of those Fred Flintstone cameras, the kind where the film canister is also the body of the camera, and I presented it to the chief. He seemed delighted and began to click off pictures. He wasn't advancing the film between shots, but since we were told we shouldn't speak unless spoken to, I wasn't able to inform him that he wasn't going to get twelve pictures, but only one, very, very complicated one.

After a couple more hours the chief lifted his hand, and there was absolute silence. All the dogs had suddenly stopped barking. We looked around and saw the dogs. All their throats had been simultaneously cut and their bodies, still breathing, pierced with rods, were turning on those pits. The chief insisted we join in the meal but Marina had turned green and I asked if we could just have ours to go. They carefully wrapped the dogs in leaves and we carried their bodies away.'

A thing of Joy is a beauty forever. For Bob and Patti and black pepper, as well, joy was about to run out. In December of 2008, the FSM court issued an order finding them in contempt for nonrepayment of their loan, and filed a lawsuit for default. After they refused to sell their shares in Apple Computer, they were found guilty of contempt of court, placed under house arrest, and their US passports were confiscated. On June 10, 2009, Bob and Patti fought back, and filed their own suit against The State of Pohnpei, the Federated States of Micronesia Development Bank, US Secretary of State Hillary Clinton, and US Secretary of the Department of the Interior Ken Salazar, for breach of contract, breach of Compact, and unjust enrichment. Two years later, the US Court of Appeals dismissed their case because of nonjurisdiction 'over the foreign state.' At the same time several different longterm land leases came due, and some landowners refused to renew. In 2013, Laurie Anderson's husband got a new liver, and The Village people, after 40 years of operation, shut down their dream.

One of the word of mouth rumors that came out of the sakau

bars was that Bob and Patti were relocating on Yap, to take advantage of the Deng Hong's big money investment, coming in from China. But like the pepper and the palisades and the pearls, it's the dark matter of dark intrigue.

'And the colored girls say
Doo do doo do doo do do doo...'
Lou Reed, *Walk on the Wild Side*

*   *   *

Happy Lucky Welcome Fun
Marshall Islands

'The bikini is the most important thing since the atom bomb.'
Diana Vreeland

Diana never saw the pathos of her remark. Also, we weren't supposed to be there. Also, we weren't supposed to be there. Robyn and I were headed from Pohnpei to Kosrae, but Continental, being the large landmass landing that it was, missed it, and we ended up in the Marshall Islands instead. Our entry point was the Kwajalein Atoll, or 'Kwaj,' as the American military missile expert sitting next to me referred to it, just before he deplaned. And that was the second reason we weren't supposed to be there. Because Kwaj, at 2174 square kilometers, was the planet's largest lagoon, and the site of the Reagan Test Site, the biggest missile catcher's mitt on Earth.

"All nonmilitary personnel must remain on the aircraft." Said the stewardess. I hadn't realized we were personnel. It felt more like we were impersonnelators.

There were some nonmilitary personnel that were getting off the plane, however. These were local Marshallese, who lived outside the Reagan Test Site area, in the adjacent *Slum of the Pacific* island-city of Ebeye. Over 13,000 residents lived in abject poverty, on 78 acres of semi-permanent project housing, in one of the most densely populated places in the world. It had been like flying over Soweto.

Every flimsy shack had up to forty inhabitants. Whatever Marlon Brando had said about privacy entitlement on Tetiaroha, hadn't sailed over on any stick and shell charts to these people. The gutters were full of aluminum cans, and the storm drains clogged with rainy season dirt.

Natives and migrant workers went from undersized children to supersized hypertensive diabetic adults, from the Ramen noodle and American potato chip and candy bar and cola junk food downtown diet. Some of it had paradoxically saved some lives, four years before Robyn and I arrived.

Ebeye's drinking water came over from the US military instillation in trucks, already chlorinated, but apparently not enough. The citric acidified sugar bomb powdered drink mixes, which some residents added to the liquid, had killed the cholera that had killed their neighbors.

The other lethal liquid that was killing them was alcohol, which accounted for most of the criminal acts, and practically all of the suicides. Ebeyites killed themselves at a rate of ten times that of the suicide rate in the States. A third of the population tested positive for syphilis, and AIDS was on its way.

For 1800 years before the Spaniards decided they owned them, the Marshallese had lived a tranquil existence in the sun and waves, on a diet of fish and coconut meat, in thatched huts to keep out the rain and wind. But then the worlds of the third and the first collided. In 1788 a British convict transport captain named John Marshall cruised through, on his way to China, and named the islands 'Lord Musgrave's Range,' before his own name was attached. Spain sold them to Germany in 1885, which ceded them to Japan in 1914, until the Americans overran everyone in 1944.

And paradise went from free, to commoditized, to lost-mournful, monotonous, and superficial. Ebeye is less than a mile long and about 200 yards wide. Trees and plants are scarce. Children swim off the crumbling pier, in water polluted by human waste and 'pampered' by disposable diapers. Sores on faces and bodies are common. They seldom return to school after lunch, if there is any. Instead, they play on run-down basketball courts, or bicycle aimlessly. Their older brothers kill time in a similar manner, circling the island in already rusted new vehicles, air conditioner and boom-box hip-hop cranked, all day every day, headed for no specific destination and less purpose. There is only one gas station and no service station. The minimum wage was a flat two dollars, and cash was king.

From the serenity and symbiosis of breadfruit trees and coconut trees pandanus trees and flame trees with brilliant red blossoms where, on the Eastern 'towards dawn' *Ralik* chain, the island of Kuwakleen had actually been named *Ri-ruk-jan-leen* for 'the people who harvested the flowers,' with an uncrowded way of life that included raising pigs and chickens and fishing and collecting snails, had become a prison.

After more than 40 years of American control, the metal and plastic and glass 'benign neglect' garbage was dumped where it fell, forming ugly rings around the Marshall Islands.

It's not as if the Americans were deliberately trying to kill them. It was simply that they were measuring how they would die, in the lethal environment they had decided to create for them. Some of the outer island migrants that had been relocated to Ebeye had come from the place that had given Diana the name of her swimsuit- the group of atolls that had originally been named in 1529 'Los Jardines,' The Gardens, by Spanish explorer Alonso de Salazar, arriving on his ship Florida, to the first place in the Marshalls he had been received with gifts, rather than stones, from amazing 30-foot outrigger canoes that could hit over 20 miles per hour. *Bikini.*

Between 1946 and 1958, the Americans did what any civilized liberating force would have done. They detonated 67 nuclear weapons in the 'Pacific Proving Grounds.' In August of 1945 what Harry Truman was trying to prove was that he could sink a warship at sea with an atomic bomb. He sent 42,000 military personnel, 242 ships, 156 aircraft, 300 cameras with 18 tons of film, and 1.3 billion dollars to sink 95 ships (including the *Nagato* flagship of the Imperial Japanese Navy, from whose bridge Admiral Yamamoto had launched the attack on Pearl Harbor), 3,350 rats, goats and pigs, sheared and smeared with suntan lotion, to the ground zero waters of

Bikini lagoon, in the most spectacular and expensive science experiment in history. He called it Operation Crossroads. The local US military governor had persuaded the 167 dutifully Christian Bikini Islanders to leave their remote idyllic paradise temporarily, 'for the good of mankind and to end all world wars.' They were shipped 125 miles east to Rongerik Atoll and given a few weeks' worth of food, with cheerful assurances that they could return as soon as the tests were over. No one could imagine that they would never come back.

The first blast, code-named Able, was a bit of a dud. The bombardier had missed his target. Baker, the second detonation, drove a half mile wide column of water into the sky in less than a second, falling as millions of tons of atomized reef and ocean collapsing back in the lagoon, sinking the 26,000 ton battleship *Arkansas*, and lifting the stern of the 880 foot *Saratoga* 43 feet in the air. Harry had his proof.

Meanwhile, 125 miles away, the Bikini islanders waiting patiently on Rongerik, had discovered that the reef fish were poisonous, the island's coconut trees had been damaged by fire, and there wasn't enough water. Benign neglect was turning to tragic neglect, and starvation set in. They tapped Uncle Sam on the shoulder. *Are we there yet?* Unfortunately Uncle Sam had discovered that Baker's shock wave had released massive amounts of radiation, and saturated the soil of Bikini with cesium 137. The isotope's half-life was thirty years. No one but the Americans was going home anytime soon. They moved the Bikinians to Kwaj, and let them camp out on a small strip of grass next to the runway. A few months later, they relocated them again, this time to the island of Kili, to a different kind of disaster. Kili was a true island, no coral fringing reef, no protected lagoon, no forested outer islands to fish and hunt, just the big breakers of the Southern Sea crashing up against rocky shores. Fishing was almost impossible. They began to starve again, saved only by an emergency airdrop.

In 1952, the first US hydrogen bomb, Ivy Mike, vaporized the island of Elugelab in the Enewetak group and, two years later, the Americans detonated another load of happy lucky welcome fun on Bikini. Because they thought that one of the isotopes, lithium 7 was inert, and it wasn't, the force of the resultant explosion would be underestimated by a factor of four. On March 1, 1954, Bravo blasted into a crimson15-megaton thermonuclear hydrogen fireball almost five miles wide within the first second, seen and felt on Kwaj over 400 kilometers away, the equivalent of a thousand Hiroshimas, and the largest US nuclear detonation in history. Expanding at 330 feet per second, the mushroom cloud was 9 miles high and 7 miles wide within the first minute, and 25 miles high and 62 miles wide, within the first ten. It raised the temperature of lagoon to 99,000 degrees, and vaporized three islands in the atoll. The crater was over a mile wide and 250 feet deep.

Bravo killed every living thing in the air, on land, and in the sea for miles around. The fallout cloud contaminated more than seven thousand square miles of the Pacific, and included some of the inhabited surrounding islands. Three to four hours after the blast, the sixty-four inhabitants of neighboring Rongelap Atoll, watched in wonder as two inches of snow-like ash covered their island. Children played in it. People drank water saturated with it. Their eyes burned, and their arms, and legs and necks swelled. Vomiting and diarrhea followed.

The Americans had not bothered to tell the Rongelapese about the bomb. They also hadn't informed the crew of the Japanese boat *Daigo Fukuryū Maru* (Lucky Dragon No. 5), which had been fishing for tuna in supposedly safe waters. Six months later chief radio operator Aikichi Kuboyama died of radiation sickness.

The other fallout came from Project 4.1, the medical study of those Bikini Atoll residents exposed to Bravo's radiation.

After the end of the Cold War, the Clinton administration declassified a number of secret documents about the test, which revealed that (1) The military knew that the winds were going to change, and detonated the device anyway, (2) The US had planned beforehand to implement the medical study, an admission of exposure premeditation, (3) It had injected radioactive substances into Rongelap residents and fed them radiation-containing drinks. Despite the adjudication of 'acceptable fallout,' the Marshallese, exposed to 4 times the radiation experienced by residents of Hiroshima and Nagasaki in 1945, began to suffer from birth defects, and die from cancer at accelerated rates. By 1956, the Atomic Energy Commission regarded the Marshall Islands as 'by far the most contaminated place in the world.'

Two years later the final American Pacific bomb, code name Fig, was detonated. The Bikinian exile continued another twenty years, until in 1968, some Atomic Energy Commission scientists convinced Lyndon Johnson that the radiation levels at Bikini Atoll no longer offered 'a significant threat to health and safety.' Lyndon ordered the 540 Bikinians living on Kili resettled 'with all dispatch,' and by the mid 1970s, over 150 islanders were living in new houses, and eating breadfruit, coconuts and pandanus from new plantings. In 1977 the scientists realized they had been terribly wrong in their estimates, recording alarming increases in cesium 137 isotope levels in the islanders. Three ships floated them all away on a sea of tears, back to Kili, and to Majuro. The only thought left on Bikini was the sign in the machine shop. *We can fix everything except broken heart.*

But wait. The scientists were back with two more Happy Lucky Welcome Fun promises in the mid 1980s. They had discovered that, by applying large amounts of potassium fertilizer to Bikini's soil, cesium levels could be reduced ten-fold. Furthermore, this combined with the simple removal of the topsoil layer, would get the Bikinians very close to the 15 millirem safety standard necessary for repatriation. And, there was other good news.

The Bikinians had come into some real money. In 1986, as part of the new Compact of Free Association with the US, they had received $75 million in damages. Two years later, they got another $90 million, designated specifically for radiological cleanup. The compact also set up a Nuclear Claims Tribunal, which meant that their grievances all the way back from the early 1980s, would be heard by a new US court. The Bikinians, 'if they desired, could go back.'

But the Bikinians had not only been living in a cultural and scientific and financial limbo for over thirty years, for over thirty years they had changed. They were the five thousand children of original 147 of the deep cobalt blue and coconut palms and breadfruit and pandanus. They no longer fished with homemade nail hooks baited with hermit crabs, nor swam in crystalline waters. They were the children of housing and food subsidies and insurance and medical plans and scholarships and health care. They were part of the Marshallese forty per cent unemployment and four per cent population growth and emigration to Oregon and Arkansas. Their trust fund balances were chopped in half by the market crashes of 2001 and 2008, and the critical mass was reached in 2010, when they lost their Nuclear Claims Tribunal case against the US government. The Supreme Court of the United States of America, the country responsible for their 66 year nuclear exile, their starvation, their irradiation and medical experimentation, their five time relocation, the loss of their way of life, and the exploitation of their generosity of spirit, determined that, like Bob and Patti on Pohnpei, it didn't have the right to rule over international agreements. The nation that had spent twenty billion dollars on the Manhattan Project, fourteen billion dollars on a thousand ICBM launch pads and silos, that had built 67,500 nuclear missiles and 4,680 nuclear bombers, and given the

Marshallese the equivalent of 7,000 Hiroshima-sized atomic bombs at the rate of eleven a week, producing 104,000,000 cubic meters of radioactive waste, had no jurisdiction over or responsibility for the few Pacific islanders they had so ignobly made permanently dispossessed and homeless. One might think that there could be no better glow, after such a Bikini waxing. But you would be wrong.

According to the Compact of Free Association, the Marshallese are not allowed to shop in the facility stores on Kwaj, or swim in the pools, play on the tennis or racquetball courts, or tee off on the golf course. They're probably teed off enough, already.

Frankie Avalon hermit crab nailed it, in *Bikini Beach*.

"Baby." He said. "I think we associate with a very unstable group."

'No longer can I stay, it's true
No longer can I live in peace and harmony
No longer can I rest on my sleeping mat and pillow
Because of my island and the life I once knew there
The thought is overwhelming
Rendering me helpless and in great despair.'
Lore Kessibuki, Rongerik horror, 1946

*   *   *

Our Continental 'island hopper' flight left the 'sunset' western Ralik chain, for the Marshall Island eastern 'sunrise' Ratak chain and capital, Majuro. On the map, it didn't really look like a country. It looked like a large expanse of empty blue nothingness, with the very odd circular flyspeck of sand, as if you took the number of people visiting Disneyland every day and dusted them over Mexico. There were only seventy square miles of land, chopped into 1200 islets, over an area of three quarter of a million miles.

As well, Marshall Island life existed in one dimension. The narrow sand halos, around most of the vast lagoons, allowed its inhabitants to live only in single file. The pig our taxi hit,

257

on the one ribbon road that encircled Majuro, had nowhere else to run.

Robyn and I had actually landed at Amata Kabua International Airport after sunset. I'm still not sure that Continental had informed our hosts that we were coming. If they had, no one was really paying attention. Its not as if we were bringing them anything they could use. The 'downtown' was actually a linear connection of three smaller settlements, code name D-U-D, not a totally inappropriate acronym, given what we were about to experience. In the middle of the dud of Delap-Uliga-Diarrit was our Continental-approved accommodation, the Outrigger Hotel.

The lobby looked promising, with a large central bouquet of flowers beneath a large illuminated inverted breast of a chandelier, under a mural of hand-painted fish stuck on a powder blue ceiling. The desk clerk handed us a room key, and noted that we would have to hurry to the restaurant, if we wanted anything to eat.

Bright and cheery disappeared down a gloomy hallway lined with food scraps, to a dingy box with battered and faded furniture. The carpet was sticky, with the unmistakable musty odor of old vomit. Water dripped from the floor above. The roaches scurried to escape the flick of the bathroom light switch, but the ants continued to circle the sink, headed for no specific destination and less purpose. The water that came out of the tap was brown, and the shower piping had come away from the wall, likely in self-defense. There were no towels. To flush the toilet, Robyn needed to hold down the handle, long enough for me to be given the task to get towels and sort out the water problem. I returned to the front desk.

"There are no towels in the room." I said.

"People steal them." He said, handing them over. They were stained. I promised I wouldn't steal them.

"The water is brown." I said.

"So is the swimming pool." He said, handing me a bottle of water, and noting that we would have to hurry to the restaurant, if we wanted anything to eat. I clubbed a roach to death on my way to fetch Robyn. She told me there was now no water, of any color.

The only anything to eat in the restaurant turned out to be pizza, which hadn't arrived after half an hour of waiting. I asked about the delay.

"The oven is broken." She said. And then she brought the pizza. It was sticky, and smelled like the carpet. Also, we weren't supposed to be there.

The Americans we had met had been under the impression that the Marshalls had been 'taken back' from the Japanese, but the islands had never been under Washington's administration, prior to the initiation of the US Trust Territory of the Pacific, after WWII. In fact, the Marshallese had been treated as Japanese subjects, which made perfect sense, since most had been educated in Japanese schools, spoke Japanese, and blended Japanese and local customs in their daily lives. A third of the islanders had Japanese ancestry. At the time of the U.S. invasion, some were applying for full Japanese citizenship, and were likely to have it granted. Some are still nostalgic for the life they enjoyed in the pre-militaristic Japanese era. I know Robyn and I were. If things had been different, we might not have ended up eating soggy pizza, after midnight, in the tropical heat.

Between the complex carbohydrates and the simple light of dawn on the lagoon, was insomnia. I rolled out of bed, and told Robyn I needed to see what I could of Majuro, before out next Continental adventure whisked us on to Kosrae, later that morning. I needed to see the result of how an ambiguous clause in the League of Nations Mandate had elevated the Marshallese into 'liberated persons under American wardship.'

The beach, that had appeared so paradisiacal, in the first rays of my twilight awakening, was strewn with trash and broken glass. There was a feeling of poverty, and indifference, and indifference to poverty. There was no indifference from the marauding packs of feral dogs, however. They were aggressively alpha American, and I quickly secured a heightened awareness, a bamboo cane, a pocket full of rocks, and an attitude, in order to continue my explorations.

The hand-painted closed shop signs conveyed no small optimism. There was the *Welcome Fun Store*, where the offer existed, without spaces, to discover the special

lowpriceherecanrefundcanchangeplywoodclothingstoreforsale.

Along the only street possible, I found the *Lucky Store*, the *Happy Store*, and the *Happy Garage*. But then, outside the pastel concrete colors and glass block windows of the Crazy Price Mart was a life-sized plastic facsimile of a coconut tree, with a yellow trunk, and six bright yellow coconuts hanging under as many lime-green fronds, sticking out the top at odd angles, just down the street from a row of real ones. Somewhere, someone, was mass-producing giant plastic coconut trees. These people were doomed.

It turns out that the Marshallese may have been doomed for more than their free association with the extended nuclear family. On Christmas Day in 2008, the government declared a state of emergency in Majuro and Ebeye. Unprecedented extreme waves, from storm surges and high tides, caused widespread flooding and the displacement of hundreds of residents from their homes. The floods hit the cemeteries, dramatically increasing the alarm about public hygiene, and the risk for contagion. The most immediate problem for people that live less than a meter above sea level, is not that their homes will soon be underwater, but that they will be uninhabitable, in less than fifty years. Even occasional 'overwash' will salinate the fresh water, and kill the land that their agriculture depends on. Climate change is also slowing the normal annual centimeter vertical coral growth in the protective fringing reefs, through ocean acidification and thermal bleaching. Even the stainless steel flushing mechanism on the urinal in the airport, was cobalt blue corroded from the Southern Sea.

If the Marshallese can't live on their islands, they will have to relocate; if they relocate, they will no longer have their country. They will lose their identity.

There is one final reason why the *Happy Lucky Welcome Fun* is about to become a quadruple oxymoron. In September of 2012, the first Ahmadiyya mosque opened in Majuro. The mosque's imam, Matiullah Joyia, was quick to publicly reject 'jihad by the sword,' a reassurance that was undoubtedly received with the most relief by Majuro's marauding packs of feral dogs. The Muslim community had committed instead to an 'intellectual jihad of the pen,' whatever that implies. Meanwhile, the bikini is now banned from the Miss World contest, and Iran is about to get nuclear weapons. Which brings us full circle to Diana Vreeland's remark. *The bikini is the most important thing since the atomic bomb.* No, Diana. Bikini is the atomic bomb, and the Marshallese have not only been designated ground zero, they're about to have zero ground.

In the three-way inundation race between Washington, Wahhabism and water, in the Marshall Island sea world of *Happy Lucky Welcome Fun*, it's awash.

'I now have absolute proof that smoking even one marijuana cigarette is equal in brain damage to being on Bikini Island during an H-bomb blast.'

Ronald Reagan

'Statistics are like a bikini. What they reveal is suggestive but what they conceal is vital.'

Aaron Levenstein

*   *   *

Mysterious Paradise of Mud
Koshrae

'Into each life some rain must fall.'
Henry Wadsworth Longfellow

I asked the lady next to me.
"Why do they call it the mysterious paradise island?"
"I don't know." She said.
"So that's why." I thought.
That's what the psychedelic sign had said, above the airport terminal door. *Welcome to Kosrae...The Mysterious Paradise Island...Home of the Sleeping Lady Mountain.*
From the air, the most eastern of the Carolines, and our last island stop in Micronesia, really did appear like a woman sleeping, although her nipples seemed a little too pointed for the proper profile. *At the beginning of time, the gods had made Kosrae in the shape of a woman, to produce the seeds known as people.* The legend said that she had been menstruating at the time of her creation, and today there is still a place in the deep lush jungle, located at the spot between her thighs, where bright red soil is found. The men used the special sacred earth to mix paint for their canoes. Only the bravest dared to collect it.
Kosrae rose in a high emerald silhouette against the stark blue surrounding ocean. We landed on the skinny coral airstrip that had been constructed within the fringing reef, connected by a causeway to the mysterious.
Bruce met us in an old rusted-out van, with a cracked windshield and missing side door. An aging hippie, he and his partner, Katrina, would have been the Bob and Patti of Kosrae, if Bob and Patti had gone more out bush, and way

more bushwhacked. In 1991 they had relocated from San Francisco, leased a parcel of land from the state tourism officer, and opened a dive eco-lodge. All the *lohm* huts had been constructed of pandanus thatch, in an attempt to recreate an old Koshraean settlement. If biodegradability had been the objective, it had certainly been a success. Ten years had taken their tropical toll on the shacks and, it would later appear, on Bruce and Katrina. Their dive eco-lodge was becoming an eco-lodge dive. Like Bob and Patti, Bruce and Katrina were from California. Like Bob and Patti, they had named their establishment the *Village*. Like Bob and Patti, their initial friendliness went a little sideways in the humidity. One day they became quite agitated, when I wanted to take their photo. The first mystery wasn't why they had come to paradise island- it was why they were still there.

Their first piece of advice was to go back the way we had come.

"If you want anything to drink, you'd better buy it today." Said Bruce. "Tomorrow's Sunday. You won't even be allowed to swim."

The unthinkable became the inspirational. Robyn and I walked out onto the only road and headed for the last bottle of rum on the island.

There were four real villages on Kosrae. Legend had them settled by the children of an old mother, who called them together, and sent them off, to live their own lives. There were three sons and a daughter. The oldest son wandered westward until he came to a heavily wooden place he named Tafunsak. It became the largest because he was the oldest. Our village was named Melem, *moon*, by the daughter, because she arrived at night when the moon was shining. The girls from Melem are said to be the most beautiful on Kosrae. The second eldest son roamed south, until he found the shore on the far side of the island. He called his village Utwe, and it would become a source for one of Kosrae's most intriguing mysteries. The last born son stayed with his mother until she died and, because his home was completely surrounded by water, named his village Lelu, meaning the inside of the lake.

We walked towards Lelu, past frangipanis and breadfruit and papaya, and pigs in pens and starving mutts in numbers, too lethargic to bark, to the Tofol shop with the last bottle of rum. Robyn posed in front of a larger than life-sized inflatable Santa. Black clouds gathered together above us, as we paid for our indulgence. The second mystery was why there wasn't more in stock. With what was coming, they should have made sure that they would never run out. We just managed to thumb a ride in the back of a covered truck, before the sky cracked open. It hosed down all night.

The showers let up for just enough time on Sunday morning, to allow Robyn and I to attend the Kosrae Pentecostal Church service. We were greeted by a mountain of flip-flops and shoes outside (to which we added our own), huge brown *muumuu* women inside, and the Pentecostal pastor on the dais, who made sure he got our names right, so he could welcome us at embarrassing length. He didn't leave out a detail of our lives that we hadn't told him about, and some that he had sleuthed out all by himself. *The Lord helps those.*

He told us how Jesus saves, baptizes, heals, and is coming again. And then he went rogue. At first it sounded like he was speaking Kosraean, but I knew it wasn't Kosraean, and so did everyone else. And they began speaking in the same language that he was speaking in, except that it wasn't a recognizable language at all. An immense hall full of brown people began swaying and shouting unintelligible gibberish, trying to connect with the gift of the holy spirit, little knowing that Robyn and I had purchased the last bottle on the island, the previous afternoon.

All the commotion inside the church had driven away all the barometric pressure outside. We exited early, to search through the mountain of footwear outside, and get back to the Village before the storm scourge arrived. It was only our second day at the eco-lodge, but the book of revelations had already been opened wide.

The consciousness that Bruce and Katrina, the San Francisco hippie eco-preservationists, thought they were bringing to Kosrae, had missed the actual ecology on the island, by several generations, and a tropical country mile. They deluded themselves into believing that the leased mangrove swamp was a simple blank California creative canvas, waiting to be painted into a paragon of living in harmony with Nature, and the envy of the real civilized world. They would provide their guests with a festival of flora and fauna. And mud. Like Woodstock. People expected mud at festivals, and would have asked for their money back if they didn't get it.

But no one had asked the heavy sticky oppressive sweltering equatorial reality of Kosrae if it wanted to fall in love with their ideology. Bruce and Katrina, with the best of temperate intentions, had built a resort in a mosquito-infested bog, *mud-licious and puddle-wonderful.* The biodegradable 'cottages' had begun degrading, from the moment of their birth. Humidity and salt had proved too much. The wall of the next shack was as shabby and filthy and dowdy and dirty and stained, with green slime and bat droppings. If the Californians had taken the time and consideration, to ask the original Kosraeans whether they would have preferred living in their natural materials, or something more durable, durable would have beaten natural to death. Bruce and Katrina ended up in a survival dance with mysterious entropic forces they had romanticized. The environmentalism they had nurtured as their salvation had so outgunned them, in the wild competition for protein and reproductive resources, that they ended up shell-shocked and paralyzed. Nature abhors a vacuum, and she filled their space with sludge.

It actually rained inside the hut. Or at least thick humidity, inside our dark space. The grey water effluent drains, that Bruce had proudly installed instead of plumbing, were an ideal breeding ground for mosquitoes. Even in the torrential downpour, plagues of them bit through our ponchos, inside

the traditional thatch, in the traditional way they had always bitten. Robyn and I lit a half dozen mosquito coils, but the traditional breeziness through the traditional thatch wafted away the healing smoke. The screens designed to keep them out were torn. We had asked for bug spray. The can was rusted shut. I prayed for more geckos. Using the barely functioning toilet at night, required crawling out from under a musty net, and into a wall of biomass. It wasn't just mosquitoes, although they had been waiting patiently. Rats and crabs and ants and gigantic spiders had made their own debut, ascending from the mud below the drains. Cobwebs that had been washed away by the shower's dripping rose, would mysteriously reappear by morning. Nature had filled the abhorrent holes in the towels and bedding and netting, with stains. There was rat shit on our table, and fleas on the feral cats in the dining room. By the fourth day there was mold on my multivitamins. It was a festival. Thankfully, we had rum. *Mud not the fountain that gave drink to thee.*
One night we braved the thatched restaurant. *Purchase of liquor in this restaurant requires a valid drinking permit and purchase of a meal as per Kosrae State Law.* Under the dim lights and sprinklings of termite dust, Robyn and I poured over the a la carte menu. Mud was one of the four food groups. *Powac — A Whole Mangrove Crab, Steamed.* I loved crab. I loved the pheromone sensuous white flakes of our Barkley Sound Dungeness crabs, the claws and legs and every morsel from the carapace, back in British Columbia. I loved coconut crab, right off the trees and rocks of the Southern Sea. Loved crab. "We have the largest mangrove trees in the Pacific." Said the waitress. I had read the Kosraean legend of their creation.
Once there was an eel who had a beautiful daughter. She was kidnapped by the king. Her heartbroken mother searched the entire island for her child, forming these channels as she swam frantically around.
"I'll have the mud crab." I said. And then I noticed the menu item below it. *Powac Parmesan — Grilled Crab... with Fresh Parmesan.* I asked Robyn.

"Why would you put parmesan on crab?" She shrugged. It was a mystery. She ordered the *Wahoo Fiesta.*
When the crab came out, he looked angry. Maybe it was because of his big vermilion spiky carapace, or his broken legs and claws, but he wasn't happy. I took in a big chunk of meat. Apparently, I frowned.
"Well?" Asked Robyn.
"Tastes like mud." I said.
"Maybe that's why they put the Parmesan on." She said. Mystery solved.
"How's the fiesta?" I asked.
"Wahoo." She said. For desert, we had more rum.

*   *   *

*   *   *

"I think I've cracked the mystery, Bruce." I said, next morning. It was raining rats and hogs.

"What's that?" He asked.

"The sun never actually comes out, does it?" I said.

"Well, it is the rainy season." He said. "You should have come some other time."

But the rain did stop, long enough for Robyn and I to go walkabout. We passed the school and studied a beautiful mural which, in a blue for the sky and one for the water, a green for the leaves and another for the land, a brown for the tree trunks and another for the traditional thatched houses, and the red of the outrigger canoe from between the sleeping lady's thighs, depicted the mysterious paradise that Kosrae had been. There was breadfruit and taro and crabs and bananas and coconuts and birds. Every man had a farm on Kosrae. Breadfruit was preserved in leaf-lined pits for times of scarcity. Coconuts were for nobles. Taro was softened and skillfully conserved as a feast food, known as *fahfah*. The men, like everywhere else in Micronesia, drank kava, which they called *sukha*. Fish came from the lagoons. The Japanese brought limes, and the Americans brought bombing runs, and tinned meat. And the missionaries and whalers had brought the rats, which killed off the birds on the mural, the Kosrae Starling and the Kosrae Crake, the only two remaining skins of which are now in the Russian Academy of Sciences, in Saint Petersburg.

But Robyn and I were walking to long before the whalers and missionaries and extinctions. We were walking to Lelu Island, the Nan Madol of Koshrae, from where the Pohnpeian Neolithic ruin had been inspired. Lelu began about 1250 AD,

269

with 150 years of moving multi-ton chunks of prismatic black basalt from the other side of Kosrae, into 67 acres of a hundred walled compounds, twenty-feet high. The streets were paved. Canoe channels ran through the city, and out to the reefs.

The first European expeditions, the French in 1824 and the Russians three years later, documented Kosraean society, as highly stratified as the stacks of basalt, piled up like enormous logs, of the royal residences and burial pyramids of the nobility. There were four main societal groups- the *tokosra* king, the *mwetleum* high chiefs and *mwetsuksuk* low chiefs, and the *mwetsrisrik* commoners, who owned no land, and paid tribute in labor, food and shell money.

Robyn and I could hear the surge of ocean waves from anywhere inside the ruins. They were still covered deep in jungle. Bursts of rain showers came and went, like they had at Nan Madol, on Pohnpei. On our way out we met an old woman, with facial solar lentigo. She smiled and bowed, as the Japanese do. It was only many years later that I learned of another Kosraean legend about Lelu. It seems there is a protective spirit called Ninamata Fatiti, who is said to guard the ruins. She appears as a grandmother with age spots on her face, and punishes people who are not respectful. One unfortunate visitor had apparently made the mistake of picking a tangerine from a sacred tree. He was wrestled to the ground, and looked up in horror to find an old woman, stuffing his mouth. With mud.

We exited under a breadfruit tree, onto a paved road, and into a group of five year olds, three little boys and seven beautiful little girls, in baby blue T-shirts, flip-flops, and serrated sarongs embroidered with flowers.

"Awshit, awshit!" They shouted, pointing at us.

"Awshit?" Asked Robyn.

"Comes from the whalers' era." I said. "They would walk around Kosrae, letting off an occasional 'Aw, shit.' And the locals decided that's what the foreigners would be called. The

whalers were often at sea for over a year, but it was worth it. The head of a ninety-ton sperm whale could yield 5,000 gallons of sperm oil. In 1845, at $1.77 a gallon, a man would only have to work one lucky year, to have enough to never work again. They had three excellent anchorages here on Kosrae- Utwe, Okat, and this one, Lelu."
Farther along the shoreline, two yachts floated in the shadow of the Sleeping Lady. Grey cotton clouds were sinking back down over her nipples.
"In this water is where the mystery is." I said. "Here be, like other Stories of the Southern Sea, a lurid tale of pirates, mutinies, castaways, sadism, a desolation of grey skies and relentless rain, impenetrable blackish-green rainforests, and shipwrecks and survival."
He was born in Cleveland in 1829, one of three sons of a grog-shanty keeper. He ran away from home to become a sailor on the Great Lakes. He left New York as a passenger on the *Canton* on March 4, 1853. By the time the ship pulled into Singapore, William Henry Hayes had become the captain. He sold the boat, even though it wasn't his, launching a thirty-year career of unparalleled depravity. He began with fraudulent forged papers, acquiring the cargo of mortgaged ships. In January of 1857, 'Bully' Hayes (for that was the name that had stuck) arrived in Freemantle, Australia, on the *C.W. Bradley*, the repurchased and renamed *Canton*. He married Amelia Littleton, despite the fact that he still had a wife back in the States. When the Singapore Ships chandlers caught up with him in Perth, Bully was bankrupted, but escaped his creditors to Melbourne, where he gained command of another vessel, heading to Vancouver. The supercargo threw him off in Honolulu, for swindling passengers, but once again, he managed to sail on to San Francisco, as captain of a new ship, where he abandoned Amelia. He lost his new boat in a storm, and others to creditors, but in between maritime adventures, found enough time to become a member of a blackface minstrel troupe back

in New South Wales.

When bankruptcy loomed again in Australia, Bully sailed to New Zealand, where he travelled the South Island Otago gold rush in a tour company of vaudeville artists. In January of 1863, he married again, to the widow Mrs. Roma 'Rosie' Buckingham, whose four sons were the vaudevillian artists, *The Masters Buckingham*. They settled in Arrowtown, where he opened a hotel, called at first the 'United States,' and then 'The Prince of Wales.' When the Buckingham's paid a barber £5 to cut his hair short, they found that he was missing an ear, lost during a discovery that he had been cheating at cards. This got Bully mocked in a popular play, and forced him to abscond with Rosie for Port Chalmers. He got his hands on a ship called the *Black Diamond*, which he hid in Croixelles Harbour, near Nelson. On the 19th of August 1864, the boat capsized, and Rosie, and Bully's infant son, drowned. Less than a year later, he had moved to Christchurch, and married Emily Mary Butler.

In May 1866, Bully had acquired the brig, *Rona*, and began operating as a blackbirder out of Apia in Samoa, and Mili Atoll, in the Marshall Islands. He was ruthless, forcibly removing entire male populations of some islands, to work as slaves in the plantations of Tahiti, Fiji, Samoa and Queensland. He would capture islanders, and send them back into their villages infected with measles, so when the rounding up began, the natives were so ravaged by fever, that no resistance was possible. Bully made a lot of money, and bought the brigantine *Samoa*, with the proceeds. But his luck was a pendulum, and he lost both of his ships off Manihiki in the Cook Islands, in March of 1869, and less than a year later, was arrested in Apia by Consul Williams for his blackbirding activities on his new schooner, *Atlantic*.

He was rescued by a worse villain. Ben Pease was an even more notorious American blackbirder, 'a satanic looking rascal with a black spade beard- more openly piratical operator than [Bully] Hayes.' Pease had been involved in the opium trade in China, and may have had greater claim than Bully Hayes as being a South Sea pirate and 'the last of the buccaneers.' Pease took Bully away in the 250-ton brig *Pioneer*, on April fool's Day, 1870. An argument developed over the ownership of the cargo. Pease died, for one of two incredulous reasons. It doesn't matter. What matters is that, when the ship arrived back in Apia, Hayes was the captain. He renamed the boat after his favorite daughter, *Leonora*, painted her white, in an effort to expunge her reputation as the 'black ship' of the blackbirding trade, and continued to deal in coconut oil, copra, and slaves. He stole another ship named the *Neva* out of Lelu harbor, installed one of his men as the captain, and brought an American warship, the *USS Jamestown*, in pursuit. He got away, until finally arrested by Captain Richard Meade of the USS Narragansett, on the 19th of February, 1872. Meade couldn't find anyone, ship's crew or otherwise, to give evidence against Bully. He was released back onto the *Leonora*, which by now had become 'the most notorious ship in the 18th century Pacific,' manned 'the last buccaneer.'

But his luck began to run out during a southern storm back in Kosrae when, on March 15, 1874, smashed onto a coral reef, the *Leonora*, with all its cargo and armaments, including four cannons, went down in tremendous seas. A number of his sailors were drowned but Hayes managed to make it ashore. Marooned at Utwe, he built a house, married a Kosraean woman, charged the local chief a bounty of almost fifty thousand coconuts to make up for lost cargo he claimed had been stolen when his ship sank, and brawled with the other European traders on the island. He didn't cut quite the figure of Captain O'Keefe on Yap. In September, almost seven months later, the HMS Rosario under Captain Dupuis arrived, to investigate a claim that Bully had raped a 9-year girl. Hayes response to being arrested consisted of two actions. He escaped in a 14-foot boat he had built from the timber of the wreck of the *Leonora*, and he hid his treasure, in three large trunks, somewhere on Kosrae. Somewhere, on the mysterious paradise of mud.

Bully reached Guam in April of 1875, and purchased the schooner *Arabia* on credit, accepting a commission to help convicts escape from prison there. Captured again, he ended up incarcerated in his own prison cell in Manila until, early in 1876, he was freed, and landed stone cold broke back in San Francisco. He tricked a Mr. and Mrs. Moody into funding the purchase of a schooner, the *Lotus*, and tricked Mr. Moody into going ashore, while he sailed off, with Jenny Ford Moody still on board. Bully arrived in Apia, Samoa on January 2, 1877, and then left for Kosrae, where he intended to collect the coconuts left at the time of the Leonora wreck. On March 31st Bully got into an argument with his cook 'Dutch Pete.' Peter Radeck shot him with a revolver, struck him on the skull with an iron implement, and threw him overboard. A Japanese sawmill employee had dug up one of Hayes' strongboxes prior to WWII. The location of the other two are still a mystery.

By the time of his demise, William Henry Hayes had stolen scores of ships, swindled countless cargos of a total worth well over a million dollars, subdued and debauched whole islands, thieved all the coconuts he could find to fuel his copra processing stations, impressed thousands of slaves, consummated three bigamous marriages and a hundred more island unions, kidnapped and raped children, and eluded 97 criminal charges, in a multitude of near escapes. As far as most anyone who knew him was concerned, Bully had died of natural causes, and the cook that done him was a hero.

Robyn and I hiked past the shell of an old concrete building strung with drying laundered dresses, an old rusted hulk of a barge the color of the soil between the island's thighs, and a giant clam nursery of a hundred pound underwater calcium vulvas, half open in the shallows. The Sleeping Lady's mysteries were dark and ephemeral, but unmistakably feminine.

In the torrential downpour of the next morning, Bruce suggested that I perform my first nitrox dive.

"It's just as wet down there in Walung Dropoff." He said. "And the hard coral is thousands of years old." The enriched oxygen content of the gas in my tank was like breathing champagne, and the coral was some of the most beautiful in the world. I lingered below to play tag with the multicolored Christmas tree worms that spiraled back into their coral recesses, with each pass of my hand, and the walking coral, dragged around by the peanut worms. There were Grey groupers, spotted rays and triggerfish, and giant clams, one of which almost ate the fin I was teasing it with.

"How'd you like the bubbly?" Bruce asked, on my return. I told him someone should bottle the stuff. He told me he did.

On our last day in Kosrae, Robyn and I hiked through the mud and dense vegetation, to the crumbling ancient Menke temples of Sinlaku, the Breadfruit goddess. We broke off giant leaves of elephant ear taro, to use as umbrellas. According to the last legend, Sinlaku had a premonition that the Boston missionaries were about to land with other gods, and left the island the day before they arrived. She had promised that, one day, she would have her revenge.

On our way out to the coral airstrip, curious about the final mystery, I asked Bruce how his windshield had ended up so shattered and smashed. He shrugged.

"Falling breadfruit." He said.

'Two men look out the same prison bars;
one sees mud and the other stars.'
Beck

*　　*　　*

275

Aground in the Abode of Love
Tonga

'You may find yourself living in a shotgun shack
You may find yourself in another part of the world
You may find yourself behind the wheel of a large
  automobile
You may find yourself in a beautiful house with a beautiful
  wife
You may ask yourself, well, how did I get here?'
Talking Heads, *Once in a Lifetime*

You know you've arrived in Polynesian waters when the vowels begin to drown the consonants. Fua'amotu International airport was 35 kilometers from Nuku'alofa, and Nuku'alofa was a light year away from caring. The Tongan immigration fullback in the blue skirt was totally wrapped up in the frayed *taovala* pandanus mat around his considerable center. Each of his solid knees was the width of my head, and his solid head was a cube of muscle. Robyn and I handed him our declaration forms. *No 'potable spirits... microorganisms... used bicycles... obscene photographs... tear gas.'* These people had taken the missionaries far too seriously.

"Talitali fiefia." He said. *Welcome.*

The Southern Sea had been a world of nothing-matters. But I was taking this trip far too seriously as well. We were on our way back to Canada from New Zealand, after finally deciding where we would live and work. It was the work part that was the problem. I wasn't sure I was really ready to commit to anything other than Robyn. We had been married for three years, and had lived in relative poverty and absolute connubial bliss, while I had finished my medical residency. Only six months earlier we had stopped off in Fiji, on the way to a new beginning in New Zealand. But the signs of a future fulfilled professional life had been inauspicious, and I had sprung our need to return to the frozen north on Robyn, on our anniversary, in a restaurant, in Rotorua. She had cried.

I promised I would make it up to her, by allowing us to stop for a month in the Friendly Islands, on the way back. I think she knew that the delay wasn't for her. She wanted to 'get on with it,' get on with the rest of our lives. *Time isn't holding us, time isn't after us. Time isn't holding us, time doesn't hold you back...*

I told her that I wanted it too, but that was only wishful. The delay was for me, to get my head around the inevitability of it all. My last kick at the can, my last island, my last diversion was the same that it ever was. *Letting the days go by, letting the days go by, letting the days go by, once in a lifetime.*

Nuku'alofa, the Abode of Love, seemed to be less comfortable with its appellation, since the arrival of the Wesleyans, and AIDS. *Koe 'eitisi 'okau' ma'u Hano faito'o ko ho'o Puke koe mate Kuo pau!* Said the sign. *Aids is incurable Once you get Death is certain Soon! Malu'I 'a Tonga.*

The annual Red Cross parade marched down Taufa'ahau Road, led by the big white Sousaphones of the uniformed marching band, and followed by floats carrying messages from both the microorganisms and the missionaries. *Avoid going for men with many women; One husband one wife; Don't shoot-see the red cross; Beware of death trap; Wickedness never was happiness.*

When the last float vanished, it left behind the most sleep-dusted royal port in the Pacific. Even the most methodical of its Methodists had been losing out to torpor and poverty and chaos. Nuku'alofa, as charming as it could be, was a center of quiet, and of quiet capitulation.

Beyond the Vuna wharf, the town straggled over a good mile of space, with flowery houses of pretty verandas, and pathways of green grass, kept short by the supersized weight of bare Tongan feet. The pork fat had begun to drown the Paradise. Tongans were eating themselves to death. The fattest population on the planet, 92% of it citizens over 30 were obese, and almost twenty per cent suffered from diabetes. The smoky scenes from roast suckling pigs, spinning on their spits through three sumptuous feasts a day, at week-long church conferences, would have given Hieronymus Bosch hallucinations, and Jabba the Hutt heartburn. Twenty-one buffets a week, for people with thrifty genes, eating suckling pig and corned beef and lamb belly 'flap,' together with the taro and sweet potato and yam carbs, in the tropical heat, who cart their leftovers home in carrier bags, is not a survival skill of the first order.

Tongans aren't actually inherently lazy, they're just not materialistic. Rather, they have more spiritual aspirations- life revolves around the church and family, and a deliberate overindulgence of both. Ten is the magic number for offspring. The bronze statue of the current King, Taufa'ahau Tupou IV, was monstrous. The grass never stood a chance.

All along the seafront was a wide double avenue of iron-bark trees and, to one side of it, the visiting facsimile of the *HMS Bounty*, which had never actually visited the place in her original form.

We came along to the Royal Palace, a white painted wooden Victorian gingerbread hybrid of Milan cathedral and German toy, with scrolled fretwork and pinnacles and gables, under a rust colored roof. It had been prefabricated in New Zealand, shipped to and erected in Tonga in 1867, and surrounded by green Norfolk pines and white orchids. A military band with a silver brass section and big bass drum changed the guard, and then came over to exchange beaming grins.

We ran in the same direction that Vuna Road did, west from the palace, the sea and reef on one side, and the stately old colonial homes on the other, to the old British High Commissioner's residence, sporting a flagpole surrounded by the four cannons from the *Port-au-Prince,* the ship captured and burned by the Tongans at Ha'apai in 1806, after they had clubbed to death all its crew, except for the castaway.

Graves of elevated powdered white coral terraces, tiers and tears outlined by pebbled rectangles, rose from the ground inside the casuarina-ringed 'tragic field' cemetery of Mala'e'aloa, along with miniature cement chapels painted white and blue and rust, and more modern burial receptacles of colored tile and block. The Tongan graves that Robyn and I would encounter elsewhere were everywhere, sometimes in the front yard, ringed and decorated with what they had-Foster's beer bottles shoved in the dirt under cloth canopies with embroidered tapestries flying in the wind, Jesus figurines, Last Supper posters, crosses, tinsel, plastic flowers, red banners, and Christmas decorations.

We came upon a shaded concrete cricket pitch, covered in an immense spread of *ngatu* tapa cloth, under grey velvet shadow patches of light falling between the golden green leaves of the trees. Here were the tapa ladies, stripping and pounding paper mulberry bark, wetting and pulping and beating it into square foot flat sheets with four-sided ridged wooden mallets, and then gluing it all together so skillfully with cassava, that no joint was visible. Fifty-two segments, representing the number of weeks in a year, were glued end-to-end, and then expanded in a matrix laterally by thirteen pieces, symbolizing the number of lunar months. The result, an immense white sheet, soft as silk, was stenciled with geometrical and symmetrical designs, in black and brown, using only the point of a triangular scrap of wood as a paint brush.

A fine pattern of ochre emerged along either edge, with a repeating cubist motif of diagonals, diamonds, checks, wings, and zigzags, extending in from the two sides, until they met perfectly in the middle. The promises of the weddings and the birthdays and the funerals of the future would be covered. Robyn and I took a left on Wellington Road, past the Centenary Church where the king and queen worshipped, to the Free Wesleyan Church of Tonga that we would attend the following day.

In between were the Mala'ekula Royal Tombs, containing the

remains of all the monarchs from the first king, George Tupou I, who died in 1892 at the age of a hundred, to the much beloved Queen Salote Tupou III, in 1965. Salote became the darling of London during the coronation of Queen Elizabeth in 1953, when she rode through the streets in an open carriage in the pouring rain, waving and smiling all the way.

The stucco gave way to wood again, with the shops of Taufa'ahau Road, scantily stocked with oversized clothing, kitsch kitchenware, and cheap perfume and jewellery. We didn't linger in the sincerity of the Sincere Variety Store, but made for the Maketi Talamahu market, to admire the whopping watermelons, coconuts, banana bunches, sugar cane, papayas, string beans, pineapples, huge taro, and cylindrical yams, each in their special open-woven green pandanus baskets. One of the smiling *lava-lava* women was weaving something three-dimensional, with several endless celluloid ribbons of old movie film.

Robyn and I checked into a decrepit Southern Sea guesthouse. On a Saturday night, in the capital of the only Island state that had never been colonized, the loud festivities that went on outside our window, were the full feral fights and flights of squealing pigs and barking dogs.

The only thing to do the next day, in fact the only thing one was allowed to do, was go to church. There was a specific clause in the constitution that covered Sundays. *The Sabbath Day shall be sacred in Tonga forever and it shall not be lawful to work, artifice, or play games, or trade on the Sabbath.*

All commerce and entertainment ceases from midnight on Saturday until midnight on Sunday. Stores are closed, airplanes don't fly, taxis don't operate, and restaurants, other than those in the hotels, don't open. Cheques dated on a Sunday would not be cashed. The penalty for breaking this rule is three months in jail at hard labor. Church people will let the air out of your tires, if you drive.

Ninety-eight per cent of the population was affiliated with one Christian church or sect, or another. But the *anothers* were making fast inroads on the Wesleyans. Nametags came knocking. We had passed 27 Mormon churches on the way into town from the airport, and some villages had more than one. It was a deadly sin for a Tongan man to be without a shirt, or for a Tongan girl to swim without full metal jacket clothing.

Most Tongans went to church three times on Sunday. We thought once would fill us with sufficient spiritual replenishment to last the week.

The Wesleyan Church had been constructed of coral block in 1888. It looked like a rib-buttressed pig thorax, with four gigantic red wax crayon points peeking out of the square stone missile silos at each corner. Inside was a large statue of Christ, crucified on the tapa cloth background above a fiberoptic Christmas tree. Robyn and I dressed as neatly as could be expected, in our sinful itinerancy. The service was long, the choir operatic. We felt pity and scorn in the glances and bellows of the believers. Perhaps I should have worn a tie, or an expression of rapture. Perhaps the faithful had detected my anxiety about our imminent return to the secular materialistic trappings of the middle class working world.

"Where do you go tomorrow?" Asked the big lady beside us.

"We're heading to the far western point of Tongatapu." I said.

"Where the Reverend Thomas first landed, and brought us the joyous word of God." She said. "Where are you staying?"

"A place called the Good Samaritan." Robyn said.

She was almost blinded by the light.

Letting the days go by, letting the days go by, letting the days go by, once in a lifetime.

*   *   *

At first there was very little to be seen, on the way to the western peninsular promontory, although once we got away from Nuku'alofa, the enchantment began to catch us up- a wonderful variety of foliage, villages, and people. Somehow, there was the eternal sameness of all tropical islands here, the whole light and joyous spirit of diversion, a *Forever Young* playground where no one had ever needed to work. Every boy, on reaching the age of eighteen, was given a half acre of land, and three acres of bush, in his own earthly paradise, in his own village, and a few coconut trees, a few fowls and pigs. For the rest, the people danced and sang, and strummed softly on their guitars. They feasted, and played football and cricket on smooth green glades in the centre of every little hamlet. There was a roughly marked-out tennis-court, with a fishing net hung across. As we drove through evening villages, people laughed and sang and called to each other in vowel-drowned words, as though garden parties were forever in session.

But, also on the way West, we came to Kolovai, the place of the gigantic trees of feathery *casuarina*, where thousands of great sacred Pacific flying foxes quarreled and defecated and dozed upside down in sheets of black drapery, and then, at precisely five o'clock every evening, took wing, and rose in a screaming cloud from the trees, like a cyclone of broken umbrellas. Black banshees with membranous wings extinguished all the light in the sky, until the streams of bats separated into long flowing tributaries, dividing away in the dusk. They would fly forty or fifty miles in the night, to islands and plantations more than twenty miles away, to feed on the bananas and mangoes and pineapples of the unhappy islanders, some of whom would lose entire crops, because only the King was allowed to hunt them. They would return shrieking and squabbling at dawn, to compete for the uppers branches, shoving and biting the toes of those already occupying the choice places they wanted, until they let go.

We turned, through the deepest potholes on the planet, headed for the western coast, and the Good Samaritan.

It was probably just as well that we arrived on sunset. A big rosy peach tumescence, with small silver stars behind, sank like the first stab of love, leaving a bloodstained rag on the long Southern Sea horizon. The white coral beach was stunning, and utterly deserted, but the Good Samaritan was also utterly deserted. It was soon pitch-black, except for the hurricane lanterns. It was just us and the bats, and the ten-dollar Australian filet mignon out of the freezer, which cost the same as our thatched *fale*, every night. Thirty bucks a day for Paradise, including animal protein.

And that was the other reason that it was just as well that we arrived on sunset. Robyn and I lived to be close to nature. Here, there were more species inside our shotgun shack, than out of doors. We fell asleep to the chirping clicks of a gecko, inches from our heads. He seemed to have a little trouble keeping up with the mosquitoes and ants, but they were assisted with enthusiasm by the gigantic spiders in all four corners of the fale. The cockroaches that came out at night, were only remnants in the morning, recycled by swarms of other insects I had been previously unfamiliar with. But the apex of the food chain, and the major nocturnal celebrants in our hut were the rats above us, who were considerate enough to wait until we were almost asleep, before beginning their roof parties. *Good Samaritans.*

In the mornings you could have either eggs or pancakes, but the choice wasn't ours. A horse and cart clip-clopped by, carrying copra. I worked on my shell collection, wading out to the reef, into brilliant pools of vivid purple and green rocks, as clear as jewels, with pink branching corals and feathery green seaweed. Tropical fish and sea anemones, and delicate silk jellyfish puffed out thick with water, were carried out and in by the tremendous roar of jade-throated waves, and then falling into laughing white foam. We had bucket baths, and Robyn did our laundry in the same plastic receptacles under the coconut trees. *Let the days go by.*

In the evening, costumed Tongan friends arrived, singing and playing their ukuleles, same as it ever was. One evening, we met an American, who, unlike most Americans enjoyed opera, but was, like most Americans, strong of opinion. He told us of his contempt for Pavarotti. I remonstrated. He presented his argument. But this was not the place to argue, as we were all immersed in one last trance before having to awake back into the real world. This was not the place for conformity. This was only the place to ask the question. *How did I get here?*

The next morning, after the unpredictable breakfast, I left my beautiful house and my beautiful wife, washing our beautiful clothes in our beautiful bucket under our beautiful coconut palms, and headed south, along the beach. I was alone on a ribbon of white powder, high green symphonic sentinel fronds and ferns on my left, and the turquoise and white foam ocean moving unsteadily under my feet, on the right.

Three beaches and as many rock promontories down, or perhaps it was four, lying on the firm sand, was a translucent castaway from the deep, glistening in the sun. Its Italian name had given us the term for fine bone china, vitrified and resonant. *Porcellana.* It didn't look as if it belonged here, but of course it did, more than I. I picked up the most spectacular gigantic spotted cowrie. The underside looked like a long toothed vulva. As I placed it in my daypack, there was movement in the corner of our eyes.

I turned to find a young boy, sitting at the end of a long shadow from the curved coconut palm protruding onto the sand. He looked like the kind of child they turned into deities or sun kings- big voluminous dark eyes, receding fine hair, poised carriage, serene countenance. Except that he was playing with a metal and plastic toy crane-excavator twice his height, and producing the noise that went along with the real ones. It was emblazoned with the name of the manufacturer. *Tonka.* Maybe it should have said *Tonga,* but it didn't. And then I caught another movement, not far from the first one. A man with sunglasses, khaki shorts, a T-shirt that said *sunbuns,* armed with a leashed corgi. I must have looked puzzled.

"King's grandson." He said. "Prince. Someday king." And then I realized whose beach I had just committed a capital offense. But no one seemed offended, and I played with the future king of Tonga's Tonka, and the once and future king.

His grandfather was like a big version of the gecko on the wall of our beautiful home. He seemed slow and impassive, like he was missing thyroid hormone but, behind the heavy eyelids and broad mandible and gravel voice, His Majesty King Tāufaʻāhau Tupou IV, wore the crown of coconuts and cannibals, on a first-class throne. *And it is, it is a glorious thing, to be a Pirate King.*

All foreign dignitaries that desired an audience had to wear a striped morning coat and silk hat. He once told a visiting Soviet naval captain that he wanted a 'titchy guitar from Hawaii.' The information was recorded on his KGB file, and because every visiting Russian brought one, the King's titchy guitar collection eventually contained over a hundred specimens.

He stretched the 180 meridian eastwards around his kingdom, enabling Tongan time to be 13 hours ahead of Greenwich, instead of 11 hours behind, allowing his subjects to be the first in the world to greet the new day. Taufa'ahau wore his favorite leather jacket to state events, even though he was over four hundred pounds, and the temperatures were tropical.

Fua'amotu International airport was closed one day a week to allow him to ride his custom-built bicycle up and down the runways. He had a gold watch on each wrist, a pair of glasses in each breast pocket, and two canes on either side of his waddle.

Taufa'ahau was a progressive sovereign, as far as medieval megaton monarchs go. He monetized the economy, and enabled commoner access to increasing material wealth, education, health care, and overseas travel.

But he wasn't without controversy. Taufa'ahau considered making the country a nuclear waste disposal site, sold Tongan Protected Persons Passports to shady outsiders, including Ferdinand and Imelda Marcos, resulting in the naturalization of the purchasers and sparking ethnicity-based concerns within Tonga, with the proceeds deposited in a US bank account; registered foreign ships engaged in illegal activities, including shipments to al-Qaeda; claimed geo-orbital satellite slots from which the revenue went to Princess Royal; held a long-term charter on an unusable Boeing 757 sidelined in Auckland Airport, resulting in the collapse of Royal Tongan Airlines; built an airport hotel and potential casino with an Interpol-accused criminal; approved a factory for exporting cigarettes to China against the advice of Tongan medical officials; imprisoned pro-democracy leaders and imposed press censorship; and lost 26 million dollars to Jesse Bogdonoff, a financial adviser who called himself the king's Court Jester. Two hundred years after Captain Cook's observation that commoners were required to touch the sole of the chief's foot as they ambled past, King Taufa'ahau had definitely touched them back.

One could be forgiven for thinking that Tongans were dimwitted bovinoids. Paul Theroux had little respect, considering them *big people with flimsy houses and island structures, not really cooperative, bereft of enterprise, slow of speech, casual of manner, indifferent to schedule, unable or unwilling to anticipate, physically clumsy, no manual dexterity, dropped things, forgot things broke promises, a society used to dealing with beachcombers, who had all the time in the world; every other day late, unapologetic, envious, abrupt, lazy, mocking, quarrelsome, sadistic to their children. Spat and swore.*

But that wasn't the way that Robyn and I had found them at all, five years after he had made these pronouncements. The locals we had met, outside the Good Samaritan, were Good Samaritans, and invited us home, for earth oven *umus*, on festive mats laid out under their mango trees.

It began with a *faikava*, the kava ceremony presided over by the *toua*, a young single woman server, unrelated to anyone else in our *kalapu*. She stirred the kava in the *kumete*, as big as a round sponge bath, legs and all carved from a single tree trunk, enameled by many years of use. The peppery dirtwater that she had poured into polished *ipu* coconut cups, were passed hand-to-hand to those sitting farthest away, in rounds. We spoke of politics and rugby and traditions, until the jokes and guitars and smiles and Robyn and the big women came out, flowers and maidenhair ferns in their maiden hair.

Then the banana leaves were raked off the umu, and the steam came up off the hot stones, together with the fish and chicken, and taro and yams and breadfruit, and the *palusami*, my favorite Polynesian dish in the world, made from chopped taro leaves and coconut milk and, here in Tonga, with tinned corned beef imported from New Zealand. There were hot dogs, go figure, because what the men took off the spit, what had originally arrived under white muslin off the flatbed truck, already gutted and stuffed with herbs and lemons, was a tremendous roast suckling pig, or two, or more- not the gaunt hump-backed long-nosed swine brought by Cook, but their thick blubbered porker hybrid descendents that had turned the Friendly Isles into one big big pig farm. One of the men would take the butt end of his large knife and smash the thick orange crackling around the throat of each hog, and we would tear it with our teeth and fingers, and eat it with salt and saliva. We got pig grease all over the back of a truck that we helped push out of the sand, and returned to our mats back under the tree, for papaya and watermelon and the young girls singing and dancing for us, advancing, retreating, beckoning. And the next day was an even bigger feast, with even bigger pigs.

The owners of the Good Samaritan gave us their big car for a day, and Robyn and I made the grand tour of Tongatapu, *behind the wheel of a large automobile*. Most of what we saw was about what men and water can do to volcanic rock. The waves that crashed into the reef near Houma village drove the Southern Sea up through the natural channels of the Mapu'a 'a Vaea blowholes, high into the air with every surge. The Tongans had two kings, one earthly, who did the hard work of government, and a heavenly king, the *Tui Tonga*, who was worshipped as a god. They were buried in great rectangular raised enclosures of rough-hewn fitted slabs of coral, 150 feet long by 90 feet wide and three-terraces high. Robyn and I found two of them near the village of Niu toua, hidden in tangled thickets of low bush, and worn by trees and traffic and time. Another structure, the Trilithon consisted of two massive limestone coral uprights, between 30 to 40 tons each and twenty feet high, linked by a lintel, built by a people who were supposedly unfamiliar with mechanics.

We stopped to ask directions from a large lady holding a blue and yellow and white umbrella, under the white and powder blue vertical wood slatted Friendly Islands Marketing Cooperative *Maketa Iki* Fish Market. She knew of the location of the monument, but not whose landing it commemorated. Perhaps it was *faka Tonga*, the Tongan way, the attitude to outsiders reflected in a history of no invasion, no occupation, no colonization, no immigrants, no investors, and no desire to look beyond. We were *palangis*, sky-bursters, and even the kids I invited and encouraged to listen to the music on my Walkman, did so out of courtesy, rather than any real interest. Still, you would think she might have known.

'Here stood formerly the great banyan "Malumalu 'o Fulilangi" or Captain Cook's tree under the branches of which the celebrated navigator came ashore on his way to visit Pau, the Tu'i Tonga (sacred King of Tonga) on the occasion of the 'Inasi (presentation of the first fruits) in the year 1777.'

*   *   *

'Letting the days go by, letting the days go by, letting the days go by, once in a lifetime
Letting the days go by, letting the days go by, letting the days go by, once in a lifetime...'

Talking Heads, *Once in a Lifetime* 1981

The crush on Queen Salote wharf was crushing. I suppose Robyn and I could have flown to Vava'u, but at this stage in our lives, we had more time than money, I was letting the days go by, and a trip like this was a unique *once in a lifetime* cultural experience.

You could barely see the red and white hull of the inter-island ferry, for the boat traffic and human commotion surrounding her. When the boarding 'process' was almost over, her name emerged from behind the cargo nets and shouting. *Olavaha*. She was slow, uncomfortable and 'bobbed like a cork,' but she had made the weekly northern trip through the Ha'apai group, and further on to the Port of Refuge, in Vava'u's principal village of Neiafu, for the previous eight years, in a mostly dependable manner. And she was cheap. Her replacement nine years later, the *MV Princess Ashika*, would sink in Ha'apai on August 5, 2009, with the loss of at least a hundred passengers. No one really knew how many were crowded below decks went she went down, before midnight, but they would have had no chance. Cargo had shifted in high seas. The only survivors had been sleeping on deck, as we were.

The *Olavahu* made several outer island stops, to more crushes of boats five deep, passing cargo and commotion and children, and gigantic upside down coir rope-bound sea turtles, from hand to hand, to upper deck. We stopped in Lifuka, the main island of Ha'apai, for half a day, to unload and reload. It was a garden of glades under a blinding sun, less than a mile wide, and less than ten long, facing west and east, steeped in sunrise and sunset, perfectly flat, and hemmed round with white sands. Lifuka had one little street, bordered with breadfruit and mangoes and coconut palms and feathery iron-bark trees, and a handful of brightly painted shops, all closed on Sunday. Robyn and I encountered an old woman, smiling a Southern Sea smile.

"Ma lo laa." She said. *It is good to be alive.* And it was, as it would have been for our castaway as well, in 1806.

Half past us, she turned, and smiled again.

"Afa atu." She said. *Love to you- health.*

The sun set to our port side, and rose on our starboard. The night on deck had been cool, almost cold. But Robyn and I had our sleeping bags, and each other, and the ship's funnels, and two hundred Tongans to keep us warm. We awoke to new islands, with four hundred foot cliffs sprinkled with red soil, and green vegetation where it had managed to find a foothold, above the deep black caves and hollows below. They were like chains of tall cakes, freshly turned out of their tins. We steered through the narrow strips of blue and white spray between them, and the clouds of sea birds about the base of every precipice. In some Asiatic languages, green and blue are one color, and should have been that way here. It was a brilliant day.

"Let's live here." I said to Robyn. But of course, we couldn't.

The cliffs gave way to clumps of trees, running down to the

Neiafu's harbor, the whitewashed church at the top, and a quay thronged with *lava-lavas* and anticipation. We watched a ghostly white muslin-wrapped body float off the lower deck of the *Olavahu*, hardly touching the hundreds of swaying arms above which it was suspended in space. There were large numbers of large women crying on the wharf, and it made a hurried retreat into the covered bed of a lorry, to escape their grief.

"What does your shirt mean?" Asked a voice to my right. I turned to find a young Swiss fellow, pointing to my chest.

"AMFYOYO." I said. "It's an acronym."

"What does it stand for?" He asked. I told him it was the parting message that every Critical Care physician had for his replacement, at the end of every shift. "Adios. You're on your own."

He started to ask about the other letters, and thought better of it. Which began our association.

Jean Pierre and his wife, Maria, were from Montreux, taking the long way home, like Robyn and I. They knew of a place to stay, with big fresh rooms and ocean views, on the hillside. There were no cars to be seen in Neiafu. We hoisted our packs, and walked it. The thin, nervous middle-aged German who greeted us, had come to paradise to unwind, but it hadn't seemed to be working out that well for him. He was too hardwired to use the software. Just reading the list of rules on the back of our door would have consumed the entire diversion. There were forces outside his control, however, that would make our stay more interesting. Not the mosquitoes, which we expected, although not in the numbers that filled our dusks and dawns.

Maria's scream announced the first *molokau*, writhing on her mosquito net. It was a foot long, the size of a small snake, and jet-black. His head rose off the mesh, before vanishing under their cupboards, like the evil alien he was. He was fast.

"Giant South Pacific centipede." I said. "They like to hide in dark, wet places."

"Are they dangerous?" Asked Jean Pierre.

"Very painful bite." I said. "Leaves two holes. Can cause temporary paralysis. Plus, they eat the geckos that eat the mosquitoes." Everyone was careful how and where we walked from then on, particularly at night.

It was not the only poison in paradise. Some had been moored in the Port of Refuge for months, avoiding the hurricanes in the Southern Sea; others for years, avoiding the ones in their lives. Bandana'd and barefoot Boat People, on *Beneteaus* rather than barges, bobbed within the offshore refugee camp at the end of the world, *Rolling Stones* and rolling cigarettes.

Yachties wanted to be apart and together at the same time, losing speed and social connectivity with each tacking manoeuvre, and futilely beating against the winds of their inevitable extinction. They had set out to become their own Robinson Crusoe, but stopped short of making the commitment, shipwrecked on their fears of becoming shipwrecked. Instead of landing, coveting, claiming, conquering, converting, they stayed in their confined cabins in their crossings in their cyclones, counting coins, avoiding the end of the world, which they had gambled would occur somewhere they were not. But there was no neutral ground on or off the water. They would either have to contend with the natives they had fooled themselves into thinking they were seeking, or their own culture, which they had fooled themselves into thinking they were escaping. When they battened down, they were only locking their demons inside. *Very painful bite. Leaves two holes. Can cause temporary paralysis.*

Still, if there was going to be an end to the world, there would be no more perfect place to meet it, than the Port of Refuge in Vava'u.

Our second day in Neiafu, Jean Pierre and Maria and Robyn and I rented a red Isuzu jeep. We drove out past the refrozen rethawed imported provisioners of Burns Philip and Morris Hedstrom, to beautiful beaches, a church that could have been a Spanish mission except for the *Koelaro Holulaumalie koe sirsi o tanga 1929* over the lintel, and a small cove, where we met a Vanilla farmer, and helped push out his small boat, loaded to the gunnels with drums of diesel, out towards his plantation island. And we ultimately came, right on course, to two young boys peeling the shavings of long yams lengthwise with big knives, which led to another kava ceremony, an old man seated in the shade, in a frayed pandanus *taovala* cummerbund, who indicated with his loaded cigarette holder, to where the roast suckling pig would come. *Same as it ever was.* Much later, we performed an impromptu concert on the village wooden slit gong, and waved to the pigtailed girls in our rearview mirror, on the way back to our hilltop refuge.

> 'If a boat ends up on a reef you don't blame the reef; you don't blame the boat; you don't blame the wind; you don't blame the waves; you blame the captain.'
>
> Tongan Proverb

*   *   *

> 'If the blood in the water is light, it is the shark's blood and the man has won; if the blood in the water is dark, it is the man's blood, and the shark has won.'
>
> Tongan Proverb

"Just hold your breath." He said. I asked him for how long.
"Until you're there." He said. I asked him how I would know.
"You'll be out of breath." He said.
I lined up on the pinkish rock in front of me, and the black

shadow ten feet below. We had come off our boat on the west wall of the north end of Nuapupu Island, a few miles southwest from our hilltop refuge in Neiafu. Robyn had decided to stay on board. She was always the smart one.

"Don't worry." He said. "There's plenty of time." But I wasn't worried about time. I was worried about space, and swimming blind through fifty feet of tunneled darkness, into a cave that was supposed to have air inside. The penalty for failure wouldn't be pretty.

"What about Captain Luce?" I asked.

"Who?" He said. In 1865 a Captain Luce, of the *HMS Esk*, had succeeded in entering the cave, but rose too soon on leaving, lacerating his back badly, against the sharp underwater coral spears. It took him a few days to die.

"Swim towards the light." He said, and jack-knifed down towards the entrance. The instruction was not quite reassuring. I bit into my snorkel, and drank in the only lungful of air I would be allowed to take onboard, for this long day's journey into night. My own movement followed his fins.

The inside of the tunnel was shot through with schools of tiny blue and black fish, jostling each other, and me. Just as I thought I was going to suffocate in one large saltwater gasp, my horizons widened out and up, onto a pink volcanic opening arching into a high blue and ochre roof. The only light was the filtered cerulean luminosity that had accompanied me through the entrance, like the glow of a nuclear reactor, the most astounding and ethereal radiance I had ever seen. The seal inside the cave was so tight that, when the swells rolled in, the water compressed the air briskly enough to create a fogbank. As the swell retreated, the air clarified to crystal, just as fast. It was sublime.

"Welcome to Mariner's Cave." He said. And I thought of him, our castaway. On December 1, 1806, William Mariner was only fifteen years old when he witnessed the captain of his ship, the *Port-au-Prince*, clubbed to death, stripped, and left lying in the sand. He watched the rest of his twenty-two crewmates outnumbered, overwhelmed, and massacred in the swift and brutal attack, beaten so badly about the head, as to be unrecognizable, before being laid out naked on deck, in regular order, to be counted, and then thrown overboard.

Will was led around unclothed and barefoot under a blistering sun, while the Tongans compared his skin to that of a scraped hog, spat at him, poked him with sticks, and threw coconuts at his head, until he was cut in several places, and led away faster than the soreness of his feet would allow him to walk.

When he finally stopped, it was to looked upon the short squat naked man responsible for the slaughter, seated with a blood-soaked seaman's jacket thrown over one shoulder, and an ironwood club splattered with blood and brains resting on the other. He appeared to Will to be about fifty years of age on both sides, with one eye blinking faster than the other, above a convulsing mouth.

How he ended up here on the *Port-au-Prince*, on the sands of Lifuka, the main island of Ha'apai, had been quite different from how Robyn and I arrived on the *Olavahu*. Will had signed on as a ship's clerk to the privateer at the age of thirteen, during the war against Napoleon. The commander, Captain Duck, had been given a 'letter of marque' from the King, permitting him to seize the cargo of any French or Spanish ship on the high seas, and loot any of their settlements along the way. The *Port-au-Prince* was 500 tons, with 24 long nine and twelve pound guns, and 8 twelve-pound carronades on the quarterdeck. Her owner, a Mr. Robert Bent of London, had given Duck a twofold commission- to pirate any New World Spanish ships and, failing that endeavor, to sail into the Southern Sea in search of whales to be rendered for their oil. They sailed on February 12, 1805, in a rough Atlantic crossing that brought them off the coast of Brazil by April, and around Cape Horn in July. They captured a number of ships, but little of value, and had a similar lack of success with the whales. When Captain Duck died of an injury, the whaling master, Mr.

Brown took over command, and embarked the *Port-au-Prince* from Hawaii in September, on a heading to Tahiti. He missed it, and instead sailed on westward, toward the Tonga islands, arriving in Ha'apai on November 9, 1806, almost two years since departing England, and leaking badly. It didn't get any better.

In the evening, a number of natives came on board with a large barbecued hog, and a quantity of ready dressed yams, as a present. With them came a Hawaiian named Tooi Tooi, who knew a little English from his former experience aboard an American ship, and convinced the ship's company that the locals were favorably disposed to them. Tonga was named the Friendly Islands by Captain Cook, on his first visit there in 1777. He had arrived during the 'Inasi Festival,' the annual donation of first fruit to the Tu'i Tonga, and invited to the festivities. What he didn't know, and what Will Mariner found out only later, was that, beneath their seemingly genial reception, the chiefs had been maturing a plot to murder him and seize his ship, but could not agree on a plan.

The few Hawaiians from the *Port-au-Prince* were not as reassured that they had weighed anchor in truly Friendly Islands, however, and advised Mr. Brown of their opinion that the Tongans were hostile, and to keep a watchful eye. Mr. Brown, to his ultimate detriment, disregarded this sage admonition. The next day he was invited ashore by the 300 natives that had swarmed the boat. For him, and most of his crew, it was their last voyage.

The naked Ha'apai chief who would determine Will Mariner's fate was Finou 'Ulukalala the First. He called to one of the Hawaiians to fire a musket at one of the Tongans high in the ship's rigging. The fall broke the man's legs and fractured his skull. When Will later asked him how he could be so cruel, Finou laughed, and explained that he had been a lowly cook, and that his life or death had been of no consequence to society.

But Will was destined to be of major consequence to society, and to Finou. Over the next three days, the ship was stripped of her iron, had her guns and powder removed, and was burnt to the waterline. The guns would help Finou consolidate his rule over the rest of Tonga, and Will would help Finou accomplish this, for which was ultimately given the name Toki 'Ukamea. *Iron Axe.*
Over the next four years, Will would teach Finou about his culture, about how taking apart a watch doesn't guarantee the ability to reassemble it, and about money.

'If money were made of iron and could be converted into knives, axes and chisels there would be some sense in placing a value on it; but as it is, I see none. If a man has more yams than he wants, let him exchange some of them away for pork. Certainly money is much handier and more convenient but then, as it will not spoil by being kept, people will store it up instead of sharing it out as a chief ought to do, and thus become selfish. I understand now very well what it is that makes the white men so selfish — it is this money!'

For his part, Finou taught Will about his culture, about his love of cooked dog meat, particularly the neck and hind quarters, and the legend of the cave inside which I was treading water in. *A young man chasing a turtle observed it dive, without surfacing. He followed it into an underwater cave of considerable size, with no outlet but the one he had entered by. The man forgot about the cave until, some months later, when the tyrannical king, who mistreated his subjects, condemned another chief and all his family to be drowned at sea, for opposing him. The young man was secretly in love with one of the condemned man's daughters, a maiden who he would otherwise be deemed socially inadequate to marry. Thinking quickly, he declared himself to her, and found that she had also been secretly in love with him. No one knew what had become of her until, one day, a boating party saw what appeared to be the ghost of girl, rising from the heart of the waves, before once again disappearing. The young man had kept her hidden for several months, bringing food, water, bedding for the rough stone couch at one end of the cave, even torches safely wrapped in leaves, until he was able to arrange to be sent on an expedition to Fiji. Outward bound from Vava'u, he stopped his canoes, leaving his men perplexed as he dived into the water, only to reappear with his maiden fair, and off they sailed to Fiji, where they lived happily, until the tyrant's death.*

There was indeed a stone couch at the end of the cave. There was also enough evocative power in the legend, to inspire Byron's use of it.

> 'The first yet voiceless wind to urge the wave
> All gently to refresh the thirsty cave,
> Where sat the Songstress with the stranger boy,
> Who taught her Passion's desolating joy...
>
> The sun-born blood suffused her neck, and threw
> O'er her clear nut-brown skin a lucid hue,
> Like coral reddening through the darkened wave,
> Which draws the diver to the crimson cave.
> Such was this daughter of the southern seas...'
>
> Lord Byron, *The Island*

But inside Mariner's Cave, I wasn't thinking about Lord Byron. I wasn't thinking about Will Mariner. I was thinking about the acoustics. Everyone that had come into the cave from our boat had left, including our guide, who told me to come when I was ready. But I wasn't ready. Inside me, inside the cave, I had a tribute I needed to get out, to the love that inspired the legend. And to Luciano Pavoratti, whose good name required a little rehabilitation, from the beating it received at the hands of the less than good Samaritan American, at the Good Samaritan. And I sent Nessun dorma, from Puccini's *Turandot*, ricocheting off the walls of the cave.

> 'Tu pure, O Principessa,
> Nella tua fredda stanza... tremano d'amoree di speranza.
> Ma il mio mistero è chiuso in me, il nome mio nessun saprà...
> Sulla tua bocca lo dirò quando la luce splenderà
> Ed il mio bacio scioglierà il silenzio che ti fa mia...
> Vincerò.'

As I sang, I thought of the riddles that the princess to which she had demanded Turandot's answers. The first, *'What is born each night and dies each dawn?'* could have only been 'hope.' The answer to the second, *'What flickers red and warm like a flame, but is not fire?'* I remembered as 'blood.' But then, I never got to the third riddle, did I? Because I also remembered, that, while I was having the most wonderful time of my life singing operatic arias at the top of my lungs inside Mariner's Cave, everyone on the boat outside Mariner's Cave was waiting for me to emerge. I had no way of knowing, of course, that Robyn, especially, was flickering red and warm like a flame and, in fact, was afire, up top, and was almost beating the skipper around the head, in her frantic attempt to get him, or anyone else, to swim back into the cave, to see if I was still alive.

I bit into my snorkel, and drank in the only lungful of air I would be allowed to take onboard, for this long day's return journey into daylight.

"Just hold your breath." He said. I asked him for how long.

"Until you're there." He said. I asked him how I would know.

"You'll be out of breath." He said.

I swam towards the light. Just as I thought I was going to suffocate in one large saltwater gasp, my horizons widened out and up, and I surfaced onto an ocean of cursing and screaming. It was a rough ride back to the hilltop.

There was no way that Robyn and I, nor Jean Pierre and Maria, as couples or even collectively, could have afforded to rent a sailboat. The islands around Vava'u were the most pristine examples of idyllic South Pacific paradise that we would ever see. And it almost didn't happen that we saw them. A wayward Spanish couple fixed that for us. We met them outside the Morris Hedstrom corned beef concession one morning. They told us they had a sailboat and, for fifteen dollars a head, they would take us on a day trip around the islands, and include a fish barbeque in the price. We quickly agreed.

Nothing quite prepared us for the experience, however. They had left Spain some fifteen years earlier, and had been trying for almost as long, to make enough money to sail home. I did the math in my head, and decided they would likely be here awhile. Their sails were original, but now the same Joseph coat of many colors as their frayed and tattered clothing, patched and quilted into a psychedelic rainbow of their nautical and personal history. It was as if Picasso had painted their trip on their canvas. But, as thin and gaunt as they were, they were also as good as their word, and we were once again the pirates, siphoning off Spanish treasure, at two bucks an hour. They sailed us through the most magnificent tropical dreamworld, of palms and frangipanis and clear liquid lagoons, to islands like little pancakes of white sand and whiter surf, where forests and other caves and serenity waited. They juggled coconuts, like the Tongan women used to, and caught parrotfish the same colors as their sails, with their held breaths and spear guns, and grilled them over an open fire on some secluded beach, on an island without a name. We were all deliriously and deliciously happy.

Live like a captain. Play like a pirate.

'Letting the days go by, let the water hold me down
Letting the days go by, water flowing underground
Into the blue again after the money's gone
Once in a lifetime, water flowing underground'
Talking Heads, *Once in a Lifetime*

*   *   *

*   *   *

They sent a dump truck. We certainly hadn't expected that. Robyn and I were back out at Fua'amotu International airport, on a day when the King had parked his bicycle. We were scheduled to leave Tongatapu, back to Fiji, on to Canada, into the blue again after the money's gone. It was time for us to 'get on with it,' get on with the rest of our lives. But time, as it turned out, was holding us, and holding us back, after all.

No one saw it coming. From where we were, at the ticket counter, more importantly, nothing was leaving. Air Pacific, Fiji's national airline, had just experienced a wildcat pilot's strike, and we were aground in the Abode of Love.

The fat Flying Dutchman ahead of us in the queue hadn't started there. He had pushed his way there, because of his obviously greater importance, relative to ours. He was an important businessman, he said, waving his obviously important arms around the solid head cube of muscle, on the other side of the desk. He needed to get out of Tonga, and he needed to get out today, and what was the solid head cube of muscle going to do about it. The solid head cube of muscle smiled. The fat Flying Dutchman wasn't flying today. In fact, it wasn't clear when any of us would fly. The strike could last several weeks. And the only place any of us were going, was the International Dateline. Not the dateline itself, the International Dateline Hotel. The fat Flying Dutchman was angry that he had just come from there. Robyn and I were delighted, that our trip had just been bumped into business class. It still might all be worth the price of the flight cancellation.

And that's where the dump truck came onto the scene. The fat Flying Dutchman had already secured his taxi back to the Dateline, and he wasn't in the mood to share his ride. Robyn and I may have been promoted to the best hotel in the country to wait out the flight delay, but no one had told Air Pacific that they owed us a deluxe way to get there. We piled our packs in the back of the dump truck, and roared the 35 kilometers back into and through the vowel-saturated streets of Nuku'alofa, to beat the fat Flying Dutchman, by a hair. It seems that his taxi driver was on a meter, and in no particular hurry, given the fact that there were no passengers at the airport from any incoming flight, whereas out dump truck driver had other places to go, and people to meet. Call it differential motivation. Of course this didn't matter to the fat Flying Dutchman. He pushed his way in front of us again, at the Dateline Hotel reception, because of his obviously greater importance, relative to ours. He was an important businessman, he said, waving his obviously important arms around the solid head cube of muscle, on the other side of the desk. The solid head cube of muscle gave him back his room, but it wouldn't be cleaned for several hours, as they hadn't expected his return. From the look on the face of the solid head cube of muscle, no one was likely to be in a hurry to accommodate him, likely because of their recent experience with him, whereas Robyn and I were brand new appreciative faces, and our room was ready for us, because Air Pacific was paying.

"Up deah." The solid head cube of muscle pointed. "Turd floah, tree-too-tree." And we carried our own bags up the stairs.

What Air Pacific was paying for was not only the room, but the meals as well. Which was about to sound the death knell for Air Pacific. For on the menu, among more plebian business fare, was an item that, since my marriage to a beautiful New Zealander, I had come to appreciate as one of the four basic Kiwi food groups. Crayfish. Big, tender, succulent, delicious lemon and butter and sauvignon blanc-compatible crayfish. At the International Dateline Hotel, although crayfish was only listed on the lunch and dinner menus, our first discovery was that, as long as Air Pacific was paying, they would serve it for breakfast as well. Robyn and I ate big crayfish for breakfast at a table by the pool, next to the fat Flying Dutchman, whose breakfast was toast.

If the time in Greenwich was mean time, the time at the Dateline, on the opposite side of the world was not only kind, it was fabulous. Every day, Robyn and I would wake up and have crayfish for breakfast. We would swim in the pool, and lounge around the pool, until it was time for lunch. We had the crayfish. In the afternoon, we would swim in the pool, or lounge around the pool, until it was time for dinner. Then we would have the crayfish. And so it went for us, aground in the Abode of Love. *Letting the days go by, letting the days go by, letting the days go by, once in a lifetime.*

Every morning we would check in with the front desk staff, to see how the pilot strike was doing. Every day we would find out the pilot strike was going well. And we would retreat back to the seemingly unending pleasures of swimming and sunbathing and crayfish.

One morning we went to the Friendly Islands Marketing Cooperative, to look at their handicrafts. In a country that produced nothing but banana-shaped postage stamps, Protected Persons Passports, and expatriate Tongans, handicrafts were the biggest local business going. The bone and wood carving, weaving, and tapa cloth were finely done, but the baskets were truly amazing, and Robyn and I bought two, to take home. Which was exactly the problem because, after a week of indulgence at the International Dateline Hotel, we were still castaways, and not only becoming shipwrecks, but at risk of becoming truly amazing basket cases. I couldn't swim another length, check out another beach towel, or look at another crayfish. In Polynesian, Tonga meant 'south,' where nothing and everything appeared to be headed. The only fun left was watching the fat Flying Dutchman decompensate slightly ahead of us.

And then, just when we thought we were marooned forever, the word came one evening that Air Pacific was sending a special charter flight next morning, to rescue us from paradise. At dinner we celebrated with crayfish. Next morning we bid farewell to the reception staff, and climbed into the back of our dump truck, for the return journey to the airport. Robyn had suggested that I dress up, 'in case of an upgrade.' I told her we didn't stand a chance, but I was wrong. Beyond the ticket counter, beyond the duty free, was a ramp to business class, and a new beginning.

Things didn't go too well for the Dateline, or the Abode of Love, after we left. Thirteen years after our salvation, the International Dateline Hotel was sold to the People's Republic of China. Five new clocks appeared behind the front desk, the biggest one in the center showing Beijing time. The Chinese manager was unavailable, and spoke no English. The swimming pool was closed because of an outbreak of disease. It was apparently bought to introduce the Tongans to the concept of Chinese fishing rights, and anger.

In 2006 riots broke out in downtown Nuku'alofa, killing six people and destroying eighty per cent of the central business district.

Pule'anga Fakatu'i 'o Tonga, a kingdom which had never been invaded, occupied, colonized, immigrated to, or invested in, which had no desire to look beyond its own archipelago of 176 islands scattered over 700,000 square kilometers of remote Southern Sea, was about to have its vowels replaced by glottal stops and palatal glides and alveolar sibilants and tones and retroflex consonants, and its *pa'anga* currency replaced by *renminbi*.

Back in the *palangi* sky-bursting Business Class, Robyn and I

were seated across from the fat Flying Dutchman.
"How did you get up here?" He asked.
Almost unconsciously, from my daypack, I pulled out my translucent castaway from the deep, the most spectacular gigantic spotted cowrie.
"Where do you get that?" He asked.
"King." I said.
We had the crayfish.

'No plane on Sunday
 Maybe be one come Monday
 Just a hopeless situation
 Make the best of it's all you can do
 'til they get through'
    Jimmy Buffett, *No Plane on Sunday*

*   *   *

Fara Way

Rotuma

'Their bodies were curiously marked with the figures of men, dogs, fishes and birds upon every part of them; so that every man was a moving landscape.'

George Hamilton, *Pandora*'s surgeon, 1791

The whole scene was a moving landscape, directly under us, just over two hundred years after Captain Edwards had arrived on the *HMS Pandora*. He had been looking for the *Bounty*. We would find another.

The pilot of our Britten-Norman banked off the huge cloud he had found over six hundred kilometers north of the rest of Fiji, and sliced down into it sideways, like he was cutting a grey soufflé. Nothing could have prepared us for the magnificence that opened up below, with the dispersal of the last gasping mists.

A fringing reef, barely holding back the eternal explosions of rabid frothing foam and every blue in the reflected cosmos, encircled every green in nature. On the edge of both creations were the most spectacular beaches in the Southern Sea. Captain Edwards had called it *Grenville Island*. Two hundred years earlier, it was named *Tuamoco* by de Quiros, before he went on to establish his doomed *New Jerusalem* in Vanuatu.

But that was less important for the moment. We had reestablished level flight, and were lining up on the dumbbell-shaped island's only rectangular open space, a long undulating patch of grass, between the mountains and the ocean. Hardly more than a lawn bowling pitch anywhere else, here it was the airstrip, beside which a tiny remote paradise was waving all its arms.

Our journey had started in the dark cold depths of our Vancouver Island winter. I was looking for a small diversion, on our annual southern migration to New Zealand. There was a need to be practical, because any excursion off the cheaper routes would carry penalty, in money, or time, or both. But this one looked to be the prize- an incredibly remote Polynesian Island in a Melanesian ocean, serviced by a new once weekly flight from Nandi, without too many hiccoughs or other gaseous threats to existence.

I went online. There was no accommodation. In order to visit, one needed an invitation from a local family, with whom one would stay. I went deeper, and looked up whom I might be able to contact to arrange such an indulgence. Somehow, in the deepest recesses of my desktop, I found a man who had originally come from there, and had actually settled here. I looked him up in my local directory. *Sosefo Avaiki*. I dialed his number.

"Hello." Said the voice.

"Hello." I said back, and introduced myself, and told him that I wanted to visit his island. Long pause.

"Why?" He asked.

"I hear it's a special place." I said. Longer pause.

"When do you want to go?" He asked. I told him.

"That's during Fara." He said.

"Fara?" I asked.

"Fara." He said. "No sleep." He said he'd get back to me. A month later he called, and told me it was all set. The family would meet us at the airstrip, and the flights had been approved.

"No sleep." He added.

Six months later, Robyn and I approached the Sunflower Airlines desk in Nandi, and were issued boarding passes for the once weekly flight to paradise. The plane was double-booked, which meant that half the king-sized Polynesians in the transit lounge would not be getting home for Christmas- at least not on this flight, despite being in possession of a valid ticket. The only other way was the once a month boat from Suva, a two day voyage that departed from the other side of Viti Levu. Robyn and I were lucky, perhaps we weighed less than others, on the scales they suspended us on, before issuing our cards.

From the air was the remnant of a massive volcano with many smaller cones, eight miles long and less than three wide, sixteen square miles of a larger eastern part, connected to a western peninsula by the low narrow Motusa isthmus, a few hundred feet across. The legend of its formation had come with Raho, who brought two baskets of earth from Samoa, and marked his creation with a coconut leaf, tied around a *fesi* tree. His rival's arrival came in the form of a Samoan chief named Tokainiua, who tied a drier coconut leaf around the same tree, claiming that he had been there first because his leaf was more dehydrated. Raho became so angry that he tore up chunks of the island, creating the smaller islands of Hafliua, Hatana, and Uea. Its original inhabitants had actually come from wither Melanesia or Micronesia, followed by Samoan and Tongan invasions just after de Quiros went by. The colonization is called the 'Westward Polynesian Backwash,' but there were also stories about a Chinese Junk that had also left a cargo of DNA in its wake, the Tikopians, who plundered the place, and the Niueans, who tried to introduce cannibalism, but were rebuffed.

We landed where the trees weren't, braking clumsily as we passed all the waving arms.

"Welcome to Rotuma." Said the big frizzy-haired Fijian stewardess. And we were. In spades.

Down the stairs and just beyond the stone tiki and the long variegated croton hedge and the coconut palms, was a single white Nissen pickup, a ponytail, and the biggest smile in the Southern Sea. She wore a blue shirt and a floral lava-lava, and nothing on her feet.

"Are you Robyn and Wink?" She asked. The odds were rhetorical.

"Are you Julie?" Robyn asked. She beamed.

"These are my three daughters." She said. And everyone felt like it was a homecoming, for the first time. We all piled in the back of the pickup, and the driver, a friend of the family, took off ahead of us. We bounced along the soft white coral sand road, in and out of potholes, towards Motusa village, near the narrow isthmus. There were seven districts on Rotuma, and Motusa was in Itu'ti'u. We came through another croton hedge, to a simple concrete house with an iron roof, and a full clothesline that went on forever, under the flame trees and coconut palms and breadfruit.

Julie's husband, John, was smiling as well, as he had laid out two big sharks out front, and was preparing to filet them, for our dinner. The flies were everywhere, and crazy. I didn't realize until later, that it wasn't just the sharks. Most of the biomass of Rotuma was flies.

Julie and her family had constructed two new tiny white shacks, with white vinyl siding and powder blue doors. She opened one, and invited us to put our packs inside. There was a sponge mattress on a linoleum floor. In a corner was a box covered with a lava-lava, on which sat a big yellow bouquet of flowers. On the only shelf was a bird of paradise. A pair of bare wires projected through the concrete, above the treated New Zealand pine paneling. Julie handed us two cold green coconuts. It was ecstasy.

We asked if we could go for a walk down the beach. I thought it was a polite formality, and it never occurred to me that, in an island culture so remote and isolated, the idea of separating awhile from your family, real or adopted, might ever be interpreted as antisocial behavior. But, for a brief movement, I saw a sag in Julie's smile, before it came on again, twice as bright.

"Of course." She said. "My daughters will go with you." And six brown feet led the way, six white soles spraying six small plumes of whiter sand in front of us, as we bolted for the water.

We didn't get very far. The girls watched Robyn and I wade into the lagoon, but they wouldn't swim themselves. Apparently they didn't know how. In it or on it, the Rotumans had long since turned their backs on the sea. Most of the fish they ate was out of a tin because, outside the thin reef were hundreds of miles of raging water, and only two or three seaworthy boats, whose outboards could consume a week's wage in petrol in less than an hour.

We rejoined the girls and continued towards the smoke. Young boys were eating mangos and throwing a rugby ball around, in the water. Beside them, some older ones played vollyball. But the smoke was a bit further, on the far side of the plaited-palm thatched roof, that appeared to be an outdoor kitchen.

"Picnic." Said one of the girls. "For Av mane'a."

"What's Av mane'a?" Robyn asked.

"Time to play." She said, explaining that *Av mane'a* was the hybrid traditional Rotuman and Christian harvest festival, the hottest season of the year, beginning in December and ending in mid-January. Time is spent on picnics, harvest festivals, kava drinking, playing cards, chatting, and going Fara. "Nobody works hard now, they take it easy."

Everyone in the picnic scene we entered was definitely taking it easy, especially the biggest ones, lounging half asleep on pandanus mats in the shade. The only movement in the heat was that of the food, which migrated to us, in huge portions of tuna and *poat kau* corned beef, cooked noodles and rice and *a'ana* taro, and watermelon and mangos. The flies were having their own festival on top of everything.

"Picnic." Was all one large Pickwickian Polynesian could muster, between puffs on a cigarette. Between the heat and the flies and the scenery, we didn't have much of an appetite, but it would have been impolite to refuse. We stayed long enough to show our interest and gratitude, and returned to Julie's, in time for dinner. The inside of the house had

Western furniture, but it was cooler on the pandanus mats. Julie brought out the shark and the pusilami (my favorite) and the fekei coconut milk and tapioca and taro pudding, while the girls used their pandanus fans to cool our heads, and keep away the flies. At sundown, there was a change of guard, when the mosquitoes took over. We had a quick shower, before the water supply was cut off, as it was every night, to allow the reserves to refill. Robyn and I felt momentarily refreshed, until we emerged from the shower, to as much heat and humidity as there would be every day. Except perhaps for that golden half an hour, just before sunrise, when it cooled off just enough to allow your sweat glands reserves to refill.

We said goodnight to Julie and the rest of our new family, and retired to the confined comfort of our tiny square shack. We lasted on the sponge mattress for less than five minutes, before rolling onto the only slighter cooler linoleum. The atmosphere was only marginally more breathable than that on Venus, and there would be no chance for Venus, in this atmosphere.

"Robyn?" It was Julie.

"Yes, Julie?" Said Robyn.

"Would you like a fan?" I watched the tension fall away from Robyn's grim perspiring face, replaced with the ecstatic delight she was anticipating, in having some moving air. I looked up at the two bare wires, protruding from the concrete, and thanked whoever had put them there.

"That would be wonderful." She said. And Julie, true to her word, handed Robyn a fan. A spade-shaped, tightly woven pandanus fan. I watched her face drop, as she thanked Julie, and began the repetitive wrist motion that would accompany her through the next week, even when she was asleep. I would watch, transfixed, as Robyn became Rotuman, able to fan herself continuously, while comatose. In the ultimate paradise of heat and flies, it was a primary habitat adaptation but an essential survival skill.

"Robyn?" It was Julie again.

"Yes Julie?" Said Robyn.

"You know tonight is the first night of Fara." She said.

"Fara?" Robyn Asked.

"Fara." Said Julie. "So much fun." And she was gone. And then, for an hour or so, so were we.

My eyes were just beginning to wobble, and then I heard it, just once.

Strummummummummummumm.

*   *   *

'Untie the dove cord; when it is free it sings'
Rotuman Proverb (applied to any girl who goes Fara)

"Was that a ukulele?" Asked Robyn, from under her fan.

"I think so." I said. But I was wrong.

It was five ukuleles, two guitars, a drum, and thirty voices, which cracked open the still softness of the tropical night, with a thunderous chorus of slow rhythmic clapping, and three-part harmony.

'Aus noa'ia , 'Aus noa'ia gagaj ne hanue te' Noa'ia
'E garue maha ma re se kiu 'a'ana
'Urtoa' het ne 'a e na se 'on la' lam lama Hea'se' ka siriag 'e av ta 'e av ta
'Ua motu lei lei sega talofa Rotuma

Greetings to you, greetings to you chiefly owner of the house.
Thank you for your hardwork in preparing a thousand of taro
The spear that you threw flew so high that I wish it broke history's record
An island so good, Greetings Rotuma

There was a knock on the window.

315

"Robyn? Wink?" It was Julie. "It's Fara time."

We threw on our clothes quickly, and opened our powder blue door onto a landscape of faces, illuminated with hurricane lamps and flashlights. Sitting and swaying on a sea of pandanus mats, was an entire village from the other side of the island, shoes on the grass around them. The women had flower garlands in their hair and *te fui* around their necks, and waved their fans and rolled their torsos in time to the music. The singing sounded Hawaiian, if the Hawaiian had been crossed with Finnish and Tongan, pushed back into their throats, and projected out in lyrical explosions. The enthusiasm of the younger children would roar into hollers or shouts. I saw Julie and the girls, moving stooped among the musicians, sprinkling them on the heads and shoulders with *nau te* perfume, or talcum powder, or both. At other houses we would get stick deodorant or Vaseline. Villagers of all ages got up to dance around the main body of minstrels. Men asked a woman to dance with a bug-eyed warrior stance, bending their knees and throwing an occasional leg sideways into the air. The women asked a man to dance more modestly, by bowing their heads and throwing their arms forward in supplication, or running a discrete hand up his back. And the men postured and the women undulated, and it was all very sexual and innocent and ridiculously romantic at the same time, and everyone was laughing and smiling and clapping, and rapturously happy, in tempo and in tune with the full moon, and the rest of the night sky and the crashing ocean just beyond. Everybody smiled like Julie smiled, and Robyn and I were exhilarated by all the excitement. We felt alive.

Between songs, the dancers, which would often make up almost half the travelling roundtrip Fara troupe, would sit down again, before the next ukulele strum and single voice would begin a new round of celebration. The songs were all about love and religion, unattainable or impossible, alone or in combination. Later in our stay, we would come to know why.

> Kepoi ka 'a e 'ofa se gou ma gou la holi se 'a e
> La 'itarua la rotuag 'esea
> Ka 'a e la na ea gou la maomaaetou
> La famori se ra ea 'a e ma gou.
> Ma gou la leuof 'e kis se 'a ea ko le' ha n te'
> La 'itarua la rotuag 'esea.

> *If you love me, I will be converted to you*
> *So that we will be in the same religion*
> *You will hide me so that I will be hard to find,*
> *And that people will not see the two of us.*
> *When will I come to you my lady?*
> *So that we will be in the same religion living together.*

They partied for almost half an hour, before the dancers sat down among the rest of the band, and Julie and her daughters, and her husband, brought out refreshments, of watermelon and bananas and pineapples and biscuits, and more sprinkling of powder and perfume. As the days went by, Robyn and I learned to recognize when this particular Fara group was about to leave, by the *Noa'ia noa'ia* song they would sing last, as a thank you to the hosts whose sleep they had interrupted.

Noa'ia, noa'ia, noa'ia 'e 'es kefkef pene'isi' ma lol pene'isi ma 'amis ta e la la'atomis... Fu'omus.
Noa'ia, noa'ia Kaunohoag gagaj
Kepoi ka teet re 'e 'otomis fara,
Ro t 'a k fu'omusa ka 'a m la 'utuof se mua.
Gagaja la hanisi a' roan 'os ma uri
Rere ta tera nit la po la 'is la haipoag hoi'a ki.

Thank you Thank you Thank you for giving us sweet smelling powder
And fragrant oil and we are leaving ... Farewell
Thank you, thank you Chiefly household
If there's anything wrong in our 'fara'
Do forgive us and we are moving on

But this wouldn't be the end of the formalities. The Fara troupe leader would express his thanks for the gifts.

Noa'ia ko gagaj 'e 'es lol pene'isi
Ma kef kef pene'isi ma vaselin pene'isi
Ma sa n pene'isi, ma 'a mis ta e la la'atomis
Fu' omus.

Thank you oh nobles for having oil, nice smelling
And powder, nice smelling and vaseline, nice smelling
And perfume, nice smelling and we will be leaving
Goodbye.

And Julie's family would thank them back.

Ma rie, ma rie, ma rie, mak lelei.

Thanks, thanks, thanks, for the good songs dances.

After a few more personal exchanges and jokes, the Fara group went off to the next house on their itinerary, Robyn and I thanked Julie and the family for the wonderful entertainment, and went back to our linoleum slumber.
Or so we thought. In our dreams.
My eyes were beginning to wobble, and then I heard it, just once.
Strummummummummummumm.
A hurricane lamp flickered into life outside our window, faster than we did inside.
"Robyn? Wink?" It was Julie. "Fara time." It was still hot and muggy and my muscles ached from the dancing and the fatigue, but I told myself that this was, after all, why we had come, and roused Robyn, to tell her the same.
It was an even larger group this time. The word was out. All over Rotuma, at different houses each night, every night for a

month, impromptu singing and dancing celebrations would burst into flame. The only difference for us was that, because we were extra special guests, it would happen at the same house every night. *No sleep.* The foreboding words of Sefo rang in my ear. But then the entire night rang into melodious song and smiles, and it didn't matter at all. We were only in Rotuma for week. Compared to other things we survived that long, *Fara fatigue* would still be more fun.

The tradition had evolved from the *manea' hune'ele* beach parties of old, where young people would picnic at the beach from late afternoon through the night, singing and dancing and courting. Here they could spend time with prospective partners, away from the suffocating tight knit social regulation of the strong Rotuman family and community pressures of collective conformity.

But then came the missionaries and the powerful church doctrine they represented. Manea' hune'ele was decreed to be immoral and licentious, and the escapades and potential loss of virginity that might occur, unacceptable. But a compromise was needed, so as to still allow some form of courtship to occur. The Methodists found a method to combine flirting with supervision, and the custom of 'going Fara' superseded the past trysts on the beach that had occurred before Jesus arrived, and spoiled all their fun. The fun was given a more precise purpose. The flirting was now the search for a life partner. The young boys were told not to 'play for nothing.' If unsuccessful they were mocked as someone who 'compresses horse manure,' *a'pat finak ne has*, accomplishing nothing by riding up and down, except spreading horseshit on the roads, until it was packed down, or *a'pat finak ne ha s' kat ma f'ia ra*, returning from a fruitless fishing trip without any fish. The boys would sometimes orchestrate having their own Fara troupe taken hostage at the house where the girl they were enamored with lived, so as to increase their chances of success. Fara literally means 'to ask,' in Rotuman. For most

islanders, all they asked was that it still be just more of a fun
social event, more frolic than flirting.

As the nights followed the Fara way, Robyn and I began to
follow the troupes to other houses as well. We would fall into
unconsciousness, like cats in the heat of the day, whether we
wanted to or not. Inevitably, inexorably, we were worn down.
I had reached my limit, and I asked Julie, if we could be
excused from that night's festivities, just to catch up on some
sleep.

I thought it was a polite formality, and it never occurred to
me that, in an island culture so remote and isolated, the idea
of separating awhile from your family, real or adopted, might
ever be interpreted as antisocial behavior. But, for a brief
movement, I saw a sag in Julie's smile. She agreed not to
wake us.

And so it was that Robyn and I looked forward to the arms
of Morpheus, even though it was far too hot to look forward
to the arms of each other. We settled into our linoleum
lethargy, and set a course for coma.

My eyes were beginning to wobble, and then I heard it, just
once.

Strummummummummummumm.

I swore out loud, and then hoped that no one in the Fara
troupe that had congregated outside our window had heard it.
And then I swore again. Robyn just looked at me, waving her
fan.

"There's no point." I said, realizing the futility of resisting the
social pressure to participate. "We're still the ambassadors of
something here." And we got up, and opened the powder
blue door, and joined the singing and clapping and perfume
in the dark. The moon was full, and the stars were bright, and
I danced with the old women and the little girls, looking away
all the time they danced, until I could dance no more. After
each they said 'Fa ieksia,' *thank you,* and I said the same. And
that, I had decided, was that. But it wasn't, was it.

An electric ripple rolled up my back, from bottom to top. I turned into a radiant reflection of where it had all started centuries ago, in songs of colliding souls swept in with the tide to the shore.

She was intoxicating, sweeter than her caramel skin, than the coconut oil in her hair, than the perfumed flowers of her *tefui* garland, than the captivating one behind her ear. She moved like the story of what had been sacrificed for us to have met here, in the gracefulness of *Mak Samoa*, the Samoan way, first with her feet together, with a subtle shuffling in-and-out in time to the music, shifting her weight from one foot to the other, then with her arms, silk ribbons flowing fluent in elegant motifs from her fingertips, like slow breezes, then, from behind and within her *titi* skirt of long leaves, hips and loins pulsating, whirling ever more exuberant, and then, and only then, with her eyes, rolling and wandering, before finally fixing on both her hands, reaching out to me.

OK, I thought. Just one more.

> '... tall and pleasant, well-built, and full of gaiety, with eyes large and full of fire, noses a little flattened, white teeth, ear lobes pierced with a sweet-smelling flower, and almost naked.'
>
> La Coquille, 1824

*   *   *

> '... as well or better cultivated and its inhabitants more numerous for its size than any of the islands we have hitherto seen.'
>
> Captain Edwards, *Pandora*, 1791

"Wink? Robyn?" It was Julie, and daylight too soon.

"I think these people are zombies." I whispered to Robyn.

"They don't seem to need any sleep." On the mats in Julie's

house at breakfast, she explained that Av mane'a was more than going Fara.

"Today we're going to Manea' 'on fa ma haina." She said, dishing out additional vowels with the sliced papaya and pineapple. The girls fanned the flies and the Fahrenheit from our faces.

"What's that, Julie?" Robyn asked.

"The harvest festival." She said. Our family walked to Motusa, past some big Mother Hubbard women carrying large rolled woven mats into the village church. I looked up at what had been carved in a curve, above the door. *Mt Sinai.* Moses and the rushes. It was allegory. *And Mount Sinai was altogether on a smoke, because the LORD descended upon it fire.* But the smoke was ahead of us, at the far end of an large expanse of lawn and a magnificent giant flame tree, under which were several open shelters, with tin roofs and pandanus mat floors, connected by upright wooden poles, each one wrapped with plaited palm fronds. Long horizontal cloth banners of red and white hibiscus flowers hung below the rooflines. Fluorescent lights were suspended from the ceilings. We were at play, in the field of the Lord's Hawaiian carports.

The playground was a fairground, an agricultural exhibition farmshow, of big yams with big pink tags, big dances by the biggest people, and big watermelon filling up the big faces of little girls.

The yam farmers who couldn't win a prize would have to give away their harvest, and go home empty-handed, but the women weavers could bring home the mats they hadn't sold. They sat sidesaddle, purses slung over their big Mother Hubbard shoulders, waving their fans, and waiting for the feasting and the dancing to begin.

The old men were already drinking kava, at head tables covered with fine petit point linen tablecloths, punctuated at intervals with bouquets of flowers and brass salt cellars, pasted with Fijian money notes. Before the arrival of the missionaries, kava had been prepared by virgin girls with limestone-caked hair, who chewed and spat it into a slurry, before it was mixed with water by the older women. Since the arrival of the missionaries, the elders had begun blending in a little additional liquid from their hip flasks, which further muddied the waters, and hastened the collapse of their livers.

The smoke from the *Koua* earth oven, that wafted through the celebration, suddenly thickened, a sign that the sand was being raked off the leaves covering the old mats, that had been placed on the banana and *papai* swamp taro leaves, on top of the hot stones that had been carefully distributed over the food, with tongs made from the midribs of coconut leaves.

This *koua* had started with a large circular hole in the ground, lined with coconut tree trunks, and filled with kindling and a mound of parallel firewood, over which had been placed the lava stones, big ones on the bottom, smaller ones on top. A shredded coconut sheath had been lit to ignite the kindling, and the men had gone off to scrape breadfruit and taro and other root crops, and to kill the hogs. The pigs were turned on the heated stones to singe off their hair, and scraped with seashells or knives. Their throats had been slit, their alimentary canals tied off at both ends, so their guts, including the gall bladders, could be cautiously removed from their sliced-open abdomens. The male pigs had their penises tied, to prevent any urine from contaminating the meat. Everything to be baked had been washed in seawater. The large hot stones were spread over the bottom of the *Koua* with long poles, and any unburned firewood removed. The smaller ones were placed inside the pigs' carcasses, together with their livers and breadfruit leaves, to keep the steam inside. The men, using the same long poles, slung the swine, belly down, onto the base of hot large stones, now covered with taro scrapings and banana leaf ribs, to regulate the temperature. The breadfruit and the root crops had been placed along the margins of the pit, because they hadn't required as much heat to bake them. When the smoke finally cleared, out of the *Koua*, came roast pork and roasted chicken and corned beef, and breadfruit and cassava and taro, and '*al'ikou* packages of taro leaves filled with coconut milk and onion, and taro *fekei* pudding. The food was hoisted with large pandanus baskets on poles, and placed beside the watermelon and pineapple and mango and pawpaw and sugar cane and jams. Some young girls fanned the food tables constantly, to keep off the flies, while others filled the closely woven *tauga* flat-bottomed coconut leaf baskets with food, to carry to the chiefs at the head table, most of which would have been too paralyzed by this time, to have fended for themselves, even if they had to. Everyone filed by the tables, filling their plates if they had one or, if not, supporting their overflowing *fono* basket in one hand, while the other held up the front edge, in a desperate race against gravity and gluttony. The feast was substantial, and superb.

But it was time to dance. Not the Fara way dancing of the night migrations, but the traditional *tautoga* rectangular rows and columns of the *hafa*, half of the group on one side men, the other half on the other side women. They wore powder blue *ha' fali* lava-lavas, red and white collared shirts and blouses, red and white and yellow pandanus fruit garlands, and tropicbird tailfeathers. The accompaniment behind them beat a pile of old mats with large sticks, to keep time. The men jumped from side to side, or in circles, or scanned the horizon back and forth, with a raised flat hand blocking the sun from their eyes, feet apart, clowning and clapping and yelping and grunting 'hui'i, hui'i, hui'i, hui'i,' in syncopated exhalations. The women were constrained to graceful subtle motion, feet together and hands clasped, until they weren't and the story-telling motifs began. They sang the third and fifth above the notes of the men, some breathing while others vocalized, spinning the music into a continuous hypnotic thread of verse. After each set, the dancers in the front would drop back, allowing the row behind them to come forward, and begin the rhythms of their ancestors all over again.

"Is your harvest festival like this in Canada, Wink?" Julie asked. I conjured up a mental image of our country fair.

"Not quite like this, Julie." I said. "Not quite."

*   *   *

The day before we ended up at Rocky Point for a cold beer, two days after the Hospital Board of Visitors decided to invite Robyn and I for lunch, the day after the harvest festival, right after our third night of Faracidal insomnia, I rolled over next to the sponge mattress, and shook Robyn awake. Her fanning didn't break Farastride.

"Do you realize that we are sleeping next to some of the most beautiful beaches on the planet, and almost halfway through our time on Rotuma, we've only seen the seashore once?" I asked. For a Kiwi, this was an unconscionable source of shame.

"Today." She said. We dressed and closed the powder blue door to our cabin, jaws grimly set to overwhelm Julie's sense of family togetherness, and escape to an isolated beach on our own. But we had no idea that, here in the most remote Polynesian paradise, this was not just impolite, or impolitic. It was treason.

Rotumans are a gentle people, culturally conservative and strongly socialized, with an emphasis on collective responsibility enforced by a sensitivity to shaming. No one did anything without everyone else's participation, except perhaps, in a rare free dove cord moment, making other Rotumans. And Julie was the perfect Polynesian Pollyanna, far too happy and in love with everything, which she believed rightly, in Motusa village at least, to derive from, and return back to, the family. She was the living Nash Equilibrium embodiment of Southern Sea survival. How could it be possible that we, in our most evil manifestation of individualistic inconsideration, even think of abandoning our adopted village, for a single day of selfish gratification? The easy answer was, of course, was that it was necessary. Robyn and I had never been creatures of collective conformity. We were mavericks, nabobs of narcissism, which is why we fell in love in the first place, and made a life together, based on not belonging. When we had first arrived on Vancouver Island, I was approached to join the local Rotary Club.

"You're not a joiner." Robyn had said. And the Rotarians were condemned to do without.

"Julie?" I asked, a mouthful of morning pawpaw in my mouth.

"Yes, Wink." She said.

"Robyn and I were thinking of hiking across the isthmus, to Vai'oa Beach." I said.

"Lovely, Wink." She said. "What time should we go?" Then it got hard.

"Well, that's what I wanted to ask you about." I said. "We thought that, for just today only, we just might go alone, to give you and the girls some time to yourselves." I looked across the floor mat, into eyes that couldn't decide whether to be hurt, or offended. I thought it was a polite formality, and it never occurred to me that, in an island culture so remote and isolated, the idea of separating awhile from your family, real or adopted, might ever be interpreted as antisocial behavior. But, for a brief movement, I saw a sag in Julie's smile. Meltdown.

"Are you sure?" She asked. I nodded.

"OK." She said. "Enjoy yourselves."

Robyn and I were gone, before anyone could reconsider. We didn't really know the way, but Julie had guided us to the soft coral path across the isthmus along Maka bay, and onto Raho's western basket of earth that had formed the Itu'muta peninsula. We came to what appeared to be an enormous Zen *sansui* garden of raked white sand, out of which colossal black lava stones protruded. It was a Rotuman cemetery. A tall structure, about twelve feet high, consisting of four inward-leaning wooden poles with streams of red and yellow and purple cloth hanging from the close-tied cross pieces, had been recently erected to commemorate a new ancestral addition to the community. From there the trail climbed into rainforest, interspersed with plantations. A Rotuman myzomela, with its black upper plumage and bright scarlet belly, announced our entrance to one farmer's yam patch. He provisioned us with mangos, and further directions through the bush. Exhilarated, walking alone together, the salt air of the most beautiful beach in the world's last Eden, danced on our noses, where the light finally split the jungle. We broke through the canopy, to a breathtaking long scimitar of white sand below, fringed with towering palms, and *niu* and *hifau* trees, framed by purple green volcanic mountains, on a cerulean-spattered watercolor bay. Large schools of fish ran in every direction, but we only ran in one, over a rock bridge and along the caster sugar crescent, to the horizontal limbs of a massive fig tree in the middle, and shade. We rolled out our towels, and lay down together, together in the faint relief of an offshore breeze, and Fara ' nuff away from the constant attention of 'Pear ta ma 'on maf,' *This Land Has Eyes.* Or so I thought.

For the first five minutes of our intimacy, Vai'oa Beach was deserted. We were in heaven.

"I think I'll go for a swim." I said to Robyn and, collecting my snorkeling gear, began to cover the short distance to the water's edge. I didn't make it.

I had just put on my mask and was adjusting my snorkel, when I realized that there were now a few other human clusters that had magically appeared on the beach, one of which was moving quickly in my direction. Two young boys got to me first.

"You can't swim yet." One said.

"Huh?" I said. "Why?"

"You need to wait." Said the other one. I looked out at the clearest bluest water in the Southern Sea, at the underwater coral forests, at the blazing schools of colored fish, at the only cool reprieve in sight.

"For what?" I asked.

"For the fishermen." Said the first one.

"I need to wait for the fishermen, before I can go for a swim?" I asked.

"Yes." The both said at the same time. It was about then that my inner renegade just about got the best of me. This is ludicrous, I thought. The heat was becoming ridiculous, the snorkeling looked brilliant, and some superstitious local custom required me to avoid the entire Pacific Ocean because it might affect the fate of a few fishermen who were nowhere to be seen. I turned around. *Robyn just looked at me, waving her fan. "There's no point." I said, realizing the futility of resisting the social pressure to participate. "We're still the ambassadors of something here."*

"How long will they be?" I asked. They shrugged. I was beaten. *The land has teeth and knows the truth.* There were now whole other villages coming out of the jungle, and spreading their pandanus mats under the palms.

Burning feet dragged my snorkeling gear and broken spirit, back to the towel beside Robyn.

"What was that all about?" She asked.

"We have to wait." I said.

"For what?" She asked.

"For the fishermen." I said. She asked me why. I had no answer.

Over the next two hours, we watched our deserted delight fill up with rotund Rotumans. Smoke rose from the far end of the beach. Finally, the sound of an outboard grew louder from Fara way in the lagoon, until we could make out from which direction it was coming. Within a few more minutes, a small open boat had beached up in front of us, and its crew warmly welcomed, as they offloaded their catch. I thought my waiting was over but, as I got up to collect my snorkeling gear, a corrective glance disabused me of the notion. Not yet.

Eventually, after another half hour, one of the young boys kneeled next to my towel.

"You can go in now." He said. I grabbed my mask and snorkel, and made for the lagoon, before anyone could reconsider. I didn't make it.

At the water's edge, I was met by a big Rotuman, eating big fish and big taro and a dozen other big things, off a big banana leaf.

"Lunch is ready." He said. I was beaten.

Burning feet dragged my snorkeling gear and broken spirit, back to the towel beside Robyn.

"What was that all about?" She asked.

"Lunch is ready." I said.

*   *   *

 *   *   *

'Don't want to hear from and cheerful Pollyannas,
Who tell me love will find a way, it's all bananas.'
George Gershwin, *But Not For Me*

The way back from Vai'oa Beach was shorter. A small red Citroën 2CV pulled over to give us a ride.

"You must be Robyn and Wink." Said the driver, a finely spoken thin gracefulness, with Nefertiti's face and air of nobility. She wore her hair piled in a bun, high towards the back of her head, and drove like she was in Paris. If Julie was the Pollyanna of Polynesia, Sanimeli Maraf was the Rotuman Eleanor of Aquitaine; they were both goddesses in their own way, one chalk and one cheese. Talcum and Tomme de Savoie.

330

"Call me Sani." She said.

"How was the beach?" Julie asked, on our return. I swallowed the word I was thinking.

"Very friendly." I said. Her smile came on twice as bright, until Sani got out of the car. It was the first time on Rotuma I felt anything like a chill.

"This is Sanimeli." I said, not believing, on reflection, that they wouldn't have previously met. Sani told Julie that the Hospital Board had arranged a luncheon for us for the following day, and what time she would pick us up. But, for a brief movement, I saw a sag in Julie's smile. And then I got it. Sani was about to introduce us to the rules. Julie had already introduced us to their transcendence.

The Hospital Board was ready for us on the lawn next morning. There were tables with tablecloths, with lemonade and little sandwiches with the crusts cut off, and the lone physician. Sani introduced us to him and the three other women board members, and they talked to Robyn, and I talked to the doctor. He was younger than I was, and there was fatigue in his eyes, and a weight on his broad Polynesian shoulders. We spoke of the frustration he experienced at watching people die, for lack of a reliable air ambulance evacuation service. He was an Old Testament minor deity and, for all his frailties and faults and failings, the people loved him all the same, for he was still a much better chance, than they used to have. We discussed the high incidence of diabetes and heart disease, in a population with thrifty genes, and pork fat as intermediary metabolites. There was a lot of premature death from heart attacks. I was suprised to learn that he didn't have a defibillator, shocked even.

"What do you do if their heart stops?" I asked.

"Have a funeral." He said. I promised him I would find him a defibrillator, as soon as I got back to Canada.

Sani drove us on the Bennett's at Itu'muta, and introduced us to Samo and his wife and two children, Rotumans home from New Zealand, for Fara. We drank lemonade and green coconut on their veranda, and promised, as travelers always do, to keep in touch.

On our tour around the rest of the island, it was along the southern coast, entering the districts of Juju and Pepjei, that things got a little strange. As we entered the village of Upu, blowing up like Notre Dame in Paris, was the Marist Catholic church of St. Michaels.

"Do you know about the wars?" Asked Sani.

"The wars?" I asked.

"Between the English Wesleyans and the French Catholics." She said. I told her I had heard about them but not much. I knew that Rotuma had experienced the usual ravages and interbreeding from the whalers and ships deserters, including the only blackbirders that hit the place on the *Velocity*, all 40 sailors from which are now represented in the gene pool. I knew that the, and other *fafisi* off the Unites States Exploring Expedition in 1840 brought grog and measles and influenza and dysentery and venereal disease. But I didn't know that most of the death and destruction was brought by the God's door to door salesmen.

"The missionaries came forth to Christianize the savages." Sani said. "But it wasn't as if the savages weren't dangerous enough already." She told us of the Great Malhaha War of 1845, when two *sau* chiefs, Riamku and Sani's husband's ancestor Maraf, from the same village of Noa'tau, each installed different saus of their choosing in our village of Motusa. The conflict killed all the young men on both sides with many villages entirely depopulated. Maraf thought he finally had the strategic advantage, when he acquired a cannon from one of the whalers but, at the battle that followed, after a few shots the falconet failed, and Riamkau's men rallied, killing Maraf and a hundred of his men. He was buried with the faulty gun serving as his headstone, and a great number of pigs were paid in indemnity.

"A year later the Catholic Marist missionaries arrived." She said." There were already few Wesleyan missionaries from

Tonga, landed by John Williams in 1839." Gradually, the southern and southeastern part of the island, and Riamkau, became converted to Catholicism, and the rest of the island, Maraf's heirs, to Wesleyan dogma. When William Fletcher established his mission in 1865, he noted that his flock had chosen to adopt a more western appearance.

> 'The contrast between the skins and garments, stained with turmeric and the clean shirts and dresses, was too marked to be overlooked. The young men of the district appeared in a sort of uniform, clean white shirts, and clean cloth wrapped about them in place of trousers. The idea was their own: the effect was good... As I reached the houses of the heathen part of the village, the difference was very marked. Everything was dirty, Turmeric was on all sides... (It was hard) to tell a Papist from a professed heathen by his outward gait and demeanour. There is the same unkempt head of long hair, the same daubing with turmeric; indeed, the same wild, and unpolished, and unwholesome appearance.'

Tumeric was the talcum powder of the traditional, of tolerance. But tolerance wasn't on tap in the pulpits of the mission churches at the end of the 1860s.

The Wesleyans were complaining about the heretical Papist 'scarlet whores' impeding their civilizing progress, and ruining the commodity accounting balance sheet of converts per unit cost. They were making the world more like Britain, measurable as much in housing and clothing as in baptisms.

The Catholics, for their part, were preaching the narrative of martyrdom, in the values of 'faith, baptism, confession, and communion,' while living among their flock in 'poverty, celibacy, and obedience.'

But differences between the two agendas were only foreground and background; what for one group was underlined, for the other was subtext, and for all their vows of poverty, the Catholics were definitely playing the money game.

'At Rotumah I was struck by the ingenious method the Roman
Catholic priests have adopted for paying the natives for their
labour. They, the priests, are all poor men, having as a rule barely
sufficient means to support themselves except in a native fashion,
and consequently they have no money to expend in wages. They
have therefore adopted a system of fines, which when enforced are
usually found to exceed in amount the sum due for service.
Absence from church is fined; smoking on Sunday, or even walking
out, is against the law. Women are fined for not wearing bonnets
when attending mass, kava drinking ensures a heavy penalty, and
fishing on holy days is strictly forbidden. The chief source of
revenue comes from absence from church, as service goes on two
or three times a day, and most probably just when the poor people
are fishing or cultivating the ground.'
Boddam-Whetham, JW, Pearls of the Pacific, 1876

Other influences stoked the fires and brimstones. European
traders provided guns and ammunition, French ship captains
drew up treaties and made threats, British colonial officials in
Fiji hovered just beyond the horizon, and Rotuman chiefs
became anxious to exercise their vested interests, kinship
alliances and grievances.

"But when push finally came to shove," Said Sani, "it was the
Rotumans who did the fighting."

"When was that?" I asked.

"The Motusa War of 1871." She said.

"You mean our village?" I asked.

"The very same." She said. "It was a strange mix of Rotuman
custom and missionary innovation."

Wars were conducted in a ceremonial, if not celebratory
fashion, in a one-day encounter only, like a sporting event.
Chiefs sent challenges announcing a particular time and place
for combat. The day before the scheduled conflict, each side
held a feast, featuring *ki* chants and war dances. Battles were
conducted on flat stretches of beach, to preclude ambushes.
Prior to engagement, each side danced menacingly and
tauntingly, sang verses proclaiming their ferocity, and then
chanted to solicit the support of their gods. Warriors dressed

in their best clothing, to make any unanticipated funerary preparations easier. They tied up their hair in topknots and wore *milomilo* conical or *suru* crescent-shaped basket hats, decorated with tapa and feathers. Round their necks they wore charms, and their bodies were smeared with coconut oil mixed with turmeric. The main weapons were spears, clubs and stones, thrown both at distant and close quarters. The goal was to kill the leading chief of the other team. When this had been accomplished, the supporters of that chief would withdraw, and the fighting would end.

> 'There were no great advantages to be gained from the war by the winning side. The villages of the vanquished might be sacked, but they were seldom burnt; their plantations might be overrun, but there was little willful destruction. All pigs were, of course, regarded as legitimate spoil. The vanquished would perhaps promise to pay to the conquerors so many baskets of provisions or so many mats and canoes, a promise which was always faithfully and speedily performed, even though they might accompany the last part of the payment with a fresh declaration of war. The victorious side obtained no territorial aggrandisement, as it was to the common interest of all to maintain the integrity of the land, and the victors might on some future occasion be themselves in the position of the vanquished... Some of the large and high *fuag ri* house foundations were built by labour from defeated districts, suggesting the possibility of labour as a form of tribute... Nominally first-fruits were claimed by the victors from the chief of the vanquished, or perhaps the victors might depose the conquered chiefs, and put nominees in their places... Such a course had, however, relatively little permanence... There was not such thing as indiscriminate slaughter or debauchery of the women after a fight.'

In the Motusa War, Communion and Christian prayers took the place of chants. Late into the previous night, Father Joseph Trouillet had baptised recently converted Catholics, sanctifying them for the expected battle. The new dress code for warriors required black dress suits, frock coats, and starched, stiffly-ironed shirts, collars and ties, although the basketware head-gear, bravely trimmed with feathers and red cloth, like an Indian head-dress put on backwards, was still considered *de rigeur*. Spears, clubs and stones had been replaced with firearms. The battle was fought on the isthmus, and the Wesleyens won, with a final score of 12 to 2. The Treaty of Hamelin was signed, and relative peace prevailed, save for the odd French warship, mediating and fomenting dissent. When the anti-Catholic Reverend Thomas Moore made landfall in 1877, the situation took a turn, and when Riamkau stole a pig and was shot in the back, he died a Catholic martyr. The war of 1878 lasted over two months, resulting in a letter to the Governor of Fiji, requesting cession to Great Britain. They got their wish.

"We call it Rotuma Day." Said Sani. "It brought us peace." And Jehovah Witnesses, Seventh Day Adventists, Mormons, and Assembly of God on Rotuma members, and an unreasonable number and variety of their churches, spread all across the island she drove us around.

Thankfully, also, it brought them cold beer, which is where we ended up late afternoon, at Rocky Point.

For our final destination, before returning to Julie and the rest of our family in Motusa, Sani took us to her home in Nao'tau, to meet her husband. He was a big solid middle-aged Polynesian, with receding grey wavy hair, a big square jaw, and a nose so wide and flat, it made you wonder how it could be an instrument of respiration. He wore his lava-lava like he had been born in it.

"Gagaj Maraf Solomone." He said, introducing himself. Which is about all he said. He was a man of few words. But he didn't appear to need many. We knew he was married to a very regal presence. We knew that he was a direct descendent of Maraf. We knew that he was also a chief, not a *sau* anymore, as the office had been terminated in the 1860's, but a chief nonetheless. We didn't know that he was a member of the Fijian parliament, or how he would slurp his soup at dinner. We asked him questions about traditional and changing Rotuman society, and he always took a very long time, before answering in as few words as were necessary, to answer the question without giving anything else away.

In the old days, when a chief died, and the day came for laying his *halaf* foundation stone, each of the five districts had to bring a healthy pretty young girl to the ceremony. At the appointed time, they were struck once on the head with a stout club, for their deaths were required to be instantaneous. If one cried out, she would have been carried away and another girl from the same district would be sacrificed in her place. They were buried, one at each of the four corners in the cemetery, and one right in the centre, their bodies resembling the five stars of the *'atarou* Southern Cross constellation, where the spirit of the kings would go.

I asked him what would happen, if someone committed a serious crime.

"It is rare in Rotuma." He said.

I pushed him for a response.

"He would make restitution to the community." He said.

I asked him what would happen if his restitution had been inadequate.

"He would go fishing." He said. Southern Cross power.

A man like this one, I thought, would have had that kind of foundation stone.

'The main island far exceeds in populousness and fertility all that we have seen in this sea...the evidently superior fertility of the island, and the seeming cheerful and friendly disposition of the natives, makes this, in our opinion, the most eligible place for ships coming from the eastward, wanting refreshments, to touch at; and with regard to missionary views...there can hardly be a place where they settle with greater advantage, as there is food in abundance; and the island, lying remote from others, can never be engaged in wars...'

William Wilson, missionary ship *Duff*, 1797

*　　　*　　　*

We spent the last magical days on Rotuma with Julie and the family on the whitest and most peaceful Motusa beach, and the nights in a Fara way kind of narcosis. Robyn had her own pandanus mat by now, and her perpetual motion fan continued to perform its double duty, keeping her cool, and the flies off her face and the watermelon.

"It's a curse and a blessing." Said Julie. She saw my puzzled look.

"The isolation." She said. "But even when the plane breaks down, and the boat doesn't come, when the shops run out of basics, we still have this, and our love. Fia'ama." *So What.*

So what if they lived to eat, and the insects and heat were as thick as each other. They had more than most of us.

"That's why the ones that came and stayed, stayed." She said. And she was right.

Our final evening, Julie's daughters danced for us, in elegant red and white layered dresses, and combed Robyn's hair, and anointed her with coconut oil, and initiated us both with lei. And then Robyn danced for us as well, and very well. We ate my favorite pusilami, and cucumber and crayfish, and steaming octopus with *tahroro* fermented coconut sauce, and pork, and a variety of stodgy fekei coconut desserts that Robyn adores.

The next morning, before the plane left, we hid along the soft sand roads of Rotuma, secretly hoping that no one would find us in time to take us to the airport. But nothing is secret on Rotuma. The land has eyes. *The islanders, passing with light footfalls and low voices in the sand of the road, lingered to observe us, unseen...*

We found ourselves on the tarmac, walking toward the Britten-Norman Islander that brung us, and Robyn dissolved into tears. And Julie dissolved into tears. And it wasn't that long before the pilot sliced back up into the huge cloud he had that he had found a week earlier, over six hundred kilometers north of the rest of Fiji, sideways, like he was cutting a grey soufflé. It wasn't that many kilometers Fara way from Julie, when our plane almost stalled. For a moment, my heart stopped, with no defibrillator on board. And then, like some noctural protective ghost from below, it cranked over. *Strummummummummummumm.*

*   *   *

13 May 1999- 'We, the members of the Rotuma Hospital Board of Visitors, are thankful for all the help and donations we received. May God bless you all. My thanks also go to Doctor Winkler and Robyn, who visited the island from Nanaimo, Canada, in December 1998 and our relatives over there. Many thanks for your kind donation of the defibrillator. We look forward to receiving it soon.'
Archived News, Rotuma Community Bulletin Board

Postscript: They did get our defibrillator. But unfortunately, they didn't realize that the power had already been transformed to accommodate Rotuman electricity. Smoke rose from the far end of the beach. It was allegory.
And Mount Sinai was altogether on a smoke, because the LORD descended upon it fire.

*   *   *

339

A Proud and Caring People
Samoa

'Outside the family there seemed to be no driving force, no loyalties; and the interdependency that was limited strictly to the family made it seem less like a society than like a simple organism, a certain type of jellyfish, perhaps, the hydrozoan that was a little colony of tentacles, some for stinging, some for eating, that sways and bloops along the surface of the sea.'

Paul Theroux, *In the Backwaters of Western Samoa*

"That's my husband's name." She said.

I looked up the hill, straining to see what she was referring to. There was nothing but our clothesline, from which projected a yellow New Zealand *AA* sign that Cousin Dave had pinched from some other place. *Equator 5702 km... London 18958 km... Hobart 1680 km... Cape Reinga 1401 km... Sydney 2000 km... Wellington...784 km...*

"Hobart?" I asked. "Your husband's name is Hobart?" She shook her head.

"No." She said. "His name is Equator."

"Equator?" I asked. "Your husbands name is Equator?" She nodded.

"Its amazing." She said. I agreed, wondering what kind of parents would name their son after an imaginary line on the Earth's surface.

"He's coming down from Auckland tomorrow." She said. "You'll get to meet him." I had just met his wife. She had hiked down the gravel driveway that Robyn and I shared with the architect's iconic bach further up the hill. Except that he didn't know that she was here, because he shared the iconic bach with his estranged ex-wife, who had shared her timeshare with her, and her family. We had met them because of the seagulls, which had ripped through the garbage they had set out, at the bottom of our shared drive. They were a big family of big people, and there were a lot of torn bags. I originally thought they were Maori, like the architect's estranged wife.

"We're Samoan." She said, emphasis on the 'Sam,' rather than the 'oan.' "We're leaving tomorrow, but Equator is coming." And he did.

Late on the following afternoon, a blue pearl low Holden Commodore Ute, on twenty-inch alloy wheels with nearly new tires, twin stainless exhaust hoods, and hi-flow cat tinted windows, boomboxed up our drive, before shutting down into sleep mode, in front of me. The Equator, as an imaginary line around the Earth's belly, is thought to have no beginning, but this one did. Like the planet he encircled, he bulged slightly in the middle, and would have been memorable to cross. He rolled out of the Holden like he had been freed from its frame, looking up the hill at his namesake on the *AA* sign, and smiling, like Samoans smile. He whipped off his hi-flow cat tinted sunglasses and, after a long Pacific pause, put out a brick-like hand for me to shake.

"Equator." He said. And why not. Samoans were renowned for naming their children with no small originality. I had met a Telefoni (telephone), a Kerisimasi (Christmas), and a Pan Am, and was thankful, at least, that their last names were all the same, so I could track them. A supersized young Polynesian girl struggled out the passenger side. Her makeup and her gum chewing slowed the rest of her down, even more than the hoop earings you could have potted a basketball through.

"This is my daughter Tyra." He said. "Named after Tyra Banks. She's thirteen." She didn't look so much like Tyra Banks at thirteen, as like thirteen Tyra Banks. I thought of Margaret Mead, and *Coming of Age in Samoa*, and Tyra, a young Samoan girl, coming of Age in New Zealand. Mead had created quite a controversy, when she published the results of her fieldwork research on adolescent Samoan girls, in 1928.

She had concluded that there was more harmony, and very little teenage rebelliousness, in nonindustrial societies where family members depended on each other through their entire lives, but that mobile industrialized communities, whose young adults were expected to move away from their nuclear families to find work, and their own neolocal paths, were a fertile culture medium for adolescent conflict. Tyra was chewing gum like she was preparing to pole vault the space and time of that great divide.

If there were almost as many Samoans living in New Zealand as in Samoa, it wasn't the fault of the Samoans. On 29 August 1914, New Zealand, at the request of the British, landed troops on the main island of Upolu, in a 'great and urgent imperial service.' The German governor surrendered without a shot being fired. Until Samoa's independence in 1962, the Kiwis were responsible for forty-eight years of trusteeship, and three atrocities.

At the beginning of November of 1918, the *SS Talune,* which had previously brought Rudyard Kipling from Wellington to Melbourne, arrived from Auckland, bringing far less poetry. The acting Port Health officer allowed the ship to berth, in breach of quarantine. The Spanish flu that disembarked, killed 8500 islanders, almost a quarter of the population. The impact of the pandemic was undoubtedly amplified by the Samoan cultural response to illness, which required the *fono* family to gather around a sick person's bedside, and the New Zealand administration's refusal of medical assistance offered by American Samoa, which had it under control.

The second iniquity occurred in Apia, on Black Saturday, 28 December 1929, in much the same way, as the Amitsar massacre in India, ten years earlier. The Mau, a nonviolent resistance movement formed to protest to the mistreatment of the Samoan population by the colonial administrations, marched in a peaceful demonstration into downtown Apia. Its new leader, Chief Tupua Tamasese Lealofi III was shot from behind and killed while trying to bring calm and order to the Mau demonstrators, who had become agitated in response to a New Zealand police attempt to arrest one of their own. That's when the mounted Lewis gun opened up on the rest of them, killing ten more and, accompanied by a hail of police batons, injuring a further fifty.

The most pernicious influence bequeathed by the Kiwis, however, was corpulence. It's not as if the Samoans needed a lot of help with this. In the vast expanse of the Southern Sea, they already had an established reputation for girth, and power.

Robert Louis Stevenson reported this, in the 1890s. *All over Polynesia, and a part of Micronesia, the rule holds good; the great ones of the isle, and even of the village, are greater of bone and muscle, and often heavier of flesh, than any commoner.*

Beatrice Grimshaw mentioned it, in 1908. *The Samoan is always ready to eat at any hour, provided there is something nice to be got.*

And Paul Theroux beat it to death, in 1992. *They valued fatness, and to make themselves physically emphatic they ate massive amounts of bananas, taro, breadfruit and such snacks as were on the menu of the eateries in Apia. Toasted spaghetti sandwich, was one I noted. (The New Zealanders have a lot to answer for.) They ate the cuts of mutton that were whitest with fat. Meat that the Kiwis and Aussies refused to eat, unsaleable parts of dead animals - chicken backs, parson's noses, trotters, withers and whatever - were frozen and exported here. A scrap of meat on a chunk of fat attached to a big bone they found toothsome. The imported canned corned beef they called pisupo was up to ninety percent fat. It was not the solid meat thing that we diced with a knife in the United States and made into hash, this Pacific corned beef was often like pudding it was so loaded with fat, and it could easily be eaten with a spoon. Not only was beef tallow added to it, but some brands contained hippo fat.*

By 1966, only four years after independence, labour disputes and a devastating cyclone had dimmed the vision of imminent prosperity. Many Samoans, including Equator's parents, emigrated to New Zealand.

"Would you like to stay for dinner?" Robyn asked. Tyra nodded at her father.

"Maybe we'll just first go up to the architect's, and change." He said. A dust cloud climbed the hill behind the rear tinted windows of the Holden.

Equator and Tyra were Kiwis of Samoan extraction. There was less racism in New Zealand than Australia, but it wasn't zero. Samoans were called 'coconuts,' and worse.

But Kiwi Samoans told their own jokes about relatives *fresh off the boat*, FOB families that lived next door in South Auckland. You knew it was their house by the amount of *lapisi* rubbish and naked kids running and playing in the uncut grass in the front yard, and the five lavalavas and three mu'umu'us and two *pule tasi* and the Bermuda shorts with a hole in it, on the laundry line next to the broken down van in the driveway. A mountain of shoes blocked the front door, every one as big as a boat, an accidental few of them from someone else's *fa'alavelave*. Inside, there were shell necklaces around the wall photos, a lifetime supply of *saimigi* ramen noodles in the kitchen cupboards, and someone else's pots and pans on the counters, still full of food brought back from their barbeque. Kiwi Samoans might have used their lavalavas as curtains, but their FOB relatives would have also used their curtains as lavalavas. There was no lock on the bathroom door and all kinds of people kept coming in and out, while whoever was on the toilet might have been pretending to relax, or playing the ukelele. The television in the living room was sited so its channels could be easily changed from the floor, with an eraser tied to a ruler.

Parental discipline was military, from the general to the corporal. In any other culture, it would have been considered child abuse. The water hose was only six feet long, because their father kept cutting off three-foot lengths, to get their attention. He could hit their heads from six feet away during the prayer at church, or have the dinner dishes cleared in less than a minute, by slapping the table and waving his hand.

Whoever ate last was the one to wash them. The toilet bowl was cleaned with a hand and a rag, because the Kiwi brush next to it couldn't do a proper job. He had a tribal witch doctor cure for most ailments, axle grease for gaping wounds, tree bark for less serious maladies, and a *pamu* enema for anything else they might have complained about. There were very few complaints. Haircut day was an outside drum solo of tapping and thumping, scissors on the comb, and the comb on the victim's head.

Grandma airdried her underwear on the bushes and sidewalks in front of the house, where she beat her *fala moe* sleeping mat into its own stupor, or cut the grass with the hair scissors. Her bedroom was cluttered with old coke bottles and the coconut oil and leaves she used for her *fofo* medicinal massages. She was the sweetest old lady on weekdays, but on Sunday she pinched and twisted the ears of her grandchildren, for their wicked sinfulness. At night she would watch wrestling, throwing her fists and her voice at the television. *Fusu fusu loa.*

The young ones learned it all, of course, made in their elders' images, since William Shaw had observed them in Samoa, in 1851. *The children are very precocious, swimming at two years old, and climbing trees with the agility of monkeys for cocoa nuts... At the birth of a child, it is the national custom to plant a plantain; which tree adding a bark ring on its trunk every year, the age of the child is easily and indubitably determined by the number of rings on the tree.* The cruelty trickled down, into sniggering and explosive mocking laughter and gratuitous hostility, reaching full expression as the need to kick any dog they walked past, or the right to throw stones at anything that didn't seem to belong to an identifiable tribal element. They would learn the same Polynesian playfulness as the Kiwi jokers they were invading, but a little more elemental, and much more savage.

Family outings were odysseys of indulgence. As everyone opened the van doors to get in, the roaches came running out. The air freshener hanging from the mirror was a toilet bowl deodorant, and the flowers decorating the dashboard had come from the cemetery. At the supermarket, the father quickly filled the first cart, with eight cans of corned beef, twelve of spam, and a twenty-pound bag of Calrose rice. *Dear Chinese people, We like rice more than you do. Luv you long dime. Samoans.* The mother loaded the second cart with pisupo, spaghetti, pilikaki, cabbage, five gallons of vegetable oil, another twenty-pound bag of rice, soy sauce, and the second hand ball gown she had just bought at the op shop, to wear to church the following Sunday. Grandma followed, wearing one white sock and one red sock with her Samoan flip flops, pushing the cart with the kids in it. Some days they would go to the beach with fishing poles and a pot full of boiled green bananas and a two-litre bottle of soda, each. On others they would go out to the airport, to see if they knew anyone coming off the plane from Apia. Some evenings they would go out to eat, taking aluminum foil to an unsuspecting All-You-Can-Eat restaurant, none of which were still in business in South Auckland. And some evenings, when they could afford it they would take in a movie, and try to time their laughter with that of the *palagis* around them, to make them think they understood what was going on on the screen.

But these were the ones that had just arrived. Equator and Tyra were second and third generation New Zealanders. They came down the drive from the architect's house on sunset, and we sat out on the patio, with a view of the ocean and the rocks below.

"I brought this for you, Wink." Said Equator, reaching into a paper bag. It was an old grey lavalava, printed in a pattern of repetitive *Samoa*'s, a simple gift, that had been well used, and well looked after. I told him I was honored, and went away, and returned with it on, and we cracked a beer. I told Equator that I was planning on writing about Samoans some day. Between sips, he had one of those Pacific pauses.

"Tau ina ta ma fa'apoi." He said. "Always gather the

breadfruit from the farthest branches first."

The farthest branches were full of thorns. The first Europeans to sight the Samoan islands, owed their survival to the fact that they hadn't landed. Jacob Roggeveen went on to Easter Island, after a sail past in 1722, and Antoine de Bougainville named them *Les Iles des Navigateurs* in 1768, when he observed the natives in canoes chasing tuna far offshore. Bougainville's compatriot Jean-Francois La Perouse, made the first landing in Samoa nine years later. The locals went about helping themselves to the intriguing bits of iron found aboard his ships, and the French sailors made examples of a few by punishing them. Word had spread westward by the following day and, while the sailors were collecting water at A'asu, the natives attacked, killing 12 crewmen, including their commander. Heads were taken. At least 39 Samoans also died during the encounter. The site of the ambush was named Massacre Bay and the French departed posthaste. When the same violent reception met Captain Edwards of the HMS Pandora in 1791, on his quest to find the Bounty mutineers, more Samoans were killed, with lessons for both sides.

The Samoans, impressed by the great ships with their white sails that seemed to have come through the slit separating the sky from the sea, had named the strange people sailing them 'Papalagi.' *Sky busters*. They learned firsthand, about European weaponry, and wanted some. They learned firsthand, from the subsequent European escaped convicts and whalers and missionaries and traders of sandalwood and beche-de-mer, about private ownership and personal greed, and didn't understand it. The essential foundation of Samoan society, the *Fa'a Samoa* way of life, was the *Aiga*, the extended communal family unit, numbering in the thousands of relatives and in-laws. Everything was possessed collectively by the Aiga and, while an individual had the right to use that property, he did not personally own it. If you needed something, there was always somebody who had what you required. The *matai* chief of the aiga was responsible for distribution, and no one went without shelter or food. And in a tropical paradise like the Navigator Islands, no one really needed anything more than a hut and a taro patch by the Southern Sea. That's not to say that they didn't have a talent for light-fingered acquisition, or trickery, ultimately able to quote the Bible, while picking your pocket. *In many quarters the Polynesian gives only to receive... a gift is regarded as a sprat to catch a whale...*

And finally, they learned firsthand about European diseases, to which they had no immunity, which they understood even less.

The Europeans, for their part, learned firsthand about Samoan warlike and hostile savagery, which had been finely honed on their 600 year-old conflicts with the neighboring Tongans and Fijians, from whom they adopted the protean protein-procuring practice of cannibalism, to compliment the headhunting. In an island archipelago destitute of animal food, came bloodstained baskets of long pig, from which the eyes of the victims were formally offered to the chief, as a delicacy. *Not many years have elapsed since he was seen striding on the beach, a dead man's arm across his shoulder. 'So does Kooamua to his enemies!' he roared to the passers-by, and took a bite from the raw flesh...*

Fighting against Samoans was unwinnable, and conciliation was deemed a sign of weakness, for which mockery, especially if any anger was shown, was dished out in portions as large as the roughness of their edges. Just when it appeared that the Samoan character was complete, and could not be influenced by anything or anyone that might make it worse, they washed up on the beach.

In the 1887s the Germans, who had began planting copra on Upolu thirty years earlier, staged a coup, backed up by naval gunboats, and a Quisling paramount chief named Malietoa, who suppressed a bloody rebellion, and exiled his rival, Mataafa, to the Marshall Islands. The Americans and British sent warships to Apia, but everyone's warships were sunk in a great storm at the end of hurricane season, killing 146 sailors. In 1889, the same year that Robert Louis Stevenson settled in Apia, the Treaty of Berlin 'legitimized' Germany's occupation. The following year, the Americans took the eastern half of the archipelago, and the Germans imported large numbers of unpaid Melanesians and poorly paid Chinese, and began making impressive fortunes from their copra and cocoa bean processing. In 1908 Governor Solf deposed the reigning king, Tupu Samoa, forcibly disarmed the Samoans, and had more warships sent from Germany. The volcanos erupted on Savai'i.

Maybe that's why they excel in sports, and in violent street gangs. Samoans have competed at every Rugby World Cup since 1991, and are forty times more likely to play in the American National Football League than any non-Samoan American. They have become some of the most successful boxers and wrestlers, and Samoans like Masuahimaru and Konishiki have reached the highest ranks in Sumo.

In any Devil's dictionary, the Sons of Samoa would come with a warning.

SAMOANS, *n.* Wild, aggressive, morbidly obese, Asian-Pacific barbarian pack animals, identified by their huge foreheads and 'groucho' eyebrows, disturbingly long, thick, matted, black hair, thighs where there should be biceps, and all clothed in humongous short pants. Wherever they have been imported, their families were allowed to follow, and immediately began setting up villages.

The males of the species are especially suited for drywalling, erecting cinder block walls, and as defensive linemen, but are also often hired as nightclub doormen. Like grizzly bears, they are usually placid, but unpredictable, and a single blow from a Samoan of either sex can be fatal. When in the presence of a Samoan, proceed with caution. Do NOT make eye contact and back away from their habitat as quickly as possible, or they will eat all your food. They are one of the hardest people to knock out. If confronted, your only chance is to go for the knees. The one and only thing that can stop a Samoan is gout.

Give them their space and, most times, they will not bother you.

Their physical appearance seems to have degraded, in proportion to the length of time in contact with the rest of us, In 1851, Shaw was enamored. *They are a singularly beautiful race, and most amiable in character... Most of the men had their short cut hair plastered snow-white with lime, because it was Saturday. Almost every Samoan limes his hair on Saturdays, partly to keep up the yellow colour produced by previous applications, partly for hygienic reasons that had better be left to the imagination. All the visitors displayed an incomparable self-possession and dignity of bearing not at all like the 'Tongan swagger,' but much more akin to the manner of what is known in society as 'really good people.' Coupled to the almost complete absence of clothes, and the copper skins, it was enough to make one perfectly giddy at first.*

Robert Louis Stevenson, their principal European advocate and benefactor, had slightly less praise, as recorded by Henry Adams, who came to visit him, in 1891. *He says that the Tahitians are by far finer men than the Samoans, and that he does not regard the Samoans as an especially fine race, or the islands here as specially beautiful... The European may chop the nut with an axe or knife till he is tired before he gets at the fruit, but the native, lacing the nut between his toes and fingers, fixes his teeth firmly into the husky substance which clings to the nut, and by the force of his jaw peals off the exterior covering.*

But it was Paul Theroux, who took the conversation uglier, from the physical to the behavioral. *I never saw anyone reading anything more demanding than a comic book. I never heard any youth express an interest in science or art. No one even talked politics. It was all idleness, and whenever I asked someone a question, no matter how simple, no matter how well the person spoke English, there was always a long pause before I got a reply, and I found these Pacific pauses maddening. And there was giggling but no humor — no wit. It was just foolery.*

I'm not sure what he expected, paddling through a people who measured time by hot hours and cool hours, responsive only to the recurring calls of hunger and sensuality; who washed their clothes and themselves in the same water at the same time, and one only needed to add a little kava to the water, to wash away time as well. In the limitless season of freedom and leisure, dozing on the mats in the heat, indolence was the only possible result. Out of the luminous vapour and dazzling smoke that accompanied their migration from Vava'u a thousand years before the Europeans, they weren't just on island time. They were island time. *It means we get deah when we get deah...*

I asked Equator how he would have me present Samoans to the rest of the world, if he could help distill their essential character. He paused his Pacific pause.

"If I could present Samoans to the rest of the world." He said. "I'd like them to think that we are a proud and caring people."

"Unlike the Europeans." I said. "Who are a proud and uncaring people." He grinned, *and took a bite from the raw flesh.*

"You wear that lavalava like a Samoan." Equator said. "You should really go."

But we had already been.

'Nothing more strongly arouses our disgust than cannibalism, yet we make the same impression on Buddhists and vegetarians, for we feed on babies, though not our own.'

Robert Louis Stevenson

*   *   *

Thirteen years earlier, possibly at the moment of Tyra's conception, Robyn and I landed in Samoa. Dropping into the torrential rains of cyclone season, we soared along the blur of small bays and coral fringing reefs pounding on the high black volcanic rocks. 'Seu le manu ae taga'i i le galu.' *Catch the bird but watch for the wave.*

At Fagali'i airport on the small main island of Upolu, we boarded a smaller Polynesian Airlines 'skyburster,' and flew on to Savai'i Island, more like us at the time, much younger, more volcanically active, lush and well-watered.

The Ma'oto terminal was just a traditional *fale*, open on all sides, and out to a small parking lot, where all the island's taxis had come to pick off the few tourists. Robyn and I were headed to the west coast, and found a bus stop, behind a red station wagon with its windows painted over with the artist owner's slogans. *Running canvas... Beautiful Expressions of Nature... No smoke drugs but only art.*

It arrived like this guy had painted it, in a blaze of color, reggae pumping out of its missing doors and windows, its name stenciled in large letters over the front window. *Heartbreaker.*

"'Talofa." Said the bus driver. "O fea 'e te alu i ai?" *My love to you. Where are you going.* I tried to pronounce our destination.

"Satuiatua?" I asked. He shrugged, and motioned us on, a much easier gesture than the gymnastics involved in our manoeuvering into the solid wall of Samoan flesh that filled our chosen conveyance. We drove off into the devastation of what Cylcones Ofa and Val had brought and wrought, ten years earlier. In February 1990 and December 1991, they had ripped the country, killing thirty-two people, and destroying villages and roads and crops and forests. The country's largest export crop, taro, was wiped out by a virulent fungus, three years later. Along with the coffee and cocoa, it had never recovered. We drove through the surviving wreckage of washed out roads and shattered culverts, uprooted trees, and a menagerie of feral animals in our path. Beyond the pigs and rats and crippled dogs and herons, at the end of the wavy charcoal bitumen ribbon, cut through all the green wavelengths in nature, our driver rolled to a stop, an hour later.

"Tofa." He said. "Goodbye." We stepped off next to the sign. *Satuiatua Beach Resort... Where Traditional Culture and Contemporary Innovation is Respectfully Balanced.*

"Jeezuz." I said to Robyn. "The cyclones have left behind contemporary innovation." But we needn't have worried.

"Talofa!" She said. I looked up to a bigboned Samoan woman, with a red hibiscus behind her right ear.

"Momma Chief." Said the little blue lavalava next to her. She was the momma chief. Leilua Vaimalu Tutogi Mailei had founded the place six years earlier. She had Little Blue show us to our fale, and the magnificent white beach in front.

Our hut could have been the very one described by William Shaw a hundred and fifty years earlier. *An oblong roof and nothing more, open with no walls, using blinds made of coconut palm fronds during the night or bad weather... thatched with grass or the leaves of the bread-fruit or palm tree externally, and lined with bamboo internally, supported by three parallel rows of posts... the inner height from the pitch of the roof is about ten feet, and the eaves slant to within three feet of the ground.*

And Robert Louis Stevenson, fifty years later. *Palm tree wood and palm-tree leaf their materials; no nail had been driven, no hammer sounded, in their building, and they were held together by lashings of palm-tree sinet.*

The elemental sounds of rain and wind and waves came up to

welcome us. Every morning, I would wrap my bright yellow Rotuman lavalava, and shave in the tiny mirror nailed to one of our posts. And Robyn and I would don our masks and float over the coral, and walk the white sand, under the tall palms and huge *pulu* Banyan trees.

Just on sunset, the wind died, the sky glowed and then faded into thickening shadow, and the stars appeared, timidly at first, and then boldly into the dark blue of the tropical night. Inside the still blackness of our fale, the moon pushed a silver belt under the roof, and drew the slow slanting shadows of our pillars on the floor. The rain came in the deepest part of our dreams, hissing and breathing and rolling in big Doppler sheets of white noise, driving us deeper still. Bang on six, the dawn pulled a radiant solar rim against the purple palms and forced the precipitant patter at longer and louder intervals to a stop and, when the last drop fell, the roosters crowed, and the day began anew.

Momma Chief would tease me mercilessly, at mealtimes.

"You hungry?" She would ask. I would nod, between bites of Polynesian portions.

"You like Samoa?" She would ask.

"I like Samoa?" I would say, holding out my plate for Samoa.

In the late afternoon, we would gather to watch young couples dance traditional Samoan *siva*. They were tattooed, as the Tahitians and Hawai'ians and Māoris had been tattooed, before they no longer were. The women had been given *malus*, fine and delicate little filigree crosses and dotted lines, extending from below the knees to the upper thighs. The men had intricate dense blue *pe'a*, a mass of straight lines and large blocks of sidewall dark cover, from the waist to the rectum to the knees.

In Samoan mythology the *tatau* originates in a myth of Tilafaiga and Taema, twin sisters who swam from Fiji to Samoa with a basket of tattoo tools. As they neared the village of Falealupo just north of us, singing a song about how only women got tattooed, they saw a clam underwater and dived down to get it. When they resurfaced, the lyrics had changed to only men being eligible.

If the Samoans believed that it had come from Fiji, the Fijians believed that tattooing had come from Samoa, and the Māoris believed that it had come from the underworld. With the extreme pain and courage, weeks to years of torment, required to finish a pe'a and become a *soga'imiti*, the Māoris had been right. Untattooed Samoan males were colloquially referred to as 'telefua.' *Naked.* Those who began the ordeal but didn't complete it because of the pain, or the inability to pay, were called 'pe'a mutu,' a mark of shame. Family members of the man getting the tattoo were often in attendance at a respectful distance, to provide words of encouragement, sometimes through song.

> 'Pity the youth now lying
> While the tufuga starts
> Alas he is crying loudly
> As the tattooing tool cuts all over
> Young fellow, young fellow, be brave
> This is the sport of male heirs
> Despite the enormous pain
> Afterwards you will swell with pride.'
> Pese o le Tatau, *Samoan Tattoo Song*

The rite of passage of every soga'imiti had begun with his birth. His grandmother started collecting the burnt candlenut soot that would dye his pe'a tattoo, and stored it in a plugged coconut. She presented it to him at puberty. When the arrangements for payment of hundreds of fine mats had been agreed upon, the *tufuga ta tatau* master tattooist could begin. He usually worked with two apprentices, whose job it was to stretch the skin and wipe off the excess ink and blood with lengths of tapa cloth. From out of a lined *tunuma* cylindrical wood container, the tufugu would carefully remove his handmade serrated *au* combs, the sharp ends of which, shark's teeth or filed boar's teeth, had been stored facing inwards. These were lashed to small tortoise shell fragments tied to a wooden handle. The hardwood *sausau* tapping mallet that would drive the candlenut soot under the skin, was as long as the master's forearm, and as wide as his thumb. The man he tattoos must not be left alone, or the *aitu* spirits might take him, like the Samoan flying fox the pe'a was also the name for.

> 'Of all the countries in the Pacific
> Samoa is the most famous
> The sogaimiti walking towards you
> With his fa'aila glistening
> Curved lines, motifs like ali
> Like centipedes, combs like wild bananas
> Like sigano and spearheads
> The greatest in the world.'
> Pese o le Tatau, *Samoan Tattoo Song*

The young leaf-collared Samoan soga'imiti on the sand in front of us didn't look like he remembered much of the pain, perhaps because he was anticipating too much of the pleasure, with the chunky girl he was about to dance with. It may have been the red hibiscus behind her ear, or the *sei* garland, or the candlenut necklace. Or it may have been where her tattoo was headed, retreating and advancing, gently twirling in front of him. Her arms waved like a field of grain in a capricious wind, in perfect time to the voices behind, singing slowly and gently at first, and then increasing in speed and volume. Dry palm-fronds rustled in the blue sky overheard, mimicking the *shushshush* whisper of forest leaves in cooler latitudes. There was a hot clean smell on the sand.

"Ai, ai!" They sang, feet and bodies quivering in rhythm, followed by loud clapping, and cries of 'Malo! Malo!' *Well done.*

In between dances, the cross-legged chorus on the grass fanned themselves, smoked cigarettes, and chattered. A big elderly Samoan grandmother with gold earrings and an oversized man's wristwatch, attached to an even bigger stainless steel wristband, held up a naked grandchild, and grinned. I asked her what the songs were about.

"Sweethearts, and the trees, and the sea." She said. "Some true, some lie."

We told Mama Chief that we would be on Manono Island on Sunday.

"Manono is the most traditional island in the most traditional Polynesian culture in the world." She said. "There are no vehicles allowed, not even bicycles, no roads, no dogs, no horses, no noise, and no shops. I asked what there would be, to see and do.

"Nothing but go to church." She said. "And you will need to show your *fa'aaloalo.*"

"Fa'aaloalo?" I asked, nearly tripping over the glottal stops.

"Fa'aaloalo is respect for the *vāfealoa'i.*" She said.

"Vāfealoa'i?" I asked.

"Vāfealoa'i is the relationships between people." She said.

"So we need to show our fa'aaloalo for vāfealoa'i." I said. Mama Chief nodded. At least I wouldn't need to buy a vowel.

Courtesy is the most important quality in Samoan society. By custom, Samoans are extremely polite to guests, so much so that some of them tend to answer all questions posed by a stranger in the affirmative. When they answer incorrectly they are not lying, just deferential. If we want real information, we should avoid asking questions that call for a 'yes or no' answer. Mama Chief taught Robyn and I some of the other nuances of Samoan culture.

"Don't talk to people while standing." She said. "And don't eat while walking around a village. Avoid stretching your legs straight out in front of you while sitting. If you're passing through a village and see a group of elderly men sitting around a fale with their legs folded, it's a gathering of matais. Do not drive by the meeting place. If you're walking, don't carry a load on your shoulders, or an open umbrella. When the empty acetylene tank gong, hanging from a tree, sounds for the *sa* evening prayer, stop until it sounds again. If you arrive at a Samoan home during a prayer session, wait outside until the family is finished with its devotions. If you are already inside, you will be expected to share in the service. Don't wear flowers to church."

And chiefs, well, chiefs were entirely different animals. Their conduct and relations were governed by strict rules. The chiefly symbol worn over their shoulders, were short brooms resembling horse's tails. The kava ritual was different than what we had experienced in Fiji. In the old days, the roots were also chewed and spit into the bowel by a virgin daughter of a chief. But in Samoa, it was a more solemn occasion, and you were expected to spill more on the floor and sip, rather than gulp, the dishwater.

We left Mama Chief to tour the rest of Savai'i, on one of the rare sparkling mornings of the rainy season. A strong man and a waterfall always channel their own path. The path to this one hiked through a coconut grove, up a muddy trail and down a rickety ladder, into a hidden vale, where a spectacular crystal cascade plunged from the rainforest, over sixty feet into a deep cool cobalt clarity.

The rock walls of the ravine stretched high into the sky, covered in rich, dense lichens and moss at the bottom, ascending into ferns, and growing into trees and vines towards the top. The tranquil pool at the bottom of the Olemoe waterfall was surrounded on all sides by this thick tropical viridescence. Robyn and I cavorted and swam in the most refreshing swimming hole in the Southern Sea, alone with the smell of misted gardenias and ozone. Or we thought we were alone. Nipping at our toes, at the shallow outer edge of the pool, were freshwater prawns, no less transparent than the moisture that sustained them. We were all ghosts together, splashing in true love, which everyone else talked about and few had ever seen. Here we lived the most we had ever lived, and died a little, as we left up the ladder.

Just up the path was the largest ancient structure in the

Pacific, a gigantic stepped stone wedding cake, two hundred feet wide and forty high, almost covered in jungle. The pyramid of Pulemelei may have been a 'star mound' platform, used in the ancient sport of pigeon-snaring. But not only did no one really know what it was for, most didn't even know of its existence. How the inhabitants of a small island, halfway between Hawai'I and New Zealand, with more legends and stories about Polynesian origins, natural features, and things that didn't even exist, could not even know about something this big, a site of some great mysterious ancient civilization, was simply incredible. The Samoans had a bagful of proverbs, which fit most of their world. Amuia le masina, e alu ma sau. *Stones rot but not words.* In Pulemelei, apparently, it was the words that had rotted, and left the stones.

Not far from the flying water and rocks of the morning, was the flying water and rocks of the afternoon. Further along the southern coast, was a perilous plateau of black volcanic cliffs, fissured with sea caves and hollows, up through which geysered the crashing ocean swells. The plumes that blew vertical through the *pupu* Taga blowholes shot over eighty feet into the sky. Each surge of the sea roared up past our ears, and into the clouds above. And no one and nothing else was there, except for the odd coconut, which we launched into orbit as canonballs, or shells from a mortar, once we got the timing right. Palm fronds chasers followed them, spinning like witches brooms in the waterspout spray.

The rollers flow through the lava holes turned to lava flow through the holy rollers, and the churches flattened in the north coast eruption and boiling river of rock surging down from Mt Matavanu, in 1905. Robyn and I stood on the convolutions inside what remained of the Methodist church, 'miraculously' spared, unlike that of the Mormons and Catholics. Methodism was that branch of Christianity that could have taken its name from its indoctrinated practice of the Rhythm Method. Nearby was the rectangular 'grave of the virgin,' a two meter deep indentation in the expanse of the lava field. Given the fact that there was only one, and molten ripples of Lucifer's licorice had still swept through the middle of their church, the Methodists might not have that much more reason to celebrate Samoan susceptibility to their missionary position. The other ripples in the hardened lava were from the old corrugated tin roof panels, and the helices of the red ginger flowers penetrating through.

Robyn and I passed a black sand beach, big bore surf breakers crashing so hard on the black volcanic rocks, it made violent white foam, and a mist of the morning. A fale, built on a lava wave, had a table and chairs inside, surrounded by large pink blossoms. Fat people sat on the steps of a whitewashed church.

We reached Falealupo, already the landing point for the twin sisters who had brought the art of the tattoo to Samoa. But Falealupo was also the gateway to the Pulotu underworld where the aitu spirits of the dead resided, and where the Samoan Goddess of War, Nafanua, was carried home by flying foxes. But it was also where the Rainforest Canopy Walkway was, that led us to Moso's footprint, the giant that had stepped here from Fiji, the Rock House cave, and a hanging swing bridge across the 100 foot gap between two big tropical trees, to the tree house view of denuded but wide regenerating green horizon and white sand beach. Past a big plastic Santa, a plaster statue of Jesus under a cupola on a tall staircase of rocks and pennants, a harbour of fishing boats with tall flagpoles and colored flags, wet kids in the sudden rain, and a Samoan cricket game, that spontaneously materialized outside a big white church with two cupolas. Cricket was different in Samoa. Firstly, it was called Kirikiti. Second, it was played with a very different bat, a three-sided war club as big as a caber. The balls were constructed from handmade rubber, wrapped with pandanus leaves. The combination guaranteed that on one would have any clue as to where the ball would go. There were no pads or face protection, there was no limitation to 22 members, losing teams could buy their way back into the match by paying a fee to the host village, and disputed calls had resulted in death by cricket bat. The stupid man, who had suggested that cricket was baseball on Valium, had never played the game in Samoa.

Robyn and I were headed to the small offshore island of Manono the next day, for it was a Saturday, and the next one was Sunday. And the only thing that happened in Samoa on a Sunday, and we we didn't want to miss it, when it did. It was pissing rain, and we were driving along the undulating Savai'I bitumen, when a thumb caught our attention. The words of Paul Theroux resonated in the back seat. *I knew I was going to meet a writer here. As soon as I saw this fucked-up place I said to myself,' I'm going to meet a writer.* We stopped, and Derek got in. "What do you do?" I asked.

"I'm a writer." He said. "From Montreal." And we drove him to our last stop on Savai'i, in Salelologa, just a few kilometers north from the ferry that would take us back to Upolu, and on to Manono, the next day. The rain continued, as we came to the Safua Hotel, *The Family and Cultural Hotel of the Island.* The manageress, Vaasaili Moelagi Jackson, goodness knew where the Jackson had come from, welcomed us, and sorted us out, to the point where, next morning on the clothesline in the sun, my towel spoke Samoan, on the rope. I asked Derek why he was here.

"I'm still searching for meaning." He said. I told him he was only halfway on the right track.

"Life is a desire, not a meaning." I said. "And you've only got the desire part correct."

*   *   *

'It was like in Samoa when they'd put up a movie screen on the beach and show movies and the locals would run behind the sheet to see where the people went. It was pretty grim.'

Dick Wolfe

Robyn and I left Derek in the Salelologa downpour next morning, for the ferry back to Upolu, a bus full of sweet wet coconut-scented hair, and a near stalemate with the small boat crew, that wanted a matai's ransom, for the short backwards crossing back in time to Manono. From the first moment that the first *palagi*, Abel Tasman, had entered the Southern Sea in 1642, every subsequent explorer was subjected to its 'traditions,' some of which involved greed and childishness and ridicule and aggression. We finally agreed on twice the local rate, just as they were about to sail and, as if in approval, the strong Samoan sun came on hot and bright, illuminating the turquoise expanse of lagoon from below.

We converged on a small black volcanic island of tin roof reflections and skybound coconut trees. Closer, we made out dozens of open-sided fales, built as thickly and as wooden as their inhabitants. Men napped inside, women wove on the stoops, and roosters and children screeched in the yards around them.

The roosters didn't come running to the black breakwaters, but the children did.

"Palagi!" They shouted, and elbowed each other out of the way, to be the first to claim what they thought we should have brought them. Those who had come before us had brought them the expectation, we brought them a bitter reality, and they had brought stones for the possibility of disappointment. But Robyn and I were experts in the art of disarmament and, despite the prevailing Polynesian position that Palagi presence was proportional to their presents, they were soon demilitarized, and anxious to show us to our chosen shelter. Manono was only a square mile in area, four small shoreline villages connected by a dirt path no more than a foot wide, edged with with yellow *lautalotalo*, banana palms, mango trees and hibiscus. The young boys left us at Uili and Tauvela Vaotu'ua's place, and an open-sided fale, shaded by enormous *tallie* trees, on stilts over the water's edge. Ulili made us welcome, with fish and deep fried eggplant.

"Manono is very traditional." Said Tauvela, explaining why Robyn would have to wear a five-piece shirt, shorts and lavalava, over her bathing suit, to go for a swim off the volcanic rocks below. We didn't have a huge problem with tradition. It was always a fascinating aspect of cultural experience in our travels. Without it, a society was rudderless. But too much tradition pulled it into drydock. Enslavement to tradition was to guarantee the corpse of creativity, the end of excellence, and the dawn of dissatisfaction. *There was something in their ill-nature that was traditional, too.* Deep inside paradise, they seemed a little annoyed.

A surgical colleague of mine, the same size and sluggishness as a kavanated matai, would often regale me with his Samoan infatuation, based mostly on his notion of how much more perfectly traditional it was, as compared to other parts of Polynesia. I doubt if he had ever met or known a Samoan, or that he had much travel experience in other parts of Polynesia, but the idea of tight Samoan traditionalism had uniquely forged his opinion about Samoan superiority.

Robyn and I were not as impressed. It was difficult, if not impossible, to meet Samoans. On Tonga the islanders included us, and dropped a pig in the ground, with little provocation; on Samoa we hadn't been properly introduced. The locals we had met were ambivalent, remaining at a neutral distance, more comfortable with their prohibitions and complex etiquette, than with any potential opportunity for engagement. Maybe it was the Germans. Most certainly it was the missionaries.

They had started with decent enough deities. Samoans worshipped a hierarchy of gods under one Supreme Being.

Before the sea, earth, sky, plants or people, Tagaloa lived in the expanse of empty space. He created a rock, and commanded it to split into clay, coral, cliffs, and stones. As it broke apart, the earth and sea and sky came into being. A spring of fresh water emerged. Next, at Saua in the Manu'a Islands, Tagaloa created man and woman, whom he named *Fatu* and *'Ele'ele*, Heart and Earth. He sent them to the area of fresh water and commanded them to multiply. He ordered the sky, *Tu'ite'elagi*, to prop itself up above the earth, and created *Po* and *Ao*, Night and Day, which bore the 'eyes of the sky'- the Sun and the Moon. The people needed government, and Tagaloa sent Manu'a, a son of Po and Ao, to be chief. Next, the world was divided into groups of islands, consisting of Manu'a, Fiji, Tonga, and Savai'i. The void that Tagaloa noticed, between Manu'a and Savai'I, he filled with 'Upolu and Tutuila. Tagaloa's final command was: 'Always respect Manu'a; anyone who fails to do so will be overtaken by catastrophe.'

They had started with wonderful legends.

The beautiful young woman Sina, who lived on Upolu, kept a pet eel named Tuna. When he grew to be as long as a man, Sina released him into the pool, where she bathed every day. The two became such close friends that Sina's fiancé became jealous of Tuna and sentenced him to death. Hearing of the plan to kill him, Tuna pleaded with Sina that she be the one to kill him. 'Plant my head in the sand on the seashore,' he said. 'From me a tree will grow that will provide for your every need. You will have food, water, and shelter always. And every time you drink from my fruit, you will be kissing me.' Whenever you drink from a coconut, Tuna's tiny face is looking back up at you.

Coconut kisses and tropical fruit were set out on the deck of our fale next morning for breakfast. We awake to the lowing of a giant conch shell.

"Church." Said Uili. Smoke from the umus for the Sunday morning feast was already rising behind us. I put on my bright yellow Rotuma lavalava and shirt and tie, and Robyn put on a dress. We passed the statue of the Reverend Peter Turner, a Methodist missionary that had come to Manono in 1835. His arrival had been arranged by the London Missionary Society, and delivered by the *Messenger of Peace*, the salvation ship built by one of the most prolific proselytizers in the Pacific.

John Williams had been a Tottenham ironmonger, before receiving his first LMS commision to Tahiti, in 1817. Thirteen years later, he was the first missionary to land in Samoa, and found fertile ground. Not only was the Tagaloa legend like the Methodist god's creation myth, a prophecy of the war goddess, Nafanua, had also prepared the message from the messenger. William's legacy resides in the large white Congregational Christian churches that dominate every village, and the fervour with which the Samoans practice his strict, puritanical version of Christianity.

There were other denominations in Samoa, of course. The *lotu Pope* Catholic Church had come with Marist missionaries from Wallis and Futuna in 1845, ploughing the way for the pernicious European rivalry between Catholics and Protestants that infected and affected Rotuma, and extended throughout the Pacific. The *lotu Mamona* Mormons arrived with two missionaries sent by a Caribbean gunrunning, rebellion-fomenting, prison-escaping, Kindom of Hawai'i Prime Minister. Walter Gibson had been trying to use religion to annex Samoa, before being excommunicated for preaching false doctrine, colony maladministration, and embezzlement of church funds. He fled and died penniless in San Francisco.

Robyn and I congregated with the congregation, outside the whitewashed church exterior. There was a stenciled curve of red above the entrance. *O le talaleilei.*

Big brown women, all dressed in white with broad white straw hats, carried their pandanas fans and bibles, up the stairs and into the simple pews in front of the cross and clock, under the iron roof inside. Someone had replaced the oxygen with the heavy sticky scent of wreaths. The stagnant air that remained, what was left of it, was hot and oppressive.

All the Samoan women love to turn out in trade finery on Sundays, and a white muslin, with lace, made exactly like a British nightdress, is the height of elegance and good form.

The preacher wore a tie, a white lavalava, flipflops, and a look of smug self-righteousness. Souls would be saved, and pockets would be emptied. The fanning women would occasionally reach out and slap a small head, or pinch a small arm during his sermon.

Reverend Williams had taught them well, but he was well repaid. In November 1839, while bringing the Gospel to a part of the New Hebrides island of Erromango, he was killed and eaten by cannibals.

At Lepuia'i village the previous day, Robyn and I had visited the Grave of 99 Stones, another monument from later in the 19th century. A high chief named Vaovasa, had 99 wives, and had been killed by villagers, as he tried to escape from Upolu with his 100th.

If you're going to get punished for your sins, root for the heathens.

'Old and young, we are all on our last cruise.'
Robert Louis Stevenson

* * *

* * *

'I should like to rise and go
Where the golden apples grow
Where below another sky
Parrot Islands anchored lie'
Robert Louis Stevenson

Everybody, soon or late, sits down to a banquet of consequences. When Robert Louis Stevenson wrote these lines, as a young man in Edinburgh, his tuberculosis and chain smoking and alcohol and opium and law degree were still in front of him.

When he arrived in Samoa, four years before his death of a hemorrhagic stroke at the age of 44, there were no parrots and no golden apples. There was the hot, clammy, humid, muddy, rainy season grey sky of Apia, at its most dismal, and salvage crews working in the harbor, still crawling over the hulks of the American, British and German warships sunk by the previous year's cyclone. But what Stevenson would find, like Lord Byron had found in Greece, was a regular postal service, and a perfect place to die.

William Shaw's arrival in Apia, fifty years earlier, had been even more convivial.

'On our arrival at Apea, swarms of natives came on board... not long since been guilty of cannibal practices, and were notorious for their attacks upon boat crews; Leprosy and elephantiasis, cutaneous eruptions and ophthalmia are common....fruit was abundant, which they offered in exchange for calico, or discarded wearing apparel; for money was not current among them. Both sexes were excellent swimmers, playing about in the water quite at their ease, as if they were amphibious; their favourite pastime being to ascend the rigging and plunge from a height into the water; which the women also did fearlessly. Two mothers with infants at their breast, ascended the shrouds, and clambering out to the end of the top-sail yard, precipitated themselves head-foremost into the sea with their babies in their arms; the plunge from such a height was tremendous, and as they disappeared the water foamed and eddyed around, but in a few seconds they rose unconcernedly a few feet beyond, as if enjoying a bath.'

The women were apparently also fond of smoking. *Lighting a pipe and taking a puff, they inhaled the smoke, emitting it through their nostrils, and then passed the pipe to their next neighbour.*

During WWII, Allied troops used Samoa as a training base for battles in the Pacific. Aggie Grey opened a hot dog and hamburger business, which morphed into one of the Southern Sea's most iconic hotels.

Paul Theroux was definitely in his *Happy Isles* grump phase, by the time he got here, referring to Apia as '*squalid... rusted and neglected... the worst Samoans and the worst Palangis come to Apia... all the failures.*' But he had just gone through a divorce.

Robyn and I had no such disappointment. We rolled in, just in time to catch the Santa Claus parade, every float throwing sweets to the mobs of children that lined it. I marched with the constabulary band, and their powder blue shirts, navy blue lavalavas, bone white pith helmets and black sandals, playing deep German-Samoan *oom-pa-pas* on their silver and white Sousaphones. *The drumbeat of the Polynesian has a strange and gloomy stimulation for the nerves of all.*

Across from the Amau Buller department store and Chan Mow supermarket was a snow cone truck with hand painted characters on its paneling. In between Donald Duck and the dwarves was a cartoon rat. It wasn't clear whether this was *Rattus exulans*, the original Polynesian rat, the same *kiore* rat of the Maoris, or *Rattus rattus*, the European black rat that, like other competitions in the Southern Sea, beat out the Polynesians every time. Even at the site of the nuclear tests at Eniewetok Atoll, only the black rats prevailed, the theory being that, in addition to their plant diet, they also ate insects. Judging by the size and color of the caricature, and the contents of the snow cones, it was the European variety. I had an American Classic, and Robyn the fish and chips, at the Kitano Fusitala, before heading off on a ninety-minute local bus trip, through villages of beautiful croton hedges and tiny houses, to the east coast turquoise water and white sands of

Lalomanu. We stayed in the #8 oceanfront shack at *Tafu Beach Fales* for two brilliant days, snorkeling in the rich coral lagoons, and gazing at uninhabited Nu'utele Island, Vailima lager in hand, as the sun went down over the clifftops behind us in the late afternoon. Love prefers twilight to daylight.

The twilight came on with a vengeance, when the clocks advanced, almost a decade after Robyn and I left our fale, and daylight saving time was cancelled that year in Samoa. Our fale was crushed by a wall of water thirty feet high, and the cliffs scoured out twenty feet higher. A mother at the Tafua Beach Fales watched her three children swept away by the tsunami, and one hospital in Apia reported it had received 79 bodies. The 2009 earthquake turned the capital into a ghost town, destroyed two whole villages outright, and left 3000 people homeless. Robyn and I were slightly ahead of our time.

But Robert Louis Stevenson was right on his. We arrived at his Vailima villa on the slopes of Mount Vaea in the morning. It was a large rambling white wooden South Seas mansion, with crisscrossed railings on the two-storied verandas, and a rust red roof. He lived here lavishly, with his wife, Fanny, eleven years his senior, his stepmother, two stepchildren, and later, his own elderly widowed mother, and his stepdaughter's drunken husband. Stevenson was the magician that some writers are, known by the islanders as *Tusitala*, the 'Teller of Tales.' He brought an enchantment to his location and, partly through insinuation and partly through recruitment, imposed himself onto and into Samoan society. He had left one cultural hierarchy of stern affection and obscure formality, of clan chiefs, and drones and hangers-on, and peasants and potwallopers, for another. He became the Scottish laird of ingratiating chieftains, and the mutual manipulation meter soared into the red zone. All his household staff wore a Royal Stuart tartan lavalava, and all his ceremonial functions were manor-mannered, and fancy dress. Stevenson and the Samoans took each other for all they were worth.

In the canonical South Sea phrase, he was 'a perfect gentleman when sober,' and also, quite fortunately, when he was not. What he wrote, of the men and women of his new culture, was of his time. *But I was now escaped out of the shadow of the Roman Empire... Something bestial, squatting on his hams in a canoe, sucking an orange and spitting it out again to alternate sides with ape-like vivacity... I have seen one lady strip up her dress, and, with cries of wonder and delight, rub herself bare-breeched upon the velvet cushions.*

He had been close friends with Oscar Wilde but he wasn't gay himself. Fanny would defend him from those who thought otherwise.

Dr. A said, 'How can anybody write books with arms like these?' I turned round indignantly and burst out with, 'He has written all his books with arms like these!'

Compared to the muscular masculine model of Samoan manhood, Stevenson wasn't it. One could be forgiven for finding similarities in Wilde's *Picture of Dorian Gray*, and Stevenson's *Dr. Jekyll and Mr. Hyde*, and wondering if he wasn't also an adherent of 'the love that dare not speak its name.' When I asked Equator for his opinion, he acknowledged Stevenson's contribution to raising the profile of his 'proud and caring people,' but also found him a bit of an effete embarrassment. In Samoa, it is acceptable, for a family that has too many sons, to raise the youngest boy as a daughter. These *fa'afafine* were given girls names, wore female clothing, and used the ladies room. Some went on to become famous transsexual entertainers in Apia.

"He was a bit of a fa'afafine." Equator would say.

"Like some Palagi youngest sons." I would say. "Some who went into the clergy." He grinned, *and took a bite from the raw flesh.*

But Robert Louis Stevenson loved the Samoans, and they loved him back. He learned their language, and wrote and translated into it. More than 200 grieving islanders hacked a 'Road of the Loving Heart,' up Mount Vaea, to a little knoll below the summit, where they placed him in a grave with an eternal view of Vailima and the town and the reef and the Southern Sea. Robyn and I found it here, with its epitaph.

In 1825, Fanny sold Vailima to a Russian merchant named Kunst, whose heirs later sold it to the German government, which converted it into the residence of the German governor of Samoa. After World War I, New Zealand turned it into British government house. Fanny died on February 18, 1914, in Santa Barbara, California, of a cerebral hemorrhage, like her late husband.

Our trip was downhill from there. We spent the afternoon flying along the sheer chute surfaces of the Papase'ea Sliding Rocks, plunging down the white waterfall, into the pool thirty feet below. Surrounded by scarlet hibiscus, pungent ginger, and mango trees, it was still the same water theme park paradise that Beatrice Grimshaw had experienced, ninety-two years earlier, as

'an unclasping of unwilling hands from the safe black rocks, a fierce tug from the tearing stream, an exceedingly unpleasant instant when one realised that there was no going back now at any price, and that the solid earth had slipped away as it does in the ghastly drop of a nightmare dream; then nothing in the world but a long loud roar, and a desperate holding of the breath, while the helpless body shot down to the bottom of the deep brown pool and up again - and at last, the warm air of heaven filling one's grateful lungs in big gasps, as one reached the surface, and swam across to the other side of the pool...'

Robyn went by, limbs spread out like a starfish, leaving behind a long, loud yell, like a train whistle going into a tunnel. We lay on the rocks above the falls, in the green shadow of the trees, drinking sweet water out of husked green coconuts, and doing nothing. The sign on the way out

was a universe of commonwealth contribution, like the one that Cicero had conceived, including both gods and men as members. *Rails donated by Australian fund... Steps donated by New Zealand fund... Watertank donated by Canadian fund.*
My memory did a backflip, to the Sunflower Airlines pilot who had flown us to Kandavu.

"G'day." He said, unapologetically. "Bloody baboons. They could have bloody told me. Where are youse two from?"
"I'm from Canada." I said. "And my wife is from New Zealand."
"Yeah, well I'm from Australia." He said. Not that there was much doubt.
"I guess we're just one big happy Commonwealth family." I said, trying to soften the edges.
"Don't give me that shit, mate." He said. "I've got no time for that bitch." *The Airline with a Heart.*

But the airline we would fly next day would have a heart. We spent our last night at the Seaside Inn, and all of the next day lounging at the pool at the Tusitala Hotel, swimming and telling tales, like Louis would have... *overcome with sodden corpulence, oppressed with drowsiness and held awake by apprehension.* Or Theroux. *By then a lazy sort of boredom had taken possession of my soul, the Oceanic malaise.*
The heart of Polynesian Airlines was a big one. It needed to be, to perfuse the peripheral tissue of the average Samoan passenger. Eighty percent of Samoans were obese, and the airline was always removing armrests or unbolting seats or levering their porcine passengers out of their toilets. In 2013, Air Samoa, Polynesian's leaner descendent, introduced the world's first 'pay as you weigh' policy, raising the bile and cheesing off some of the more rotund reservations. *Step 4. You travel happy, knowing full well that you are only paying for exactly what you weigh... nothing more."*
There had been a long tradition, among all the others, of moving big things around in Samoa. At precisely 06:00, on September 8, 2009, all the drivers in the archipelago switched over to driving on the left side of the road, the order to

formally switch sides formally broadcast on national radio by the Prime Minister. Horns honked, sirens wailed and church bells rang. Steering wheels would continued to be allowed on either side of the vehicle, but the bigger problem was with the country's buses, whose doors were mounted on the right side, which meant that passengers had to board from the middle of the road.

Two years later, the Prime Minister outdid himself, and moved the International Date Line to the east of the country, so that Samoa would lie to its west, and making it one of the first, rather than one of the last places to greet the new dawn. He also took an entire day out of the calendar to do it.

Big money was also moved around. Corruption was rife in Samoa. In 1997 the country had made international news with a scam involving the sale of Samoan passports for up to US$3300 in Hong Kong. *'Mo' betta.'*

I looked up to our plane on the tarmac, to find an airline employee with a roll of duct tape, wrapping the leading edge of the tail section. And Paul Theroux came back to mock me, for mocking him. *And at those moments when I was most exasperated I would look up; and see the oddest thing - a man holding a pig in his lap, or a man standing up to his neck in the lagoon, smoking a cigarette - and I would laugh the witless Samoan laugh and think: Take this seriously and you're dead.*

But we took off on time, and the big heart pumped hard. In the forty-minute flight back to Nandi, the Polynesian Airlines stewardesses, in the tradition of moving big things around in Samoa, did what no other airline in the world could have accomplished. They served a hot meal to everyone on the plane.

'Then we climbed back too the road, and drove home, six buggies full of laughing brown and white humanity, crowned and wreathed with green ferns, and singing the sweet, sad song of Samoa 'Good-bye, my flennie' - the song that was written by a native only a few years ago, and has already become famous over the whole Pacific. It is the farewell song of every island lover, the melody that soars above the melancholy rattling of the anchor chains on every outward-bound schooner that spreads her white wings upon the breast of the great South Seas. And for those who have known the moonlight nights of those enchanted shores, have smelt the frangipani flower, and listened to the soft singing girls in the endless, golden afternoons, and watched the sun go down upon an empty, sailless sea, behind the weird pandanus and drooping palms - the sweet song of the islands will ring in the heart for ever... the Samoan air will whisper, calling, calling, calling, - back to the murmur of the palms, and the singing of the coral reef, and the purple tropic night once more.'

Beatrice Grimshaw, In the Stange South Seas, 1908

Tofa my feleni, 'ole'a 'ou te'a
'ai folau i le vasa le ali'i pule i meleke
 ne'i galo mai Samoa, si o ta 'ele'ele
'ae manatua mai pea, le 'aupasese

Goodbye my friend, we are departing
As you travel overseas
Don't forget our homeland Samoa
Always remember us
Hold Samoa in your memories

Oh, I never will forget you, Samoa e ne'i galo atu
Goodbye, I never will forget you, Samoa e ne'i galo atu

Faatui Fuimaono Voa, Tofa My Feleni

*　　　*　　　*

375

One Foot
Cook Islands

'Ambition leads me not only farther than any other man has been before me, but as far as I think it possible for man to go.'

James Cook

Ambition aspires to descend, and when that's over, happiness begins.

Our flight from Auckland ended in a night landing. I wasn't sure I believed what I thought I was seeing, looking out our window on the final approach. It looked like the entire 'Heart of Polynesia,' as our destination had defined itself, was hanging on the sea wall at the end of the runway, to personally intercept our touchdown.

"They're jetblasting." Said the fleshy Kiwi Cook Islander, seated like a broad unfinished Rodin sculpture next to me. I couldn't take my eyes of his feet, which filled the space under the seat in front of him, even without his flip-flops, which he had stashed in the overhead bin.

"Jetblasting?" I asked.

"Yeah, jetblasting." He said. "The planes come in ten feet above their heads, and they love the noise and the wind they make. The ones that are really addicted prefer standing behind the takeoffs." I tried to get my head around the act of standing in the jet engine wake of a modern airliner launch, for the sensory experience.

"There's not a lot of nightlife here in Rarotonga, is there?" I asked.

"No, not really." He said. The ground came up to begin our happiness.

We descended the ramp, losing the bright rectangular slit and silhouetted mountains behind us, crossed the night sky star smoke above the tarmac, and entered the orange luminescence inside the terminal. There was the smell of frangipanis and coconut oil and humid sweat and heavy tropical air, and the sound of elated reunions unencumbered by consonants. The Cook Islanders were another big Polynesian people, and the ones returning from New Zealand were bigger yet. The local legends had propounded the theory that the great Maori migrations to *Aoteoroa* began from here 1500 years earlier, from a gap in Rarotonga's fringing reef, at the widest eastern part of the lagoon. Third generation kids, some in their own first time reverse migration, had left New Zealand with their directions and baseball caps and attitudes on backwards.

The true blue Kiwis on the flight, by comparison, were pale and scrawny, like they had another terminal condition, which had developed along with, or perhaps even from, their comparative agitation. They paced in front of the growing pile of luggage, on spindle-shanked shillelaghs.

Everyone eventually lined up in front of desk of the only immigration officer, uniformed in a flowered shirt and shorts. His flip flops had become deformed by his sheer mass, like he had just stepped on a cake.

Outside, the few minivans had arrived from town, two kilometers away in Avarua. Robyn and I piled in with as many as could be accommodated, which wasn't many, and spent the next hour in a circumnavigation of Raratonga, having drawn the short straw, the last at the end of a long line to reach our lodging.

The geometric figure of maximum area and given perimeter is a circle. Rarotonga is a submerged volcano sloping steeply upwards, almost 15,000 feet above the ocean floor, 20 miles in circumference with an area of 26 square miles. Most everyone lives on or near the two outside radial roads. The ancient inner one, Ara Metua, was constructed in the 11th century, paved with large slab stones, and peppered with several important *marae*, including Arai Te Tonga, the most sacred shrine in Rarotonga. The newer outer one, Ara Tapu, is paved with bitumen, and peppered with hotels and bungalows. There are only two bus routes- clockwise, and anticlockwise. For the number of chickens and coconuts and dogs that wandered into the roadway, it was remarkable that everyone got to where they were heading. When we finally arrived at our southeast lagoon accommodation, I realized how stupid it had been, for me to have booked anything this far around the circle's circumference this late at night, if we were flying on again the next morning, to Aitutaki, but if I had been at any risk of forgetting this, I needn't have worried. Robyn reminded me for the last time, just as I was drifting onto the reef.

"Why did we come all the way down here, if we're leaving tomorrow?" She asked. I was gratified to be able to answer promptly, and I did. I said I didn't know.

But Aitutaki would be the next island, and Rarotonga was still this one. Our return the following week was in daylight, and magnificent. We flew back over the high needle-shaped rock peak of Te Rua Manga, the agricultural terraces and flats and swamps surrounding the eroded central volcanic peaks cloaked in dense vegetation, palm-studded white sandy beaches lighting the circle and, and radiating further outward, over three hundred feet beyond the shore, the fringing reef that enclosed the lagoon.

The second Rarotongan holiday shack we rented was near Muri, with a simple open veranda and ceiling, and everything we needed- beach, barbeque, fridge, mosquito nets, hardwood slatted louvers and terra cotta floors. We spent our days snorkeling, on the offshore coral islets across from the shack, or opposite Fruits of Rarotonga, where grilled fish burgers and smoothies waited for us back onshore.

Robyn and I thought that a swim at Papua Falls would be like other Southern Sea waterfall experiences. It was, and it wasn't. The murmur of the falls was as much mosquitoes as water, but we escaped and cooled off with a swim in the dark pool below. There hadn't been any escape from the darker pools beyond the faded sign off the dirt track that took us there. *Hilton Rarotonga Resort... apartments and hotel suites for sale.* A more recent banner, *Stage 1 "Sold Out" Investment Opportunity- not timeshare*, had been pasted across some of the original script. *On site showroom open... Construction commencing soon.* Which brought us to the original script, of the Curse of Vaima'anga, and the Sheraton Resort debacle.

The waterfall was also called Wigmore Falls, after a planter named William John Wigmore who, in 1891, signed a twenty- year lease with More Uriatua for fifty dollars a year, for the land 'situated at Vaima'anga, boundary between the two streams Te Vai Tanga o Te Maanga from the sea to the hills.' What More Uriatua wouldn't know, was that, eleven years later, the New Zealand House of Representatives would enact the *Rules and Regulations of the Cook and Islands Land Titles Court*, creating land ownership title on the basis of written application. On July 9, 1903, the appointed Rarotongan High Court judge, Pa Ariki, claimed More Uriatua's land, and then released it to Wigmore. *I claim this piece of land (Vaima'anga 4) as mine. I claim it for myself only.*

When More Uriatua came to see Wigmore to ask for his land back, on Sunday, March 12 1911, Wigmore told him that he was no longer the owner, and to pound sand. In the bitter argument that followed, Wigmore shot More Uriatua dead, with his 303 rifle.

In his trial for manslaughter that began three months later, Wigmore was found guilty, with 'a very strong recommendation to mercy.' Chief Justice Stout sentenced him to six months hard labor in Rarotonga, followed by deportation. This was appealed in Wellington and, over a year later, Wigmore was back on his homestead.

Meanwhile, More Uriatua's daughter, Metua, who had sought the return of her father's land from Wigmore on numerous occasions, enlisted the help of her gods. In 1913, she carried out an act of *purepure* sorcery, by pacing a *taumaa* curse on the property.

*Any business (kimi'anga puapinga) activity operated on the land
Vaimaanga 4 will fail unless the land is returned to Ngati More and
the rightful owners.*

William John Wigmore failed. Between the 1950s and 1980s,
a pineapple plantation developer and one of New Zealand's
food giants, Greggs, attempting to run a citrus orchard, failed.
In 1987 the Cook Islands government signed a $52 million
deal with an Italian bank to build a Sheraton resort hotel, and
the project was insured by the Italian government. It looked
like Metua's curse had met its match. Except that Metua's
grandson, More Rua, returned to his great-grandfather's land
on May 25, 1990, fully adorned in his *Kaka'u* and *Rakei Taunga*
high priest traditional regalia. And laid on another one.

He struck the rock, on which sat the plaque commemorating
the agreement between the Cook Islands and Italian
Governments, with the butt of his spear, and cursed the land
again. The impact shattered the stone, cracking it all the way
down into the earth. Earlier in the day, in front of the Prime
Minister Sir Geoffrey Henry and hundreds of guests at the
official Sheraton Hotel Project launch, More Rua had
protested and proclaimed it would never succeed, reminding
them of his grandmother's curse. He knew, in his actions, he
had sentenced himself to death. He passed away a short time
later.

But just as the grounds and buildings were eighty percent
complete, the laundered Mafia money ran out, the debt rose
to $120 million, and between 10 and 20 million dollars
disappeared. The Italian contractor who had begun the
project failed.

In 1993, a second Italian company, that had almost
completed the 200-room luxury resort, had its funding pulled
by Rome amid allegations of more Mafia-related corruption,
and failed. And the biggest effect of the curse was still to
come.

In 1996, after a crisis meeting in Fiji regarding debt defaults
on loans from the Pacific state of Nauru and the Asian

development Bank, twenty thousand people unable to service a national debt of over $100 million, declared bankruptcy. The government of the Cook Islands failed.

Two years later a group of Japanese and Hawaiian investors paid a NZ$300,000 advance on the lease, before the Japanese investor who had been given control, was arrested for tax fraud. Failed.

In 2000, an attempt to convert it into a casino-equipped Hilton was disrupted by persistent local anti-gambling activists. Failed.

Two years later, the government sacrificed an opportunity to have Outrigger Hotels of Hawaii manage the property and, in 2003, former Auckland developer Mark Lyon announced plans to buy Vaima'anga, until his appearance in Auckland District Court, on charges of unlawful possession of a pistol, four knives and ammunition, stirred up the Rarotongans enough to demand he be put on a plane back home. Tim Tepaki, of the Tapaki Group, in a partnership with the McEwan Group of Auckland, tried in 2008, and both went into receivership. Strategic Finance was the last, and is now in liquidation. Failed. Failed. Failed. Failed.

Robyn and I wandered through a post-apocalyptic film set, sinking into tropical overgrowth, humidity bubbling through the stucco and drywall, and graffiti with far too many vowels.

The current land-owner Pa Marie Ariki rejects the idea that any curse is affecting business at the site, saying the failure of hotel plans in recent decades has come down to economics. If there is any lesson for the Pa Ariki dynasty, it may be that, in the battle between black lawyers and black magic, more ambition is no guarantee of more ambrosia.

*　　　*　　　*

The universe is not required to be in perfect harmony with human ambition, but what it sent, on the evening breezes through the shoreline shack of our own planet, was in perfect harmony with us. Robyn had bought a black pearl, which she strung in the middle of a strand of irregular freshwater cousins I had found, for less than a buck in Cambodia. She sat at the bamboo and rattan and pandanus, while I poured her a Matua Judd estate chardonnay, or some other libation, and served up barbequed chicken, with rice, and long beans and pawpaw, and the memories of One Foot Island.

Soon it was a Sunday, and there was nothing else to do.

"CICC Day?" She asked.

"Cook Islands Christian Church." I said.

"Why that one?" She asked. It was an excellent question. The place had been overthumped and overbashed and overrun by churches and crucifixes and nametag cruisers.

"The Catholics don't sing, the Seventh Day Adventists don't dance, the Jehovah's Witnesses don't smoke, and the Mormons don't drink." I said. "At least these guys are still trying to have a good time." Like they used to, before we brought them our worldview.

The Pre-Christian Cook Islanders didn't separate existence into spiritual and physical components. The rituals that Nature required were indivisible. Every important physical action, birth, death, making a canoe, going to war, or a fishing expedition, required the propitiation of favorable spiritual connections, through *'akatapu* consecration, *ta ma* purification, *karakia* prayers, *atinga* offerings, and *apinga 'akaariu* charms. Every one required every one. Worship required intermediaries and mediators- the chiefs, the *taura* occult prophets (receiving revelations from the gods and discerning the trend of events), and the *ta'unga* priests, experts in sacred lore and ritual. *Mana* was the concentrated procreative power that resulted from the dynamism of the culture's cumulative intelligence, skill, and accomplishment potential, and the *marae* the sacred stone temple where it all happened. The Polynesian forbidden, tapu, was either divine, or corrupt, or both, and required isolation. Those who broke a tapu, and angered the gods, were thrown live onto a red-hot *umu* oven. In war, the first enemy killed was a 'first fruit' offering.

This is the stage that Captain Cook arrived on, in 1773. He called them the Hervey Islands. They were only named after him, on a Russian naval chart published in the 1820's. If there had been any place on the earth that could have deserved to be named after the quality of this man, here would have been fine. The Cook Islanders wouldn't be taken down without demonstrating their character. When sailors from the *Cumberland*, a commercial sandalwood expedition from the Antipodes, rocked up and onshore in 1814, trouble blew up almost immediately, and many were killed on both sides. The captain's girlfriend, Ann Butchers, was eaten, and her bones were buried in Muri, a few feet from where Robyn and I toasted them again, with our Antipodean white wine. *Cheers, Ann.*

But the history of the Cook Islands was the history of missionaries. It would become a God-fearing archipelago, the history of the bluestockings and the Rechabites, of sought after souls.

The principal proselytizer was the very same London Missionary Society ironmonger, John Williams, who would eventually end up to become one with the gastric juices of the Big Nambas of Erromango, who would eventually become one with Vanuatu.

Before his namba was up, in 1821, he had landed on Aitutaki with a Bora Bora backup believer named Papeiha, before leaving him there, while he sought out more corporeal care for his infirmities, in Sydney. Two years later, he returned on his *Endeavor* (a very different venture vessel from that of

James Cook's), delighted to find that Papeiha had evangelized the entire island. Williams took Papeiha, together with a new cohort of converts, and landed at Avarua on July 23, 1823. The first night was a bit awkward, when the Ariki tried to rape the wife of one of the Tahitian ministers. Once again it was Papeiha who was left behind on Rarotonga, to end cannibalism, destroy the main marae, build a chapel, and burn the carved wooden ancestral 'idols.'

By October, only one wife was permitted, causing considerable anguish for men with multiple spouses, who were forced to choose which one they would keep and which ones they would send back, with their children, to the wife's relatives. Serious punishment awaited those involved in 'fornication and adultery.' A system of surveillance was established on every island, comprised of married church *rikos* appointed by the missionary, charged with pursuing the delinquencies of their neighbors, with the greatest diligence. *We are going to implement... a system of collective surveillance where everybody will know who lives on their block and... and what they devote themselves to; who they meet with; what activities they are involved in.* Actually, that was what Fidel Castro would say almost 150 years later, on the other side of the world, when he created the *Committee for the Defense of the Revolution* CDRs that lived in every neighborhood, a mechanism of ideological control, marked by informers and mistrust, modeled on Hitler's *Committees of Territorial Vigilance.* But in the Cook Islands in the early 1800s, it hadn't been much different.

And inside John William's original whitewashed coral limestone church in Avarua, under its rust-colored metal roof, the missionary zeal had worked like a hot damn. Robyn and I stood in the balcony wooden pews, next to the simple stained glass windows, and looked down over a Southern Sea of fine white coconut palm fiber *rito* hats, each with a band of painted and stitched-on pupa shells, on singing brown women in bone white dresses. The tropical pages of my prayer book, lagging behind the pace of the service, began to turn themselves, with the help of the deacon standing next to me. We spoke after the sermon. I asked him about the collusion of the CICC in the history of Cook Islands blackbirding.

"The London Missionary Society earned money from it." He said. They sent their teachers along with the blackbirds, and some of us wanted to go." And that part was true. In 1857, a devastating disease wiped out their coconut palms, and people were starving. When the Peruvian blackbirding boats arrived in the Cook Islands in 1862, over 700 natives were recruited without having to be kidnapped. They were duped into thinking that they would be employed in easy work, like gathering cotton or planting sugar cane, and would be returned within a year. Conscription was aided with the complicity of local European beachcombers, like Paddy Cooney and Ben Hughes, who were well paid for their efforts. Some islanders who hadn't volunteered received a standard welcome onboard drink of brandy and opium mixed by the ships' doctors, and abducted outright. They were held in compartments separated by iron gratings, which also covered the hatches, to prevent escape. The crews were heavily armed and extra hands had been hired on, to guard the hatches day and night. Armed swivel guns were mounted by the hatches and on top of the surrounding decks. The Peruvian transports came in fast and efficient- the 151 ton barque *Adelante*, the 98 ton schooner *Genara*, and the brigs *Trujillo* and *Ellen Elizabeth* were quickly followed by the *Rosa y Carmen* and the *Jorge Zahara*. By the time the barque *Dolores Carolina* blew in, there was no one left to take. On their arrival at the port of Callao, the Cook Islanders were sold at 200 dollars for men, 150 dollars for women and 100 dollars for boys. No one ever returned.

The deacon seemed a bit dazed and distracted.

"My wife has gotten fat." He said. "But we now have many grandchildren and great-grandchildren. The grandchildren are mostly boys for a rugby team, and the great-grandchildren are mostly girls for a netball team. And then he laughed, and took off on his motorbike.

History may not ultimately show the blackbirders of the 19th century to be the darkest evil lurking offshore in the Cook Islands. One afternoon, Robyn and I found ourselves at the Cook's Corner main bus stop, outside Tangee's Hideaway Bar, the one with the big cans of Foster's and VB above the entrance. Beyond the flame tree and before the misty mountains in the background, was BCI House, and a list of interesting companies on the nameplates. I was enticed by the fact that most of them displayed the word 'trust' in their title, a rare sought after quality that I thought was worth pursuing. Some of them also had the words 'assets' and 'wealth' in theirs, additional features that were not, in and of themselves, unattractive. We went into one of the offices, and asked to speak to someone trustworthy. The young Kiwi lawyer who spoke with us, told us that he was not really speaking with us. Apparently, trust, once it made it offshore, was a very *hush hush* commodity. I asked him about the assets and wealth part, and he asked me about mine. My answer was so unimpressive, that within less than a minute, Robyn and I were back outside, under the flame tree.

The first European who landed on the Cook Islands had come in the form of the same Portuguese-Spanish explorer, Pedro Fernández de Quirós, had also been the first to land in Vanuatu, to 'discover gold and spread the word of Christianity, in that order.' Not much had changed. When de Quirós had set foot here in 1606, the same year he abandoned his New Jerusalem in the New Hebrides, he called it 'Gente Hermosa.' *Beautiful People*. He was prescient. The other beautiful people, from all over the world, returned in the 1980s, and brought their money. The Blackbirders may have had guns and money, but they didn't have lawyers. Ambition is but avarice on stilts, and masked. It can creep as well as soar.

In June of 2013, the Washington-based *International Consortium of Investigative Journalists* (ICIJ) would expose an entire secret conspiracy of wealthy investors, some of which had used the Cook Islands as their flag of convenience. I had studied all the ship rats, and Polynesian rats, that had dramatically reduced the bird population in the Cook Islands, and the others that came later that had dramatically reduced the real trust in the Cook Islands. Most of these were Chinese, or Russians acting through their Cypriot vehicles, but a prominent fellow Canadian was a black pearl.

Tony Merchant might not have qualified as a jolly good version, but he most certainly taken ambition to a new level. The Merchant of Menace was a class action lawyer from Saskatchewan, whose exploits and exploitations had grown into twelve offices across Canada. Some of his more successful lawsuits had included awards against GM over its manifold gaskets, Merck over its arthritis drug, Vioxx, and Maple Leaf Foods over its tainted meat. His biggest windfall, however, came from his class action suit against the Federal Government, on behalf of native residential school abuses. Even though the government and churches had already admitted wrongdoing, Tony walked away with $25 million dollars. *We thought we would do well financially and I think we will do well financially.*

Tony was a well-known Liberal, and husband of a Liberal Senator, who herself had been a past fundraising chair of the provincial Liberal Party.

In 1986, Tony was fined $1000 for having interfered in the lawful use of property. In 1989 he was fined $500 for having failed to reply to correspondence from the Law Society. In 1998 he was criticized by a panel of three judges for 'unacceptable conduct' for filing a legal memorandum in 'eye-straining extra-small type,' and by a Tax Court judge for 'stonewalling' Revenue Canada auditors. In 2002 Tony was found guilty of conduct unbecoming a lawyer by the Law Society. In 2006 he was reprimanded twice again, and fined $5000. His wife, the senator, sued the Saskatchewan government insurance for damages the family dog had inflicted on their son's car, also claiming 'punitive and exemplary damages,' for bad faith conduct. In 2007, the Supreme Court of British Columbia awarded one of Tony's clients more than $300,000 in damages, for a wrongful billing of a quarter million dollars. In 2012 Tony appealed a six-month suspension issued after he was found guilty of two more counts of conduct unbecoming a lawyer.

In June of 2013, Tony Merchant was named by the ICIJ as a holder of offshore money in the Cook Islands. It had already been there fifteen years.

Two other fellow Canadians, Ken and Diane, in the shack adjacent to ours on Muri beach, had told me about the ukuleles, made by the prisoners in Ararangi. Ken had been gracious enough to scooter down there one day, and pick one up for me.

I think of Ken more often than I think of Tony. But when I think of Tony, I think of Robert Louis Stevenson. *I never knew a man who had more words in his command, or less truth to communicate.*

To the ancient Rarotongans, the breath was the medium on which uttered words were carried into the spiritual world. The Cook Islander who made my ukulele, and brought harmony to the universe and human ambition, was a prisoner. The Canadian who had blown so hard on the flames of human misery, and created so much 'trust' on the other side of the world, was a prosecutor.

In Oceania, there is no law. Or far too much of it.

> 'Blackbird singing in the dead of night,
> Take these broken wings and learn to fly
> All your life,
> You were only waiting for this moment to arise.'
> Beatles, *Blackbird*

*   *   *

In between the onshore and offshore intrigues on Rarotonga, Robyn and I flew to Aitutaki. Eight years later, Tony Wheeler, the founder of the Lonely Planet travel guide series would nominate it 'the world's most beautiful island.' But beauty is an emotion, and that hadn't happened yet.

Lime green mountains sat languid large against a morning sky. We boarded our white Air Rarotonga turboprop, with its three fuchsia frangipanis on its two-toned blue tail. Other inter-island planes arrived as we took off, banking north on a forty-five minute flight to the 'almost atoll,' 230 kilometers away. Aitutaki is a large amoeba in the shape of an equilateral triangle, twelve kilometers long on each side. The fertile volcanic main island nucleus extends south into its brilliant turquoise central lagoon from the apex. The southern edge of the triangle is almost entirely submerged below the Southern Sea, the western side an even larger open boat passage through the barrier reef, and the eastern side hangs off the nucleus as the Ootu Peninsula, continuing further south as a string of uninhabited small palm-fringed coral *motu*s, extending to the southeastern tip. I pointed down to the second last islet, surrounded by sunshine and wonderful organelles of reefs and sandbars.

"That's it." I said. "Tapuaetai. One Foot Island."

"Is that where we're going?" Asked Robyn. I nodded.

"And that's where the flying boats used to land." I said, directing my finger slightly further north. "Near Akaiami." The first plane that landed on Aitutaki in 1942 was an American light bomber. Looking down into the lagoon, you couldn't blame the crew members who didn't leave after the war. In the 1950s, the Tasman Empire Airways Limited (TEAL) landed their big Short Solent flying boats on the lagoon, a refueling stopover on the rich and famous interisland *Coral Route* between Auckland and Tahiti.

Robyn and I didn't land on the lagoon. We landed at the airfield the Americans had built as a forward base to bomb the Japanese, at the apex of the ameoba, next to the powder blue terminal building that still had its tin roof, before Cyclone Pat would tear it off, eight years later. Belinda and two of her brothers piled us into the back of their jeep, and roared southwest through Arutanga town, on the way to the jetty. It was almost an afterthought, on the wind and in the rear view mirror.

"Youse want some food?" Asked the driver. "Just in case?" Robyn gave me one of her rhetorical glances. It seemed like an idea.

"Food is good." I said. And he hauled a hard right, into what passed for a supermarket in Arutanga. They didn't tell us how much or what we would need, nor that we wouldn't need any, anyway. So we wandered the three small aisles, like we had just won an all you can grab shopping contest, before the look on our host's faces would turn to stone. There were tins of sardines and beans and corned beef that went into our basket, an old loaf of bread from Auckland, and a big rich and famous jar of Nescafé. There was no way we were going to One Foot Island without coffee.

"That it?" Belinda asked, at the till, which made us wonder if we were going to starve. We nodded.

"Let's go." She said. And we piled back into the back, and made the turn onto the breakwater. An old aluminum Kiwi 'tinnie,' with half a cabin, and a seventy-horse outboard, was already coughing and sputtering at the end of the pier. We made the jump from the back of the jeep to the back of the boat. The nucleus of our amoeba pulled away behind us, and there was salt spray and laughter. I wondered how my fingers didn't come out of the lagoon sapphire-tinted, as I pulled them out of the water. And I thought how, in the middle of this vivid tropical jewel, and mass of brown arms and legs, how dull our own northern colors would seem to them, if they knew. The pure white sugar sand we approached melted our blue talc water into clearer glass. Coconut palms soared above the motu that advanced towards us. Belinda pointed at a two-story shack, barely visible against the trees. A cat paced back and forth on the foreshore. Six years after we landed on the beach at One Foot Island, the World Travel Awards, two years before Tony Wheeler would nominate Aitutaki the world's most beautiful island, would award Tapuaetai 'Australasia's Leading Beach.' But we didn't know any of that, and wouldn't have cared, and wouldn't have cared to. It was the kind of place that made you cry, and you didn't even know why. *Its floor was nothing but white coral sand brought from the beach. The house stood sheltered by tall palms, and the sea was so near that all day one could watch the soft sparkle of the creaming surf through the half-transparent walls...*

Belinda and the boys went to work in the open kitchen. It appears there had been food. Robyn rolled into a hammock and I went walkabout with the cat.

"Lunch!" Rang out a short time later, and a small pinched-off piece of taro flew by, into the bush. *Motoro, here is your taro. O eat.*

But what remained was magnificent. Woven palm leaf baskets held *ika mata* poisson cru ceviche and yam salad and fermented *mitiore* shellfish and *moina tai* coconut cream sauce and fresh grilled teriyaki tuna.

"Kentucky Fried tuna." Said one of the boys. And Belinda brought out pineapple and star fruit and pawpaw and guavas and watermelon, and donuts.

"Donuts?" Asked Robyn. I shrugged, watching the cat do cartwheels on the sand, around the grilled tuna.

"Enjoy." Belinda said. Within a few minutes they had loaded everything back on the tinnie, and were receding into the lagoon. And there was silence, except for the sound of the occasional breeze, or the fine metallic ring of the broken coral limestone, like volcanic clinkers, under our feet, or the meow of Sniveller, for that is what we called him, after the cat I had in Cape Town.

It wasn't as if Belinda hadn't given us any guidance, before they left. One Foot Island was all ours, except for two hours in the morning when a wedding party would arrive. They would land at ten o'clock, the bride would have her photos taken on the beach in front of the shack, the marriage ceremony would go by, a sumptuous wedding feast would be laid on for the guests, and they would leave, and leave us with the rest of the feast. We hadn't needed the tinned sardines, or anything else.

"Some people get tired of grilled fish, and Cook Island food." Belinda had said. Some other people, I thought.

Robyn and I adjusted to the new environmental challenges immediately. All our clothes came off, and would only come back on for the two hours every morning when we attended the wedding in our front yard. We abandoned time, but it would keep track of us, counting down paradise. Robyn made us mango and passion fruit and banana smoothies for breakfast. I would think of shaving, but wouldn't. We snorkeled naked in the turquoise and black pepper rocks, and schools of tropical fish of other colors, and played with the octopus, until it was time for our Japanese wedding, and buffet. When the sound of the tinnie's outboard went over the lagoon horizon, we would fall asleep naked in the hammocks, and Sniveler would fall asleep on the sand beside us, in the midday heat. We would awake to lengthening shadows of the coconut palms on the long white beach, and fluffy clouds overhead. Sniveler and I would walk the long strand of cinder coral or, if the tide was out, the sandbank that went off into the Southern Sea forever. I would look back, to Robyn waving from the balcony. The sunset flamed across the lagoon, against the last blue clouds, and we brought out candles, for the last of our feast, until we didn't need them, under the full moonlight and star smoke. We fell asleep in our stretcher bed on the upper floor of the shack, open through the wooden railing to the expansive cobalt luminescence of the sand and the sea and the serenity. *And all night long one slept to the matchless lullaby of the humming reef.*

As we lost days, we gained knowledge. We learned that the ants found everything in the kitchen that hadn't been hung up or covered, or both. We learned about the *arapo* 'night of the moon,' and how root crops were planted in the full phase and fruits in the new moon, and how, in ancient times, fishing and war and love-making and stealing and other activities were guided by the arapo, but this is now long gone.

We learned that there were so many hermit crabs, the entire beach would occasionally pick itself up and move off sideways. We learned how black bêche-de-mer sea slugs would squirt strands of white slime goo if you disturbed them, and how sheets of small silver fish would careen across your compass, even if you didn't.

We learned about fishing, and how the men did the deep-sea stuff, and the women gathered in the lagoon, how they would go out at night with flaming torches of coconut fronds and catch crabs and, next morning break them, and put them in coconut shells, to catch *patuki* cod; how they would catch parrot fish by stepping on them in the seaweed, and reaching down to pull them up with your fingers in their eye sockets; how they drove mackeral into fish weirs; and how they caught sharks in the lagoon.

There were sharks in the lagoon. I had seen them. But in Aitutaki, they used to catch them like cowboys. In the middle of the day, when the sun had heated the shallow water to unbearable, the sharks would head for shelter, on the sand in the coral patches. An islander jumped in with a strong rope, noosed in a ship-knot at one end, and moved along the shark, tickling his ribs, like a trout in a stream, until he was able to lasso the shark's tail. The half dozen men in the boat above him, armed with knives and axes, hauled hard, until the real battle began on a rocking gunwale, and ended as a fin in a Chinese soup.

And finally, we learned about the legend of One Foot Island, about how it got its name.

Long ago, one of the chiefs, seeing that there was not enough food for his people, created a reserve to protect the lagoon. No one was allowed to fish here at any time. But Nga, a simple fisherman, although he respected the chief's wishes, had a hungry family. During his village's dance festival, Nga and his son Taongo slipped, unnoticed, into the lagoon and paddled to where the fish were still plentiful. The journey was long, and difficult to navigate in the dark. When they reached the reserve both father and son were tired but they caught their fish and prepared to return to the mainland. As the sun rose, one of the villagers coming home late from the festival spotted the silhouette of an outrigger. The chief was outraged that anyone had dared disobey his orders, and sent a war party to capture whoever was fishing in the reserve. Nga spotted them in the distance and knew they that escape was futile. He shouted at Taongo to paddle to Tapuaetui as fast as they could, and then to run to the center of the motu. Nga ran behind him, careful to step in his son's footprints as he did. Soon the warriors could be heard on the shore. Nga lifted his son high into the arms of a banana tree, where he could hide. Do not come down until dark,' he whispered, and continued running to the other side of the island. Taongo watched the warriors, covered in tattoos and carrying long spears, chase the footprints on the beach. He watched them lead his father at spear point, demanding to know if anyone else was with him. 'No.' Said Nga. 'Just me.' Because the warriors had only seen one set of footprints, they believed him, and then killed him. After sunset, Taongo climbed down from the tree and paddled his father's outrigger back home. His mother couldn't believe her eyes. He told his mother how his father had saved him and, in time, Motu Tapuaetai became known as 'One Foot Island.'

Of such bones are coral made.

*   *   *

*   *   *

'Say you were standing with one foot in the oven and one foot in an ice bucket. According to the percentage people, you would be perfectly comfortable.'

Bobby Bragan

I will leave it to the reader's imagination, how depressing it was to leave One Foot. Belinda and the boys must have been used to seeing this gloom, as the other side of the elation they likely saw in people on the outward passage. They didn't say a word on the return voyage to Arutanga. The sentinals of their ancestors would have spotted the HMS Bounty from the top of Mt Maungapu on April 11, 1789, just 17 days before Fletcher Christian mutinied against Captain Bligh. Belinda and the boys would have been prepared for such a contingency from any Europeans that came after. We didn't risk it.

Bligh had brought papaya trees to the Cook Islands, and the papayas had brought other unhappy men. Paul Theroux had met David Lange, the ex-Prime Minister of New Zealand, here, both licking their wounds from their divorces and both, although Theroux only described one of them as such, 'fucked up and far from home.'

There were no dogs or telephones or movement, except for Fanny, a Tahitian woman whose house we had rented from Belinda, for the rest of our stay on the almost atoll. Fanny was on holiday, in Tahiti. Fanny was nuts.

In retrospect, its not that Fanny's house was that bad, although it actually was that bad. It was shabby, and unventilated, and the heavy drapes and furniture and dark interior colors and cockroaches and mosquitoes and French perfume and cigarette smoke odors inside made it worse. It's just that, after One Foot, there was no other place on earth that would have been acceptable.

We needed to escape Fanny's house and, in the evening, we went into Arutanaga, for Island Night. In a bar under the gigantic Banyan trees, we joined some American mutineer boat people, fresh off their yacht, for the dinner and dance. Large local women stood near the buffet table fanning away the flies, while we filled our plates with roast pig and ika mata and kumara and octopus in coconut milk and banana fritters and fruit salad.

Young men, and women in grass skirts came in through the croton hedges off the dirt road. The five *pate* slit drummers hit the most frenetic resonant complex rhythms I've ever heard, and hips began to convulse and shimmy and shake and jiggle and vibrate and move in ways I had never seen hips move. These *ura* dancers were believed capable of rousing and stimulating the passions of the gods, and their *mana* had procreative powers. They certainly had my vote. With their hands and bodies, they told stories of birds and flowers, the ocean of love and loss, and sadness and joy.

Our return to Fanny's was like dying.

In ancient Aitutaki, the dead were either buried in a cave, in the ground, or wrapped in cloth and laid on a raised platform, heads turned towards the rising sun. Relatives slashed themselves with shark's teeth to make their blood flow. Their faces were blackened, hair shorn, and their front teeth knocked out, to show their grief. Personal names were changed, in memory of the deceased. Mourning ceremonies were long and arduous, six months or more.

The next morning, Robyn and I awoke with our heads turned towards the rising sun. We decided to go for a walk, and dropped off a note at Belinda's house, on the way.

> 'Dear Belinda,
> Robyn and I are just hiking up Hospital Hill; If its OK with you, we would be fine with staying here until we leave Wednesday. If you want us to go back to One Foot, that's OK too.
>
> Thanks, Wink'

Belinda knew a mutiny when she saw one. We made the jump from the back of the jeep to the back of the boat. The nucleus of our amoeba pulled away behind us, and there was salt spray and laughter.

> 'There is not one Pacific
> Only one common theme
> That development is certain
> Though foreign
> And coconuts will continue
> To fall
> The Pacific Ocean will camouflage
> superficial dreams
> and the faint sound of drums
> will still be heard
> if we pause a while to listen"
> Vaine Rasmussen (Cook Islands)

*   *   *

Luxury Link
Tahiti

'Pain does not create a long-lasting memory, but the memory of luxury exerts itself for ever.'

Paul Theroux, *The Happy Isles of Oceania*

The last white orchid dropped onto my office carpet. I was ready. Robyn had been all over the Southern Sea with me, but never here.

There had been many reasons. Tahiti was, above all else, expensive. I don't mean costly; I mean first born limb amputation extortion. Second, it was French. Robyn, as a true blue Kiwi, ever since the sinking of the Rainbow Warrior in Auckland harbor, and her near starvation for calories and cordial communication on a Parisian tour, had considered all Gauls intolerably arrogant, hirsute, and 'smelly.' Third, Tahiti was a bit off the direct flight route from Vancouver Island, and required a diversion through Los Angeles, which, since the World Trade Center tragedy, had become apocalyptically paranoid. But it was my intention to show her the other side and, during the global financial meltdown of 2008, Tahiti reappeared over our horizon with a random click on a website I would never have otherwise thought to visit.

I typed it into the search engine of *Luxury Link*. What appeared was astounding, and I began to tick off the boxes in my head. Bora Bora. *Check*. Right time. *Check*. Amazing reviews on travel websites. *Check*. Auction, with no minimum. *Check*. Enough time to bid strategically, but not too much to become discouraging. *Check*. Enter bid now. *No. Wait*.

Three days later, three minutes before the close of the auction, there had been fifteen lowball bids. Two minutes later there was at least one more. A minute after that, an email appeared in my inbox.

It began with 'Congratulations,' and ended with 'Conditions.' I read the conditions, and paid the amount shown. For less than a third of what would normally cost, in a contest with a tribe of other vacation vultures from around the world, I had won four days and nights of paradise at the Bora Bora Lagoon Resort & Spa, *located on Motu Toopua, a small island in the middle of the Bora Bora Lagoon, and surrounded by clear tri-color blue waters and views of the enchanted emerald peaks of Mt. Otemanu.*

It was still expensive, first born limb amputation extortion. But I thought I had it covered, until I told Robyn the good news.

"How much?" She asked, with what might have been misconstrued as incredulity, if you had watched the subsequent contractions. And then, she did what any other woman would have done, when faced with the reality of how much love her husband had brought to the table.

"Well." She said. "I've never been to Tahiti." And so it was.

There followed a car trip and a ferry and a bus and a sky train and two planes and, near the end of the ordeal, two old Tahitian garland heads playing the ukulele and guitar in Pape'ete's Faa'a Airport. As we waited for the puddle jumper to Bora Bora, our two-liter bottle of *Barcardi* began to tumble like a shinbone in a space odyssey. Its touchdown turned every set of ears in the terminal, and their eyes formed a common pool of empathy with the one on the floor.

"Pas de problem, Monsieur." Said the agent behind the counter. "Prenez votre vol." No problem for him. He wasn't about to pay first born limb amputation extortion prices for his intoxicants. The gap our puddle jumper crossed was less than 150 miles, and more than the sum of its colors and history. We were greeted in chirpy French by the big smiling Tahitian woman, with our names on her handheld placard.

"Je m'appelle Gloria." She said, floating two white *tiare* gardenia leis over our heads. "Suivez-moi."

An oversized van swallowed the three of us, for the brief ride to an enormous launch idling at the jetty, glistening white fiberglass and brass in the Tahitian sun. We entered an enclave of teak and white leather, alchemically woven with stainless steel bar sinks and air conditioning vents. The inboards didn't grumble; for this kind of money, their only option was to purr. We passed a *motu* with two isosceles palms, and then there was the canvas of the French tricolour against *the enchanted emerald peaks* of Mount Otemanu behind the overwater bungalows and pandanus-thatched roofs of the main resort. Our launch glided past the dormant torches on the wooden boardwalks. Everything went silent, except for the breeze through the coconut fronds.

"Bienvenue au paradis." Said Gloria. And so it seemed to be. Robyn and I were first shown to the spa where, in Euros or CFA, we could enjoy an unsurpassable period of Parisien-Polynesian paradisial pampering, whenever the impulse impelled us. The adjacent shop didn't appear to be offering any sales on its selection of black pearl jewelry and French luxury goods. As the *invités spéciaux* who had finagled an astounding discount package for one of the already cheaper 'Garden rooms,' our introduction to the resort amenities was shorter than it otherwise might have been.

"Bon vacance." Said Gloria, and left us at our bungalow. It was an authentic Tahitian *fare* by night, with an authentic Tahitian pandanus roof above, authentic Tahitian geckos on the walls inside, and authentic Tahitian mud crabs, under the greenery outside. But the authenticity of the amenities collided with the colonial. There was a great kingsize white bed strewn and festooned with giant red hibiscus flowers and white gardenia garlands, Indonesian teak excess, Japanese slippers, and square-rigged nautical double sinks and mirrors in our ensuite. A copy of Gauguin's 'Arearea' *Joyfulness* (I think it was a copy) hung over the white expanse of mattress, one authentic Tahitian woman raising her eyebrow at what must have gone on in our room, and the dog in the painting's foreground trying to remain inconspicuous enough to stay off the authentic Tahitian menu.

The menu in the resort restaurant was an embarrassment of riches, but we never dared ordered a la carte. There was always an overly sumptuous buffet, groaning boards of four distinct cuisines- French, Polynesian, Japanese, and dessert. Mountains of food were perfectly prepared and presented at every meal, for all the guests who, for most of our stay, were only Robyn and I. *Even on the equator, the sun gives one time to dress for dinner (if the toilet is not a very elaborate one) while it is setting, and after it has set.* Even Robyn's sweet tooth could hardly make a dent in the patisserie on parade.

Most of the days were spent at the large teardrop pool, under white puffy clouds and whiter umbrellas, and the tall green coconut palms *surrounded by clear tri-color blue waters and views of the enchanted emerald peaks of Mt. Otemanu.* A four-masted schooner, the *Polynesia*, almost 250 feet long, a ghost on our horizon, like the *Caleuche* or the *Flying Dutchman*, magically stalked our Tahitian idyll through every island. Originally built as the last windjammer of the Portuguese Grand Banks fishing fleet in 1938, she had been originally christened *Argus*, and left Tahiti forever, the same year we did. Her streamlined white hull and sixteen white sails, including three triangular jibs, floating against the mountains and palms, turned our romantic into ridiculously romantic, an iconic canvas memory of slowed motion. We swam laps to keep up with her, and moved our parasols and paperbacks ahead of the sun's parabola. *Rascals in Paradise.* Sometimes, I would sneak off in the afternoon over the Japanese garden suspension bridge, to the stranded gazebo in the middle of a pond of lily pads, and wrestle with the only French keyboard that offered access to the outside world, before deciding that it wasn't worth the crossing. Utility is when you have one telephone, luxury is when you have two, opulence is when you have three - and paradise is when you have none.

Other days we made the other crossing, to Vaitape town, to play with the *vahine* and *tāne* bronze statues and big pretty mille franc bills, and baguettes, and vanilla, and in the pink and white church with the red spindled steeple, or the other small white one with the imposing red cross against the green mountains and dark clouds above. We rented a car, and drove around the island, past large local ladies, other resorts, a car splattered with colorful fiberglass ice cream scoops, a *Va'a* outrigger festival, and a blue scene, bluer than the flow of life in Gauguin's *D'où Venons Nous? Que Sommes Nous? Où Allons Nous?* Robyn, in a blue pareu with a big blue umbrella against the two blues above the beach, hovered far beyond the blue idol of his masterpice. The air was heavy with vanilla.

Our last night at the *Lagon* filled the rest of the air with noble gases, but none were inert. The full moon provided silver photons. Guitars and ukuleles and shark skin drums and torches and hips and pelvises filled the rest of our eyes and eyes with *'Ōte'a* dances, the men gesturing sailing and warfare, the women enacting more natural themes, combing their hair, or becoming butterflies. Which brought Robyn and I full circle around the moon to Gauguin's question. *Where do we come from? Who are we? Where are we going?* And why were there no butterflies in paradise?

The least inert and most ignoble gas supplied the answer. It came in a fine spray from the compressor nozzle attached to the mobile tank rolling past our garden bungalow. I had thought there had been too few geckos. Luxury is a state of mind.

"Pour les insects." Said the driver. "Pour les ravageurs." *The pests.*

The problem with living in the lap of luxury is that you never know when luxury is going to stand up.

'The first day one is a guest, the second a burden, and the third a pest.'
Jean de la Bruyere

*   *   *

Only one island over was the weakest luxury link in the chain. Robyn and I had booked the catamaran because 'it was just like Bora Bora had been fifty years earlier.' Bardot would have loved the place. The French tricolor rippled off the stern, and the waterspouts and flying fish skimmed and skittered over the surface of the waves.

Green. We had arrived there. There was no other landing place. Maupiti was green. Then there was blue. We continued there. Maupiti was blue. Blue barrels full of *noni*, blue sky, and blue water. Other than for the soaring grey cliffs and white sand and the occasional rust red roof, Maupiti was green and blue.

Alain, who met us with his boat at the jetty, had brought the customary fragrant *tiare* leis, but he tossed them over our necks like he'd rather be doing the driving than the welcoming. I don't think we ever heard him speak. But his smile, and the wrap-around sunglasses pasted to his head, told us he was glad to have us there. He was aiming for the small lagoon islet of Motu Tuanai, and Pension Poe Iti. The owners, José and Gerald, were away, but their dream was still awake. The pension was self-sustained in power, from photovoltaic cells and a tall wind turbine. It had solar hot water heaters, and potable water from a desalinization system on the property. Gerald may have been self-sufficient, but he would eventually realize that this was not the same as secure.

There were flowers, and coconut and other fruit trees. Two of the flowers had come down to the white sand shoreline to greet us. They couldn't have been more different. One was Polynesian, the other Parisian. The French woman was thin and pale, with puffy eyes, long black forehead bangs and a ponytail off to the side, and not quite white teeth. She wore sandals, a stainless steel wristwatch halfway up her arm, and a pink gardenia behind her right ear. The large canvas handbag hung over her shoulder seemed out of place, until you realized where she kept her *Gitanes*, and her lighter. Monique was a guest, on her mission abroad to update travel information for the more urbane *citoyens* of the Fifth Republic. In contrast, the Tahitian woman was the picture of health. Brown and barefoot, rotund and raucous, the ivory smile below her flat nose reflected the afternoon sunlight above the two giant green leaf imprints on her fuschia dress. Yoyo was José and Gerald's chef, chambermaid, and *chargé d'affaires.*

She looked like Bloody Mary would have, if Rodgers and Hammerstein had portrayed Bloody Mary without betel nut and rough skin, and the opposite of vulgarity. Yoyo was all class. *If you try, you'll find me, where the sky meets the sea. Here am I your special island. Come to me. Come to me.*

Four tan dogs were asleep against the breakwater.

"Maeva." Said Yoyo, welcoming us. "Ils sont tous frères et sœurs. Comme nous." *Brothers and sisters, like us.* She showed Robyn and I to our small bungalow. The red hibiscus scattered on the bed were large enough to sleep in their own shadows.

By the time we unpacked, the dogs were dozing again, on our porch. But when Robyn and I tried to sneak off for an early evening walk around our motu, they sprang into life, as if they had been trained to lead the way. Four upright curled tails, wallaby-bounced ahead of us, on the clanking clinker coral strand. They led us over cracked volcanic rock shelves along a beach lined with more scrublike vegetation and more sea smell than we had found on Bora Bora, whose mountains still loomed on the horizon in the distance. Perhaps it had been like this, fifty years earlier, before the luxury link had forever weakened the primeval Tahitian food chain. But even here, the hundreds of red and white crabs that formed a missing link, looked French, like Citroëns or Renaults in a continually moving territorial traffic jam, defending their turf far too sideways to progress, ours, the dogs, or that of the Fifth Republic. The Mount Tiriano cliffs on the main island were rugged and square, like the white church with the red roof under them, in Vaiea across the lagoon.

Poisson cru and *poulet fafa* waited for us on the plastic tablecloth of the Poe Iti dining hall on our return. We shared our wine with Monique, but Yoyo didn't drink.

"Je reçois heureux sur les étoiles." She said. *I get happy on the stars.* When they came out later, they put the grapes to shame.

The dogs were still asleep on our porch next morning, where Robyn and I left them after breakfast, to walk around the main island. Alain took us across to Vaiea, and arranged to pick us up a few hours later. The town appeared abandoned, and the first interesting sign of human habitation, was an interesting sign. *Stop! Filariose.* I had thought that Elephantiasis, and the swollen limbs and basketball-size scrotums I had seen in books of human oddities and tropical medicine, had been eradicated, as did many imperfect experts on the disease. But roundworms were still peddling their life cycles through mosquito proboscises, and I had another reason to encourage Robyn to keep the screens closed.

We passed a right-angled breadfruit tree, with a shark's tail nailed to its trunk. Its fruit were gigantic, like green basketball scrotums afflicted with filariasis. Beyond the turtle petroglyphs were a vanilla plantation, walls of coral and concrete and conch, and a boy and girl on bicycles, who stopped just long enough under a mango tree, to charm Robyn out of a pen. Our one path circumambulation continued past an outrigger canoe stenciled with shark and dolphin fish, through beautiful lush valleys and mountains, and into an ancient stone marae, under a pillbox–like mountain redoubt, with three lonely coconut palms on its top. Closer to Vaiea were front yard cement block square graves, painted white, on which pots of plastic flowers slowly faded in the sun. There was a strangely inappropriate mural of two fat Polynesians dancing tango, and a handpainted Hinano beer label poster, that brought us back to Alain's smile and sunglasses, and the fast wake of his outboard home. The dogs

got up to welcome us back, Yoyo prepared another excellent
fish dinner, and even Alain accompanied us on his solar
powered keyboard, after the homemade coconut ice cream.
Yoyo and Monique waved to us from the shore next
morning, as Alain cut the boat on an arc towards the airstrip.
The dogs went back to sleep as the motu disappeared into
our slipstream. We waited in the hot sun for the weekly flight
back to Pape'ete, beside a chalk mural of pink tiares and fish
and a four-masted windjammer. I thought of how I would
have liked to meet Gerald, and link to the luxury he had
created on his motu. But one person's luxury is another
person's loathing. Gerald's innovations had generated more
than one kind of power. During his birthday party, the
electrical room was set on fire, and a counterweight
turnbuckle bolt on one of his expensive wind turbines was
unscrewed, causing the entire structure to buckle. Resentment
is like taking poison and waiting for the other person to die.
The strangest thing of all, to me, however, was that the dogs
hadn't barked.

'Some people think luxury is the opposite of poverty. It is not. It is the
opposite of vulgarity.'

Coco Chanel

*   *   *

*   *   *

'Then we plow'd the South Ocean, such land to discover
As amongst other nations has made such a pother.
We found it, my boys, and with joy be it told,
For beauty such islands you ne'er did behold.'
Dolphiner's *Song of Tahiti*, 1768

The voyage across the Sea of the Moon took an hour, and
another quarter century. The last Mo'orea ferry I boarded had
been half the speed and size of this one. Through the only
blazing jewel break in the reef towards the landing at Vaiare,
the *Aremiti* crossed from the fresh flaming sapphire tumbling
open ocean to the molten emerald glow of the lagoon basin.

My eyes rose to tall angular volcanic peaks spiring eight thousand feet up into the violet sky, splitting the sun into dark shadows and pearl light. Sharp steep skeletal slopes slid off black escarpments into hard narrow hollows, where cadaveric crags set loose sparkling waterfalls over the ridgelines. Enormous greenfire palm plumes swayed in the warmth of the trades, far above the aching blinding surf spray, the cloud powder salted starch of the white sand beaches, and flamboyant trees ablaze with vermilion flowers, spilling their own cataracts of flame through the surrounding thick green foliage. *Does any dim grey North dweller really know what light and colour are?* It was as if the mountains were trying to escape from the paradise below them.

The disembarking chaos of soft French and softer Tahitian vowels flowed into a few round *voitures*, one long rectangular *Le Truck*, with big open wooden windows and a village of primary colors painted on its side panels, and silence. Ten minutes after we made our Vaiare landing, it was deserted again. And Robyn and I had the wind on our faces, running counterclockwise around Mo'orea's heart-shaped coastal road, past Teavaro, Temae, and Maharepa, to Cook's Bay, where Vaita's prophecy had been fulfilled. *The glorious children of Tetumu will come... Their body is different, our body is different... And this land will be taken by them... The old rules will be destroyed and sacred birds of the land and sea... will come and lament over that which this lopped tree has to teach. They are coming on a canoe without an outrigger.'*

Cook had observed that Polynesia had been settled from west to east, but Robyn and I were committed contrarians. Streams of sunlight fell over the mountains onto our arrival at the old Hotel Kaveka. There were stingrays below our deck that night, and refuge from the heartwrenching beauty and the French verbs that surrounded us, next morning.

It was a Sunday, and Robyn and I decided to walk down and around the bay, past sailboats and cages full of *Gaz de Tahiti* butane tanks, a shop selling *pareus*, a *Nestlé* rebar man sculpture outside vending 'citrons,' an old fishing boat, a fishmonger tattooed in the same blue and white as his *Rava'ai* marlin mural, and a wall made of abalone shells, before passing through the sleeping town and near empty Chinese *supermarché* of Pau Pau at the bottom of the blue invagination. We turned north again, past the *Salle Omnisports de Pau Pau* and wild red ginger and small yellow roadside flowers, under jagged mountain cliffs and towering coconut palms. Mangos and an empty honesty box covered a green and white floral pareu-covered table. A red version further along was piled with small orange pineapples, each with a 5 CFA price tag. A tall papaya tree reached above the diminutive church of St. Joseph, whitewashed with pink trim, enclosed by a rock wall, between two broad flame trees, under the prominence Mount Tearai. Masks of bald wooden Tahitian faces with poignant expression of pain, carved from seemingly random planks, lined the road further north, of the same trees with the buttressed roots that tried to trip us, as we took refuge from the sun on the shore. Our four-masted horizon ghost windjammer, *Polynesia*, sailed by, just as Robyn found a red hibiscus to place behind her left ear, put a forefinger in her right dimple, and assumed her saucy French girl pose under the flowering red mimosa. It was midday hot, and we were headed for the tropical beverages at the *Jus de Fruits de Moorea*. Our throats were parched when we arrived, and the 'ouvert' sign, outside the gates of the processing plant, was reassuring. Until we encountered two problems. The first was that, there were no fruit juices available in what should have been a tropical torrent of fruit juice. Instead, there were fruit juice liqueurs to sample, as many as we wanted. Liqueurs and dehydration were a bad marriage. Our head divorced the rest of our bodies just before the tour buses arrived. When they did, those who descended the stairs were New Zealanders, blue collar Kiwi Maoris from Auckland, who were reveling in their Polynesian relationship with their obviously more erudite French-influenced Tahitian cousins, and the opportunity to drink as much high alcohol dessert libations as was possible in the half an hour of off-road adventure that their tour allowed. George Forster, who had travelled with Cook on his second *Endeavour* expedition, the unofficial account of which he published as *A Voyage Round the World* in 1777, had expressed a confidence in the ability of his Tahitian navigator and translator, Tupaia, to 'raise the New Zeelanders to a state of civilization similar to that of his own islands...' The differential calculus of fruit liqueur volume disappearing down Maori throats in a time-dependent fashion, was not supportive of this conviction. Robyn and I struggled back to the Hotel Kaveka for water, and the burgers and freedom fries, which tasted very French.

The next morning we departed for the second of the three places we had intended to spend our nights in, on Mo'orea. The first had been Tahitian, the third would be French, but this one was All-American. The Club Bali-Hai was a Southern Sea romantic legend and, poolside at 5:30 pm, every night except Wednesday, the narrative was retold by one of its original wayfarers.

"Pull up a chair." Said the old guy with the silver crew cut. "Swing in. Swing in." He was sporting two small airline bottles of *José Cuero* tequila, and a grey sweatshirt. *Hammered and Happy.*

"Welcome to Happy Hour with Muk." He said, pouring the contents of one of his bottles over ice. "I'm Muk."

In 1959, Donald 'Muk' McCallum was in his early '30s, and a salesman in his family's Southern California sporting goods business during the day. By night, he ran a tiki bar called *Miss Boo's* in Costa Mesa on the side. He shared an apartment in Corona del Mar on Acacia street, with two friends. Jay had gone to Newport Harbor High School with Muk, and then to USC, and then to work as a broker at the Pacific Stock Exchange in Los Angeles, leaving every day before dawn. Hugh was an attorney, and had been a classmate of Jay's at USC. It was the end of the Eisenhower era, and the beginning of their disenchantment. Every night, they traded their suits and slacks for Hawaiian shorts, cranked up the Tahitian music on the stereo, consumed prodigious amounts of exotic potent mixed drinks, and dreamed of different lives beyond their sunsets. They'd end up down at the harbor full of sailboats, and wished that one of them would take them away from the rat race. Then one day, Hugh signed onto a ninety-foot yacht, which had entered a race to Honolulu. It sailed on to Tahiti, and Hugh got off in paradise. The sultry scenery and opportunities for romance hooked him through the gills, and he found an elderly California couple that wanted to sell their vanilla plantation on Mo'orea. Hugh rolled the name around on his tongue, and in his head. *Urufara.* He returned home to willing accomplices. Muk sold Miss Boo's, Jay sold his stock-exchange seat, and their friends bought shares in the scheme.

By June of 1960 the stockbroker, the attorney and the salesman had sailed across the Sea of the Moon on a smoky diesel freighter, vowing never to return. But it turned out that Hugh had been a better lawyer than a farmer. Only two of their nearly 400 acres could be cultivated. The price of vanilla crashed when African farmers flooded the market. French authorities, determined to prevent their islands from becoming a haven for poor foreign dreamers, would only grant them six-month visas. Their farming failures by day were more than offset by their successes with the local vahines at night, drinking and dancing and singing in the *One Chicken Inn*, where the barstools were overturned crates.

"I'll tell you this." Muk winked. "Sex on the Beach wasn't just the name of a drink in those days. We lived in a beat-up old shack with coconut fronds on top, from a local politician who had four bungalows at a hotel he was desperate to get rid of. Jay and Hugh and I were desperate to stay. We made a deal."

The hotelier got the Americans three much-coveted renewable five-year visas, and the boys got a new learning curve. They knew as much about running a hotel as about vanilla farming, but it all came together slowly. Hugh drew up the business papers, and went about making repairs and upgrading the shacks. Jay was the business brain, restricting their rampant aspirations to a strict budget. And Muk, always the jovial public salesman, greeted the freighters at the dock, and cajoled visitors to stay at the Hotel Bali Hai instead of one of the spots near the harbor.

"We used local workers to run the restaurant and do most everything. We knew them all." Muk said, looking around. "Hell, we probably all dated their mothers."

"Things were pretty wild in the old days." He said. "We used to be the TV for the whole island. People would come down and watch us."

In 1962, a *Life* magazine writer and photographer named Carl Mydans, returning from an atomic bomb test at Johnston Island, stumbled across their South Pacific playboy inn. There were airline stewardesses. Mydan's plan to stay one night turned to three weeks, and the making of a myth. The boys thought they were relating a folk tale of hardship and endurance in the face of adversity, but the photos in the December issue told a different story- the trio of muscular, tanned smiling American Bali Hai boys, in swim trunks and sandals, carousing with beautiful girls in tropical pools by day, and partying deep into each Polynesian night became an overnight sensation in tens of millions of eyeballs, back in the States. Their phones ran hot with reservations, and the hotel rapidly grew from a small collection of ramshackle bungalows to a 65-unit resort, one of the largest in these most Society of islands. By the early 1970s, the boys had built new hotels on Raitea and Huahine, and introduced the first overwater bungalow, which became an icon of the quintessential tropical escape to paradise. Jay appeared on *What's My Line* and Muk did ads for *Camel* cigarettes. The Bali Hai boys started incidental families with local women, and even occasionally married. They were living the dream.

But then, gradually, the very grind they had sought to leave behind in Southern California, caught up to them. There were real estate deals and construction deadlines, ledger books, maintenance issues, labor strife, dollar-exchange fluctuations, fires, and competition from a new Club Med, and other more modern resort complexes. The very success that created their luxury link to prosperity and treasure began to unravel their pirate freedom, simplicity and happiness. Hugh and Jay are gone now, and Muk, who used to look after the plumbing, has plumbing problems of his own. And arthritis. The boys had sold off or shut all of their properties except the Club Bali Hai, where, *in the last small outpost of a once far-slung enterprise*, Muk had it in his will that he is 'to be stuffed and set out here, so there will be 'Muk's Happy Hour' forever.'

For some in the plastic chairs, seated around the table by the pool in the sun setting against the magnificent mountain backdrop of Cook's Bay, Muk's message was a celebration of the success of the American pursuit of happiness. Cook had observed that Polynesia had been settled from the west to the east, and the unsettled had come the other way. The story that Muk told, in the same way every night for decades, had become increasingly inflexible. Whenever I tried to ask a question, his annoyance with any deviation from the gruff gospel by which he had defined his reality, would show. Muk the missionary. His Happy Hour had become less about happiness than homily, an attempt to solemnize a life of self-absorption and debauchery. Hugh Heffner may have been a hero to a lost decade of eternal adolescents but the legacies that would link luxury to decadence and dissipation, required the uncoupling from, and abandonment of, the most singular fundamental element of existence. *Meaning.*

*   *   *

'Oh Tane, god of beauty, Lord of the fleets, of the deep ocean Take care of your people Carry us in the hand of your mana, right to our destination Give us a wind astern, a wind from the east Let us sail as fast as a child's canoe with a coconut leaf for a sail Let us sail as smoothly as on a sea of oil, or a bed, Let the crests of the waves be low.'

Robyn and I needed to find something that could link us to a more authentic Mo'orea, before it had got all muk'd up. We rented a white Peugeot. It turned out to be just the sort of time machine we needed.

We drove by an old white church with red caps on its two steeples, like candles, past a hand-painted mural of a pineapple, to a giant warrior statue with a *paua* paddle in one hand, and an outstretched palm in the other. Everybody wants something. We scraped the underside of the Peugeot on the rocks and roots of the old forest, on our way to swim naked in its waterfall. Another hot bush walk brought us to stony streams, big ripe orange coconuts on the ground to quench our thirst, and shiny burnt sienna bracket fungi and round white mushrooms and curved buttressed trunks and roots leading to the ancient rock walls of the marae.

'Marae were the sanctity and glory of the land... the pride of the people... A place of dread and of great silence ...When the people approached... they gave it a wide berth, they lowered their clothes from their shoulders down to their waists, and carried low their burdens in their hands until they got out of sight of it... They were places of stupendous silence; places of pain... dark and shadowy among the great trees... the basis of the ordinances... the basis of royalty; It wakened the gods; it fixed the red feather girdle of the high chiefs.'

The Tahitians that worshipped here had individual names for over two hundred stars, seventy different species of coconut tree, and a marvelously complex oral history of their flowers, trees, rocks, fish, birds, insects, winds, and physical geography. The highly intricate lapita pottery they had brought with them on their great twin-hulled sailing vessels had become increasingly plainer, until it was abandoned for baking their food in *ahima'a* earth ovens. They had no knowledge of the wheel, using rollers to move their gigantic canoes ashore instead, some on logs, some on human bodies. Because of how steep Mo'orea was, the wheel would have been of no use to them. They had migrated here around the time of the birth of Christ, but they had brought a different deity. *The dark land above... The light land below... Surrounded by birds... At the flash of sunrise.*

> He was there Taaroa was his name
> All about him was emptiness
> Nowhere the land. Nowhere the sky
> Nowhere the sea. Nowhere man
> Taaroa called out. No echo to answer
> Then in this solitude he became the world
> This knot of roots it is Taaroa
> The rocks are him again.
> Taaroa. The song of the sea
> Taaroa. He names himself
> Taaroa. Transparence
> Taaroa. Eternity
> Taaroa. The Powerful
> Creator of the Universe which is
> but the shell of Taaroa.
> Who bestows on it life in
> beautiful harmony.

The old warriors of Tutaha's army were as serious as the Bali Hai boys were not.

'Be like the blasting north wind Weed out the water mint (refugees) Look for the red taro (able-bodied survivors) Leave no one alive Disembowel the hen (the enemy clan) Do not leave a red root behind Be deaf to their entreaties Be like the roaring ocean Put the sky (the chief) beneath your feet Let us have the anger Of Ta'aroa, whose curse is death!'

We emerged to the smile of a swath of afternoon sun on the far forested peaks of the island. And moved forward again in time. The ancient Tahitian war canoes had carried their fresh water supply in hollow bamboo tubes, and set sail after offerings of 'a fine mat, *ura* feathers, *arioi* cloth, a pig, half a breadfruit, and a bunch of braided coconut leaves.' *Let your shadow be one of aroha.*

The two passing modern catamaran ferries carried their fresh water in little plastic bottles labeled *Evian* and *Perrier*, and set sail after offerings of an uneventfull passage. *They are coming on a canoe without an outrigger.*

We drove by the fimbriae and flagellae of overwater bungalows, elongating further out into the lagoon with each of Muk's birthdays. The abandoned Club Med lay in ruins above our road, luxury linked to oblivion.

Our final shelter from vulgarity was French. And how. The staff at *Les Tipaniers* was uniformly surly, the Parisian women waded topless on the shallow beach and on the long powder blue pier, and the kite-surfing legionnaires cutting arcs through the atmosphere obviously considered the small children making sand castles under their aerobatic *Activités nautiques* collateral damage. All the yachts at anchor were first born limb amputation extortion expensive. Fluffy orange clouds hovered *en flambé* above. Even the roosters and mosquitoes and heat that kept us awake all night did it with classical Gallic insouciance. And the signpost near the road that would take us back to Pape'ete promised to take us even further. *Ile de Paques 4257 km.*

But that wouldn't happen until later.

'This may well be called the Cytheria of the southern hemisphere...where the earth without tillage produces both food and clothing, the trees loaded with the richest fruit, the carpet of nature spread with the most odiferous flowers, and the fair ones ever willing to fill your arms with love... contradicting an opinion propagated by philosophers of a less bountiful soil, who maintain that every virtuous or charitable act a man commits, is from selfish or interested views.'

George Hamilton, Surgeon Of the *Pandora*

Here, of course, was where it really all began. Below us was Faa'a Airport, reclaimed land on the offshore coral reef, beside the original island that, in less than thirty years, had been claimed by offshore European imaginations, and had claimed them back even more. *Otaheite*.

When Samuel Wallis' *Dolphin* entered Matavai Bay in 1767, he had no idea that the physical integrity of his ship would fall into hard jeopardy, from the nails that would begin to go missing in his crew's search for soft paradise. A year later, the deprived sailors on Bougainville's *Boudeuse*, watched a smiling Tahitian girl climb onto their quarterdeck, and drop her *pareu* like a gauntlet. If Botticelli's *Birth of Venus* had made a simultaneous appearance, she wouldn't have held a candle. When Cook's *Endeavour* arrived a year after that, to follow the Transit of Venus, his crew's endeavours were similarly focused. The history of ships and Shangri-la culminated in Bligh's *Bounty* entrance in 1788, and Edward's *Pandora* pursuit of his mutineers, three years later.

Tahiti would have been paradise to any European, even without the months of abject misery any male crew would suffer just to get there. In a melange of recorded impressions from these first ships, the island itself was achingly beautiful.

'We saw the whole coast full of Canoes, and the country had the most Beautiful appearance its posable to Imagin, from the shore side one two and three miles Back...a fine Leavel country appears to be all laid out in plantations, and the regular built Houses seems to be without number, with Great Numbers of Cocoa Nut Trees and several other trees...all along the Coast. There is beautiful valleys between the Mountains- from the foot of the Mountains half way up the Country appears to be all fine pasture land- from that to the very tops of the Mountains is all full of tall Trees... The country is as beautiful as it could be, forests, fertile vales, streams and gardens make up a charming setting in which the inhabitants have located their houses... Nature was pleased to grant them perfect bodies... We found companies of men and women sitting under the shade of their fruit-trees: they all greeted us with signs of friendship: those who met us upon the road stood aside to let us pass by; everywhere we found hospitality, ease, innocent joy, and every appearance of happiness amongst them...We walk'd for 4 or 5 miles under groves of Cocoa nut and bread fruit trees loaded with a profusion of fruit and giving the most greatefull shade I have ever experienced, under these were the habitations of the people most of them without walls: in short the scene we saw was the truest picture of an arcadia of which we were going to be kings and the imagination can form...'

The Polynesian women, that came out to greet their boats, turned it into the Garden of Eden.

'We have discovered a large, fertile and extremely populous Island in the South Seas... Women... endeavoured to engage the Attention of out Sailors, by exposing their beauties to their View... The men...pressed us to choose a woman, and to come on shore with her; and their gestures denoted in what manner we should form an acquaintance with her. It was very difficult, amidst such a sight, to keep at their work four hundred French sailors, who had seen no women for six months. In spite of all our precautions, a young girl came on board, and place herself upon the quarterdeck, near one of the hatchways, which was open, in order to give air to those who were heaving at the capstern below it. The girl carelessly dropt a cloth, which covered her, and appeared to the eyes of all beholders, such as Venus showed herself to the Phrygian shepherd, having indeed the celestial form of that goddess... At last our cares succeeded in keeping these bewitched fellows in order, though it was no less difficult to keep the command of ourselves... I was told by one of the Young Gentlemen that a new sort of trade took up most of their attention that day, but it might be more properly called the old trade...The Women were far from being Coy. For when a Man Found a Girl to his Mind, which he might Easily Do Amongst so many, there was not much Ceremony on Either Side, and I believe whoever comes here after will find Evident Proofs that they are not the First Discoveries. The men are so far from having Objection to an Intercourse of this Kind that they Brought down their Women & Recommend them to us with the Greatest Eagerness... I sheltered in a small house where I found six of the prettiest girls in the locality. They welcomed me with all the gentleness this charming sex can display. Each one removed her clothing, an adornment which is bothersome for pleasure and, spreading all these charms, showed me in detail the gracefulness and contours of the most perfect bodies. They also removed my clothing... They hastened to see whether I was made like the locals and pleasure quickened this research. Many were... the tender kisses I received!...I thought I was transported into the garden of Eden... In the Island of Otaheite where Love is the Chief Occupation, the favorite, nay almost the Sole Luxury of the inhabitants; both the bodies and souls of the women are modeled into the utmost perfection for that soft science...I have nowhere seen such Elegant women as those of

Otaheite... The Luxury of their appearance is also not a little aided by a freedom which their differing from us in their opinion of what Consitutes modesty. (A) European thinks nothing of Laying bare her breast to a certain point but a hairs breadth Lower no mortal eye must Peirce. An Otaheitean on the other hand will by a motion of her dress in a moment lay open an arm and half her breast the next maybe the whole...and all this with as much innocence and genuine modesty as an English woman can shew her arm... Most of these were young women, who put themselves into several lascivious postures... At certain parts they put their garments aside and exposd with seemingly very little sense of shame those parts which most nations have thought it modest to conceal, & a woman more advanc'd in years stood in front, held her cloaths continually up with one hand and danced with uncommon vigour and effrontery, as if to raise in the spectators the most libidinous desires... The Over flowing plenty, the Ease in which men live and the Softness and Delightfulness of the Clime, the women are Extremely Handsome and fond of the European, prodigiously insisting and Constantly Importuning them to stay, and their Insinuations are Backed by the Courtesy of the Chiefs and the admiration of the people in general. It is Infinitely too much for sailors to withstand... Otaheite... has every allurement both to luxury and ease, and is the Paradise of the World. The Women are handsome, mild in their Manners and conversation, possessed of great sensibility, and have sufficient delicacy to make them admired and loved. I can only conjecture that (the mutineers) have Ideally assured themselves of a more happy life among the Otaheitans than they could possible have in England, which joined to some Female connections has most likely been the cause of the Whole business... The women have too great an intercourse with different Men. ... it is considered no infidelity, for I have known a Man to have done the Act in the presence of his own Wife, and it is a common thing for the Wife to assist the Husband in these Amours... Inclination seems to be the only binding law of Marriage in this Country, for a Woman will quit her husband if she pleases...'

The explorers had found Rousseau's Noble savages living in the Southern Sea, afloat on a Golden Age of freedom, free fruit, and free love. They had landed to find no one working very hard at anything. Which was what Robyn and I also discovered, when we tried to find an inexpensive way into town. Pape'ete wasn't quite the enchanting little *In the Strange South Seas* hamlet that Beatrice Grimshaw had found in 1908.

But it also wasn't Theroux's 'ugly plundered-looking town with scruffy, ill-assorted and flimsy buildings.' Pape'ete was a cultured black pearl, not the 26 mm baroque-shaped AAA 8.7 gram Tahitian Silver in Robert Wan's museum collection in on Boulevard Pomare, but more like the fat mongrel bitch with the big nipples that continually rolled on her stomach to have her belly scratched, in the cafeteria that Robyn and I grabbed an overpriced croque-monsieur in, on our way to the market. We visited the *Galerie Winkler*, still open, thirty years after I had originally thrilled to its discovery, on the last leg of my Final Cartwheel. I still couldn't afford anything inside, and the original owners had taken their Happy Hours back to California.

From the balcony, the market was still a tableau riot of pareus and pandanus and plastic grass skirts, shell strand necklaces and *rito* hats, scarlet ginger flowers and yellow and orange bird of paradise, and stalls of opalescent fish and primary-colored produce. Downstairs, in the toilet, was a red-lipped urinal in the shape of an open female mouth, with a sign. *Pour répondre à tous vos envies.* To answer all your desires.

Back outside of the steps, we met Santa, and his heavenly helper, scantily clad in red and white, both sweltering in the midday heat. Robyn wore a garland gift of white *tiare* gardenias, and I waved a baguette baton to stop traffic, as we charged through the sidewalk vendors and fois gras and wine shops, luxury-linked to the fresh shipments of pink and blue Chinese plastic bicycles next door.

On our final day in paradise, we did the unthinkable, and took a bus tour around Tahiti Nui. It is said that King Pomare built the Old Broom Road that encircles it out of alcohol, inside so many of his more inebriated subjects that were sentenced to its construction. Its convolutions took us at French *autoroutes* speeds, to caves and cataracts and a café for fish, and on to the Gauguin Museum. He had lived in Tahiti until he decided his proclivities and perversions were more suitably situated in the Marquesas. Most of his paintings had emigrated as well, but what had survived still conveyed the mysterious shadowy spirit of the tropical Tahitian rainforest, and the primitive essence of its natives. 'D'ou Venons Nous Que Sommes Nous Où Allons Nous.' *Where Do We Come From What Are We Where Are We Going.*

Where we were going was under an immense waterfall, and Matavai Bay where it all began, and the Fare Suisse, to spend the last night, before our redeye flight Out of Eden to Easter Island. And in the late twilight of my last few hours in Tahiti, I reflected on the luxury link to paradise that we had double-clicked on. Had Dr. Hamilton been right? Before the colliding colonial creeds and commerce and casks and contagion and cast iron and cannons, had Tahiti really been the New Cytherea? Or was it a hopeful alternative to the Seven Year's War, a disastrous conflagration that both the English and French were looking for a way out of?

If Tahiti had been paradise, the Europeans would soon change that forever, almost immediately, according to the musings of Cook.

'I have reason to think that we had brought venereal disease along with us which gave me no small uneasiness and did all in my power to prevent its progress, but all I could do was to little purpose for I may safely say that I was not assisted by any one person in ye Ship, was oblige'd to have the most part of the Ships Compney a Shore every day to work upon the Fort and a Strong guard every night and the Women were so very liberal with their favours, or else Nails, Shirts &c were temptations that they could not withstand, that this distemper very soon spread it self over the greater part of the Ships Compney...'

It didn't take long for the whalers, the merchants from the

Australian penal colonies (bringing arms and alcohol and prostitution), the Methodist and Baptist and Calvinist and Wesleyan and Presbyterian missionaries, ultimately replaced by the Catholics, to bring the apple to Adam and Eve.

And then, there came the French, who simply shrug, when confronted with the odiousness of their oppression. The République got rid of their own monarchy, and did the same for the Tahitians. But, as Montesquieu had insightfully observed, luxury ruins republics, and poverty ruins monarchies. And the French had brought both ruinations, and worse, to paradise.

The worst endowment, without question, was radioactive. From 1960 to 1996, France detonated 193 nuclear bombs in the Society Islands. The one that exploded 17 July 1974 exposed Tahiti to 500 times the maximum accepted level of radiation exposure, showering the island with plutonium for two whole days. Thyroid cancers and leukemia spiked all over French Polynesia. Observers stationed 15 miles away, in shorts and T-shirts without so much a pair of sunglasses, were told to 'look the other way' when the 'test' occurred, and then sent into the mushroom cloud to inspect the damage. Only 11 people have received reparations.

Tahiti was hit 36 more times by plutonium 239 fallout, and isotope so toxic that it has to be contained for 240,000 years before it can reenter the wider environment. Almost half the New Zealanders on observer ships have died of cancer-related deaths, as well as one photographer, blown up by French secret agents in Auckland Harbor in 1985, who had entered the country with the intention of sinking the Rainbow Warrior, leaving to protest the next planned detonation at Mururoa atoll. The agents were released. And French President Jacque Chirac, resumed nuclear explosions in the South Pacific, after being elected in 1995.

The French also brought hypocrisy. The dogs that the Tahitians had as pets and food, now stand guard against their old masters as fierce *chiens méchants.* The French girls cavort around naked, while the Tahitian *vahines* have to dress more modestly. And the Heiva Tahiti festival 'celebration,' the day the French forced Queen Pomare IV to abdicate, is held on Bastille Day.

Paul Theroux, despite his surname, hadn't thought much of the French, referring to them as 'the most self-serving, manipulative, trivial-minded, obnoxious, cynical, and corrupting nations on the face of the earth.'

I asked the Tahitian sitting next to me on our Lan Chile redeye, how he felt about his paradise.

"The French have taken our freedom, the Japanese have taken our fish, and the Americans have taken our Happy Hours."

'The land is like our mother. People come from the land. We must always respect our mother, not explode bombs in her belly.'
Jacques Ihorai

*   *   *

Birdman
Easter Island

'A myth is far truer than a history, for a history only gives a story of the shadows, whereas a myth gives a story of the substances that cast the shadows.'

Annie Besant

Wet Horses. When the aft door swung open, a mustang moisture rode into the cabin, instead of that mix of tropical rot and jet fuel that usually pries you half awake, on any twilight torpid flight through the Southern Sea. This air was all wild wet horses.

Robyn and I had flown out of one legend into another, from the story of the New Cytherea, to a saga of societal collapse. We landed on the eastern tip of the Polynesian triangle, on a triangle-shaped island of multiple mythologies. There were myths of origin, of ancestry, of the Birdman Cult, and of death and rebirth. The Dutch captain that made the first European sighting on April 5, 1722, had no idea how appropriate was the name he had chosen. Paasch-Eyland. *Easter Island.* Jacob Roggeveen had been in trouble in Holland, for publishing a religious pamphlet called 'De Val van's Werelds Afgod.' *The Fall of the World's Idol.* In the ocean of mythical metaphor, Jake was on a roll.

We had all arrived on the most remote inhabited island on Earth, over two thousand kilometers from the nearest human thought, and that was on Pitcairn. Unlike the year it had taken Roggeveen to get here, Robyn and I had arrived on a LAN Chile Boeing 767 in only a few hours. The original 7th century Polynesians that had spawned the Myth of Origin had taken four months in two doubled-hulled canoes, each ninety feet long. They didn't pass through Customs, they brought them, along with warriors, tradesmen, farmers, fecundity, and *ariki* nobles. And 'fowl, cat, turtle, dog, banana plant, paper

425

mulberry, hibiscus, ti, sandalwood, gourd, and yam.' Hotu Matu'a had led the first expedition, from the legendary land of Hiva, either the Marquesas or Mangareva in the Gambiers. When one of his wives gave birth to a son after the long voyage, the severed umbilical cord gave birth to the name of their new home. Pito-o-te-henua. *Navel of the Land.* Or maybe *Land's End.* It was the sanctification of the greatest ocean journey of human colonization in history.

Our arrival was a little less auspicious. There was the same salt wind and pounding surf and mud and marsh, but the crowing roosters and barking dogs had been here awhile. The *ariki* noble that met us outside the terminal was named Bill.

"G'day." He said, removing a little of the shine off our discovery. But William Howe was a bit of a local legend as well, and no small hero of his own myth. An Australian film set construction manager, he had arrived on Easter Island in 1993 to coordinate the production of Ken Costner's *Rapa Nui*, the one with the great scenery, far too condensed history, and Puerto Rican and mixed Chinese actors speaking New Zealand-accented English, emoting to a background beat of African *booga-booga* music. None of these results had much to do with Bill, of course, who related the nightmare of producing a complex film in the most remote location on the planet, and a hybrid world of Latin American and Polynesian efficiency.

"It was just like the theme of the movie." He said. "A continuous war against the landscape." Until Bill met Edith Pakarati, and his own world collapsed in a burning hunk of love. Edith was Rapa Nui wild horse woman, whose father, one of one of Thor Heyerdahl's informants, had told her when she was 12, that her husband wouldn't come from Chile, but from west of Tahiti. She met Bill in the disco, and he eventually met her 22 brothers and sisters, all of whom were descended from the only 36 ancestors out of the 111 Rapanui inhabitants still alive on the island in 1877.

Edith greeted us at their Taura'a Hotel, with soft words in English and Polynesian, and hard edges to some others in Chilean Spanish. Bill said goodbye, and set off to work on their 'new house in the country.' I wondered to myself what country he thought he was working in.

Robyn hung up our Tahitian laundry in the bathroom, I grabbed the umbrella from its shadow against the ochre wall, and we walked into the alternating rain and sunshine of an early Sunday morning in the middle of nowhere.

The waves crashed into the coast near the cemetery, its ornate graves with the crosses and bright plastic flowers and Polynesian names, beautiful against the open sea. Farther along the shore, past the row of standing stone *moai* at Ahu Mahai, one with a red scoria topknot, and eyes made from similar red irises, black obsidian pupils, and white coral conjunctivas, we found a huge sentinel brother, at Ahu Akapu. Its massive size hadn't been accurately suggested by any of the photos I had previously seen, now so imposing against the breeze-blown grass and volcanic rock in the foreground, and the clouds and wide Pacific surf behind. Chestnut horses grazed on the greener areas of brown expanse. We stopped to pose before an inverted boat-shaped skeleton of a more traditional *hare paenga* dwelling, and to wonder at the baby banana plant, hiding from the winds inside an individual round lava rock wall formation, especially constructed for its protection.

The dirt road led on to the one room Museo Antropológico Padre Sebastián Englert, named for the 'strict, authoritarian and patriarchal' Bavarian Catholic priest who, in collusion with the Chilean authorities, prevented the Rapanui from working, traveling, or buying imported goods, and publicly censured churchgoers in his sermons based on their private confessions. Inside the museum were their ancestors' skulls and fishhooks, the most ancient oblong stone 'potato heads,' and grotesque emaciated Toromiro pine *Moai kavakava* statues, with goatees, exposed ribs and vertebrae, and expressions of pain. The humidity had taken its toll on some of the older historical photographs.

Back out along the shore, towards the township of Hanga Roa, a Christmas festival of balloons and bicycles and a carousel for the children to fly around on, was in full merry go round. The local fire truck had been polished to a fine cherry red, and three young boys with their own topknots, were scraping a large pig with knives, under one of the few struggling coconut trees that had been originally brought from a more conducive Tahitian climate. The only conifer in sight, a Chilean cedar, drooped under the weight of the tinsel and presents and heat and guilt that hung from its own branches.

Hanga Roa was supposed to have three thousand inhabitants, but they seemed to be hiding from us today, like they had hidden from the Peruvian blackbirders who had looked for them 150 years earlier. It was Christmas on Easter Island. Still, there were signs of sprawling habitation- a dog and a pile of BMX bikes on a porch, kitchen gardens with evidence of recent harvest, vehicles on steep sloped twin cement drives, each the width of a tire, and the odd burst of Tahitian or Chilean pop music from behind a curtain. A cow skull, painted brown, was tied to a post. Down Avenida Atamu Tekana, the movie playing in the theater was *Rapa Nui*. A life-sized Santa stood guard outside a closed shop selling brown Barbie dolls, and Coca-cola. There were almost no other street names, and no street numbers. On the village walls between two far-flung volcanoes, sharp contrast lines of light and darkness cut between the bright subtropical sun, illuminating the motives, and the simple dark empty shadows, hiding the deeds.

We finished down Caleta Hanga Roa, watching the colorful open Chilean fishing boats move up and down in the harbor. On an island where all the other statues faced inland, there was one lonely statue of Christ, celebrating his birthday in the place named after his resurrection, looking out to sea.

∗   ∗   ∗

'Myth is an attempt to narrate a whole human experience, of which the purpose is too deep, going too deep in the blood and soul, for mental explanation or description.'

D. H. Lawrence

And the Myth of Origin gave way to the Myth of the Ancestor Cult. Geography determines climate; climate determines culture.

The sixty square miles of Easter Island arose from three coalesced volcanoes, as extinct as the culture that had erupted on them. Terevaka is the largest, the youngest, the highest, the most northerly, and the least culturally significant, lava field and wind. The far eastern stoneless headland is Poike, the oldest, most weathered and once separate volcano, the site of the 'Poike Ditch' and the Battle of Poike, between the Long Ears and the Short Ears, that changed the course of Rapa Nui history. The last large volcano, Ranu Kau, in the southwest, has high sea cliffs that have eroded back from the blue ocean, chewing into the wall of the mile wide crater filled by an eerie freshwater lake, speckled with totara reed islands and its own microclimate. Sheltered from the wind, figs and oranges and vines and bananas flourish inside the caldera. The last native toromiro tree was cut down on the inner slope in 1960, for firewood. Here is the abandoned ceremonial village of Orongo, on the cusp of where the sea cliff and the inner crater wall, and the Ancestor Cult and Birdman Cult histories, converge. Robyn and I would come here last.

Before the descendents were the ancestors, and I was anxious to see where their birth and descent had occurred. We had negotiated the red and gunmetal Suzuki SUV in town the day before, from a Chilean mainlander who had given us a deal, because I had negotiated in Spanish. I asked him why the petrol was cheaper than on the mainland, almost four thousand kilometers away.

"No hay impuestos." He said. *No tax.* For which we were grateful.

In the early morning, we headed east along the southern coast road, through the Polynesian vowels and glottal stops of all the bays we passed. *Ahu Hanga Te'e, Ahu Ura Uranga Te Mahina, Ahu Akahanga, Ahu Oroi, Ahu Runga Va'e, Ahu Hanga Tetanga.* The sun shot fibrous streams and shafts of quicksilver through the smoky clouds above us, onto rivers of twin tire track light on the mud road ahead, and broad pewter patches of the following sea, off to our right. Wild wet horses galloped across our path, and we rolled down our windows to smell them. When the sun pushed through the black sky blanket above, it turned the ocean the bluest of blue, just for a moment, before it was overwhelmed and enveloped again. We drove the grey line between wide expanses of coarse straw tussock spattered with cold chunks of coal-colored lava rock, past random red stone topknots, out of the quarry at Puna Pau, and an immense solitary broken dead prone moai I lay beside, out of empathy. And as we turned left, climbing away from the Southern Sea, the sun pushed through in a final burst of determination, and illuminated a convoluted crested crater cone at the top of the road. Here was where the ancestors lived. Here is where their descendents descended with them, and the nursery we ascended to. *Rano Raraku.*

On the most remote island in the world, Robyn and I found ourselves at the most famous mystery in the world, alone except for the forest of a hundred stone faces, looking right through us. It wasn't anything like we had imagined it would be. It was like finding your own remains, and those of everyone who ever looked like you, in an attic- strange, spooky, surreal, ghostly, unearthly, hair-raising. The Rapanui believed that the *akuaku* spirits of their ancestors provided for all the needs of their living- fitness, fertility, and fortune. In turn, their descendents made offerings that provided the dead with a better place in the spirit world. It was a symbiosis.

The *aringa ora* living faces were made to watch over the settlements before them, with their backs toward the spirit world in the sea. No one dares to go near them at night.

When Roggeveen arrived in 1722, he found 887 upright stony-faced moai statues. They had been carved from 1100 to 1680 AD, almost all with basalt hand chisels out of the solidified volcanic *tuff* ash at the Rano Raraku quarry. Each clan had it's own territory. It took six men a year to complete a single moai. The largest ever made was over 69 feet high, and weighed 270 tons, although most averaged a paltry 13 feet high, and 14 tons.

Nearly half of all the moai ever created were still staring at Robyn and I, at Rano Raruku, waiting to descend to their descendents. They were gigantic chess pieces in the game of Southern Sea survival, carved in minimalist flat planes, with proud unfathomable faces on overly large heads. The ones that had made it off the slopes were meant to have rust red scoria *pukao* topknots added at the bottom. Their brows were heavy, over orbits, slit deep to receive the rocks and coral that would color their eye parts. Ears were elongated oblong rectangles, and their sharp chins set their strong jaws out over truncated necks on heavy torsos with subtly outlined clavicles. White lichens had appeared, a few millimeters every decade, as age spots, for that many years. Their noses were long and broad with sneering fishhook-curled nostrils, over protruding lips pursed into a thin pout. The message was anything but blithe, except for the Percy Shelley Ozymandian kind. *Look upon my works, ye Mighty, and despair.*

A theory, and when it comes to Easter Island, there are always theories that come to Easter Island, exists that the physical features of the moai represent essential signs of leprosy in a reversed overcorrected form, in an attempt to ritually 'undo' the ravages and 'existential shock' that the disease had visited on the general population. It was propounded by Dr. Anneliese Pontius, a psychiatrist from Harvard, to explain the aesthetic preference of a people whose main diet, before they began to eat each other, was probably the Polynesian rat. I'm thinking no.

The big mystery about the moai, however, was not how they were created, but how they got to where they were going. What we do know is that, by the time Roggeveen arrived in 1722, the island was treeless. *These stone figures caused us to be filled with wonder, for we could not understand how it was possible that people who are destitute of heavy or thick timber, and also of stout cordage, out of which to construct gear, had been able to erect them.*

We know from the pollen record that it was totally forested up to 1200 AD, and that tree pollen was gone by 1650. Because that's when the statues stopped being made, we infer a relationship with the trees. The latest theory about transportation was that the moai were literally 'walked' to their *ahu* terraces by rocking and tilting them down the hill, from side to side. Whether the 250 men needed to move each stone statue employed ropes, sledges, lubricated rollers, tracks, A-frames, or cantilevered posts, is of specialized interest, but doesn't change the fact that Rapanui obsession with their Ancestor Cult was the principal instrument of their own destruction.

Robyn and I posed for the usual foolish optically delusional photos of us pushing up falling moai, lying down beside the ones with broken backs and whispering in their oblong ears, and generally celebrating our own private festival of indecorous desecration.

We hiked around the crested corner, past lone striated moai on the internal caldera slopes, to the freshwater volcanic lake, its rushes and wild horses, and a massive murmuring nest of bees, in a rock hollow, on the way back out. Where had they come from?

And where had the maroon and white painted upright Ancestral statues gone? By the time that Cook arrived in 1754, he had a similar impression as that of his predecessor. *We could hardly conceive how these islanders, wholly unacquainted with any mechanical power, could raise such stupendous figures, and afterwards place the large cylindric stones upon their heads.*

But he also had another observation, that the islanders no longer sculpted, preserved, or worshipped the moai. If he had travelled inland, he would have seen them littering the pathways like the discarded toys of giants. The moai had started to come down more than the hill. They had started to come down, like the trees that came down before them. The Ancestors were being pushed over, their necks deliberately broken. The last upright statues were reported by Abel Thouars in 1838. There were none standing, other than those that Robyn and I had played with on the outer slopes of Rano Raraku, by 1868. Other indignities were to follow. Eleven were removed from the island, and others re-erected at museums elsewhere. The tsunami that swept away the Tongariki ahu in 1960, had its summer solstice sunset-facing 15 moai restored, including an 86 ton monster, with the help of the Japanese, thirty years later. Just after we left, a Finnish tourist chipped a piece off an ear of one. He was fined $17,000 and banned for the island for three years. Forever would have been better but, as the Rapanui ancestors would substantiate, if they had been talking heads, nothing lasts forever.

Robyn and I descended with the nursery's descendents, marching past those still frozen in time and space on the slopes. We drove across the navel of the land to the north coast, past Bahia de La Perouse, and the steep long path down to swim naked at the red sand beach at Ovahe. The white sands of Anakena were wider, and there were seven beautiful moia, complete with cylindrical topknots, that Thor Heyerdahl had put right, before he put everything else wrong. Others had been decapitated, and weren't coming back. Robyn changed behind the blue and white triangles of our hotel umbrella, and we lay under a palm tree from a more conducive Tahitian climate, that had stopped struggling so hard.

A sudden rain put us back in our Suzuki, for the return

around the Terevaka northern road, to Hanga Roa. Bill was heading out of the Taura'a, as we were heading in.

"How'd ya go, mate?" He asked.

"Great." I said.

"Bonza." He said, condensing the experience of a lifetime and a thousand years of mystery into a quintessential Australian abstraction. And was gone.

We decided to celebrate our wonderful day with a wonderful evening, and took a stroll back down to the harbor, to look for seafood. I spotted a place near the fishing boats, beside the dive shops, and put a little more speed and traction on Robyn's arm.

"It's French." She said. And so it appeared. *La Taverne du Pecheur.* "Probably more hoity-toity than fish." And she was right. And she was wrong.

The hoity-toity part was unmistakable, and immediate. The big potbellied owner, Giles, was gigabyte grumpy Gaul, and had just thrown out one customer, for asking for ketchup. His huge handlebar mustache moved more quickly when he was agitated, and he was agitated all the time. The décor was more rustic than it had a right to be, for the print and prices on the menu, but I reminded myself how far away we were from France, or anywhere else. His waitress installed us in a rough-hewn wooden booth, surrounded by more plants than on the entire rest of the island. I could feel him watching me peruse the wine list. Frowning, when he wasn't barking at the staff. I ordered something midrange, from a decent Puligny vintage. His expression softened ever so slightly, until another couple asked to sit upstairs.

"Non!" He said. And that was all. I summoned up the courage to ask him where he was from.

"Normandie." He said.

"Calvados." I said. And we were good. I ordered the seafood platter, and the prawns *pil pil,* and we were better. It turned out that Giles had ended up in Hanga Roa by marrying a Rapanui woman. Whatever she had done to him, his crustacean crustiness had become a local legend, and he was known to the Chileans as El Vikingo. The food was magnificent.

I cringed when the accent of the new couple landed in the booth beside us. When their order emerged from the kitchen, I didn't wait long, before a Midwestern whine accompanied it, next door. I think it was something about moisture and the fish. Giles closed the distance from where he had been, to where he would be, without any leather touching the floor.

"The aioli." He shouted. "The aioli! You have to use the aioli." I ordered the Crêpes Suzette, figuring he was finished. But I was wrong. The female half of the booth had decided to have an opinion.

"You're American." He said." You don't know how to eat."

Perhaps, I thought. But the Polynesians did.

*   *   *

'The myth of unlimited production brings war in its train as inevitably
 as clouds announce a storm'

Albert Camus

And the Myth of the Ancestor Cult gave way to the Myth of the Birdman Cult.

Wherever Polynesians had landed, they started eating. Not that they had ever stopped. Food on their long ocean voyages had been undoubtedly rationed, and they had likely arrived hungry. But they had still arrived, with the seeds of their new prosperity, and their ultimate destruction. The Polynesians ate the rats, but the rats, lacking any other natural predators, ate them back. The Rapanui couldn't eat the rats as fast as the rats could eat the *Paschalococos disperta* Easter Island palm tree nuts. The palms took a hundred years to reach maturity. The rats took eight months. It was a massacre. The rodent population soared, until the trees were gone, and then it crashed.

In the rapid destruction of the Rapa Nui forest, the rats had all kinds of human help. Polynesians were farmers, not fishermen, and their staple diet consisted mainly of cultivated taro root, sweet potato, yams, cassava, and bananas. Slash-and-burn agriculture cleared vast tracts of woodland. Palm and *Sophora toromiro* trees were needed for building settlement dwellings, boats, and tools. The Ancestor Cult required more and more logs and lubrication to move the moai. From about 1650 to 1850, the climatic effects of the Little Ice Age may have hastened deforestation. Whatever the relative contribution of each of these factors, the total destruction for Easter Island's original subtropical moist broadleaf forests became inexorable, and total. This resulted in considerably less rainfall as a result of less condensation, and a dependence on either wells or the three volcanic lakes for fresh water, as there were no permanent streams or rivers on Rapa Nui because its volcanic soil was so porous.

With no trees to protect their crops, soil erosion, the sudden reduction in fresh water flow, and the increased salinity from sea spray, led to harvest failures. The islanders took to planting below the collapsed ceilings of caves, covering the soil with rocks to reduce evaporation. With no wood to construct the kind of fishing vessels that were necessary to provide the main protein sources of tuna and dolphin, the Polynesians didn't stop eating. Before the arrival of humans, Easter Island had vast seabird colonies containing probably over 30 resident species, perhaps the world's richest. There were five species of landbirds, two rails, two parrots and a heron. Midden history began to show a drop in fish bones and a corresponding rise in bird skeletons. With the disappearance of the last trees, no more moai were made. If the *akuaku* ancestor spirits could no longer provide for all the needs of the living, the allegiances of their descendents would change, and venerate the creatures that could. The symbiosis continued, but was now interspecific. You can't eat ancestors. Geography determines climate; climate determines culture.

Robyn and I had lined up for most of the morning, to change a traveler's cheque, at the BancoEstado. The hours, like Hanga Roa's street plan, and the commission charges, were irregular. We left the bank for the long wind-blown grassy slopes of the speckled water caldera of Rano Kau. Here, from 1540, inside the low entrances of the elliptical stone houses at Orongo, was born the Birdman Cult, rising in megalithic structures of flat basalt, as the hardened volcanic ash ancestors were *huri moai* tumbled to the ground. Nearby were the richest collections of petroglyphs in Polynesia, carved and painted in homage to the chief god Make-Make, *komari* vulvas, and sea turtles. Fitness, fertility, and fortune. At this ceremonial village, every Austral spring September for more than a century, the *ivi-atua* priests, the 'kinsmen of the gods,' held a competition to determine who would hold and administer the island's new *mana*, for the coming year. The young male *hopu* competitors raced down the sheer southwestern cliff face of the volcano, until its increasing verticality forced them to dive off into the boiling surf a thousand feet further below and, on the small totara reed paddleboards they had jumped with, swim across the two kilometer shark-infested expanse, to the last of three islands in the deepest of Southern Seas swells, the summits of seamounts another thousand feet tall. Robyn and I stared down in disbelief at the physical dimensions of the challenge, and wondered how anyone would have survived even that part of the ordeal. The race contestants continued, past the tall fang-shaped spire of Moto Iti. They finally reached Moto Nui, and scrambled up its steep ledges to search for the first eggs of the nesting Frigate birds, back from their annual migration. Each candidate tied one into a small forehead basket, like a Jewish phylactery, with all the prayers outside. He swam back across the treacherous sea, and climbed up the precipitous volcanic rock face, to present it to the waiting priests. No one knew if any egg had broken during the ordeal until its basket was open. The one with the first intact egg to see daylight on the Orongo side would be named Tangata manu, *Birdman*. His head and eyebrows were shaved, eyelashes plucked, and his body painted, before he was locked in total darkness with just a priest for company for the next twelve months. Not even his wife could enter the dwelling. His nails grew until they curled like claws. In exchange for this enforced eccentric reclusiveness, the Birdman was imbued with a spiritual mana so powerful, that he could take the land and lives of other tribes, including the consumption of their flesh in sacrificial ceremony. And a year later, he would be squinting into the sun, screaming the start of the next race for the next Birdman. The film critic Gene Siskel had thought that the Rapa Nui 'egg hunt' sequence was ridiculous.' But the ritual was as real, as the birdman's avatar was a scary swirling image, a goggle-eyed, curved beak-egg-clutching idol, carved into the rock of ages and myth, and the glyphic Mayan-like mysteries of the still-undeciphered Rongorongo script.

The village of Orongo is just over the hill from Mataveri airport. And I wondered what a Birdman would have made of our 200-ton Lan Chile Boeing 767, landing on the other side of his volcano.

As the number of bird bones in the middens began to decrease, a new style of art emerged, showing people with exposed ribs and distended bellies. But the Polynesians had landed, and had started eating, and had never stopped, and knew how to eat. All the eggs had been broken. All the birds had been eaten, and then the pigs, and then the dogs. The islanders had moved into fortified caves, with narrowed entrances and crawl spaces with ambush points. One was known as *Anakai Tangata*, the 'Cave where Men are Eaten,' where fingers and toes were considered the most palatable bits of *kai-tangata*, and the age of warfare and cannibalism had begun.

In the evening after Robyn and I had visited Orongo, we ate in a restaurant that served a variety of local fish- piafi, toremo, atun, po'o po, kana kana, mata huira. The fishermen had spoken Spanish. The boats were from the mainland, painted wood. Our dinner arrived on an elliptical metal pan, with little nametags stuck in the flesh of the fillets. The Chilean owner set it on an imported wooden slice of tree slab, burnt with a Birdman design in the center, and rough bark still around the outside. She brought a bottle of *Los Vascos* sauvignon blanc from Santiago, covered in a blue plastic insulator, decorated in Mandarin script, and a Chinese pagoda. Her son was obese, and sat in a corner, brown eyes glued to the television, both hands in a bag of *Chis pop*. We finished at another place for ice cream. Frangipanis had been sprinkled on the tablecloth.

Later, I dreamt. Of trees and frangipanis and fish and ice cream, and eggs unbroken.

'As for the men in power, they are so anxious to establish the myth of infallibility that they do their utmost to ignore truth.'
Boris Pasternak

*   *   *

*　　　*　　　*

'A myth is the name of a terrible lie told by a smelly little brown person
to a man in a white suit with a pair of binoculars.'

David Antin

And the Myth of the Birdman Cult gave way underneath
them all.

The hardships that the Rapanui had brought upon
themselves, were about to be dwarfed by the shipfuls of
sorrow the rest of the world was about to unload on them.
Rongeveen's men had shot a dozen locals stone cold, before
he even hit the beach. Whalers brought smallpox and leprosy
and tuberculosis and venereal disease, and blackbirders

plundered and kidnapped the survivors. In 1804, the American ship *Nancy* abducted 12 men and 10 women as slaves to work in Mas Afuera, in the Juan Fernández Islands, where our first story began. The Polynesians jumped ship after 3 days, drowning in the direction of home. In 1822, an American whaler skipper seized a group of girls, and threw them overboard next day. One of the officers shot one, for sport. In December 1862, Peruvian slave raiders struck. Violent abductions continued for months, capturing around 1,500 men and women, half the island's population. They carried off paramount chief Kaimakoi, together with his son and all those who knew how to read and write rongorongo script, to Peru's guano islands. When the blackbirders were finally forced to repatriate the people they had kidnapped, they disembarked carriers of smallpox together with a few survivors on each of the islands, unleashing devastating epidemics all the way to the Marquesas. Easter Island's population was reduced to the point where the dead were not even buried.

By 1900 there were only 214 inhabitants on the island, 84 of them children. The missionaries took care of them, and what remained of their collective memory. In the end it was disease and enslavement, genocide not ecocide, which caused the physical demise and cultural ruination of the Rapanui.

But the forests of 21 tree species, including the largest palms in the world at the time, *Alphitonia zizypoides*, and *Elaeocarpus rarotongensis*, that had grown 50 feet and more, were still gone, replaced by introduced weeds and grassland and erosion. Carpetbaggers and missionaries would buy up the 'newly available lands of the deceased,' exile even more of the Rapanui, and turn the island into a sheep ranch.

The worst of these was Jean-Baptiste Dutrou-Bornier, a French artillery officer in the Crimean War, who abandoned his wife and young son in France, and was subsequently arrested in Peru for arms-dealing. By the time he arrived on Easter Island in 1868, he had amassed huge gambling debts, and burnt his boat to the waterline. A year later he kidnapped Koreto, the wife of a Rapanui, and married her. With rifles, a cannon, and some hut burning, he and his supporters managed to acquire all the land, apart from what the missionaries had around Hanga Roa, and ran the island as its 'governor,' appointing Koreto as Queen. By the time that Dutrou-Bournier had moved his natives to Tahiti to work on the plantations, and the missionaries had evacuated theirs to the Gambiers, to prevent him from recruiting even more, in less than a decade there were just over a hundred, or around 3 per cent, of the original Polynesians left alive, mostly older men. In 1876, the megalomaniac murderer himself was murdered, in an argument over a dress, or perhaps for his other habit of abducting pubescent girls.

The man who would take over Dutrou-Bornier's kingdom was more benevolent. Alexander Ariipaea Vehiaitipare Salmon Jr. was the son of an English Jewish merchant, Alexander Soloman, and a Pōmare dynasty Tahitian princess, Oehau. While one of his sisters was becoming Queen of Tahiti, another had married a Scottish merchant named John Brander. Alex inherited his father's business interests, co-owned with Brander as the *Maison Brander* copra and coconut oil plantations in Tahiti, the Marquesas, and the Cook Islands, one of which would acquire the sheep station on Easter Island.

In October 1878, he set off with twenty Tahitian workers, and a number of Rapanui whose indentures had expired, to manage the wool exports. He introduced the coconut, developed a tourist industry, and encouraged the manufacture of Rapanui artworks, including imitation rongorongo tablets, which he helped them sell to passing ships for good prices. Alex also sent three genuine rongorongo inscriptions to his niece's husband, Heinrich August Schlubach, the German consul of Valparaíso, which are now kept in Vienna and Berlin.

When the British and German and American archeological expeditions came to the island in 1882 and 1886, Alex provided his services as a guide, translator, and hotelier. As owner of nearly all the island, and the sole source of employment, Alex was its de facto ruler, a fact not lost on Dr. Cooke, the surgeon of the *USS Mohican*.

> 'Mr Salmon, who is guide, philosopher, and friend to these people, unites in his person (and being a giant in stature, he can well contain them) the duties of referee, arbiter, judge. They entertain the greatest respect for him; evince the utmost affection; look up to him as their master; go to him with all their troubles; refer to him all their disputes and grievances. His word is law, and his decisions final and undisputed.'

Salmon was one of the few honest men that had ever set foot on Rapa Nui, with a sincere interest in the welfare of the people. He worked to repatriate Rapanui workers from the inherited copra plantations in the Society Islands. Under his patronage, the population and culture started to recover, albeit with a Tahitian influence so strong, that the language spoken by the surviving natives would be more intelligible in today's Pape'ete market, than to any of the *ariki* nobles on Hotu Matu'a's first expedition to the island.

Alex sold his holdings to the Chilean government on January 2, 1888 and signed as a witness to the cession of the island. His return to Tahiti was scarred by his arrest and imprisonment for assault and battery, resulting in his departure for the remote Tuamotus, where the original double-hulled canoes had left for Rapa Nui. Here he collected oral histories, at the very same time and place that Robert Louis Stevenson was inventing his own account of *In the South Seas*.

But even in paradise, there are no Jews without Nazis. In 1947, sixty years after Alexander Salmon arrived in the Tuamotu archipelago, a quarter century before the French mushroom clouds would appear on its horizon, a balsa raft named *Kon-tiki* washed up on Raroia. It had covered over 5000 miles in 101 days, and its navigator-adventurer would capture the imagination of every kid of the next generation, including mine. Thor Heyerdahl grew up with a collection of snakes in his house, as did I. He set off to prove it was possible to travel long distances with the most primitive of resources, as did I. He had three wives, but this didn't necessarily make me an underachiever.

Heyerdahl saw the stonework and totara reed islands in the lakes on Rapa Nui and had come to the conclusion that Easter Island had been settled by pre-Incan South Americans. It wasn't that hard to make a connection. I had stood beside the 14-cornered stone in Cusco, which would resonate wildly in my head, with my first glimpse of the seamless basalt constructions on the island. *You can't slip a piece of paper between the stones.*

"One thing is for certain." He said. "This was not the work of a canoe load of Polynesian wood carvers."

He considered the moai were 'characteristic of the pre-Inca period of northwestern South America,' similar to monolithic structures in Tiahuanaco, and he rocked their replicas back and forth like refrigerators, in an attempt to prove how simple it had been to move them. Heyerdahl asserted that the stone architecture was hardly found elsewhere in Polynesia, and that the picks used to carve the volcanic rock, the huts built like reed boats, the reed boats themselves, the bottle gourds, the sweet potatoes, and the practice of elongating ear lobes with heavy earrings, could all be traced to pre-Inca South America indigenes. His theories coincided with native myths. Ancient Rapanui folklore told of the island being initially settled by a divine king, Machaa, who 'steered in the direction of the setting sun,' to find the island. These Hanua Eepe "Corpulent People' (later mistranslated as the 'Long Ears') began to sculpt the moai, presumably to honour their first deceased ancestor. The myth continues with the arrival of the Hanau Momoko 'Thin People' (later mistranslated as the 'Short Ears'), overwhelming the Long Ears at the Battle of Poike Ditch, and then toppling their statues.

Heyerdahl was charismatic. He had lived and made his own romantic sagas, and a series of best-selling books of his exploits and deductions. In 1989, with the publication of *Easter Island: The Mystery Solved*, he was surfing tides that would carry him way beyond where they had taken his raft.

But, even as I was eating up the novel excitement that his voyage generated, I felt that there was something too facile and shallow and patronizingly comic book about Thor's theorem. He seemed to be looking down the noses of the moai, at his own analytical superiority. In 1968 a Chilean-American cooperative effort, the Rapa Nui Archeological Survey, began to unravel Heyerdahl's hack detective version of Easter Island settlement, mapping and measuring 19,000 items, including 3224 house foundations, 2536 earth ovens, 886 moai, and 240 ahu. These were more similar to stone altars in the rest of Polynesia, than to the ruins of Tiahuanaco. In 1976, anthropologist Ben Finney, sailed a traditional Polynesian double hulled canoe from Hawaii to Tahiti and back. By contrast, the South American Indians had no history of long distance sea voyages. Heyerdahl had postulated that the pre-Incans had brought the reeds with them, but pollen analysis showed that the reeds on Easter Island had been growing there for 28,000 years. DNA had sunk the Kon Tiki.

Heyerdahl's thinking was *hyperdiffusionistic*. Instead of searching for evidence that diffusion had taken place, he spent his life 'testing' whether the requisite sea travel could have taken place in antiquity. He had no conception of convergent cultural evolution, of the possibility of independent invention. He may have been a Norwegian national icon, and a 'hero for the atomic age,' but he was also a man with a great many honorary doctorates, but no university degree. Sailing had come before the science.

In 1938 Heyerdahl had sent a Marquesan skull to Professor

Hans Günther, one of the leading 'racial scientist' ideologues in Nazi Germany, with a note, effusive about the 'character-solid German race.' In a letter to his mother, he had praised 'the firmness of the German character after having had so much to do with France... shifty, uninformed, selfish, immoral and rude in all senses except phrases and words.' *Myth is neither a lie nor a confession: it is an inflexion.*

The fleshy Polynesian lady with the pink skirt, yellow shirt, old boots and floppy hat, looked subjugated and sad, like the indigenous mixed blood and bloodied of Chiloé. The Chileans had treated them the same way. Their *cara-cara* hawks, circling overhead, were hunting Polynesian rats with the same mainland metaphorical madness.

In 1888, as Alex Salmon and Robert Louis Stevenson were converging on the Tuamotus, as the paramount chief was being poisoned in Valaparíso, and when enough other Polynesians had been extinguished by the epidemics, the Chileans annexed Easter Island. The naval officer responsible, Policarpo Toro, who had also been a second lieutenant in the British Navy, had the main street of Hanga Roa named in his honor. The Rapanui couldn't miss it, as they were confined within the town by a wall constructed by the *Compañía Explotadora de la Isla de Pascua*, a subsidiary of the Scottish Williamson-Balfour Company, which had rented the rest of the island as a sheep farm, until the Navy took it back in 1953. They didn't let the locals out of their gulag until 1960. In the next decade the Rapanui were granted citizenship and, when Pinochet came to power, forbidden to speak their own language.

Two years after Robyn and I arrived, members of the Hitorangi family would occupy the Hanga Roa Eco Village and Spa, a hotel bought from the Pinochet government, in violation of the ancestral ownership of the land. They created a standoff. The titular owner, industrialist Christoph Schiess, of the powerful holding company *Empresas Transoceania*, had close ties with the former billionaire businessman, Chilean

President Sebastián Piñera. Schiess, whose name translates as 'shooter' in German, and whose father was a German soldier on the Russian front in WWII, would provide the two shuttle buses for the 50 heavily-armed *carabineros*, Chile's uniformed police, who would burst into the hotel on an early Sunday morning, six months after the Hitos had occupied the US$800 per night resort. The national motto of Chile is 'Por la razon o la fuerza.' *By reason or force.* The violent actions of the carbineros, on the families and children inside, and in the bloody brutal raids and point blank pellets that came later, would leave little doubt of their loyalty to the mantra.

But that hadn't happened yet, and the Rapanui and their invaders were still enjoying a measure of entente, when Robyn and I took a last wander around the back lanes of Hanga Roa. We had attended many Sunday church services in other parts of the Pacific, and were usually enraptured by the tight choral singing, that flowed in honeyed harmonies out of Polynesian parishioners. The sound that came out of the rounded mouths and off the outstretched hands of the these worshippers, however, was more tentative, didn't quite fill the space, and had an *oom-pa-pa* beat, like the Teutonic martial music of a Latin American army. Heyerdahl's theory of the direction of corpulent colonization had turned out to be correct. He was just off by a few hundred years.

A mother and daughter rode by on a horse, with a blanket where the saddle would have been, each with a hibiscus behind an ear. A bunch of ripe bananas hung off to our side. They smiled and waved.

Edith had allowed us to hang out at the empty Taura'a, to wait for our flight, on our last afternoon in a deserted Hanga Roa. She and Bill, and everyone else, had left to prepare for their New Year's Eve party, at their new place in the country. Whatever country that might have been. Robyn and I sat in the open patio, surrounded by hanging bunches of bananas. We played Scrabble until Bill returned, in a hurry to take us out to the airfield. His parting words were not quite profound. "Invest in commercial real estate." He said.

We lay on the ground beside the runway, in front of a volcanic wall, hand decorated with images of goggle-eye birdmen. The size and power of the Boeing 767 that came out of the sky shook us back into our own time. Halfway up the airstairs, Robyn and I turned to look behind. We were leaving an island of half as many people as wild horses, the descendents of 36 dead voices who had survived the most intrepid collective ocean journey in human history, ecological disaster and famine, civil war and epidemics, and slave raids and violent imperialism. We found our seats and looked out at the angry clouds of a brooding storm... *At this time, make sure your seat backs and tray tables are in their full upright position. Also make sure your seat belt is correctly fastened.*

Lightning flashed outside. There was thunder. *Flight attendants, Cabin Crew, doors on automatic, cross-check and report.* We began to roll.

It was then I heard the music, reverberating from our overhead speakers. *Wild wild horses couldn't drag me away...*

Like the Rapanui, Rolling Stones...*If you have any questions, please don't hesitate to ask one of our crewmembers. We wish you all an enjoyable flight.*

Scary, swirling images, then silence.

'As human beings, our greatness lies not so much in being able to remake the world- that is the myth of the atomic age- as in being able to remake ourselves.'

Mahatma Gandhi

*   *   *

Ghosts of the Rock
Niue

'A rock pile ceases to be a rock pile the moment a single man
contemplates it, bearing within him the image of a cathedral.'

Antoine de Saint-Exupery

"You won't have any New Years Eve." He said. A glass of
bubbly had arrived with the usual preflight palaver of rugby,
hobbits, and syrupy cuteness mixed with sexual innuendo.
The Air New Zealand stewardess was wearing red reindeer
antlers. *Ladies and gentlemen, boys and girls...*
"But you get to celebrate Christmas twice." He said. I looked
across the aisle to a brown Polynesian, dressed as Santa. His
red and white suit, and fake belly and white beard, were
authentic enough, but the red cowboy hat trimmed with
white fur and silver tinsel, and the wrap around sunglasses,
were all Kiwi joker. His wife had a matching green cowboy
hat, trimmed with the same festivity.
"Where yooz fullas frum?" He asked.
"Canada." I said. He sat a little taller in his seat.
"First time to Nuie?" He asked. We nodded in the
affirmative.
"Captain Cook called it Savage Island." He said. "Cuz we
wooden let him land." I expressed the hope that we would
have better luck.
"No worries, mate." He said. "You're goin' to the Rock of
Polynesia."
Santa was right about all of that. Through the only western
break in the fringing reef of one the world's largest coral
atolls, the sea smashes into precipitous limestone cliffs rising
sixty-five feet into the air. Behind the coastal blowholes, Niue
is an eleven mile-wide oval rock, with the finest crags and
crevices and caves in the Southern Sea, a hat with two
terraces, levitating over two hundred feet to a central plateau.

In 1774, James Cook did indeed call it Savage Island, and the US postal service still requires that denomination in the address of any item to be sent there. Niue is separated from New Zealand by the International Date Line, and despite being only 15 degrees of longitude apart, the time difference between Niue and mainland New Zealand is 24 hours. We were leaving Auckland on Christmas Day and would be landing in time for Christmas Eve. We would return in the afternoon, just before New Years Eve, and arrive back in Auckland, not three hours later, on New Year's Day, after supper. Should old acquaintance be forgot, this year it wasn't even going to happen.

The plane, full of jubilant Niueans returning home for the holidays, cheered on takeoff. There were twenty thousand of them living in New Zealand, and only fifteen hundred of them still back home on the Rock. We were bringing the gift of the Magi.

"Welcome to the KFC flight." Said the only other white male face on the flight. "The whole cargo bay is loaded with Kentucky Fried Chicken." His name was Murray. He didn't look like a Murray. He looked like Rodney Dangerfield. Murray was a consultant with the International Monetary Fund, and his Hawaiian shirt, Bermuda shorts and Aussie flip-flops served as living testament to his globalized expertise. He introduced Janet, his portly partner. They were *Rothmans* smokers.

Robyn and I joined them in the exit row.

Murray had been to Niue before, and was bringing Janet, to show her the sights. His planning had been as organized and methodical as the World Bank- he had just enough happy hour bottles of duty free liquor to get him to the case of mixed white wine for each of the seafood dinners he had carefully scheduled, and matching sets of postprandial libations, to see them off to lullaby land each of the six nights they were away. He had secured a special rate at the best resort on the island, and for the rental car they would use, to reach the scenic highlights of the island, at the optimal time they should each be visited. It turned out that Robyn and I were at least staying at the same lodging, and he seemed pleased when I told him I would take his lead on where to go and what to see.

"We'll all have Christmas lunch tomorrow at Juanna's." He said, as our flight path broke from the World Bank through the cloudbank, and all the brown passengers erupted in applause. We shuffled down the airstairs, to the vowels at the edge of the tarmac. *Fakaalofa Lahi Atu.   Welcome to Niue...undiscovered unspoiled unbelievable.*

Behind the white picket fence was a makeshift stage of woven palm fronds, with large clusters of ripe orange coconuts and black rocks at each of the four corners. A young dancer greeted us, rotund in a red dress, weaving stories with her hands and hips. Murray and Janet disappeared into the welcoming throng inside the open terminal in front of us. It seemed like all 1500 remaining residents of the island had come to meet the plane. Fleshy ladies, in multicolored Mother Hubbards, with tinseled leis and tiaras, either barefoot or with extra sized flip-flops, sat in rows of long connected picnic tables, shouting to the arriving passengers. You could tell the ones that had lived too long in New Zealand by their backwards baseball caps and sunglasses, and leather sandals and big full suitcases. They were the ones receiving frangipani garlands. Long wagons of enormous Styrofoam boxes began to arrive from behind the *Tapu* sign, along with the KFC shipment. Other enormous Styrofoam boxes were positioned to be loaded back onto the plane. I asked the immigration guy behind the podium.

"Meat coming off." He said. "Fish going on." In Polynesia, like everywhere else, survival was still all about protein. *Outwit Outlast Outplay.*

Like Murray and Janet, who were already long gone, Robyn and I had booked a rental car, and John was waiting for us to turn it over.

"The keys are in the ignition." He said, pointing to the old New Zealand Japanese reject out in the field in front of Hanan International Airport. I asked him if he wasn't worried about theft.

"Where would they take it?" He asked, explaining that it was still a thousand miles to the next nearest landmass on Fiji or Wallis and Futuna, or the Cook Islands. And then he, too, was gone. As was every other human being. Less than thirty minutes after landing, everyone had left the airport. It was just us, and our Japanese rental. Robyn cranked the ignition, and we had fire. For a moment. Not twenty feet outside the airport, we died, near the climate change sign, the one with the cartoonish blue globe and the umbrella and fan. *'Global Warming' a Dangerous reality...Act Now while we can make a difference or risk losing everything.* Robyn and I made it to the last employee at warp speed, and John soon appeared on his landline.

"I was a bit worried about that one." He said. "Karked out on me this morning, but I thought I had it done and dusted." I made a noise into the phone. John was back within five minutes, with another car in tow. Olive green, same profile.

"Don't we need a Niue driver's license, John?" I asked.

"Anytime this week should be fine." He said. "The jail's closed." "How do we pay you?" I shouted too late, at the trail of dust he had already left behind, in the rush to get back to his Christmas party. By now the field was completely deserted. Robyn turned a key in what appeared to be the only ignition on a remote planet. The engine rolled over.

"Where to?" She asked.

"Follow the road." I said. Around the southern end of the airstrip, past breadfruit and mango trees and empty grassland, we eventually emerged on the coastal road towards Avalele.

Six months earlier Robyn had written Niue's tourism agent in Auckland about accommodation, *looking for a quiet little spot to escape to.* You could hear the chortle in his response.

Hi Robyn, the only true resort on the island is the Matavai, even with
27 rooms... it is still small and intimate... restaurant a popular choice.
Let us know accordingly. Regards.

Some additional digging found out that since the name had changed from the Niue Hotel, the resort had never had an occupancy rate over fifteen percent, the government subsidized its operation, and there were plans to upgrade the facility in the year after our visit. We had waited until the very last minute, and offered to stay for a week, for a deeply discounted rate. Celia had written back, to acknowledge that they would be essentially empty between Christmas and New Years, except for another couple from New Zealand.

Two fresh cold coconuts, waiting for us at the front desk, sealed the deal, and Robyn and I walked out through the French doors onto an expansive aerie multileveled patio of faded wooden decks, with views of coconut palms and green escarpments, soaring over the wide coastal reef, the color of marrow and bone, with black specks far below, collecting shellfish on an outgoing tide. Long-tailed red-billed *tuaki* tropicbirds hovered overhead, stark white against an immense slate blue waterspout offshore. There were wekas and swamp hens and parakeets and terns in the surrounding forest, and a winding rock garden path of beautiful ferns and wild red poinsettias and rhododendrons, that led up the hill to our accommodation. The walls were alive with busy geckos. Our balcony looked out on a sea that would turn to quicksilver, in the full moonlight.

"We need to go into town." Said Robyn. It was coming on Christmas Eve, and everything was about shut down for the next three days. We drove into Alofi village, past where Captain Cook had been driven off the Opaahi reef opposite the Mormon church, to almost where the kings Tuitoga and Fataaiki were buried near the Ekalesia church, and the Post Office. There were five churches in Alofi, one for every hundred residents. But Robyn and I weren't looking for deliverance; we were seeking dispensation. Inside the police station, we met the same Niuean, now in a slightly different uniform, who had stamped us into the country less than two hours previously.

"You need a driver's license?" He asked. Given the fact that there was no actual crime on the island, it was a perfectly reasonable question. Robyn had her picture taken under the *tau ika he uluulu ha niue* fish poster and, not two minutes later, was in possession of an official Niue driving permit.

"How do we know if we're doing something wrong?" I asked. "It's Christmas." He said. "Jail's closed." So we went to the supermarket, to stock up on staples. Swan's and Sons appeared to specialize in both the frozen fatty cuts of meat that the Kiwis wouldn't go near, and the Tip-top ice cream confections for those days when you couldn't get your fill of other kinds of saturated fat, or what remained of the wilted root vegetables. Every Alofi church member was inside, stocking up on last-minute comestibles, all of which were unbelievably expensive. Robyn and I bought biscuits and Canadian sardines, and I still turned my pockets under the coconut palms, inside out in the parking lot.

"It's how they named the country." I said. "'Niu' means coconut, and 'e' means behold."

And behold, back at Matavai, Murray and Janet appeared on the deck that Christmas Evening, outside the teal-colored recreation room, with its walls of spears and clubs and baskets. We ate fish and taro, under the stars, like the Niueans off the first canoes from Samoa might have done, in their new island of mosquitoes and torrential rain and underfoot sharp-edge limestone.

I dreamt of their ghosts.

*   *   *

'Nothing in Niue is quite so curious as the native fancies about ghosts and devils. In spite of their Christianity they still hold fast to all their ancient superstitions about about the powers of evil. Every Savage Islander believes, quite as a matter of course, that ghosts walk the roads and patrol the lonely bush, all night long. Some are harmless spirits, many are malignant devils. After dark has fallen, about six o'clock, no one dares to leave his house except for some very important errand; and if it is necessary to go out so late as nine or ten o'clock, a large party will go together- this even in the town itself. Every native has a dog or two, of a good barking watchdog breed, not to protect the property, for theft is unknown, but to drive away ghosts at night! Devil possession is believed in firmly. When a man takes sick, his neighbors try, in a friendly manner, to 'drive the devil out of him.' Perhaps they hand him up by his thumbs; possibly they put his feet in boiling water, causing fearful scalds; or they may drive sharks' teeth into him here and there. But the most popular method of plain and simple squeezing, to squeeze the devil out! This often results in broken ribs, and occasionally in death. It is a curious fact, in connection with this 'squeezing,' that the natives are remarkably expert 'masseurs,' and can 'drive the devil' out of a sprain, or a headache, or an attack of neuralgia, by what seems to be a clever combination of the 'petrissage' and 'screw' movement of massage. This, they say, annoys the devil so much that he goes away. Applied to the trunk, however, and carried out with the utmost strength of two or three powerful men, Savage Islander massage is often fatal- and small wonder!'

Beatrice Grimshaw, *In the Strange South Seas*, 1908

The devil is just God after a few glasses of wine. Murray and Janet and Robyn and I had arrived at Juanna's midmorning, for her *Xmas Special Buffet*. The effects of our *Somersault* sauvignon blanc-semillon were as good as its appellation and, although somewhat worse for its transportation and markup, afforded us a few degrees of exorcism from the Ghosts of Christmas Past. We took two tables on the veranda, beside a South African in a red jester's hat, whose bells jingled with every mirthful insight. Martin was a stocky exile, on holiday with his wife and son, from their new home in Perth. We did *Somersaults* together, waiting for the promised seafood buffet to emerge from under its petit point muslin gauze. None of us had suspected that, as impervious as the barrier was to the flies, it would prove totally inadequate against the young

Niuean boys, whose quick probing fingers made off with the best pieces of crayfish and prawns, and small crabs. When I finally got up to chase them away, the heavens opened up, and so much rain poured off the coconut frond roof, that individual pools on the ground below us coalesced into a lake. Perhaps it was a sign of ancestral displeasure. After a welcome speech and a prayer, we were invited to queue for what was left of the shellfish, and ham, and traditional *faikai* fish chunks marinated in coconut cream, and pipis and pawpaw.

The rain had lifted by mid-afternoon. All the holy spirits had been toasted, but more secular phantoms lay in ambush, on our accidental route back to the Matavai. Murray drove us through an abandoned village of lifeless boxes. The houses were empty and derelict, roof iron rusted, water collection systems collapsed, doors boarded up or completely missing, window frames devoid of glass, and tropical vines growing through the open spaces. Old washing machines collected spider webs on some porches, and some properties had become dumping grounds. But there were neatly mown verges and an immaculate village green, like we had entered a medieval hamlet struck by plague.

"About a third of the homes on Niue are like this." Said Murray. "Entire villages are deserted. Ghost towns." We drove by an abandoned school, and an occasional dog. A large flock of chickens had taken up residence on a vacated veranda, and another in a living room, further down the road. They were the only sound.

"Where did they all go?" Robyn asked.

"Mostly New Zealand." Said Murray. But they had gone other places too.

In 1825, George Byron, captain of the British warship *Blonde*, discovered another small island in the Southern Sea. A cousin of the famous poet, and another grandson of Captain John 'Foulweather Jack' Byron, our Chiloé castaway, George had been given the task of repatriating the remains of the young king and queen of Hawaii, who had died of measles during a visit to England. After he dropped off the bodies, and helped himself to the wooden carvings and other artifacts from the Hawaiian temple ruins of Puʻuhonua O Hōnaunau (with the 'consent of the Christian missionaries'), Captain George found a low arid atoll almost three thousand miles further south, and named it after his navigator, Lt. Charles Robert Malden. He also named the next nearest island, over two hundred kilometers away, Starbuck Island, after Valentine Starbuck, an American whaler and likely inspiration for Herman Melville's first mate on Moby Dick's *Perquod*, after which the multinational coffee company was named. But I digress.

Malden Island is a triangle, consisting mostly of a shallow irregularly shaped lagoon, containing a number of small islets, like Aitutaki. It's interior is depressed below sea level, from where the surrounding Southern Sea cannot be seen, as if it was meant to be hidden from the rest of the world.

Captain George had found mysterious prehistoric ruins of previous Polynesian habitation, abandoned marae temple platforms, graves, and house sites, as well as dry or brackish wells.

But the Polynesians would return, with the assistance of Peruvian Blackbirders, and men like Bully Hayes, who *would capture islanders, and send them back into their villages infected with measles, so when the rounding up began, the natives were so ravaged by fever, that no resistance was possible.*

The Niueans may have been 'enticed' rather than abducted, but they ended up digging the same bird shit, under the same conditions, for just about the same wages. They and their Aitutaki cousins, joined the Hermit Crabs and Snake-Eye Skinks and Mourning Geckos in mourning, working twelve hour days in the guano. When Beatrice Grimshaw visited the 'glaring barreness' of Malden's 'desolate plain of low greyish-green herbage, relieved here and there by small bushes bearing insignificant yellow flowers,' she noted what was missing... 'shade, coolness, refreshing fruit, pleasant sights and sounds: there are none. For those who live on the island, it is the scene of an exile which has to be endured somehow or other.' The Niueans and Cook Islanders were housed in 'big, barn-like shelters... large, bare, shady buildings fitted with wide shelves, on which the men spread their mats and pillows to sleep.' Their food consisted of 'rice, biscuits, yams, tinned beef, and tea, with a few cocoanuts for those who may fall sick.' Water came from large distillation plants, since no fresh water wells could be successfully dug on the island. The laborers constructed a unique railroad, with cars propelled by large sails, which often jumped their tracks.

"But what happened on Malden Island isn't why these villages on Niue are so desolate." I said.

"Not at all." Said Murray. "Since New Zealand began to administer the island's free-association, Niueans have been migrating to the bright lights of Auckland in droves. Cyclone Heta, which smashed the rock to pieces in 2004, and wiped out Alofi, didn't help. There are now about 1400 people living here, almost ninety percent of whom work for the government, compared to the 25,000 Niueans living in New Zealand. It's an almost empty country."

"Can they fix it?" I asked.

"That's the question." He said. "Every attempt to create permanent jobs here seems to have been doomed to failure. The huge Niue Fish Processors plant closed in 2007, after only two years in operation, because of poor catches, rising costs and problems with whales. Vanilla, which requires hand-pollination within hours of flowering, has never found a stable market. Every year, a hundred thousand liters of noni juice is shipped to China and Japan, but the company, Pure Pacifika, is struggling. New Zealand currently subsidizes Niuean public service payrolls, to the tune of quarter of a million dollars annually. There is talk of turning the abandoned villages into tourist accommodation or retirement communities for Kiwis, although I'm not sure how the local *taulaatua* traditional healers and herbalists would be able to cope with the workload."

In 1956 Malden Island became a site of the first British H-bomb tests, in Operation Grapple. *Goodbye, said the captain. Goodbye, said the islander. Next time test in your own country, perhaps New York or Paris.* But the Niueans who managed to return would eventually grapple with another fact. It seems that the soils of the Rock of Polynesia have exceedingly high levels of natural radioactivity... *undiscovered unspoiled unbelievable.*

'The houses stand down one side, as is the invariable custom of South Sea towns. They are whitewashed concrete for the most part, built by the natives out of materials furnished by the coral reef. The roofs are plaited pandanus thatch, high and steep. The floors are mostly windows, or the windows doors - it would be hard to say which. They are simply long openings filled in with wooden slats, which can be sloped to suit the wind and weather. Mats and cooking pots and the inevitable Chinese camphor-wood box, for keeping clothes in, are all the furniture. Round the doorways grow palms and gay hibiscus, and cerise-flowered poinsettia, and here and there a native will have set up an old decoration of glittering stalactites from the caves on the shore, to sparkle to the sun by his doorstep.'

Beatrice Grimshaw, In the Strange South Seas, 1908

*   *   *

'It was so very far away, to begin with. In other islands, with regular steamers, people concerned themselves to some degree about thedoings of the outer world, and used to wonder how things were getting on, beyond the still blue bar of sea. Newspapers arrived, people came and went, things were done at set times, more or less. One was still in touch with the world, though out of sight. But in Niue, the isolation was complete. There was my come and go. We were on the road to nowhere. Nobody knew when any communication with anywhere would be possible, so nobody troubled, and save for as occasional delirious day

459

when a ship really did come in, and waked us all from our enchanted slumber for just so long as you might turn round and look about you before dropping off into dreams again, we were asleep to all that lay beyond the long horizon line below the seaward-leaning palms. Niue was the world. The rest was a cloudy dream.'

Beatrice Grimshaw, In the Strange South Seas, 1908

The sky met the sea on the deck next morning, and floated us above the reef below. It was Boxing Day and Sunday, and the sunshine and warm breezes rose up in celebration.

Robyn and I packed the snorkeling gear, and drove up through Alofi, heading north. We stopped briefly at the grave of Nukai Peniamina, the Niuean who first introduced the island to Christianity, and all its pleasures. He didn't have an easy time of it. In 1830, John Williams of the London Missionary Society had been thrown back by force. When the Samoan-trained Peniamina arrived back on the *Messenger of Peace* in 1846, he was initially rebuffed by several large villages. Some wanted to kill him. When he was finally allowed to land at Mutulau village, the chief assigned over sixty warriors to protect him day and night, at the fort in Fupiu. Periwinkles and plastic garlands decorated his rocky memorial. Today over two thirds of islanders belong to his Ekalesia Niue congregation, although there are other denominations. The second highest proportion of Jehovah's Witnesses live here, but they must be increasingly frustrated by all the boarded up and open doorways, when they come knocking for converts.

We passed a sign outside the Coral Gardens. *Slow Down Uga Crossing*. It wasn't that far-fetched. The coconut crab is the largest land-living arthropod in the world, and can grow up to nine pounds, and over three feet from leg to leg.

Our first snorkeling stop was at Limu Pools, and down a ladder into the sheltered calm clear turquoise, full of vibrantly colored fish. But our arrival in the aquarium was about to be also thrown back by force. Robyn saw him first, and was out of the pools before my eyes adjusted to the undulating black and white striped barber pole heading toward me. It was a meter long, with a flattened fin-like tail, and existed only here in the waters of Niue. The katuali is the biggest sea snake in the world, highly venomous, and one of the most dangerous creatures on the planet. It's *a* and *b endotoxins* are the same as those released by gram-negative bacteria, and cause the same shock, and death. We were rebuffed.

But just a little further north, near the village of Hakutavake, we pulled into a forest clearing, and a path that would take us to one of the most enchanting places in the Southern Sea. A jungle track led us down a soft incline cut into the coral cliff, lined with beautiful dense foliage. We were surrounded by butterflies, which guided us along, towards the sound of the ocean. We emerged into a magnificent vertical clearing that opened into the long narrow pool and high rock walls of Matapa Chasm, the former bathing spot for the kings and royalty of Niue. A Japanese garden of scattered plump succulents, and maroon and green bromeliads, grew straight out of the limestone on our left. We entered from the shelf on our right, through the cold fresh surface stream trickling into the pool, and into the most spectacular deep fissure in the Rock of Polynesia. The water was warm, but the midday sun directly above poured onto our faces through a crack in the heavens, and we were radiantly reinvigorated, and reborn a hundredfold more than any form of baptism that Peniamina would have brought from Samoa. We snorkeled and surfaced, and snorkeled again. The water was so clear enough to make out the shells on the bottom of the chasm, twenty feet below. It was breathtaking. When we tired, the long rock bump that ran the entire left-sided length of the crevasse, provided us a resting place, a pew from which we could shout echoes across the walls of our cathedral canyon. Neither of us wanted to leave.

We drove ever so slightly inland, and inward. I picked a giant red hibiscus, for Robyn to place behind an ear. There were no people, only occasional road signs. One was for the Lady Farmer Piggery. *Pigs for sale, Pigs for Hair Cutting, Pigs for Ear*

Piercing, Pigs for Weddings, 21ˢᵗ and Anniversaries, See the Lady Farmer: Ini Taufitu Ph: 3202 Fax: 4010 Self-funded Piggery.

"What's that all about?" Robyn asked.

"The coming of age ceremonies for Niuean children consist of ear-piercing for the girls, and a first haircut for the boys."

We passed an intricate white-tiled roadside grave, and a tinseled 'Merry Christmas' sign strung across its roof.

"What's that all about?" She asked, again.

"I've no idea." I said.

We came to Toi village, and a sign that some of its inhabitants were still inhabiting. *Toi Village Hall (Fale fono maaga ha toi)- Village meetings, kindergarten-centre, national general elections, national meetings: government, churches, politics, business, sports, youths, Womens weaving, Womens gossip, Womens handicraft centre, Hall-for-hire: aerobics, concerts, cinemas, weddings, shows, bingo, 21ˢᵗ parties, raffle, hair-cuttings, ear-piercings, etc., all welcome, management: Toi village council.*

A muscle-bound caricature of a long-haired Niuean boy was illustrated, on another billboard further on, breaking the chains of something with his strength. *Strive to Overcome POPS.* "I have no idea." I said again, learning only much later that POPS stood for persistent organic pollutants. These people were clearly more erudite than we were... *undiscovered unspoiled unbelievable.* But then we passed a large cement grave with the name and the date embossed in white on its cross stone face. *Meleani. Dead. 10-10-53.* A rooster pecked around the base.

Meleani, it seemed was not the only one dead. The entire village of Mutalau was empty and abandoned and forsaken. Ferns grew around the perimeter of what had once been a respectable whitewashed Queenslander, and was now a derelict collapsing ruin of crooked uprights and powder blue framing, rusted tin roof, blown open doors and windows, another ghost of the rock. An ancient raised limestone marae, and the flame tree it led to, was still in better condition than the church that lay just beyond.

Robyn and I would reach Uluvehi Landing, the main arrival slipway in the early days. Beatrice Grimshaw would have come ashore here, through the keyhole from the beach and the blue Pacific at the bottom, past the outrigger we found stored in the cave up the steep path, to the coconut palms at the top of the climb. Japanese car bodies lay silent in the surrounding bush. *Dead.*

That evening Robyn and I met Murray and Janet, and Martin and his wife, under the T-shirts and floats and flags around the central circular wooden bar of the Washaway Café. The owner, Willie Santeli, offered to take Murray and Martin and I fishing. Captain George's cousin, Lord Byron, was in attendance. *There's naught, no doubt, so much the spirit calms as rum and true religion.*

The day after Boxing Day began bright, breakfast on the deck with Murray and Janet. The tide was out, and Robyn and I watched the locals collecting shellfish on the reef below. She posed with a frangipani, where the giant red hibiscus had been, the day before, and held her palms up to the ocean and sky. We hiked down the steep slopes through the other palms and the shadows, to the flame trees and aquamarine and beach and *bêche-de-mer* at the bottom.

And then, just as we made it back to the Matavai, it rained. That would be an inaccurate description of the volume of water that dropped out of the sky, but for our purposes, then and for the entire next day, it rained. The average annual rainfall in Niue is two liters. I assumed that most of it landed on us over the following 48 hours, but I couldn't see my hand in front of me. The ocean and sky had become one. The geckos on the roof of the restaurant that evening flew into a feeding frenzy, on the gigantic triangular moths that had taken refuge around the lights, in the overhanging eaves above. Moth juice fell into our wine glasses, and onto our lamb dinners.

The second liter of rainfall arrived next morning, determined to wash away the Rock of Polynesia. We had spiked a Cabin fever, and needed to get away from our getaway. Our drive into Alofi slowed to a deliberate appreciation of all of the nuances we might have missed the first few times. We noticed wreaths and giant fake presents and candy canes on bushes and hedges, a snowman in front of the *Welcome to Fatalupe* sign, and further north again, *Welcome to Tuapa smokefree village.*

Tuapa was where the last *patu-iki* king of Niue was buried. Togia-Pulu-taoki had given away his island's independence to the British Empire, and enacted laws forbidding the sale of land to foreigners, and liquor to his countrymen. And now, two years before Robyn and I arrived, Niue declared its intent to become entirely smoke-free. They needn't have given it much thought. Fully recumbent, bare feet on the dash, trapped inside our Noah's ark on the side of the road, I concluded that anyone able to light a cigarette in this torrential rain, should not only be allowed to, but should be sold alcohol, as well. Besides, the already dwindling population could ill afford to lose a battalion of 250 smoking islanders, who just might decide to pack their blindfolds, and leave. But again, they needn't have given it much thought. In Niue, even the dogs chase the cats at a slow walk.

Wednesday was the day that Murray and Martin and I had planned to go fishing. I awoke before dawn, to stare the horizon into relinquishing the water in its sky. The rain slowly shuttered to a stop. I packed up quickly, and kissed Robyn goodbye, while she was still half asleep. Murray met me downstairs with the packed lunches, and whatever hadn't rusted off Willie's old blue and white HiAce van careened into the Matavai gravel parking lot. Martin was already in the front passenger seat. Down at the pier, while Willie hooked and winched his *Sarah* into the air and down over the side of the high concrete jetty with the hoist, Martin made quiet commentary on the state of Willie's vehicle.

"Seat belts. Check." There was an old canvas belt.

"Air conditioning. Check." No doors.

"Central locking. Check" No locks or handles.

"Rust-proofing. Check." We could see through the floor.

Thankfully, his Senator fishing tinnie and 70HP Mercury outboard were in better condition and, not long after Willie found water, we were smashing across the rough swells, along the sky-high limestone cliffs and caves and coastal blowholes of Savage Island. And the lines went down, and we all prayed to the ancient Nuiean gods of the sea. Hake mai! Hake mai! Ha ika kili kahi. Ha ika ulutafatalei. *Come up! Come up! Oh dark-brown fish. Oh barb-headed fish.*

But, despite the middle-aged men fun we were having, there were no wahoo nor blue trevally nor yellow fin nor mahi mahi, nor even a shark to rip one off your line. What there was were mackerel, and plenty, which Willie hand-gutted and gilled, with just his thumbnail. I asked him what would happen if he tried that with an uga.

"You'd lose your fingers, mate." He said.

Seabirds filled the air above and behind.

On land, Martin took the mackerel back to the Coral Gardens Motel, and invited us all for a barbeque. I helped him filet the catch, and we all fed finely.

Robyn and I drove back to the last rays of the sunset, streaming out behind the outriggers on the broad golden carpet of ocean, in front of the Matavai.

As the stars had filled the black sky above us, a commotion of clanking clamor drew us to a juggernaut invasion of the rock pinnacles, down off the deck below. Celia handed us torches.

Our flashlights caught the movement of an army of armored panzers, three-foot alien exoskeletons, climbing the sharp fangs of limestone in slow motion, to the coconut-baited snares on top.

"Tomorrow night." She said. "Uga feast."

*   *   *

*   *   *

'Everyone has a rock bottom.'
Prince

On our last full day in Niue, Robyn and I took the southern road through the central plateau villages of Vaiea and Hakupu, and crossed to the east coast. The jungle swallowed more and more of the gravel track, until it opened again into a small clearing to our left. Tall coconut palms framed the arrowed sign. *Togo Chasm*. For the next half hour we hiked through the garroting garden of strangler fig fingers and vine-

466

choked buttressed trunks, and the philodendrons and ferns and orchids of the Huvalu forest. Soft suffusing liquid light floated onto the protruding brackets of striped orange fungi, and the radial filigree of huge spider webs, stretched beyond their central heartbeats. We emerged to a spectacle of rock and roaring surf. Far off and below the ocean boomed, pounding its breakers into invisible cliffs at the bottom. The rope on the path helped stabilize the steep sloping irregular green and grey vertigo. Giant karst limestone spearpoints stabbed into the sky, a surreal *Grande Armée* panorama of stone warriors, sculpted by the elements. Robyn and I weaved around them, through a breathtaking maze of thirty-foot razor sharp slabs. *Pinnacles of fantastic grey rock, all spiked and spired, started up unexpectedly in the midst of the riotous green, and every pinnacle was garlanded cunningly with wreaths and fronds of flowering vines.* Delicate plants with perfectly round jade leaves, with white fimbriated flowers far too fragile for such irregular and savage terrain, germinated in a few sheltered rocky recesses. After another thirty minutes the coral track ended abruptly, at the top of a huge ladder, a ladder for giants, as solid and as steep as the rocks it connected. Thirty-two steps took us down to a white sand beach in a grove of colossal palms, surrounded on all sides by the craggy turrets. Waves broke over the sea arch, through a cave. We had hit rock bottom. The feeling was indistinctly North African. Three years after our visit, the government of New Zealand announced a plan to use Niue as an elephant quarantine station for the Auckland Zoo. If the locals don't want their bananas and taro trampled, they'll have to hide the coconut crabs.

Robyn and I drove on up the east coast to the Hikulagi Sculpture Park, described by its New Zealand creator as a *'an on-going and interactive art project with no perception of any finite conclusion.'* The flip-flops nailed to a wooden post, the totem pole of beer cans, and the 'Protean Habitat' of nailed-on pots and pans and fan blades would firmly support the mission statement. *Based on a wooden substructure the sculpture's construction is fundamentally constructivist in its utilization of the found object that can easily be attached with the most basic of tools.* There are no crazier artists in the world than Kiwi artists, and the craziest ones finish up in the islands, with the rest of the bananas. Robyn and I found a starving puppy in the not so Protean Habitat, *with no perception of any finite conclusion.* All we had were biscuits.

Another gravestone went by, this one of cement, topped with a crown and spear tip, and decorated with rivets. *Barned 4-7-21 Died 20-7-42.*

At the end of the twin-tracked road, and our intended destination, was the village of Liku, celebrating whatever celebration falls between Boxing Day and New Years. The fairground festival was in full swing. It was a coconut carnival under flame trees and palms, and the old national red and blue flag emblazoned with the Southern Cross. Inside the long marquees were massive yams and tall tied taro stalks, and new green pandanus baskets of breadfruit and coconut and bananas and onions and cucumbers. There were old girls in their Mother Hubbard dresses and big coconut leafbud straw hats, carrying oversized purses half as big as they were; there were men with baggy shorts and *opshop* T-shirts and sponge cake *jandals*; and there were kids wearing the last generation of where all that had come from. A young girl was feeding her pet fruit bat lollipops and papaya.

The country's entire police force, or Immigration service, were out on the pitch in their uniforms, playing cricket, and golfing between liquor bottles, some empty and, apparently the objects of the enterprise, some full. Niuean *Tame* music flooded out of the public address system and over the improvised stage on the village green, moving the three hips and six hands of the same sturdy young dancers who had greeted our plane. It was here you could see that the Niueans had come from Samoan and Tongan, and not Tahitian, canoes.

But the stars of the show were being walked on their leashes, or tethered to poles with fishing line, or bandaged up with rubber bands. The orange ones were the most valuable, but I thought the blue ones the most fetching. The best were fetching up to $NZ50, a princely sum for us, but for the ninety-seven percent of the population whose income came from New Zealand, it was probably harder to go out and trap a coconut crab, as it was to work as a public service employee.

We met two plump Polynesian ladies who held up their ugas on nylon lines, like they were about to launch into a synchronized yoyo routine.

"Some of them live over sixty years old." One said.

"What happens if he gets you with a claw?" I asked.

"No problem." She said. "You just turn him upside down and tickle his soft parts, and he'll let go." I wasn't convinced. To my eye, they looked like a mescaline vision version of a Sherman tank. I thought of Amelia Earhart's remains, and how she probably ended up in a number of uga burrows, on the coconut husk bedding. These were some tough crustaceans, capable of killing and eating Polynesian rats. They could husk a coconut by ripping off strips of coir, carry it back up the thirty foot tree it fell from to drop it, so that it cracked on the rocks below, and plummet from half the same height itself, totally unhurt. Its claws can break the hard coconut shell into smaller pieces, or take your thumb.

"You have to be careful." Said the other plump lady. "Sometimes they're poisonous." If your uga feast has previously gorged on sea mangos, you'll have a cardiac arrest for dessert.

But our uga feast wasn't until later, and there was still one more place to visit.

The symbol of Nuie, its representation to the world, were the Talava arches and caves. *He like a rock in the sea unshaken stands his ground.*

We started in the same clearing that had taken us to Matapa Chasm but, this time, we took the path to our right, down an uneven trail of sharp coral and hermit crabs and lizards and butterflies. Signs indicating that we had arrived at a 'Rest Area' appeared occasionally, but there was no real place or inducement to rest. After thirty minutes we came upon the entrance to a cave, with a low ceiling, and an immense central stalagmite which, once you decided which way around it you wanted to move, opened up into breathtakingly colored massive columns of stalactites and stalagmites. The floor of the cave was slippery to the edge of lethality, especially the brown and green parts, inclined laterally, straight down off the high cliff, into the rocks and surging ocean waves. We walked on our backs, like crabs, moving from handhold to foothold, one limb at a time. Gradually, we came around the curved corner into a magnificent semicircular gorge with towering limestone walls, and the iconic Arch of Talava. Brilliant colored marine invertebrates undulated below us, in the clearest tidal pools in the world. On the return leg, I was slightly ahead of Robyn. I stopped in the cave, to listen to the waves crashing over the reef, and water dripping from the cave and arches, falling in the small water pools that the centuries had made.

I left a long white datura flower for her to find, behind me.

And so it came to pass, that we would spend the last night in Niue on the deck of the Matavai, with the monster moths and their gecko stalkers, and with Murray and Janet, and Martin and his wife and son, and other travelers who had heard the word. And Celia and her helpers brought out the steaming platters of uga, and those of prawns, and drawn butter, and sauvignon blanc-semillon, and we all did Somersaults. As did the geckos, and the moth juice fell, squirting from the ceiling. It was glorious.

I met Murray at the front desk next morning. He warned me to check the bill, as it was 'always wrong.' He was right. Every meal had been recorded incorrectly, and not in our favor. He

asked me what room rate Robyn and I had paid from Canada.
When I told him, he began to sputter like Willie's outboard.
"But how on earth did you ever get that kind of price?" He
asked.
"You're the World Bank, Murray." I said. "You should have
negotiated."
We left our cars on the same grassy field we had driven them
off, a week earlier, keys in the ignition, tank full of petrol.
The same young dancer, and her two stocky friends, rippled
and rolled their hips and hands, to the guitar and ukulele in
the big hands of the big guys behind them. An old girl played
the wooden drum, to keep time, and prevent eternity from
leaving. More of us would be going, than coming. The big Air
New Zealand A320 pulled up behind them, slowly and
quietly, like a ghost.

'There were never, in all my island wanderings, such shadows or such
sunsets, as I saw in lonely Niue. The little house was far away from others,
and the palms stood up round it close to the very door. In the white,
white moonlight, silver-clear and still as snow, I used to stay for half a
night on my verandah, sitting cross-legged in the darkness of the eaves,
and watching the wonderful great stars of shadow drawn out, as if in ink,
round the foot of every palm-tree. The perfect circle of tenderly curving
rays lay for the most part still as some wonderful drawing about the foot
of the tree; but at rare intervals, when the hour was very late, and even the
whisper of the surf upon the reef seemed to have grown tired and dim
and far away, the night would turn and sigh in its sleep for just a moment,
and all the palm-tree fronds would begin to sway and shiver up in the
sparkling moon-rays, glancing like burnished silver in the light. Then the
star at the foot would dance and sway as well, and weave itself into forms
of indescribable beauty, as if the spirit of Giotto of the marvelous circles
were hovering unseen in the warm air of this alien country that he never
knew, and penciling forms more lovely than his mortal fingers ever drew
on earth. . . . Yes, it was worth losing one's sleep for, in those magic island
nights.'

Beatrice Grimshaw, In the Strange South Seas, 1908

Postscript: Cook had originally named Niue 'Savage Island' because the natives came out to his ship, painted in what appeared to be blood. However, the substance on their teeth was actually *hulahula*, the native red banana.
In 2003, Niue became the first territory to offer free Internet to all its inhabitants. They'd come a long way, but they may not be going back.

*　　*　　*

The Blood in Wineglass Bay
Tasmania

'Nothing is softer or more flexible than water, yet nothing can resist it.'
Lao Tzu

Water. I keep coming back to Tasmania. Most of those who carved its history only wanted to escape, but I kept coming back. It was elemental. Water and wind and earth and fire. But water first.

Robyn and I returned to Tasmania just over a decade after our banishment by the Medical Council bureaucrats, for the sin of having not attended one of the imaginary schools on their register of recognized epicenters of higher learning. Mr. Lemon was likely long gone, and the scotch-slugging president gynecologist had likely perished in the *delirium tremens* horrors in front of him.

Familiar faces met our reemergence. Debbie and JB, Robyn's sister and brother-in-law, also a decade older, greeted us in the arrival hall of the Hobart airport. Their two children, little Kate and Ryan, had stayed at home in Montagu Bay, with JB's elderly mother, Win. We laughed and hugged each other, the reunion closing the gap of elapsed time in only minutes. Robyn told them of our visit to Jules and Mark in the Snowy Mountains of New South Wales, just a few days earlier. Julie had been traveling with Robyn when I first met her in Pakistan, and both her and Mark, and his big handlebar moustache, had welcomed me to Sydney, on my first touchdown in the Antipodes. And now they had received us at their wooden shack in the wop-wops, tall tin chimney, corrugated iron water tank and matching roof, and a ballet of giant red kangaroos bounding through their property at dusk. We drove through the brick bungalow edges of Hobart, across the kilometer-long Tasman Bridge, to the eastern shore of the Derwent. I looked over the side, 200 feet down, where the motorists, who had found out too late that the white line had gone, had also gone, over the gap in the old bridge, created by the pylon collision of the bulk zinc ore carrier, *Illawara*, and into the watery whirlpool of death below. Of the twelve people killed, five had been occupants of the four cars that drove off, and seven had been crewmembers, trapped and crushed by falling debris. Two drivers managed to stop their vehicles at the edge, but not before their front wheels had dropped over the lip of the bridge deck. They balanced on their automatic transmissions, until they were rescued. Although the loss of life was less than it could have been (it was a Sunday night), the social debonding and isolation that hit the communities of Hobart's eastern shore, took a toll anyway. In the six months after the disaster, neighborhood quarrels and complaints rose 300%, crime rose 41%, and car theft rose almost 50%. On the western side of the Derwent, crime rates fell.

Squeezed in between Rosny, Rose Bay and Lindisfarne, Montagu Bay was named after one of the usual type of political picaroon that had administered the early days of the penal colony. Algernon Montagu was known as a quarrelsome 'Mad Judge,' before he was himself exiled to Sierra Leone, finishing his days with more scandal, a Creole mistress, and two illegitimate children.

The bay named after him had a boat ramp and jetty, filled with yachts at anchor. The trans-Derwent swim, a difficult crossing of almost two kilometers, in incredibly strong currents, began from here. We passed a boatbuilding shed from the early 1920s, and the Clarence War Memorial Pool, covered with a white inflatable bubble. Montagu Bay was fed by a freshwater creek, whose aboriginal dialect word for it, meant 'drinking place.'

"Cascade?" Asked JB, handing me a cold beer. *Q. Why is Australian beer served cold? A. So you can tell it from urine.*

"You and Robbie have a bed made up in the garage." Said

Deb.

"We think we've cleared out all the redbacks." JB added, referring to one of the indigenous venomous spiders. I asked him why, with a diet that consisted of small insects, their venom had to be extravagantly toxic enough to drop a large horse.

"Tough neighborhood." He said. "There are no survivors with sissy poison in Tassie." JB explained that, since the arrival of his convict ancestors, entire species had been shot, hunted or worn into extinction. Facing this type of accelerated evolutionary existential challenge, any red-blooded redback would have automatically developed stronger venom and learned how to hide in the shoes of the invader.

"Either that, or its the justice of a vengeful God." We shook out our bedding.

Whatever it was that burst through the garage door next morning, landed on my chest like a lost section of the old Tasman Bridge.

"Did you bring me a lolly from Santa?" She asked. I looked up into the eyes of my sugar-seeking niece, relieved that we had bought the jumbo size *Toblerone* in duty-free. In coming days, the garage would become the secret bolthole, where everyone snuck in, to wrap their Christmas presents they had bought for each other, in shifts so no one would see.

And JB and I would head for the water, to provision the family for Christmas Day brunch. He would dive for crayfish and abalone, and then we would drop our lines, for fish. But this was Tasmania, and nothing you hooked, wouldn't try to hook you back.

"Watch the spines, mate." JB said, as I pulled up the slimy brown mottled puffy prehistoric Pisces off the bottom. "They're poisonous." Like the adjective wouldn't be surplus.

"Watch the teeth, too." He said. "Flatheads bite." I thought of romantic Polynesian words for other fish in the Southern Sea. *Mahimahi, kawakawa, ahi, wahoo.* But there was only one fish in this Tasmanian water. *Flathead.*

"Easy to catch, mate." He said. "They'll bite everything." As we would do on Christmas Day.

There was bubbly with orange juice to start the festivities. In Australia, unlike in France, appetizers were called entrées, and for the size of them, could have been. Shiraz and chardonnay accompanied the main course. Debbie had baked a big ham, and assembled several salads, to go with our fish and seafood. And Win, not to be outdone, had three kinds of Christmas 'pud' on the table, each one more poisonous that the last. There were rum balls (with rum), trifle (with sherry), and Win's own homemade Christmas cake (with enough brandy to bring down the new Tasman bridge).

"I like my sweets, Wink." She said. "And my cuppa tea." She settled back to watch her family, as full as bulls' arses in the middle of spring, charge into the new above ground swimming pool, in the back yard. Uncle Wink put a dance CD on the blaster, and everyone waded around the water, churning the water around, waving their arms, in time to the music.

> 'This summer I did the backstroke
> And you know that's not all
> I did the breast stroke and the butterfly
> And the old Australian crawl, the old Australian crawl.'

Some of the purest water on the planet is in Tasmania, and its use and abuse has often unleashed a cascade of controversy in a population of rogues and rebels. In the 1970s, as the result of the state government's announcement of a plan to flood Lake Pedder, the world's first green party was established. Ten years later a dam proposed on the Gordon River, that would have impacted the environmentally sensitive Franklin River was damned and bulldozed by a populist blockade, resulting in 1217 arrests, and the subsequent imprisonment of almost half of them, for

breaking the terms of their bail. In one of the oldest and most notorious penal settlements in the world, they had run out of cells to hold them. *Let the Franklin flow, let the wild lands be.*
Just east of Hobart, on the other side of the Carlton River, was the family shack on Susan's Bay at Primrose Sands. Every landscape was a watercolor. We headed there on Boxing Day, and built primrose sandcastles. *To see a world in a grain of sand And a heaven in a wild flower, Hold infinity in the palm of your hand And eternity in an hour.*

> 'In one drop of water are found all the secrets of all the oceans; in one aspect of You are found all the aspects of existence.'
> Khalil Gibran

*   *   *

> 'No wind is of service to him that is bound for nowhere.'
> French Proverb

Wind. JB and I would sit out the back of the shack, and play our didgeridoos. He had a real Yidaki eucalypt drone pipe, six feet long, hollowed out by termites, painted by a Yolngu from Arnhem Land, with wild black beeswax around the 'sugarbag' mouthpiece, and the non-harmonic spaced resonances that he produced with his asymmetric instrument.
I had length of PVC plastic pipe with a rubber stopper, but I kept up the circular breathing and vocalizations of my own *aural kaleidoscope of timbres*, imitating dingoes and kookaburras and thunder, and wind.

During the Age of Sail, it was another kind of wind, the Roaring Forties that 'ran the easting down,' and took the last breath from the last *thylacine* tiger, and the indigenous people that had lived there for at least 35,000 years. *It was the site of the worst atrocities against the black man, the place of bread buttered with arsenic for the unsuspecting, and the terminal Black Line beating, in the hunt for the last survivors.*

During the Royal visit of 1868, the Duke of Edinburgh, Prince Alfred, at the 28th Derwent River regatta, met 'the last representative of the Tasmanian Aboriginal race, King Billy and the old woman Trugannini.' King Billy's other name was William Lanne, and he was the last captured male to die.

Even his death in 1869 gave him no respect. Dr Lodewyk Crowther removed his head at the Colonial Hospital, in the name of science. Neither it, nor the tobacco pouch that was made out of his scrotum, has ever been found. By 1876, the entire population of Tasmanian aborigines had been annihilated.

In the 50 years from 1803 to 1853, those same winds had brought more than 75,000 convicts to Van Diemen's Land.

'They call it the end of the world, and for vice it is truly so. For here wickedness flourishes unchecked.'

Tasmania, haunted by extinction, was the first place in the Southern Sea where the headhunters and the cannibals had been the white guys.

Alexander Pearce had eaten all seven of the other convicts that escaped with him from Macquarie Harbor in 1822. He had originally been transported from Ireland for 'the theft of six pairs of shoes, but he did himself one better, as he and his mates traversed the west coast, on the way back to Hobart.

> 'And I said, right there's another one, don't you frown,
> Chew the meat and hold it down, It's a tale they won't believe
> When I get down to Hobart town.'
> Weddings Parties Anything, *A Tale they Won't Believe*

His captors eventually found parts of one of the bodies in Pearce's pockets. He was executed at the Hobart Town Gaol at 9am on July 19, 1824, after receiving the last rites from Father Connolly. Just before he was hanged, Pearce said, 'Man's flesh is delicious. It tastes far better than fish or pork.'

The wind caused more tragedy, when Robyn and I returned to Tassie, in 1998. The Bluewater Classic Sydney to Hobart Yacht Race, over a thousand miles of high winds and difficult seas and 'southerly buster' storms, was widely considered to be one of the most difficult yacht races in the world. Of the 115 boats that left Sydney on Boxing Day, only 44 eventually made it to Hobart. Five boats sank and six people died. We hung around the winner's boat, *Sayonara*, but no one was in a celebratory mood.

The winds of Tasmania, which keep the green-patterned ground parrot from even thinking about nesting higher up in the trees, may be finally finding a benevolence. One of the most galvanized of Australian icons. Southern Cross windmills, produced by the thousands at the Griffiths brothers factory in Toowooba, still pump water all over the back of beyond. But a new generation of wind power is in the works for King Island, off the northwest corner of the Fatal Shore, in the Roaring Forties of the Bass Strait. A 300-turbine wind farm had been proposed which, if built, would make it the largest wind farm in the Southern Hemisphere. When the winds of change blow, some people build walls and others build windmills.

'If you reveal your secrets to the wind, you should not blame the wind
  for revealing them to the trees.'

Khalil Gibran

*   *   *

Earth. King Island was not only known for what could come out of its wind, but what could come out of its earth. Every last morsel of Black Label cloth-wrapped Cheddar and Brie and Reblochon and Blue Triple Cream and Roaring Forties Blue were brilliant, and every one could be found at the *Taste of Tassie* celebration at Salamanca Place, following the culmination of the Sydney to Hobart Yacht Race. Debbie and Robyn and JB and I took it all in, the hundred of stalls of artisanal local foods, the bistro and carnival atmosphere, and the random street performers that had infiltrated the festivities. We found a table beside a large group of *papier mâché* skeletal zombies and a huge black raven puppet mime. Lao Hmong people had the garden market produce covered, outside the laneways and squares, in the sandstone shadows of the former warehouses, built during the whaling industry boom of Hobart port, in the early 19th century. I loved the exterior lead plumbing.

Crayfish and orange roughy and oyster and salmon mongers shared space with the microbrewery owners and, most exciting for me, as a vintner and patron of the Heartbreak Grape the largest collection of pinot noir winemakers, outside of Beaune, under one roof.

"Let's go taste Tassie." I said to JB. Though not strictly an oenophile, JB had several remarkable traits that would serve to enhance the adventure we were about to embark on. First, he was of good convict stock, and was discriminating in his choice of beverages. Second, he had a knowlege of local lore, and knew some of the pinot purveyors personally. But it was his third attribute that would take us beyond plebian and into the patrician. JB's brother, Jimmy, was the owner of the most famous seafood restaurant in Hobart. Robyn and I had eaten there, and its reputation was well deserved. Any budding yeast winemaker would give his first born, to have a fair go at the restaurant's sommelier, a fact that I was not about to leave unexploited.

The only brakes on our escapade, were the tasting fees that each winery imposed on prospective buyers, to ensure that the descendants of half the original population of Van Dieman's Land, was not unfairly rewarded for their thirst. Because of the stars in the eyes of the pinot pourers, however, this turned out to be a totally ineffectual impediment. Perhaps it was my initial introductory pitch.

"Hello." I said. "I'm an international pinot aficionado from Canada. I'm sure you know JB, whose brother Jimmy is the proprietor of the finest seafood restaurant in town, and is always looking for exceptional wines to showcase from his cellar." The response was immediate, and generous.

"No worries." They would say, pouring out large samples of their reserve pinot, in the large glasses they kept under the counter for their special customers. No money crossed hands. I took their card, and JB and I went on to the next one.

This strategy worked fabulously for the first few suppliers, until the cumulative effects of their serial indulgences came up and whacked our heads. It became increasingly more difficult to maintain coherent speech, or strategy. Our final attempt to procure a free *méthode champenoise* fizzled rather than fizzed.

"Hello." I believe I said. " This is JB. His brother is a big bastard. Let's have some bubbly." We were done. Out of the earth of the *Natural State*, the *Island of Inspiration*, and *A World Apart, Not A World Away*, we had gone to ground.

Even in the world's most remote penal colony, wine and terroir were inextricably shackled. On another day we had picnic at Morilla Estate. It was for sale, and I seriously considered making an offer, before Robyn made a more serious counteroffer. JB knew one of the originally transported, who baited his sale of an ancient Grange Hermitage, with a half decent 1967 Seppelt Great Western

Colin Preece Memorial Burgundy. I should have known it wasn't worth it by the ullage hanging below the neck of the bottle. I did manage to score a 1990 Henscke Hill of Grace at a local wine shop, and this would prove magnificent, ten years later.

We took Win out to a winery lunch out up the Freycinet Penisula, an outcrop of wild, pristine coastland on Tasmania's east coast, eighty miles north of Hobart. And then JB suggested we leave everyone, and go walkabout.

"Where are we going, JB?" I asked.

"Wineglass Bay." He said. And we began our trek along a path lined with white-flowering *Kunzea* myrtle, buzzing with insects, past eucalypts with moth larvae scribbles, climbing uphill through the three bare jagged pink and grey Devonian granite peaks of the Hazards, rising in a line from the sea like the Pillars of Hercules.

About forty-five minutes in, we came to a ridge, flanked by rock walls dappled with bright orange lichen. It was the same lookout view that Louisa Meredith wrote about, in 1853.

> 'On either side of the ravine rose the towering summits of the mountain, bare masses of granite heaped up on high like giant altars, or rising abruptly from belts of shrubs and trees, like ancient fortress walls and turrets. But the downward and onward view was like enchantment! Far below my giddy perch...lay, calmly slumbering in the bright sunshine, that blue and beautiful nook of the Pacific named Wineglass Bay.'

I drank in my first sight of Wineglass Bay, a flawless dazzling white sand crescent fringed by a sapphire-colored sea, framed by sparkling roseate granite sea cliffs. A wombat crossed our path.

A sea eagle soared above us, black cockatoos and green rosellas flitted through the trees, native hens scurried through the scrub, and penguins waddled up the beach to their burrows. Pacific Gulls and Pied Oystercatchers waddled on the beach. Seals and bottlenose dolphins and a southern right whale played offshore.

"I see why they called it Wineglass Bay." I said, appreciate the symmetry.

"That's not why." Said JB. And we continued downhill, towards the beach, through a wild hinterland of heath and *Casuarina* forest, punctuated with banksia, orchids, wattle and honeysuckle, melaleuca, and Oyster Bay pine.

A half hour later we emerged to a Bennett's Wallaby on the beach, waiting for us, with a joey in her pouch. There were dunes behind the beach and, at the other end, there was a backwater, tea-stained from the Leptospermum 'tea tree'. The odd 'blue bottle' Portuguese Man' o war lay on the white sand with loaded tentacles, waiting. Even here, was a Fatal Shore. But not as fatal as what named it.

The peninsula had once been the exclusive domain of the Pydairrerme people- the Oyster Bay tribe, the last place the last Tasmanian aborigines were held. For some 30,000 years they lived there off the bounty of the sea and the forest. With the coming of Europeans, they fought a desperate guerrilla war to defend it until disease and deprivation did what musketry could not. By the 1850s, the Pydairrerme had been pushed out and the whalers had moved in, and then came sheep and cattle grazing, and coal and tin mining. Even the ancient Aboriginal middens were scoured for oyster shells to make lime.

"So what's the story of the bay?" I asked.

"In the 1820s, whalers came to Wineglass Bay." Said JB. "There was no job more laborious, more hazardous, and more disgusting."

The Southern Right whales swam past Wineglass Bay in the winter months, on their annual migration from Antarctica. The shore bases that were set up, precipitated violent and fatal clashes with the local Aborigines. The whalers set out in small boats to chase and harpoon passing whales. They laboriously towed the dead cetaceans back to shore, where the carcasses were butchered, and the fat rendered in large iron trypots. The slices of blubber, known as 'bible leaves,' were kept as thin as possible for the processing. The extracted oil, cooled and barreled, was shipped to Britain, where it was used for lighting and industrial lubricants, and the whalebone for ladies' skirt hoops and corsets.

In less than fifty years, by 1750, the North Atlantic Right Whale had been nearly exterminated. It took less that twenty to do the same to the Southern Right Whale on the Freycinet peninsula, in the mid-1800s.

"In that short time," Said JB. "Whenever the whalers went about their grisly business, the sparkling bay was dyed red with blood- like rich red wine in a glass." Between the two near extinctions, the London Morning Post, on November 1, 1786, printed a propitious prognosis for Tasmania. *This thief colony might hereafter become a great empire, whose nobles will probably, like the nobles of Rome, boast of their blood.* The nobles wouldn't likely be terribly disposed, to boast of the blood of the Aborigines or the Southern Right whales that they had slaughtered, to contrive their great empire.

By the 1840s shore-based whaling was in decline. Whale stocks had been severely reduced due to years of ruthless exploitation. Deep-sea *pelagic* whaling, with the sperm whale as the main quarry, would dominate the industry until the 1880s. The Southern Right whale would continue to suffer.

Waste from fish processing plants allowed seagull populations to soar, without any real reliably sustainable increase in their protein source. They turned to attacking and feeding on live Right whales. Because they need to spend up to a third of their time and energy performing evasive maneuvers, the mothers spend less time nursing, and the calves are thinner and weaker.

"This is one of the ten best beaches in the world." Said JB. "Its climate is similar to that of France." And how appropriate. The peninsula had been named for one of the Freycinet brothers, senior officers on Nicholas Baudin's exploration of the region in 1802, on the vessels *Le Geographe* and *Le Naturaliste.*

'High granitic mountains whose summits are almost completely barren,
form the whole eastern coast of this part of Van Diemen's Land. They
rise sheer from the base. The country which adjoins them is extremely
low and cannot be seen unless viewed from only a little distance at sea.
It is to this strange formation that we must doubtless attribute the
errors of the navigators who had preceded us into these waters and
who had mistaken these high mountains for as many separate islands.'

But there had been a history of loss and sadness, over the
wine dark sea.

'And forget not that the earth delights to feel your bare feet and
the winds long to play with your hair.'

Khalil Gibran

*　　　*　　　*

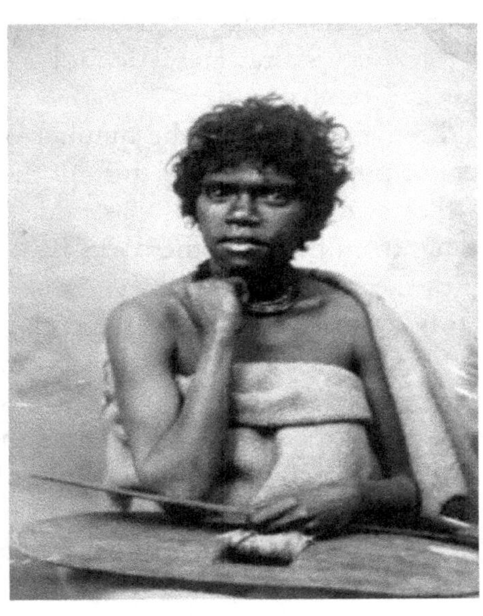

*　　　*　　　*

'Fire has always been and, seemingly, will always remain, the most terrible of the elements.'

Harry Houdini

Fire. Australians, despite their avowed dislike of Arabs, are not all that different from the object of their disaffection. Both tribes live in geographically isolated, mostly desert, hostile environments. Both are dependant on minerals and resources, foreign cheap labor, and western nations for development and investment. Both are ambivalent about their monarchies. Both have institutionalized racism, hostility and intolerance towards immigrants, non-whites and refugees. And both treat their women almost as well as their camels. But there are important differences. Australians show their maidens and hide their emotions, except at barbies where, as in most other cathartic social occasions, the men congregate near an outdoor source of fire, and the sheilas huddle together in an interior space.

And the tiebreaker, the one compelling distinction, separating the *habibis* from the *hoons*, is firewater. Alcohol is what makes Australia 'The Lucky Country.'

The most I could remember, about the number of bottles of wine it had taken, to put enough corks around the rim of my hat to keep the flies away, was that it was odd. As were the stories I was telling, from the wine the corks had come from. There were a lot of flies.

Smutty and the other mates, and JB and I, were raging on out the back of the shack in Susan's Bay. I knew we were getting along famously, because everyone was a 'bastard.' The conversation turned to barbeque lore. Fire dreaming. I believe I had made a disparaging comment about how Antipodean barbeques, reliant on a single large metal plate to cook the meat, was nothing more than a glorified frying pan, and lacked the finesse that aerated wood smoke and grill marks could achieve.

The criticism was received with more considered mental activity and less derision than I deserved, and I was invited to 'give it a burl.' In Tasmania, there was still sympathy for the devil.

The corks wobbled about my head, as I pulled the iron plate off the barbie, and dropped it into the dust. JB brought over a pile of blackwood and tea tree. I filled the bottom of the grill to the top, and lit a match.

Tasmania had certainly seen fires before I had arrived. In 1967, the Black Tuesday bushfires left 62 people dead, 900 injured, and over 7000 homeless. I wasn't trying for a new state record, but my enthusiasm to bring sophistication to my out scrub relatives, was far too untempered by the ecology I was operating in. JB was the first to offer feedback.

"Fair Dinkum." He said, as the flames licked the top of the carport.

Fifteen years after I had almost turned the east coast of Tasmania into an inferno, the Angry Summer did. A heat wave that brought 41.8°C to Hobart on January 4, 2013, the highest temperature in 120 years, kindled a six month conflagration of forty fires that burnt out fifty thousand acres of bushland, and destroyed over a hundred properties. One of them came down with the northwest wind, over the hill into Susan's Bay. *The sky was just scarlet... It burnt right to the waterline. It was just unbelievable.*

Luckily for JB and Debbie, daughter Kate and her boyfriend were at the shack, and managed to save it with a lot of quick thinking, and even more water.

The elements of earth, water, fire and wind, which pumped through the heart of Aboriginal myth, also gave life to their rock paintings. Earth was the first element, from which water was liberated, from which fire was taken, from which smoke became wind. From the blood of the Tasmanian Aborigines, and the Southern Right whales in Wineglass Bay, only the elements remained.

A red and black and yellow and white sunrise broke open the

morning that Robyn and I left Susan's Bay. Just after our departure, a strange form of facial tumor, capable of dissolving parts of the skull, began destroying most of Tasmania's devils. In 2008 high levels of carcinogenic flame retardant chemicals were found in the affected animals. It seems that, in the race to prevent any more blood from being shed into the water, the new settlers of Van Dieman's Land are caught in a perpetual struggle, between the devil and the deep blue sea.

'Human kinds cling to earthly things, but I seek ever to embrace the torch of love so it will purify me by its fire and sear inhumanity from my heart.'

Khalil Gibran

*   *   *

A Speck under the Forefinger of God
Norfolk Island

'Come out mine I show you foot dem callet God's Country,
hengen up een myse kitchen.'

Merv Buffett

Most departure lounges smell of freedom. This one was more complicated.

"Why would you want to go there?" Our Kiwi relatives had asked. "Unless you're newly wed or nearly dead."

"Maybe I'll win some money at cards." I said. We bought four bottles of wine and one of rum in Duty Free, and found a long row of bored prospective passengers, for the NZ794 weekly flight from Auckland. The geriatric gathering they warned us about was there in such profusion, I bet Robyn that so many more would be boarding than arriving, and so much more leg room would become available, that we would be able to stretch out in ever increasing comfort, as the flight progressed. An island girl with short denim shorts, black stockings, and ankle boots, swung a crossed leg up and down, in time to the muzak.

Air New Zealand had recently won an Australian government tender to provide the service, if winning actually occurs in anything other than surgery and war. If being memorable was more important than winning, they were about to become very important indeed.

I read the immigration form. *Do you have any criminal convictions or have you been deported or removed from any country?* And I wondered. Are these criteria for exclusion, or entry?

We dropped down over a volcanic landscape softened to rolling green hills by time, and tribulation. *Fech em jet daun ya.*

An overhead voice announced our imminent landing, but its owner wasn't quite as switched on.

"If you are connecting to a domestic flight..." She said, before taking it back. A lot happened on the Southern Sea, but not as much as what happened after landfall. There was nowhere else to go from here, and in the old days on this island, domestic flight would have gotten you shot.

Robyn and I filed off the plane, into the terminal.

The immigration guy wasn't sure what to do with me. I had an entry permit from some agent profiteer, the validity of which had been confirmed by the Australian government. No one had told the Norf'ker perusing my passport. He was clearly conflicted about my legitimacy.

"You've let in worse." I said. He scowled, but his stamp fell hard. *Welcam tu Norfuk Ailen.*

We had landed on a subtropical oasis, three tranquil miles by five, home to eighteen hundred natives of the most unusual pedigree.

"It looks even more beautiful than the photos." Said Robyn, before we landed. It did.

We emerged to find the proprietor of our cottage, standing under a one-acre Banyan tree.

"G'day." He said. Wayne was a former Kiwi car salesman from Tauranaga, who'd married a local girl. He was unimpressed with the work ethic of the Islanders, but even less 'dazzled' by the Australians.

"They're the ones drinking." He said. "Aussies, mozzies, same damn thing." But Norfolk was also curiously reminiscent of rural Australia in the 1960s, especially those trees, which grew up in small town parks all over the country, with predictable regularity.

Wayne drove us into the only town of Burnt Pine, and a short diversion to the Farmer's Market. Under the flame trees, a handful of stalls sold giant papayas, bananas, kumara, peaches, guavas, cauliflower, winter squash, guava jam, and roast pork smoked over pinewood.

On returning, he pointed to an old silver Mazda, and handed over a set of keys. The license plate had four digits.

"Here's your car." He said. "I'll give you a brief tour. Follow me." Robyn asked about road rules. He laughed.

"This is the only place in the world where the cattle are on the outside of the enclosures. Driveway cattle grids are to keep them out. Cows have right of way, and the fine for killing one with your car is about five hundred dollars. They're our watchdogs. The fencing is made from recycled Marsden matting, which was used to construct the runway during the war. Our potholes are huge, because we ran out of tar. Petrol is $2.50 per litre. Seatbelts are optional. We have one roundabout, and one streetlight. Everyone waves at passing drivers. The safest place to leave your car keys is in your car. Any questions?" We had no questions.

"I'll point out the shortcuts." He said, and was gone over the first hill, almost before Robyn had found the gearbox. Hundreds of swallows lined the hydro wires. We caught up to Wayne, and watched as he motioned right, then left, then right, and we took it too soon, and kept going, past a statue of a sleeping Mexican with a sombrero over his head.

"What's he doing here?" Asked Robyn, tooting the horn at some cows in the road, and dodging chickens and potholes. "And why haven't they thought of filling the potholes with cowpies?" A police car drove by, and waved. We finally stopped at a parking spot on Mission Road. Each space seemed to be spoken for. *Prison Wardens... Glass Blowers... Nose Pickers... Corrupt Politicians... Yogi Bears... Plant Lovers... Horse and Carriage... Tandems... Mopeds... Surfboards... Skateboards... Broomsticks... Faeries.*

"I think these people are going to be a little different." I said, as Wayne finally caught up with us, flailing his arms feverishly. We flailed back.

Up to the left of Bullocks Hut Road, Wayne led us into a wonderful bucolic setting, adjacent to the National Park. The garden was full of orange and grapefruit trees, and palms, with 'choir boy' tin collars around their trunks, cartoon crimson rosellas and local green parakeets darted in and out of the forest, strafing the English blackbirds on the lawn.

"Restorative justice." I said.

"Welcome to Anson Bay Lodge." Said Wayne, guiding us to our cottage. "Anson Bay is just over the hill, named after the famous admiral, the one that introduced rum rations to the Royal Navy." But I already knew about George Anson, and offered Wayne a rum.

"Wet with Anson's tear?" He said. "Bit early." And he wished us a Merry Christmas, and goodbye.

"No need to lock it." He said. Robyn and I opened the open door to the cottage, and a blowfly flew out, liberated from incarceration. I wondered why there was a coat rack over the mirror. The temperamental Telefunken television improved with an aerial, fashioned from aluminum foil, but it took some time to figure out that the channels would only change by pressing the volume buttons.

Robyn put the jug on, and I checked my messages.

> 'Someone recently tried to use an application to sign in to your mail. We prevented the attempt in case this was a hijacker trying to access your account.'

The death sentence was still valid on Norfolk Island. I reached for the telephone book, and quickly realized three important things about the islanders. Almost everyone had the name of one of the original Bounty mutineers- Adams and Christians and Evans and McCoys and Youngs and Nobbs and Quintals and Buffetts. Consequently, not many last names were available to go around. It had become necessary to list people by their nicknames. As a result, there was a veritable smorgasbord of sobriquets to be fascinatingly found, in the *Faasfain Salan Bai Dems Nikniem* directory:

Aussie, Baldie, Barley, Bash, Bear, Bebs, Beef, Bella, Bing, Blackie, Blitti, Bonnet, Boo, Bookie, Boot, Borgy, Borry, Boy, Bubby, Bugs, Bunt, Cane Toad, Carrots, Cat, Chine, Chinney, Cocky, Coon, Crocket, Cowboy,

Crowbar, Culla, Dar Bizziebee, Derms, Devil, Dids, Diesel, Doby, Doodus, Drill, Father, Feathers, Fishy, Fletch, Foxy, Frenzy, Freshie, Gags, Garnet, Geek, George, Glover, Goldie, Goof, Golla Jnr, Golla Snr, Gotty, Grace Proud, Gran, Griffo, Gumboots, Hat, Honey, Honkey-Dorey, Hook, Hose, Hover, Huggy, Hussein, Ippy, Ikey, Jap, Junny, Kik kik, Kik, Kissard, Kitha, Knuckles, Koota, Lettuce Leaf, Little Pooh, Loppy, Maa Aelis, Macka, Mami, Massport, Millie, Minnie, Monkey, Moochie, Moonie, Moose, Morg, Muff, Mutty, Nippa, Noon, Onion, Oodie, Pash, Pedro, Pelly, Perko, Philly Foxtel, Pinky, Pip, Pixie, Plumber, Plute, Pooh, Pops, Poppa, Possum, Puffa, Puk, Pumbles, Pumper, Pumpkin, Puss, Quack, Quent, Rossco, Ruffy, Sarlu, Scotty, Short, Shorty, Skeeters, Slack, Slick, Sluggy, Smitty, Smudgie, Snapper, Snobbles, Snoop, Snowy, Sparks, Sparrow, Spider, Spindles, Sputt, Storky, Strutts, Tardy, Tet, Tiny, Toyboy, Trigger, Trix, Truck, Umi, Wiggy, Willie, Winnie, Wolf, Yarm

Either something bad had happened to Binky, Duck, Oot, Paw Paw, Skeeters, and Tarzan, or they had taken out unlisted numbers. I looked at a map of street names and locations (Burglars Lane and Stink Corners and Pig Heads Corners and The Meat Tree) and another of local fishing grounds (Oodles and No Trouble Reef and No Reason and Side ar Whale Es and Side Suff Fly Pass and Side Eddie find ar Anchor and Ar Yes! and 10 O'Clock Bank and Ikes), and I reflected on the bizarre blend of 18th century Tahitian and West County English dialect that had become N'folkese.

Wut-a-wey yorlye?	How are you?
Webaut yu gwen?	Where are you going?
Dii Elduu f'mada	They'll do for dumplings
Swiit tieti	Kumera
Grawy	Gravy
Koknat pai	Coconut pie
Glaas bohtam boet	Glass bottom boat
Bussup	Broken in pieces

Even in the ATM I had accessed, up town. *You no got nuff money in dees account.*

"We'll need *wettles*." Said Robyn. It was coming on Christmas fast, and we drove back up town, for victuals. The first surprise at the supermarket was how normal it appeared. There were rows of this and that, with aisles that were not quite empty. The second surprise was what kind of this and that there was, and wasn't. Tinned goods from the Antipodes were in good supply, as was longlife UHT milk, cheaper to import than to pasteurize the real stuff locally. There was no dairy industry on the island. Despite the fact that the roads were full of cattle, over sixty per cent of the beef, most of the chicken, and all of the lamb, was still imported. Island feral chickens were tough enough to bounce off the kitchen floor, and the sheep on Norfolk were afflicted with footrot. The signs over the butchers were befittingly banal. *Please don't prick our sausages. A steak a day keeps the doctor away.*

Norfolk has no working harbor. Two piers, at either end of island, are the only means of bringing in freight, and which landing to use must be decided on the day of arrival. Cargo must be loaded on to smaller craft and brought to shore in military-style manoeuvres, against a four-knot current. Such tricky logistics, coupled with strict quarantine regulations, means that little fresh produce, except potatoes, onions, ginger and garlic, can be imported. The crops that can be grown above the steep escarpments, citrus, bananas, guavas, kumera, cauliflowers and winter squash, only last so long. Peaches are available for two weeks. *The people throw dead horses down to prove... The cliffs are what the island grows above.*

The climate is too cold for coconuts. Guavas grow wild, and make excellent preserves. American whalers introduced Thanksgiving, turkeys and pumpkin pie, and cornbread, and the British convict system introduced the wind and water and manpower methods to grind the corn.

But it wasn't Thanksgiving; it was Christmas, and most everything that had been on the supermarket shelves was now there in spirit only. Someone had stolen every mincemeat manifest morsel but the music. There was no bread, and no fresh vegetables. And what was left was the third surprise. The prices were in scientific notation.

"It's hard to believe how much money I earned last year." I said, "And here I am on the worst convict island in the South Pacific looking for the cheapest soup mix." An Aussie mainlander shopper had overhead my comment, and hove to my starboard side.

"You should try living here." She said. "The eggman will be giving away free cartons of eggs at the P&R in a few days." Robyn and I got directions.

Between the *Huggies* nappies and the *Wondersoft*, we managed to cobble together a Yule basket.

"Here for the holidays?" Asked the checkout girl. It appeared so, and we inquired if she knew a good place for lunch.

"Dino's at Bumboras is good." She said.

About fifteen minutes from up town, we drove over a set of cattle-dissuading judder bars, to a venerable crumbling tin-roofed homestead with palms and pines, and lovely gardens. Old straw Pitcairn hats lined the dark interior timbered hallway. It appeared initially that the restaurant was empty, except for the owner, Helen, who inquired as to our intentions.

"Lunch." I said, and she found us the perfectly sunlit table with a rich red tablecloth, set with Georgian glassware and silver flatware and contorted crockery. The artwork on the wall was a little off the wall. Robyn had the seafood linguine and I ordered a T-bone with rosemary potatoes. Helen dropped the steak cutlery in a parabola, and a near miss, over my shoulder.

"You could have had a knife in your back, mate." She said.

"Its an old tradition here, isn't it?" I asked. It would be one of the best meals of our visit. I put a plastic card in a machine in a place where, unlike every other machine there that had formerly represented a form of torture, I was legitimized. Helen told us to drive a little further south, to the Bumbora reserve.

Tangerine and blue rosellas screamed around our arrival, before blasting apart down the path through the trees.

Magnificent trees. Trees with textured bark and breadth of pachyderm proportion, ponderous pillars of elephant trunk rising into the sky, throwing off green-fingered triangular fans of coniferous confidence, separate and sideways. Their shallow roots went as wide as the trees were tall.

"Cook thought that he had found the mother lode source of ship's masts." I said. "The real Meat Tree. But they have too many knots to make good spars. Norfolk pines soak up salt, so the locals never park under them. There's a lone tree down in Kingston that was already mature when the First Fleet made landfall in 1788. The original convicts planted a tremendous 'Avenue of Pines' windbreak, containing a giant old 'Tree of Knowledge.' Mitchener wrote about how the Americans had it all cut down to construct the airfield during the war. *The American landscape has no foreground and the American mind no background.* They removed 26 homes and 240 islanders, used bulldozers to knock the tops off several hills, and filled the valleys with hilltops and Marsden matting mesh. It was never used as a major base. The Army Corps of Engineers didn't know any geography; they were too busy making it."

We identified the four remaining rare endemic Norfolk Island euphorbia, among the white oak or Norfolk Island hibiscus with its bright pink flowers and yellow stamens. There were large land snails, enough for escargots, patches of taro, and trees of white paperbark, black peppered with spots. The path became a boardwalk, zigzagging down to the silver surf in the bottom of an amphitheatre of tall pines soaring stratospheric out of a cliff of grazed lawn, like the final green on God's golf course. Big scattered piles of gray rocks protruded out from a white sand beach into some of the clearest seawater in the Southern Sea. We noticed a colony of breeding white terns off to the left, but were completely ignored by some local bathers on our other flank. Clouds rolled over the sun and dropped a few drops of rain, and then retreated, before returning to repeat the performance.

"It's the kind of climate that can't decide what it wants to be when it grows up." Said Robyn. But it became more a more decisive drizzle as we left, up town on Ferny Lane, on our way back to the lodge. We stopped in at Governor's Lodge, to check on the rich tour accommodation.

"Are you coming for dinner on Christmas Day?" Asked the Papuan receptionist. We hadn't thought that far. "The menu is on the door of Bailey's restaurant there." It looked quite wonderful, a panoply promise of prawns and crayfish and mussels and oysters and Norfolk Blue roast beef, and other classic Australian indulgences. Robyn saw the price before I did.

"A hundred dollars?" She said, more than asked.

"That includes your drinks." Said the receptionist.

"I guess you'd need to charge that much." I said. " To break even on a roomful of Aussies." She half-cracked a smile.

Another place caught Robyn's eye, on the other side of Burnt Pine. We pulled into the South Pacific Resort, to check out their rates. The receptionist, Verney, pointed out their Christmas Day dinner offering, posted on the bulletin board. It was forty dollars cheaper than the celebration at Governor's Lodge and, although of more modest proportions, promised seafood and turkey and ham. I asked if it included liquid refreshments.

"One drink." She said. "But if you're discreet, you might be able to BYO the rest in a paper bag." A bargain is something you can't use, at a price you can't resist. With the shops still closed for another two days, Robyn and I would be requiring some form of revictualization by the day after next. We signed up for the South Pacific's holiday banquet, and would dream sugarplums, until it was spread out before us.

Up Grassy Road, along moss-covered fence posts and through the cows and the potholes, was the Botanical Garden. Drizzle and mist turned the light suffusing through the canopy a glistening green, and our *trip ina stik* became primordial. Before European colonization, before the clearing and the grazing and the weeds, Norfolk Island had covered with subtropical *Araucaria* rain forest of 174 native plants, a third of them found nowhere else on earth. Robyn and I walked under the tallest tree ferns in the world, in an understory thick with lianas and broadleafs, undulating over the forest floor. We weaved around contorted open vines and wrapped vines, green berry clusters, tiny yellow and orange orchids, barks of various textures and colors, and a large carved punga tiki. There had been only one native mammal on Norfolk Island, Gould's Wattled Bat, now most probably extinct. But the tin 'choirboy collars' around the palms gave a hint of what the colonists had brought along for the ride. I had asked Wayne what they were for, back at the lodge.

"Fate didn't arrive here like an eagle." He said. "It crawled off with the rats."

*   *   *

'The said Island... is nearly as large as the Isle of Wight. Lieutenant King... gives the most flattering portrayal of it. The island is fully wooded. Its timber is in the opinion of everyone the most beautiful and finest in the world... most suitable for masts, yards, spars and such. The New Zealand flax-plant grows there in abundance... It only lacks a good port and suitable landing places...How far these deficiencies can be improved by art and the hand of man, time must decide.'

Letter from an Officer of Marines, 16 November 1788

"Noisy bastards." I said, waking to the larrikan rosellas, boomeranging around their Norfolk parakeet cousins. Robyn was already brewing the coffee.

"You need to get up anyway." She said. It was the day before Christmas. "Beat the other noisy Aussies to the bread shop."

The Mazda was already moving when I shut the passenger door, and Robyn headed off up town. We stopped for a brief look at Puppy's Point, a lone Norfolk pine coupled to a sheer coastal cliff over 200 feet high, sloping down to the Pacific foam, raging below. Cattle contentedly chewed, in time to the view. A little further along, an honesty box sat outside the entrance to Strawberry Fields maze. *Admission $7.*

"This is a convict island." I said. "You think they'd charge you to get out."

"Nothing to get hungabout." Said Robyn.

Saunder's *Meat-Foodstuffs-Electrical* was closed, and so was the supermarket, but we got our loaf at the P&R.

"Did you pay for the bread?" Asked the proprietress, as we were leaving.

"On the counter." I shouted back. It wasn't as if there was anywhere we could have escaped to. We left our prize in the trunk of the Mazda, and went walkabout.

"We might have been a bit overenthusiastic." Robyn said. The rest of Burnt Pine was still asleep, except for the golden silk orb-weaver spiders and the gossamer they danced on, shimmering in the rising sun, a gilded cage for the unsuspecting. Fishermen on other coasts of the Indopacific had formed the webs into a ball, and thrown them into the ocean where, unfolding, they would catch their bait fish.

I patted the white-patched forehead of a chestnut mare, leaning over a rail. She seemed sad to see me go.

We passed through the closed commercial heart of Burnt Pine. *Tahitian Fish. Bounty Centre Shop. Four Corners. Pigs Can Fly $$$.* A plastered Santa posed in a red and white suit without a hat in a display window, next to a provocative female mannequin with a partially awry short satin bathrobe, and a tennis visor over her eyes. We walked by the Anson Coffee Club. *The only place for a cup of coffee- closed until further notice.* The

Anson Bay plantation had been for sale on an international property website. I had thought of buying it.

Robyn put a red hibiscus behind her ear, and I took a photo of her standing under a gigantic spreading *dracaena*, a fountain of leaves, engorged with venous blood.

"We should go back." I said. Wayne had booked us on the mandatory free bus tour of the island, and I could see people beginning to congregate, back down Taylors Road.

The clipboard guy called out our names.

"You're with Max." He said. Right on cue, a bus pulled off the curb, and the driver swung open the door. "That's Max."

He was difficult to age precisely, but Max had sacrificed most of his years to the sun. There were bits chopped out of the edges of his ears that spoke of cancer. He was a thinner version of Paul Hogan, or Robyn's father, or any other Antipodean everyman, with a strong sense of duty and honour and family devotion, good-natured and blessed with humour and the common touch, the kind of man the English wasted in heaps, in the trenches of the Somme and Gallipoli.

"Thank you for spending Christmas with us." He said, motioning us to board. "Lets have a nice morning." I recognized one of the tourists from the South Pacific resort the day before. The front half of her hair was white, the back half black, and her over-injected lips were painted bright pink. Max must have seen it all.

From the moment we drove out of Burnt Pine, Max was an overhead encyclopedia.

"Norfolk Island is eighty-four hundred acres, five by three miles, three extinct volcanoes now one sixteenth its former size, forty-three indigenous plants, fifty-two birds, only three native, the green parrot, bubuck owl, and long-billed silvereye, fifteen hundred people, a third descended from the Bounty. We use tank water from out annual fifty inches of rainfall..." He began, between waving to every passing vehicle, swinging his bus around the cows and the corners, with skill, and Norfolk Primordial.

"The island was first settled at Emily Bay by 14th century Polynesians from either the Kermadecs or North Island New Zealand. They left behind stone tools, banana trees, New Zealand flax, and the Polynesian Rat, before disappearing. When Captain Cook arrived on 11 October, 1774, he called it a 'paradise,' a word he had never used before. He made special note of the impressive tall trees, and the flax."

> 'It was uninhabited; and the first persons that ever set foot on it were unquestionably our English navigators. Various trees and plants were observed that are common at New Zealand; and in particular, the flax plant, which is rather more luxuriant here than in any other part of that country. The chief produce of the island is a kind of spruce pine, exceedingly straight and tall, which grows in great abundance. Such is the size of many of the trees that, breast high, they are as thick as two men can fathom.'

Ships masts from New England would soon become unavailable, with the opening shots of the American War of Independence. In addition, all the flax that the Royal Navy required to make sailcloth came from Russia. When Catherine the Great restricted its sale to Britain twelve years later, the English were desperate to find another source. New Zealand flax at source was impossible to procure because of the bellicosity of the Maoris, but Norfolk was uninhabited, and quickly planned for 'dual colonization' with Botany Bay."

Max told us of the three phases of Norfolk settlement- the First Convict Settlement from 1788, abandoned in 1814; the 'planned hell' of the Second Convict Settlement, from 1825 to 1855; and the 1856 relocation of the entire population of Pitcairn Island.

The First Settlement began with six women convicts 'whose characters stood fairest' (and whose fair feet hadn't even touched the ground in Australia), nine male convicts, and eight free men, 'the best of a bad lot.' The *H.M.S. Supply* made the thousand-mile journey from Botany Bay, in a race to beat the French, but La Perouse had already been, and described it as a place fit only for 'angels and eagles.' *It was obvious that I would have had to wait maybe for a very long time for a moment suitable for a landing and a visit to this island was not worth this sacrifice.*

The British commandant, Philip Gidley King, had similar misgivings. *I now began to think it was impossible to land on ye isle.* Unlike the French, however, he had no choice and, after spending five days sailing around the island's 300-foot high cliffs, forced a landfall on the 'huge rainforest.' King wasted no time trying to turn the island into a garden, to feed the struggling barren settlement back in Australia. He meted out flogging punishments for stealing rum, forbade the building of any boat longer than twenty feet, and took himself a mistress. In only a matter of months, his convicts had cleared ground, constructed a road from the landing place to Anson Bay via Mount Pitt, located sources of limestone, and fathered the settlement's first son, which he proudly named 'Norfolk.' By April of 1789, he had food crops in the ground-groves of Rio bananas, orange trees, sugar cane, wheat and barley and rice, squash, potatoes, artichokes, turnips, onions, leeks, lettuce, parsley and celery. But as far north as they had come, it was all about to go back south.

The pines were not resilient enough to make good masts. Because none of the settlers had the necessary skills to prepare the flax for manufacturing, two Maoris, Woodoo and Tookee, were kidnapped onto and off of the *H.M.S. Daedelus*, the first record of blackbirding in Southern Sea history. But flax weaving was considered women's work, and the Maori men had no idea or interest in what to do. The crops failed due to the salty wind and caterpillars and the rats. The absence of a decent harbour would hinder supply and communication. A convict insurrection in 1789, the same year as a synchronistic mutiny half an ocean away, was almost the end of the First Settlement. But it was not far off.

On 19 March 1790, the *H.M.S. Sirius*, sent from Sydney to relieve the colony, was shipwrecked on the foreshore, and marooned for a year until they could be rescued back to England. Three years later, the decision was taken to abandon Norfolk. A small party remained to slaughter the stock and destroy all the buildings, until the final remnants were removed in 1813. For another dozen years, the only visitors would be the whalers.

Max drove us around to the abandoned whaling 'factory' on Cascade Bay. He spoke of the 26,000 whales that had been killed, until the last one in 1962 *Far down below the whale boatmen row, as after the Humpback the Norfolk men go.* He spoke of the convict cooking pots, and of whale vertebrae used for milking stools. *With backs nearly broken, and blistered hands sore, the boatmen at last reach the isle's rocky shore.* But most heartbreaking, he spoke of the whale cow he saw, give birth to her calf, while being sliced into pieces on the deck ramp. *The joy on friends' faces, what pleasure to see, their loved ones return with the prize of the sea.* The smell of burning rubbish was thick in our throats.

Max cut the bus back inland, past a kentia palm plantation, to the perfection of St. Barnabas chapel. Founded by Bishop John Coleridge Patteson, five years before his habit of coming ashore off his *Southern Cross*, wearing only a top hat, got him speared and eaten in the Solomons, the St. Barnabas training college brought in 200 'students' from all parts of Melanesia, for whatever abuses would occur. The chapel, though small, was lavishly constructed with tiled marble floors, Solomon Island mother-of-pearl inlaid, intricately carved pews, and the most beautiful red and green rose stained glass windows, one by William Morris, and the other by Edward Burne-Jones. The kauri and Norfolk Island pine open timbered ceiling was built in the shape of an inverted boat, and stained with whale oil. Max locked the door in a half-serious way, and made an appeal for donations. We sang a hymn, in honour of the acoustics. *Let the lower light be burning, send a gleam across the wave, some poor, fainting, struggling seaman, you may rescue, you may save.*

He was more at ease toward the end of the tour, when we stopped for tea and scones with jam and cream at the tour company owner's estate. We thsat among large whaling pots converted into planters, in a magnificent precisely pruned garden of palms and bromeliads and staghorn ferns and all other manner of other tropical verdure. The slower Christchurch passengers were still queuing up for carbohydrates and theophylline, beside a chubby wooden tiki with open arms and a tinsel headband. You could hear the painful rumblings of their recent earthquake, clipping their consonants short. I asked him how he could do this job, day after day.

"You meet some others." He said. "Is the island surrounded by water? Who planted the first pine? Why do the feral chickens look so real? What spider makes a noise like a cricket? How do you say 'Cockadoodledoo' in Norfolk language?" I overheard a beefy Aussie at the next patio table.

"I can't understand why the prisoners didn't like it here." He said. "Its such a beautiful spot." Max rolled his eyes, just a little.

By the time we made it back to Burnt Pine, he was back to gracious. He thanked us for taking his tour.

"Merry Christmas." He said. "Drink plenty."

Robyn and I headed back to Anson Bay lodge, via the honesty jar in the roadside kiosk at *Barnaby's Fresh Fruit & Veg*. The cows surrounded us, as we picked out our wettles, from the courgettes, lemons, onions, beans, Roma tomatoes, passion fruit, and winter squash on the pine boards. 'Twas the night before Christmas. A bubuck owl hooted at the full moon, calling back the whales.

*   *   *

'Still I search the constellations
And the tiny grains of sand
Where the song of the ocean
Meets the salty piece of land.'
      Jimmy Buffett, *A Salty Piece of Land*

Our cottage at Anson Bay Lodge abutted hard up against the national park, and the distinct probability of being clipped by a low flying parrot, unless you kept your head down. On the morning of the third day, Robyn and I decided to drive the upward spiral around to the other side, and the summit of Mount Pitt. The views out to the Southern Sea took their own breaths between the occasional open breaks into vertigo. Norfolk pinetops fell behind the sky in a path of evergreen Christmas shooting stars, melting into a receding mist. We walked along the trails until, entering one Arcadian glade, Robyn broke into a Tai Chi set. As she arched upward, after her 'put a little pin to the sea,' a congregation of tan and yellow and black and white Norfolk Golden Whistlers gathered on the branches around her.

"As friendly as our Whiskey Jacks in Canada, or our Fantails in New Zealand." I said. As if on cue, a stray grey fantail joined them. "The locals call them Tameys."

"I see why." Said Robyn. And the birds broke into a chatter of chirpy whistles, going up at the end of their sentences.

"Sound like Aussies." Robyn said.

"They're also called Thickheads." I said, with an epiphanic nod. "This is the only place on Earth to find them and, with the black rats and feral cats finding them as well, there may soon not be many left to find."

"They shouldn't be so friendly." She said.

Back at the cottage I found a French picnic basket, which Robyn proceded to load with leftover chicken, a salad assembled from the purchases of Barnaby's honesty box, and one of our bottles of Kiwi *sauvblanc*. Packed in the boot, we drove it out, via a northern tour to Fisherman's Lane- past the grey moss-covered south-facing fence posts, and a yellow blue, grey and red faced wooden fish carving, on our way to Anson Bay, for a Christmas lunch, in the place our lodge was named for. We arrived at the picnic area at the top of the reserve, and looked down over and onto and into a deep crescent of pale blue sky becoming beautiful cobalt horizon becoming turquoise bay becoming broad eggbeater waves becoming sugar sand shore.

"Should we hike down first or have lunch first?" Asked Robyn, knowing immediately after she asked, what the right answer was. "Lunch."

We found a picnic table under one of the white oaks between two Norfolk pines, and laid out our spread. The only other person in the reserve was dressed in overalls and a cap, wearing sunglasses and sub-dermal ink, and trans-dermal metal. He wandered over cautiously, to chat.

Darren was a painter and a mushroom grower, but wasn't making much of a go of it.

"It's all the rules, mate." He said. I asked him if the island hadn't been built out of rocks, and rules. Darren told us he was an Islander, and resentful of the increasing invasive 'Mainlanders' that were ruining his paradise.

"They're just like that kikuyu grass there." He said. "Bullies. What have they brought us? Canberra gave us four million dollars, about what they'd spend in a year on fireworks. They've brought us crime. There hasn't been a murder on the island since 1893, and we had two in four years. In 2002, Janelle Patton was murdered. The killer ran her over with his car, fractured her skull, and stabbed her 64 times, before pulling down her panties, and dumping her in the Cockpit waterfall reserve over there. The Aussie cops ran around with no guns in their holsters, and announced that they were going to test the DNA of everyone on the island, including our religious elders, before they found the Kiwi chef that did it. The Aussies are the bad drivers and the petty thieves. Before they came here was never any crime on Norfolk." I must have been staring.

"Well, not for a long while, anyway." He said. "Look, the Aussies can come here and live anytime they want, and there's more and more of them doing just that. If I want to go to Australia, I need an Australian passport. And what do they want from us? They want to impose an income tax. We already pay higher freight charges than anywhere else in the world. You've been in the supermarket. Milk is seven bucks a litre. A kilo of yogurt is almost twenty dollars. We've got oil and gas offshore. You don't think they know that? That's really the reason why they want to turn our legislature into a local council, and send our self-government down the gurgler. It's breaking the hearts of the old people."

"We're Pitcairners." He said. "In 1856, Queen Victoria gave us this land. Every year we celebrate Bounty Day. Our national anthem is *God Save the Queen*, not bloody *Advance Australia Fair*. Norfolk is our homeland. If less than two thousand people can manage our own customs service, schools, stamps, phones, and rubbish, we can go the rest of it alone." I told Darren about the toxic smell of the plastic burning near the old whale factory. He told me he didn't think the Aussies would be carting it all away. I asked him who he thought was going to win this battle for Norfolk Island.

"We're mutineers mate." He said. "We know how to deal with them." Darren shook our hands, and wished us a merry Christmas, and a happy time on the island. We wished him the same, and finished our picnic lunch.

The adjacent grassy track switchbacks would bring us down three hundred feet of steep coastal cliffs onto the outstanding sand beach seascape of Anson Bay. Robyn and I walked through wind-pruned white oak and native flax, moo-oo and coastal lily, and porpieh and shade tree and a single euphorbia. African olive and Hawaiian holly and lantana had invaded, long before the Australians. There were weird miniature purple corncob candelabras, with tiny symmetrical pink flowers around the top, and the inverted parasolic profiles of Norfolk evergreen branches, against the upper atmosphere. We passed under high vertical crenulated columnar cliffs of basalt lava, pale yellow and purple and red layers of volcanic ash and scoria, seemingly afflicted with elephantiasis or like the Thing's thick integument, or Wyoming's Devil's Tower, eroded, and threatening to slide down on top of us. Fallen rocks flowed down grey to become cream sand, and the Norfolk Island beans and native *vignas* on the dunes below. Robyn ran ahead, and had the empty wide beach all to herself, except for the blue bottle jellyfish, and the sign. *Strong current- can be dangerous to swimmers.*

White terns and the rarest of red-tailed tropicbirds hovered overhead, or plunged dived beside us, likely the reason why I found one of his thin red tail feathers on the sand. We sat and played with the curled calcium castings of long departed marine worms, and danced with each other's own deep footprints in the sand, until one of the deep footprints decided to dance back. The hornet that stung my left foot was trying for the third murder on Norfolk since 1893, but I managed to hobble all the way back up to the top of the reserve, *where the song of the ocean met the salty piece of land,* without giving him the satisfaction.

We were looking forward to our Christmas dinner at the South Pacific resort that evening. And didn't we just get a better deal than the hoity-toits who had spent a hundred dollars, for a similar experience at Governor's Lodge? The easy answer was about to become 'no.'

Robyn and I arrived to an abominable assembly of ancient Aussie males wrapped around young Oriental girls, or comparable horrible old Antipodean couplings, wearing too much perfume, but not enough to disguise the miasma of death.

"Bring me a gin!" resonated through the lobby, as a layered stack of plastic chairs rolled off into the swimming pool in slow motion. Paper bags were discretely poured, from under tables, everywhere. Whatever young people were in attendance, had either skirts that didn't cover the bits that should have been covered, or fabric tension, that accentuated things that should have been left more discreet. We were in the company of Australians. Inside the dining room, some attempt had been made at celebratory decoration. Lime green nylon bows and wreaths had been draped over black velour chairs, lining pink tablecloths on which decade-old '*Best By*' crackers and Cadbury's products had been formed into centerpieces. Balloons floated across the ceiling, and spherical white paper Japanese lanterns deliberately stole light from the buffet. Robyn and I got to sit at table #22, across from Ed, an eighty-some year-old civil engineer from Auckland ('He owns twenty-four houses, don't you know?'), and his paramour, Diane, a post-menopausal English surveyor from Hawke's Bay, now a travel consultant. Ed wore a crêpe paper crown around his head. He looked right at home, and started in with the jokes, long before our table was advised to get up, and hit the buffet.

Q. What happened when the butcher sat on the meat slicer? A. He got a little behind in his work. Q. Why don't elephants like playing cards in the jungle? A. Because of all the cheetahs. Q. What do you get if you cross a cocker spaniel, a poodle, and a rooster? A. A cockerpoodledoo.

We got called to the buffet. Moment of truth. And it was immediately apparent that we had made the wrong decision. The prawns were so salty, they must have come from another age. The back of the pig was so flayed, he could have started his own religion. I asked for a turkey leg, and was admonished for being 'too selfish.' I came back to get the other leg. The mayo was off. The Filipino servers ran out of chowder, unless you spoke a little Talagog. If you did, you could get them to turn the lights up or down. We figured out how to get more than one free glass of bad wine, from several pourers, by pouring on our own charm. Over at Governor's Lodge, they were chowing down, on mussels and oysters and fish. But they didn't have what we had- 'Puffy,' slicked hair, old Elvis tunes and a boom box, Neil Diamond, and an overwhelming urge to slit our own wrists. You could hear the old commandants laughing.

Robyn and I left early, to save ourselves.

"Is there a fine if we don't wear our seatbelts?" I asked. Robyn was prosaic.

"They'll probably throw you in jail." She said. "But the food, the food will definitely be better."

*   *   *

'The famous ruins rotting on the shore,
A carrion perch from governmental crows.
There is no town at Kingstone anymore...'
Bruce Beaver, *From Norfolk Island, I Kingstone*

Boxing Day. I traded the French picnic basket from the lodge shed, for the snorkeling gear. First in, first served.

"Do you think it'll be safe to leave it in the car?" Asked Robyn.

"They'd flog anyone trying to steal it." I said.

Burnt Pine had flat lined overnight, and we drove through it, climbing up to the viewpoint on Rooty Hill Road, for an early morning aerial view of Kingston.

"So this is where." Said Robyn.

"This is where." I said. *Infamy of crimes upon the wind that neither salt nor sun can quite dispel.*

But what first caught our eye were not the remains of the Second Settlement, on the beach below. It was the barren hairdryer-shaped reddish brown offshore island, nozzle pointing to Pitcairn, almost four thousand miles away, and Easter Island, another thousand miles further east.

"Remember the Birdman cult?" Asked Robyn. *They finally reached Moto Nui, and scrambled up its steep ledges to search for the first eggs of the nesting Frigate birds, back from their annual migration.* It's bigger and farther than Moto nui, and the frigate eggs are long gone. Max had told us of the only remaining life on the island, carnivorous rabbits, eating each other's lucky hind feet. How late it had become. *The isle's eroded carcase, angry red, alive with rodents, otherwise quite dead.*

Our view came ashore from Philip's Island, to the roof parapet rosellas and rich ochre stone walls of the Georgian row houses and military barracks, and prison, below.

"If you were bad you ended up in Botany Bay. I said. "If you were bad in Botany Bay, you ended up in Tasmania; if you were bad in Tasmania, you ended up here."

"And if you were bad here?" Robyn asked.

"You still ended up here." I said. *For the Term of His Natural Life.*

In 1824, the British government sent instructions for NSW governor, Thomas Brisbane, to recolonize Norfolk Island. The station to be established was designed for the 'worst of the worst,' the 'lees and dregs of mankind,' criminal lunatics, half-crazed, warped and perverted in mind and body, brutes of low mentality, or rotten with every vice produced by the degraded instincts of the worst types of sub-human beings.

Its construction would not just create an impression, but give birth to a myth.

Norfolk would become the *ne plus ultra* of convict degradation, a *great Hulk or Penitentiary* for the incarceration of reconvicted incorrigibles, a place of the severest punishment short of death, a *Hell in Paradise*. Reformation was not an objective.

"The felon who is sent there is forever excluded from all hope of return." Brisbane wrote. His successor, Ralph Darling, was as severe. *Every man should be worked in irons that the example may deter others from the commission of crime... to hold out Norfolk Island as a place of the extremest punishment short of death.*

Darling's fellow Tasmanian confederate, Governor Arthur, offered the same. *When prisoners are sent to Norfolk Island, they should on no account be permitted to return. Transportation thither should be considered as the ultimate limit and a punishment short only of death.*

But of the 6500 convicts that would be transported into the 'machine for extinguishing hope,' over the thirty years of the Second Settlement, only a minority would be as bad as advertised. Less than half had been the 'doubly-convicted' perpetrators of additional crimes committed since arriving in New South Wales. Nearly 70 per cent of original offences were non-violent crimes against property, the burglars and pickpockets and highwaymen who stole cheeses and ducks and shawls and watches and handkerchiefs and livestock, or the clerks and embezzlers and forgers and fraudsters and utterers of more 'gentlemanly' crimes. There were rapists and gang rapists and arsonists and murderers, but fewer than 4 per cent had been transported for explicitly violent offences, the same proportion that were under the age of fifteen. Most had been farm laborers, and the average sentence had been three years, a far cry from forever.

Far more cries were in their Orwellian future, inhuman boots forever stamping on human faces.

From the moment of landing, discipline was abusively enforced. Military guards never walked alone. Almost two hundred cubit yards of earth was moved by hand, to reclaim the swamp's 'slow-motion water' on Slaughter Bay. Kingston arose, one stone wall at a time, into a 'miasma of sin, where horror and vice beyond sane imaginings grew like poisonous fungus on a dung heap...a place of perverted values where evil was reckoned to be good and where the unbelievable became the norm.'

By the mid-nineteenth century, Norfolk was the most notorious penal station in the English-speaking world and represented all that was evil about the convict system. One of the most sadistic commandants was James Morrisset who, during his five-year reign of terror, 'delighted in applying the lash in person.' One Second Settlement observer remarked that

> 'If the wretches of Norfolk Island were fiends and not men, they could not be worse treated. There is no parallel to the cruelties practised on them. I beg to observe, my Lord, that in the report of Mr. Commisioner Bigge he notices that he examined the backs of prisoners at Newcastle and found them knotted and furrowed in consequence of severe scourging. That scourging was inflicted by Colonel Morisset, the present Commandant at Norfolk Island who is, save for the late Captain Logan of Moreton Bay, one of the most improper that could have been selected.'

Morisset flayed convicts 'for having a pipe... for having fat in his possession... for not walking fast enough... for doing up his shoelaces when Muster called... for not pushing hard enough on a cartload of stone... for asking the Gaoler for a chew of tobacco, for having a tamed bird... for saying 'O my God' while on the chain... for smiling while on the chain... for having some raveling from an old pair of trousers in his possession... for walking across the prison yard to make an enquiry... for singing a song. *His collarbones looked 'very much like two ivory polished horns. Another half pound off the beggar's ribs! Next time we'd better try the soles of his feet.*

It was no wonder that, in January of 1834, the prisoners rebelled, planning to capture Morisset and 'cut him into four pieces to be divided about the island.' It didn't work. The mutineers were captured and tried. '*Their... once manly limbs shriveled and withered up as if by premature old age, created horror among those in court. There was not one... who had not undergone from time to time, a thousand lashes each and more. They looked less like human beings than the shadow of gnomes who had risen from their sepulchral abode... grey, wizened and shrunken, their eyes dull and unseeing, the skin stretched taut on the cheeks; they spoke in whispers and were awful to behold.*

Father William Ullathorne, the Vicar General of Sydney, arrived to comfort those convicts due for execution.

> 'I have to record the most heart-rendering scene that I have ever witnessed. The turnkey unlocked the cell door and... then came forth a yellow exhalation, the produce of the bodies of the men confined therein. I announced to them who were reprieved from death and which of them were to die. It is a literal fact that each man who heard his reprieve wept bitterly, and each man who heard his condemnation of death went down on his knees and, with dry eyes, thanked God they were to be delivered from this horrid place. The morning came, they received on their knees the sentence as the will of God. Loosened from their chains, they fell down in the dust, and, in the warmth of their gratitude, kissed the very feet that had brought them peace.'

The bishop was to learn of the existence of 'suicide lotteries,' and the murders, performed 'without malice and with very little excitement,' that could get a man hanged who wanted to be, if he found it easier to kill another than himself. *They knew they should be hanged, but it was better than being where they were.*

In all, before the end of the Second Settlement, eight-six prisoners would be hanged and three thousand would take their own lives.

Not all the commandants were as brutal, of course. Alex Maconochie's four years in the early 1840s were a positively enlightened experiment in penal reform, for the place and the age. But he was dubbed in by the resident priest for expecting *to make good subjects out of bad ones, by good feeding, good clothing, some amusement and light labour and by holding out a speedy prospect of returning to society to earn an honest livelihood. This is very plausible and very fine in theory, but he does not seem to pay proper attention to the constituent parts of the dregs of human nature on which he is experimenting.*

Maconachie was replaced by Major Joseph Childs, reputedly a strict disciplinarian, but no match for the convict 'old hands.' His wife wrote a most compelling narrative of his 'utter imbecility,' during the subsequent Mutiny of 1846.

'The Major's turn came for doing duty at Norfolk Island as Commandant, and we went to that terrestrial paradise, where the clanking of chains and the fall of the lash rang in the ear from daylight til dark- these sounds accompanied occasionally by the report of a discharged musket, and the shriek of some wretch who had fallen mortally wounded. These shots became so frequent that at last they ceased to disturb us, even at our meals. Our house was behind rampart, surmounted by a battery of guns, loaded to the muzzles with bullets, bits of iron, tenpenny nails, and tender-hooks. By day and night sentries guarded the door with loaded muskets and fixed bayonets. 'Kill the Commandant' was always the first article of the agreement these desperate monsters came to when they entertained an idea of escape. In the morning when they were brought out heavily ironed to go to work, the guard that had been on duty came from the barracks, and, in the presence of the Commandant, obeyed the order 'Prime and load.' Then came the ringing of the iron ramrod in the barrel. Then the order, 'Fix bayonets.' Followed by the flashing of the bright steel in the sun's rays. Many a time have I, from my window, seen these incorrigibles smile and grin during this ceremony, albeit they knew that upon very slight provocation they would receive the bullet or taste the steel. During the twelve months that we were on the island, one hundred and nine were shot by the sentries in self-defence, and sixty-three bayoneted to death, while the average number of lashes administered every day was six hundred. Yet, to my certain knowledge, almost every officer who acted as Commandant at Norfolk Island tried to be as lenient as possible, but soon discovered that, instead of making matters better, they made them worse, and they were, in consequence, compelled to resort, for security's sake, to the ready use of the bullet and the bayonet, and the constant use of the lash. That part of the punishment which galled these wretched prisoners most was the perpetual silence that was insisted upon. They were not allowed to speak a word to each other. One day, when The Major was inspecting them, they addressed him through a spokesman, who had originally been a surgeon, and who had been transported for a most diabolical offence. He was a very plausible man, and made a most ingenious speech, which finished thus: 'Double, if you will, the weight of our irons and our arm-chains, reduce the amount of food we now receive by way of ration, but, in the name of humanity, permit us the use of our tongues and our ears, that we may at least have the consolation of confessing to each other the justice of the punishment we have to undergo. The Major turned a deaf ear to this harangue and, when he related it to me, laughed at it. I, however, foolishly took a different view of the case, and teased him into trying the effect of such indulgence. What was the result? The use they made of their tongues was to concoct a plan for butchering the garrison and every free man and seizing the next vessel that brought a fresh cargo of convicts to the island.'

When the revolt occurred, four officials were murdered, Childs was fired, and thirteen convicts were immediately hung by his heir, a monocled monster named John Price, 'privileged, amoral and ruthlessly contemptuous of human suffering.' His family crest was a dragon's head in whose mouth was a human hand, dripping blood. A visiting magistrate later exposed his horrifying tortures and incessant flogging, overseer corruption, and inadequacy of the prison's housing and food.

In 1854, the colony was totally abandoned and its convicts transported to Van Diemen's land, to finish their lives in the town founded by the old exiled exiles from the First Settlement. They had called it New Norfolk.

Robyn and I took a deep breath, and drove down the hill, to the *ne plus ultra* of *Hell in Paradise*. We landed in the middle of a festival. There was a live band and a surfing competition, and sausages and ice cream, and medieval tents and banners flying in the wind.

"I can't understand why the prisoners didn't like it here." I said. "Its such a beautiful spot." The Georgian box buildings had less ochre now, Monopoly pieces of lemon and pink pastel-painted stuccoed squares and concrete cylinders and equilateral triangles, covered in hipped slate or shingle, or having no roof at all. Tall chimneys soared out of both edges of each edifice. Old dories lay about, one dripping and oozing wide rust down otherwise white panels, one flattened out into the ground, like it had melted into the lawn growing up through its bulkhead. The column-flanked gray Palladian entry to the yellow cream *Royal Engineer Office A.D. 1851*, still looked open for business, but it wasn't. Neither was the stone carcass of the Crank Mill, although you could feel the agony in the limbs of the convict teams, shifting the unbearably heavy grindstone capstans, the suffering sounds of which could be heard all the way back to Anson Bay. What was open was the rock relic workshop of the tattooed Aussie shingle-makers, seated and surrounded by stacks of Eucalyptus shakes and whittling piles.

"I do it 'cause I like the smell." One said, swinging his maul into a fresh plank.

"I do it for the money." Said the other, a little slower.

Robyn and I walked around the walls of the penitentiary, trying to absorb the magnitude of what had happened here. I got nothing from the vast expanse of walls and what was left standing of the beveled block buildings, until I honed into the ruin and rubble tilted footprint of the pentagonal congested cellblocks, and the one lower corner of each of them that drained off the dysenteric feces and calcium concreted urine, of the 'lees and dregs of mankind.' We left them for the Commissariat Store, in the basement of the Pitcairner's All Saints Church, and the glass beads and ceramic pieces from the First Settlement and the whips, leg irons and crankwheels from the Second. The attendant was a brusque, ruddy-faced shorthaired Aussie matron, who insisted we buy the entire museum package, and was clearly unimpressed with the hypercritical alacrity we employed to navigate the displays. If Disney had transported dwarfs to Norfolk, this one would have been 'Grumpy.' I could almost hear her wrinkled harrumphs, echoing off the history. A far friendlier face greeted us at the former Protestant chapel, in the H.M.S. Sirius Museum. She admitted to just beginning her job, but let us have the run of the place, to play with its ill-fated Jeremy Benthamoid masthead, and black-painted rescued knobbled iron anchor.

But it was back to the Pier Store Museum for what had been billed as a 'Tagalong Tour,' offered by a resident archeologist with a resident expert on the Second Settlement.

"All I want to do is see the broken china." Said Joan, an elderly lady from Melbourne, confused about the difference between museum opening hours, and the optional tours.

"Helen should be here any minute." Said the attendant. "She's very knowledgeable." And in walked Grumpy.

"Whose for the tour?" She asked. Robyn and I and some others put up our hands. Helen explained how it would go.

"Any questions?" I asked where the fifth museum was, the one the new attendant in the Sirius Museum had told us about.

"Five museums? She doesn't know what she's talking about." Said Helen. "She's new. Put ya crook."

We moved through the main floor of the exhibits. She showed us the original bell from the H.M.S. Bounty, and other relics from Pitcairn Island. Her tour went on to places we had already been, and we lingered behind upstairs, to take in a video of Norfolk history, on the Telfunken television. *To watch the DVD, please call the museum attendant for assistance (there is a trick to getting it started).* The attendant came upstairs.

"You change the channels with the volume buttons." She said.

"Just like our other one at Anson Bay Lodge." Said Robyn. And we learned about the four mutineers drowned in Pandora's Box, the Codex Pitcairniensis, how the Melanesian Mission had created Pitcairner resentment by commandeering an eighth of their land, how the ship they built for transporting goods to remote markets, the *AV Resolution*, was impounded in Auckland for being unable to pay port duties and ended up in Vila harbor, and how the US airstrip generators replaced the whale oil lamps in 1945, and how the grid is now flooded with electricity from home panels.

We set off down along the beautiful residences of Military Row, one of which now customarily houses the rotating doctor from Australia.

"What do you think?" I asked. "Should we come back and do a locum? But Robyn had already read about the medical conditions of the brutal Second Settlement.

'The hospital is a low stone building containing three wards, two of them accommodating 5 beds each, the other 10 but they are too confined for this number. The mode of ventilation is objectionable, as a thorough draft cannot be avoided, the wards are exceedingly hot in summer and cold and damp in winter. They open under a narrow verandah into an enclosed yard of about 80 feet by 20. This is the only place in which the patient can take exercise. Opposite the verandah is a wall with a privy mid-way, the smell from which is very offensive... but during the hot season when the wind prevails from the northward, the stench is excessive...the dispensary and office shows symptoms of damp from which cause I believe the medicines and instruments become injured. This building affords quite insufficient hospital accommodation...on an island wherein, during summer, attacks of dysentery of epidemic character, occasionally assuming a malignant type are common.'

I assured her that the facilities were now much better, and the illnesses more amenable to treatment.

> 'The internal applications of poisonous matter was frequently
> resorted to, to produce sickness, and not withstanding the great
> attention of the Medical Officer, Death in many cases occurred.
> The most dangerous Wounds and Ulcers were produced by a
> means of Manchinial and other poisonous herbs; severe cuts were
> purposely inflicted with the Hoe; intentional burning, scalds, forced
> dysentery and tampering with the eyes to produce blindness, were
> common practice. So numerous were cases of this nature that in
> addition to a crowded hospital there were daily from 80 to 100
> locked up and grouped together in a room measuring 16 feet long
> by 12 feet wide. It was a filthy and suffocating hole, and yet the
> greater number would prefer it on bread and water, to performing
> labour which at that time was extracted from them. It was the last
> resort of a debilitated man worn down by hunger and fatigue.'

I tried to point out how beautiful it was, how *Hell in Paradise* had become *Paradise in Hell*. She said she'd think about it. As we walked by No.10, we saw Helen on the front porch, sitting with Joan. We asked her about medical care on the island.

"There's not much that's much good." She said. "Anything serious costs $A25,000 to fly off the island. Most older residents have to leave to spend the last part of their lives in New Zealand or Australia." She invited us to have a look inside.

"It was built in 1844, as the residence for Thomas Seller, the first Foreman of the Works, and his manservant." She said. "The Young family who moved in for 34 years, from 1856, had fifteen children." The pink and mustard and apricot interior seemed far too small to house that many, but it had been lovingly restored with white wainscoting and fireplaces, fine desks and dressers and round tables, and elegant display cases for the blue and white Wedgewood that Joan had found so fascinating. A wall of pink and white periwinkle and red geraniums lined the interior colonial period garden, with a red hibiscus over 150 years old.

We reemerged onto the front veranda. Helen had pulled up the aerial on her red and metal 'Vintage' radio.

"I like to listen to the cricket." She said. "It's starting soon." But we still had time to see how she had softened, with knowing us a little better.

"I could tell you stories." She said. "There are more here than anywhere else on the Southern Sea." I told her about Darren and his comment about how the Pitcairners would know how to deal with the Aussies, if and when the time came.

"Live in hope, die in agony." She said. "Which Darren was it?" I gave a general description.

"That's Darren X." She said. I asked how many Darrens they had.

"Too many." She said. "Those boys are on a permanent tagalong tour." Helen told us about the old days of the Pitcairn arrival, when 'nobody slept in the same bed twice.'

"And no one was really sure who their father was. No. 5 Quality Row over there was the brothel." She said, pointing over to the curved stone wall of Government House. "The Aussies aren't much better. Labour sends career bureaucrats, and the Liberals send retired politicians. The police helicopter runs interference for the chief's trysts. When the governor flies home, the only thing left is the dining room table. A carrion perch." The talk turned briefly to the current prime minister.

"She's giving the country away." Said Helen.

"Beech." Joan agreed, not alluding to the tree.

"And there's no more archeology allowed for me to do here," Said Helen. "Since they made the place a World Heritage Site in 1965. I've got three cats at home. The other day one of them brought me a rat with a five inch tail." She pulled a can opener out of her handbag, and then a can.

"I always have creamed rice for lunch." She said, and turned up the cricket game on the radio.

And then I saw it. Despite all her knowledge, she didn't know how to get back to her native Australia. Helen, the free inquiring authority on all things Norfolk, had become a captive lifer in her own area of expertise, too poor to go home. She must have seen my look. The cricket volume was squelched, for one last musing.

"You know, the horses start to run around the common before someone dies." She said. "And they don't stop until the funeral is over." The crack of a fly ball careened off the roar of the crowd. *For the field is full of shades as I near a shadowy coast, And a ghostly batsman plays to the bowling of a ghost, And I look through my tears on a soundless-clapping host, As the run stealers flicker to and fro...*

It was another ball game venue we pulled up to, just a few meters further down Quality Row. It could have been a Canadian flag flying over the Point Hunter Reserve, but the red was green and the maple leaf was a Norfolk pine.

"Where else can you play golf on a World Heritage Site for just seventy bucks a week?" I asked. Robyn and I checked out the pro shop, where a cartoon depicted a convict swinging his ball and chain over his head in an arc. *Norfolk Island Ball Game.* The single harried Boxing Day worker in the clubhouse kitchen was having a back-and-forth cheeseless meltdown of palindromic proportions. *Golf? No sir, prefer prison-flog.*

"I've got no food." She agonized. "I can make you a foccacia, if you're desperate." We were no longer sure what that word meant actually on this island, but we knew it didn't apply to us. Even the sign in the washroom was ambivalent about what was being locked in, and what was being locked out. *Please Keep Door Closed Due to Birds, Thank You.*

But if Golf is a game to be played between cricket and death, our next Quality Row stop appeared right on cue. Two days earlier, Max had told us that, if we wanted a cheap funeral, and arrived on a one-way ticket, Norfolk would still bury you. "If you've kak'ed it," He said. You'll arrive on a different part of the aircraft, bearing two cold cartons of beer for the diggers, and a backhander for the clergyman." There were no crematoria, stonemasons or undertakers on the island. The government would provide you with a coffin and a wooden cross. If you wanted a headstone, you would need to bring one from overseas.

Although that hadn't been a problem in the old graveyard on Cemetery Bay. Here the headstones stood resilient against the headwinds buffeting the southern coast. And here there was a bounty of buffetts, and a buffet of Buffetts from the Bounty. *In Loving Memory of David Buffett Native of Pitcairn Island Died Aug 7th 1924 Aged 96 Years Thy Will Be Done.* There had been John Buffet and Cup a Tea' Buffett and Leekee Roof Buffett, and in 1996, aboard his Grumman HU-16 Albatross seaplane, *Hemisphere Dancer*, even Jimmy Buffett came to have a look.

"There was this huge clan of Buffetts." He said. "They were all there."

They were all there with the convicts and soldiers, children and murderers, side by side, beside the same beautiful ocean that could have taken them home. *Sacred to the Memory of Ja's Neale: private in the 4th or King's Own Regmt.who departed this Life on the 4th of Feby 1832 Aged 32 years. He met with an untimely end by the accidental discharge of a gun while shooting in the woods and was deeply lamented by all who knew him. Come all ye comrades standing by As you now are once was I As I am now so you must be Prepare for death and follow me... Thomas York Private in 4th K.O. Regmt Aged 22 Years who was accidentally Shot by a Brother Soldier on the night of 17th January 1834 while in pursuit of Mutineers engaged with others in a disgraceful attempt against the peace of the Settlement... In Memory of Willm McGulloch who was executed on the 23 of Septer for the Mutiny on this Island 1834 Ages 21 Years. who having spent 16 years in warning sinners to flee the wrath to come entered to... Catherine Hurley.Infant Daughter of John Hurley who departed this Life on the 19th of Sept. 1837. Aged Nine Months... Sacred to the Memory of Stephen Smith, 40, Native of Dublin.free overseer at Norfolk Island.who was barbarously murdered by a body of prisoners on the 1st of July 1846.whilst in the execution of his duty at the Settlement Cook house leaving a wife and three children to lament his loss... Beneath this stone are deposited the remains of Michael Mansfield.Pt in H.M. XIth Regt of Infantry. Who died Sep 13th 1847 from the effects of a fall from a Horse the 22 years of his age... Sacred to the Memory of Frank A. Warren Native of Providence Rhode Island U.S.A. who was brutally murdered by a Greek Miscreant on board Am. Ship Hope August 11, 1861, in the eighteenth year of his age. Alas my brother...*

There were Freemasons buried here, and Pitcairners interred with a Star of David carved over their remains, for whatever reason. *In Memory of Arthur Quintal Native of Pitcairns Isle Died Nov 19ᵗʰ 1873 Aged 79. Seek and Ye shall find. Knock and it shall be open to you...*

The snorkeling gear in the back of the Mazda was beginning to cry out for release. Robyn and I crossed over the legend of Bloody Bridge.

In the time of Major Anderson, a labour gang was constructing this beautiful little bridge. Leg irons, some weighing as much as 22 pounds, impeded every step of every convict. Rations had been adulterated by 'Potato Joe,' a merciless one-eyed Scot who substituted spuds for the bread the men were meant to have. Dysentery constantly gnawed at their vitals. Already half-crazy, they were relentlessly provoked by the overseer, hoping for a flicker of protest. Immediate retribution, in the form of the cat-o'-nine-tails, would fly at any offender. One of the prisoners exploded, and drove a pick through the brain of his tormentor. Knowing that every one of them would be horribly punished, the gang walled up the bleeding corpse in the bridge. When the overseer's relief turned up at midday, he asked where his predecessor was.

"Oh." They said. "He went for a swim down in the bay. We think he must have drowned." But then, and unfortunately for them, something bloody began to ooze through the still wet mortar between the bluestones.

We parked in the shade of a tall pine, put on mask and snorkel and fins, and slid into Emily Bay. The water came as a cool crystalline relief from the hot blood and gore of the day. Robyn and I held hands with each other and the current, and undulated among the parrot fish and 'sweet lips' pink trumpeters, and even the big sting ray with a humped head like a wide-body 747 cockpit.

That night we splurged at Hilli Restaurant, fully discharging the credit card and recharging our souls, with slow braised pork belly *in a sticky Asian sauce served with seared prawns and crushed peas*, a lamb roast rump *with a sun-dried tomato crust, potato and artichoke mash, zucchini and an olive anise jus*, and a crispy skin confit duck leg *with garlic sauteed potatoes, vegetables, and cherry port reduction*. For dessert, we engorged on an affagato, *three scoops of vanilla ice cream, crushed meringue, crisp biscotti and a nip of coffee (Chef's suggestion: For a really decadent experience add Frangelico or your favourite liqueur)*, and a *decadent* chocolate creme brulee, *served with homemade cinnamon ice cream and crisp biscotti*. I couldn't help but notice the word 'decadent' decorating the menu, as if 'a state of moral decline' truly needed defining on Norfolk.

The real decadence returned in my dreams, with visions of bloodstains between the grains, seeping through the creamed rice.

'Not for the buried but the wide awake
Audience of the ever watchfull dead...

The elders, privileged, bend each to each
In front rows of their grey embodied stones,

While farther back the young latecomers stand.
Self-conscious still, though hearing with one ear
The same bright prelude blessing rock and sand,
Laving the lawn with tide serene and clear.'
   Bruce Beaver, *From Norfolk Island, IV Cemetery Bay*

*   *   *

*   *   *

'The object of all the former voyages to the South Seas
undertaken by the command of his present majesty,
has been the advancement of science and the increase of
knowledge.'

William Bligh

"They have a winery here?" I asked. "The climate's all wrong."

"Its listed as an attraction." Said Robyn. "Two Chimneys Wines. Opens at ten." We drove to Bucks Point, to stretch out on the grass of the steep reserve, letting the sun play on our faces. The cows had breakfast around us.

The owner of Two Chimneys, Rod McAlpine, was already in the tasting room.

"G'day." He said.

"Morning." I said. "It's 10:00, bit early but we'd like to try your wines before we go off for a bit of a snorkel."

"Well, we'll see how smooth it is." He said. "I wouldn't hope for much." I told him he didn't seem to have much confidence in his libations.

"I was talking about the snorkeling." He said. Rod imported his wines from New South Wales, 'until we can make our own.' He was also the president of the local gaming commission. The vines outside were struggling with unfavorable odds. I asked him about French varietals.

"We don't serve any Froggie plonk 'round these parts." He said

I bought a bottle of bubbly for a planned New Years Eve celebration back in New Zealand, and drove back towards our lodge through Burnt Pine. We pulled into the Returned and Services League driveway. *N.I. RSL. Sub-Branch Boer War 1899-1902... 1914-1918... 1939-1945... Visitors Welcome.*

"You want to have lunch at the club?" She asked.

"Just have a look around." I said. "There's always history inside." Robyn and I had fond memories of the 'meals' we

526

had with her parents, at the Huntly RSA, in the early days of our courtship.

The first thing that greeted us was a hallway of glass gun cases, behind which were likely most of the weapons used in all three of the wars. The second welcome came from a massive aborigine behind the bar.

"First time?" He asked, keeping an eye on some of the more intoxicated patrons at the adjacent pool table, with a peculiar blue velum. An old tin helmet lay on the bar, a rough slit in the top, for tips. The word 'Legacy' was written in marker under the slash. *Ring for Drinks*. The walls were covered with desert photos of 'Departed Comrades,' in shorts and Aussie slouch hats. On this island, conflict was inescapable. The suspicious manager approached us.

"You come to the bistro for lunch, or what?" He asked. I told him we were thinking about it. He shoved two menus into our hands, and waited.

"That's alright." I said, after absorbing the sticker shock, the melange of mealtime and murdered mates on the walls, and the incongruity of the description of the place as a 'bistro.' "We're not that hungry."

But by the time we had a snorkel, and made it to the market, and back to the cottage in the late afternoon, our appetites had sharpened considerably. We had purchased two steaks at the butchers, an imported one from New South Wales, and another local leaner Norfolk Blue specimen.

I lit up the brick barbeque, under the choirboy-collared palms and tree ferns in the back yard, and waited for the heavily scented Norfolk pine to burn down into embers. Even still, the meat would taste of sap. The Aussie steak won, hands down.

The day before we were due to leave, Robyn and I set out to see most of what we had missed so far. The most liberated lifeforms in Norfolk had always been the birds, and Max had suggested we take in the One Hundred Acres Reserve, up Rocky Point.

"Go early." He said. We left the lodge between the dawn chorus of the Pacific Robins and the rush hour traffic of the Golden Whistlers. I didn't expect much. Norfolk Island and Lord Howe have by far the worst record of bird extinctions in Australia.

When the *Sirius* was wrecked on Norfolk Island in 1790, and 270 extra people joined the few first settlers, there was too little food to feed them all. They soon discovered that by lighting fires at dusk, a type of petrel would 'drop down out of the air as fast as the people can take them up and kill them.' Three thousand birds was taken, every night for two months, and named the bird of providence. But fate frowns quickly and, not long after, the deafening aerial chatter of courting Providence Petrels became extinct on Norfolk Island.

Since 1774, four endemic bird species and five subspecies have disappeared. The Norfolk Island kaka and pigeon, which were so common when members of the First Fleet landed in 1788 that they described them as pests, were exterminated by hunting and forest loss. But the rats and cats took out the Grounds Doves, Starlings, Trillers, Guavabird Thrushes and pure Boobook Owls, and the White-chested White-eye is on the verge of annihilation.

The entry to the reserve was darkened by heavy branches, reaching overhead from enormous Morton Bay fig trees on high curved buttressed roots, a forest from the innermost recesses of Tolkien's imagination. It spoke of ghosts and fallen comrades. *'Caution-Tracks may be Uneven and Slippery Beware of cliff edges, muttonbird holes, wear proper walking shoes, remain on walking trails.'*

For the first ten minutes we saw nothing. Then two ethereal white terns appeared on their bough at black beak and eye level, inches away, watching us watching them. As the track wound down to the ridge, the Black Noddies began to surround us everywhere, in the air and in their flimsy nests in the pines. Fluffy Masked Booby chicks, bigger than their parents, swayed precariously on branches or, if less fortunate, waddling in hedges underfoot. Here were the eggs of the same Sooty Tern that had produced the Rapa Nui Birdman cult, had been seasonally harvested by the Islanders, who called them Whale Birds. And here were other kinds of petrel and shearwater and gannet and ternlet, soaring and nesting. We emerged onto magnificent precipice, where turquoise and green collided with the rocks under the Tropicbirds, hanging in the wind blowing up the cliffs.

The trail turned into a copse of White Oak, and I made a big heart of their China pink hibiscus flowers for Robyn, like I had in Sulawesi. An arrow pointed towards our destination. *Rocky Point- Exposed Roots, Muttonbird Holes.* And the path wound into a big green moss Eden, under beautiful tall tree ferns, and towering ficus, and pentagonal starred Norfolk pine saplings sprinkled with red flowers from their neighbours. It was like strolling through Christmas.

Robyn and I have always avoided cruises and guided tours, more because of our own need to define the experience as independently as possible, rather than out of any contempt for those who require paths with more prescription. The Salty Theatre on Norfolk was where tour operators took their groups to experience the local canned version of *Mutiny on the Bounty.* I had no burning desire in the performance, but there was something about the idea of posing and playing on the outdoor Bounty replica stage that required a break-in. And so, I found myself a bounty hunter, crawling through the vegetation allowed to flourish to prevent such a raid, and appearing on the deck in front of hundreds of empty seats, and Robyn.

As cosmic time is counted, Norfolk Island and Pitcairn Island were twin volcanic peaks, rocketing out of the ocean floor. Both lay uninhabited for three million years until, in the closing years of the 1700s, Norfolk became a penal colony, and Pitcairn a hiding place for Bligh's mutineers. In 1789, as Sirius died on the rocks of Norfolk, Bounty was incinerated at Pitcairn. In a bizarre cyclic saga, the Pitcairners, whose ancestors had escaped transportation to Norfolk as convicts, found themselves its new owners, the bounty from the mutiny. Max had provided us with an abridged version of the original. "In 1789, a mongrel mob stole a ship, picked up their mates, burnt the ship, and marooned and unable to speak to each other." He said. "Wound up climbing up the wall and blowing spit bubbles." It was still the recipe for a classic Story of the Southern Sea- iconic sailing ships and stormy seas and muskets arriving in an exotic romantic tropical Shangri-la, good-natured good guys having good-natured fun, but this time becoming their own pirates and castaways, on their own islands. When Bligh and that portion of his crew was set adrift in their longboat, had he known that the new Norfolk colony was thousands of miles closer that the Timor he was making for, the island might have seen the descendents of loyalists living alongside those of the mutineers.

But it didn't happen like that. It happened that, after all the bloodshed between the English mutineers and the Tahitian men, only one adult male, a Cockney orphan named John Adams, was left alive. He spent his days filling himself with the holy spirits from the salvaged Bounty Bible and prayer book, and those made from Pitcairn ti-tree root juice. The second was more potent. One night a vivid hallucination of the Archangel Michael attacking him with a dart remade him as a Patrirach. Moses of the Mutiny, he transformed the twenty-three young hybrid minds left on the island into 'the world's most pious and perfect community,' one of the great historical ironies. They hid from the world for eighteen years, ensuring that no fires burned during the day.

When Captain Folger arrived at Pitcairn on the American whaler, *Topaz*, he described a Rousseauian race of 'Noble Savages... tall, robust, golden-limbed and good-natured of countenance.' He had discovered a community of athletic surfers with an unquestioning belief in Divine Providence, scrupulously honest, and all working for the common good. No one had ever seen all that nailed together before. But it would become too successful to be self-sustaining.

In 1855, because of overpopulation on Pitcairn, Queen Victoria generously offered Norfolk Island to the mutineers' descendents. At least that's what they thought the terms were. For the 194 Pitcairners that sailed the hideously seasick five-week journey on the *Morayshire* in 1856, their first impressions on landing were those of gratitude, joy, grief, and astonishment.

Massive stone buildings appeared as castles, and the cattle and horses were the first they had ever seen, as were gardens of English flowers and exotic new fruits and vegetables. Lavatories were a complete mystery. Anything with wheels became novel sport, pushed down the nearest hill and smashed. Furniture exceeding the bounds of functionality became fuel. The Bubuck owls, and the moaning echo calls of the 'ghost bird' wedge-tailed shearwaters, terrified their nights.

But the most horrific revelation came with the realization of what had happened on Norfolk before their arrival. The inhumanity of the punishments meted out to the convicts terrorized them to their marrow. Who were the criminals? Who were the virtuous? The gibbet in front of the prison was hurled into the sea.

Captain Denham had left them well-provisioned.

'Pending harvest time, I leave their community of 194 persons provided with 45,000 lbs of biscuits, flour, maize, rice, with groceries of proportion, and an abundance of milk at hand, 22 horses, 10 swine in sties, domestic fowls, 16000 lbs of hay, 5000 lbs of straw, and a number of wild pigs and fowls. And lest the first crop should fall short, I have arranged with the Governor for a supply of potatoes, rice, and peas as an extent of aid.'

And Governor Dennison gave each Pitcairn family a fifty-acre block of land. But he also gave them an annulment of their ownership of the island, as instructed to by the Colonial Office, a betrayal that formed today's seeds of Darren's new mutiny.

And so the question, again. Who truly represents the savage and who the civilized? Rousseau would pick the barefoot, uneducated Pitcairner as the very best society; Hobbes, the social contractor, insisting that the nature of man in nature is inherently evil, and must cede rights to government as the price of peace, had never experienced the 'peace' on Norfolk. The ironic reality that his Leviathan government brought to the island had been the exact argument he made against the 'Natural Condition of Mankind.' *...worst of all, continual fear, and danger of violent death; and the life of man, solitary, poor, nasty, brutish, and short.*

Thankfully, there is no record of my own performance of *Mutiny on the Bounty*, from that thespian day on the deck of the replica. Instead of being driven from the stage, we drove from the stage, past an iconic scene of a derelict old moss-covered dory on its side, under a Norfolk palm, under a Norfolk pine. The owner of the property caused us red-handed, taking photos, and waved the Norfolk wave as she went down her drive.

For what we thought would be our last night in the *ne plus ultra*, Robyn and I drove back under the Morton Bay fig trees, and the Norfolk Blue Restaurant. We had met the charming pioneer of the blue grey breed of native hybrid cattle, earlier in the day, chasing a reservation after our walk through the reserve. Her first name was also Robyn, and her last name came from Paul 'Jap' Menghetti, the owner of the hundred-acre farm of rolling hills and a 19th-century Norfolk-pine homestead of eclectic artworks, old photographs and crystal chandeliers, whom she married in 2002. Robyn had originally come from Melbourne, after working on a dried fruit farm in Mildaura. She seated us in front of an imprinted water carafe. *Mildaura.*

"You collect crockery like you collect cattle?" I asked. And she grinned. Robyn had collected every one of the 'mongrel' blue cows she could find on the island, all thought derived from an Angus-Shorthorn blue bull cross, that had played with the other Herefords and Friesians and Red Devons and Murray Greys.

"We're not just paddock-to-plate here." She said. "We're conception-to-plate. You must try our house specialty." A waitress appeared in short order, with a large tattoo on her neck, and a Norfolk Blue beef pâté, with caperberries, crostini and homemade chutney. We spent the evening sandwiched between the New Zealand High Commissioner, and the current Governor, to whom Robyn later admitted she had been 'absolutely septic to.' We loved her style, and wished her all success, as we left.

The weather changed on the morning we were supposed to leave, and my Robyn, who gets a bit more concerned about the forces of nature that I do, was obviously less placid than the cows we ate the previous evening. I knew this because she told off the Japanese greeting that came out of the Mazda's speakers whenever we started it up.

We had enough time before our flight to drive Up Cooks, to see the compulsory Captain Cook monument, just north from our cottage. We pulled up at sign next to another moss-covered fence beside the Xanadu farmstead. *Yorlyi Kam Luk Orn.*

We walked out to the statue at the headland, surrounded by pink hibiscus, and magnificent views of the plate-shaped rocks offshore. *Captain James Cook R.N. On his second voyage around the world discovered and named this island Norfolk Island Landing in the vicinity of this point on 10th October 1774.*

We drove past a basalt formation decorated with strange pale green-painted egg-shaped rocks, into Burnt Pine. The only taxi rolled by, a black London cab, which charged $5 for journeys inside the cattle grid that keeps the cows out of the commercial centre, and $10 to anywhere outside it. The

Chucky doll on the model of the Bounty was not an auspicious sign. *Norfolk Island Chamber of Commerce and Westpac wish the 653 Visitor to Norfolk Island a very memorable stay.*

Our stay was about to get even more memorable. We drove round ar airport, round ar plane, and left the Mazda to its own devices, keys in the ignition. We checked our baggage and our emails, and stood around in the terminal, clutching our boarding passes. I watched the Air New Zealand flight bounce off the runway.

"That must've hurt." Said Murray, an engineer from Christchurch.

"Bloody Oath!" Agreed a nearby Aussie. I just watched the poor plane trying to do an impression of the *Sirius* shipwreck, until the pilot managed to regain some kind of control from his hard landing.

Murray, and one of the Maori Christchurchers from Max's tour, congregated to conversation, as the time for us to board, left without us.

"Must be mechanical." Said the Maori bloke.

"Must be." Said Murray and I, in unison. And as if he had been prompted, the pilot appeared in the boarding lounge, confirming that like the many who had come before, he had landed a 'machine for extinguishing hope.' The flight, for today, was 'delayed.' But if we weren't leaving today, shouldn't the more appropriate description be cancelled? And the more he tried to reassure us that everything was being done, the more we became convinced that he didn't really know if anything could be.

"It's kind of like your lawnmower." He said, apparently drawing a comparison to what had happened to the hydraulic landing gear.

"Jeezuz." I said. "If this bloke thinks he flying a lawnmower..."

"Bloody oath!" Said the Aussie. Murray and the Maori and I looked around, and then at each other. Another day in *Hell in Paradise.*

"Governor's Lodge for lunch?" Asked Murray.

"Bloody Oath!" Said the Maori and I, in unison. So we walked with our wonderful wives to Governor's, and Robyn got up on the Bailey's restaurant stage and using her camera as a microphone, pretended to sing, which was the only sane thing to do. We had the focaccia sandwiches. Australians love focaccia because they like the sound of saying it, because it sounds Italian and Australian at the same time, and they don't know any other kinds of Italian bread. An entire airplane had arrived unexpectedly for lunch. The black waiters lost their smiles, and the skies opened up with black rain.

We asked about staying at Governor's, at the front desk.

'Its just been sprung on us too." Said the Papuan receptionist. "We'll have to see what Air New Zealand says." What Air New Zealand said, when they finally got around to saying it, was that they couldn't put us up at Governor's but they had similar accommodation at a nearby location. I asked where that might me.

"It's within walking distance." Said the agent. This much was no news.

"It's the South Pacific Resort." She said. Now, I don't really have any precise idea of what had gone through Christian Fletcher's mind, when he made the irreversible decision to mutiny, but I do know it was the same train that thundered through mine. We had already suffered the indignity of Christmas dinner *where the song of the ocean met the salty piece of land*. The possibility of New Years Eve in the same prison was unfathomable. Murray and the Maori and I looked at each other, and our shoulders drooped in a collective defeat. We gathered our spouses, and what was left of our strength, and marched in formation down the road.

"Are you the delayed flight?" Asked Verney.

"No, Verney." I said. "We're the cancelled flight." I asked how we would know when we would be able to leave. The strains of *Hotel California* reverberated in my brain.

"Listen to the radio." She said. I told her that we didn't have a radio.

"Check the bulletin board." She said. And she gave us keys to a terrible room that smelled, and then other keys to a terrible room that didn't, with a view of nothing.

Unlike Murray and the Maori. I didn't think of actually going over to eat at Governor's that evening, and for that, I should have been given a harsher sentence. In fact, that was the harsher sentence. As we waited for the dining room doors to open, we played a game of billiards on a table with a peculiar purple velum, and the Robyn listened to a conch, hoping for news of a reprieve. We got to sit with Ed and Dianne again.

"You're the bloody aeronautical engineer." He said, as if it was my fault the pilot smashed his plane all over the tarmac. The food was up to its usual standard, even more unfit for human consumption because of the rush on the unfortunate Filipino servers, who discharged the bland-colored contents of the heating units into the plates of the discharged detritus from the plane. They served horrible ham, and terrible trevally, and chunderful chicken. And there wasn't enough of it, or too much.

"Is this your second time?" Asked the overseer, as I was thinking about how to mortar her remains into the bridge.

"It's not a reward." I said, helping myself. We checked the 'Disruption Advice' notice on the bulletin board later. The advice was the same as the 'Disruption Advice' notice on the *Sirius*. Come back tomorrow. *"You still ended up here." I said. For the Term of His Natural Life.* Back in the terrible room that didn't smell, I broke my right fifth metacarpal on the ceiling fan. Jimmy Buffett swam underneath the prop wash. *Listen to the night birds cry, Sit and watch the sunset die, Well, I hope you understand, I just had to go back to the island.*

The sun cracked the heavens wide next morning. Breakfast is a notoriously difficult meal to serve with a flourish, but no one needed to have worried.

The excitement among the castaways was palpable. Even the abominable assembly of young wraparound Oriental girls

kissed their ancient Aussie benefactors. We were had received reprieve, and suddenly, to 'be transported' was good again. Murray and the Maori and I, and our loved ones, had a final lunch at Governor's, and boarded the bus that followed the big open dump truck of our luggage, out to the airport.
Most departure lounges smell of freedom. This one was more complicated. *Yorlye kum baek sun.*

'The voices of all the Islanders are remarkably low and musical. They are the voices of those whose ancestors for many generations have never known hurry or anxiety; of people dwelling in 'a land where it is always afternoon'- of a gentle, dreamy folk, living slow, sweet lives as changeless as the empty sea that rings round their island home.'
Beatrice Grimshaw

*　　*　　*

White Villa Blues
New Zealand

'I can shelter from the wind.
But I cannot shelter from the longing for my daughter.
I shall venture as far as Hokianga, and beyond.
Your task should I die shall be to catch my spirit.'
                    Tōhē, Ngāti Kahu Chief

Robyn pulled the shade up, just a fraction. Twenty thousand feet below the crack of dawn, we had crossed over the northern edge of a scalloped fishtail, the first land in fourteen hours.

"Spirits Bay." I said, pointing at the central coastal crenulation. Its Māori name, Kapowairua, meant to 'catch the spirit,' and described the sacred jumping off point where the ghosts of the dead moved down the beach to gather at the large old pohutakawa tree, where they were launched into the afterlife of their ancestral home. Robyn looked around outside our window.

"Nope." She said.

But this is not a ghost story, but an exorcism, and before you can have an exorcism you need a possession, and that had happened ten months earlier, in the depths of a cold Canadian winter.

I had known that this was coming for a very long time. Robyn's New Zealand childhood had been a bit of a fairytale. Her eyes would get all dreamy, and glisten, whenever she related one of her springtime stories of the Southern Sea- how she used to go floundering with her father by lamplight, half-asleep with a spear in her hands, and how good it tasted for breakfast at daybreak. Tales of seashore foraging and surfing and waterskiing rolled into character descriptions of far-field family and friends, lost to time or space or both. Reminiscences of smells and tastes, of Nana Pitcon's baking, pineapple lumps and pavlova, and passion fruit and feijoas made her yearning more poignant, her homesickness more acute. The hard short winter days seasonally affected her, beyond what any artificial light could soften.

One particularly frosted evening I caught her on *Trade Me*, a Kiwi version of *ebay*, on the Real Estate pages. She had ticked off the 'Waterfront' box. My retirement plan jumped the clock forward another decade.

"Just looking." She said. "It doesn't hurt to look." But it would.

"If you're searching for a snowbird bolt-hole." I said. "At least get one with some character." I had always loved the romance of the old kauri villas, white wedding cakes of gabled hips and polychrome brick chimneys and terra cotta pots, leadlight corner angled bays, fretwork verandas and Italianate balusters and balustrades, and interior scotias and architraves. "Maybe you can find one on the ocean."

But that sort of architectural and geographical synchrony no longer existed. The old bay villas near the sea had either long since been dissolved in salt water, or were only preserved by the prosperity of the most expensive established neighborhoods in the biggest cities. We spent many evenings revving the search engines to nowhere.

One night I was scrolling through the listings, when it jumped off the screen.

"Robyn." I said. "Where the hell is Takou Bay?"

"Northland." She said. "Far North."

And we hovered over the most beautiful white villa in the world.

YESTERYEAR

303B TAKOU BAY RD KERIKERI

Come and share the ambience of this 1930's restored kauri villa, a real rare find in the Bay of Islands. Set on 3 1/2 acres, this private residence has four bedrooms, formal dining room, separate lounge, study, master bedroom with ensuite, triple garaging and views to die for. 150 olive trees which produced 7 litres of oil last year. The peace and tranquility are deafening.

We found pictures of Takou Bay, just down the road from the villa. The deserted beach surf scenery threatened to pound our hearts to pieces.

"It's a lot of money." She said. We had already been through this exercise. New Zealand real estate prices were on the same trajectory as the Spirits Bay Māori ghosts, launched into the ether from the beach. Every time we thought we could afford something, the price jumped off the old pohutakawa tree and into the sky, between bids.

"Go big or go home. " I said.

"Or both." Said Robyn.

The agent's name was Joanne. She was delighted to hear from us. We asked as many questions as we could think of. Why were the owners selling? *They were retiring and needed to downsize.* How motivated were they? *Very motivated. The villa had been on the market a year earlier for fifty thousand more.* Who were the neighbors? *Just a Dutch farmer and his wife, and a lovely Māori family, who had bought their property from the vendors.* Were there any other offers on the property? *Not yet, but an English couple had just gone off to their bank to see if they could borrow enough to put in a bid.* This was hardly a welcome complication. We thanked Joanne, and promised to get back.

"Remember Ian and Åsa?" I asked. Didn't they move to Kawakawa, in Northland?" Ian and I had shared a medical internship year, but he had gone into general practice, and exile in New Zealand, while I stayed on the frozen Canadian prairie, to finish my residency. It didn't take much to find him.

"Why don't I go up and have a look?" He said, between echoes. "It's only forty minutes away." A weekend went by, before we got his email.

"It depends what you want." It began, and proceeded to outline precisely what we wanted. Ian also knew the farmer, Rudi, who had worked with him as a nurse, before retiring to his farm.

And so it passed that we found ourselves the owners of an olive farm in New Zealand, sight unseen. We spent the next few months in our own heads, redecorating the white villa, pruning trees and crushing oil, driving tractors and each other crazy with anticipation, until the day arrived and so did we, at the boarding gate in Los Angeles.

"What kind of plane is it?" I asked the attendant.

"Sivvon suxty sivvon." She said, reminding me how Kiwis shift every vowel over to the next one along.

Below was the Land of the Long White Cloud, and the end of the long wait to see what we had done.

*   *   *

'There's a real purity in New Zealand that doesn't exist in the States. It's actually not an easy thing to find in our world anymore. It's a unique place because it is so far away from the rest of the world. There is a sense of isolation and also being protected.'
Elijah Wood

I caught her trajectory out of the corner of my half-open eyes. The full impact from her freefall belly flop emptied my lungs.

"I like eating the eyes out of fush." She said, on landing. Such was the delicacy of my young niece Millie, sharing her joy at seeing her Uncle Wink again. The eye is a cannibal dainty. Marquesan spirits sometimes tore them out of unsuspecting travelers.

Millie's brother, Sam, piled onto the blankets, and into the roughhousing, and Robyn and I finally had to get out of bed for air. We had arrived across to the island on the last ferry the night before, and were catching up on our jetlag, in the small shack at the end of the drive.

Nikki was already making coffee and Carl was outside on the deck of the main house, overlooking the sailboats and turquoise of Anzac Bay.

"Waiheke's still as beautiful as ever." I said, pulling up a cuppa.

"Yeh, mate." He said, as Kiwis do. Sam and Millie went off to teach their hamsters acrobatics, and Nikki and Robyn joined us at the table, and the view.

"You sure you know what you're doing?" Asked Carl. Waiheke translates as 'descending waters,' from when the Māori explorer Kahumatamomoe landed on the island and urinated. This was going to be a bit like that.

"You've never even seen this place you bought" He said.

"You want to live in Northland?" I responded with another question.

"Why not?" I asked. "It's got a subtropical climate, and great beaches and bush. There's history, and I think we've found the perfect quiet place in the country."

"It won't be quiet, mate." He said. "And you'll have more history than you can handle." I asked him what he meant.

"They didn't call the Bay of Islands the 'Hellhole of the Pacific' for no reason." He said. "In those early days, the problem was only vice and alcohol."

"And now?" I asked.

"And now there's all sorts." He said. "Northland has twice as many Māoris as the rest of the country. Heaps. They're historically disadvantaged, socially and economically. More of them are unemployed, underemployed, and on the dole, because of the poverty and poor education levels. They're less than thirteen per cent of the citizenry, but more than half of those in jail. Sixty per cent of the female prison population is Māori. Some think the corrections system is racist."

"What does that have to do with Northland?" I asked.

"There are real consequences of the demographic inequity that exists up there." Said Nikki. "More crime, more violent crime, more drug-related crime, more anti-social offences, and more family violence. A lot of it goes unreported because of a general mistrust of authority.”

“Woodpigeons get sozzled on fermented kaka berries.” He said. “And there’s cannabis and methamphetamine. And burglary and murder.”

“And unresolved land claims.” Said Nikki. “So you need to make sure your new rural paradise is actually yours.”

“But it should be sweet as.” Said Carl, finally, in recognition of our aspirations and intrepidness, and Sam went by in his Mexican sombrero, two thumbs up.

Robyn and I spent a few days with Nikki and Carl on Waiheke, as we now always do, before heading off to our own paradise. I had read stories to Millie and Sam, and Robyn played her ukulele. We all went into town, to find Santa riding a *Buzzy Bee* decal in the window of one of the shops, and big red sunglasses threaded with lights over a set of big red lips nailed to the trunk of a palm tree. It was Christmas. We dined on Humble meat pies from the village butcher. *All animals are equal... but some are tastier.* A septic truck drove by. *Hugh’s Takeaways.*

One evening we met Bas, an architect who had previously allowed Robyn and I to camp out in his olive shed, waking every morning to magnificent views of Wharetana Bay. I told Bas about our own olive farm.

“It’s the gritty end of the country up there.” He said, and told us of how the children of Kaikohe attacked Santa in the parade, one Christmas, for running out of candy and balloons. It wasn’t an easy image to dislodge. “The Far North of Northland is the Deep South of New Zealand. They add treads to their tyres with a chainsaw.”

On our last day before heading north, we went to Sam and Millie’s school, to watch them play on the monkey bars, and participate in their athletic events. We cheered when Sam put on a final burst of speed, and crossed the finish line ahead of his classmate competitors.

“Sammie won.” I said.

"We're all winners, aren't we?" Said the assertive voice next to me, attached to a peasant dress with unshaved axillae, and subdermal ink and transdermal metal. Waiheke had always been a countercultural refuge, and now that all the class warfare battles had been lost, was an epicenter of political correctness.

"Nope." I smiled. "Sam won."

That last evening on the deck we clinked wineglasses full of Sauvignon blanc, looked out to the blue water, and toasted Sam's victory and our northern journey to the white villa next morning. The setting sun suffused through the olive trees, and Millie in the wildflowers, behind us.

Because of its remoteness, New Zealand was one of the last places on Earth to be settled by humans. Where we were going it still hadn't.

Back in the city, we picked up our rental red RAV with the yellow bush lights, and set off across the 'Nippon clip-ons' of the coathanger-shaped Auckland Harbour bridge. Most Kiwi roads were so convoluted that it seemed they had been built by white *pākehās* chased around and through the curly ti tree bush by the Māoris, but this one was a fairly straight effort, 250 kilometers north to the Bay of Islands, where we would veer off northeast on State Highway 10 towards Kerikeri. *So nice they named it twice.* We only stopped once, for a thin sandwich at a roadside tearoom. *Please Remove Filthy Footwear.* The traffic safety signs began to have more than one interpretation. *Mind wandering?*

"Don't mind at all." I said, blowing through the lush beauty of the kiwifruit hedges and citrus orchards and forestry north of Waipapa, until the sign we had waited for all day, rose up on our right. *Takou Bay Road.*

We turned onto a gravel road, into rolling countryside of green pastures filled with herds of Black Angus among solitary Monterrey cypress macrocarpa, and red-tailed hawks overhead. In the late afternoon we finally arrived, to the deafening peace and tranquility. A red mailbox was missing the zero, of 303B Takou Bay Road, but we recognized the access entry from our northern hemispheric soaring on Google Earth. The Phoenix palms that lined our driveway had poisonous spines, but we didn't know that yet. They would become host to Australian strangler figs, but we didn't know that either. The approach to the residence was much shorter than the virtual impression we had of it on the Internet, but none of that mattered now. Robyn turned past the last tree and into the circular drive that wound us in front of a 1930's Mt Eden white kauri villa. Wrap-around decks and wrap-around French doors and wrap-around dreams.

Robyn spread her arms and spun. For a moment I thought she was going to do a Julie Andrews. We ran, exploring like children, landing in the waning sun on a new planet, palm trees and olives, and the smell of the ocean on the breeze. Around the back the hills rolled into rows of *frantoio* and *koreneiki* olive trees on our left, scattered hills and houses and farms on our right, and down the steep bank into native bush in between. Our minds were frantic and fevered, building carriage houses and swimming pools, and planting more olive trees and fruit orchards and gardens. When the peace and tranquility became deafening again, we held hands back around the front.

A young Māori was standing in the circular drive.

"You the new fellas?" He asked. We made introductions. His name was Shane.

"Weh's yo' lounge suite?" He asked. We told him that we didn't have one.

"No lounge suite. Mhuh. Weh's yo' bed?" Same answer.

"Weh's yo' teevee?" The concern began to show on his face. For every inquiry, all we had was a shoulder shrug.

"Well, what have youz got?" He finally asked, very disturbed by all of this scarcity, us being his new neighbours and all.

"A quiche, bottle of wine, and sleeping bags." I said. He jumped back into his truck, and was gone.

"Maybe we're travelling a little light." Robyn said.

Fifteen minutes later, Shane returned, with a trailer, full of all those missing things he had asked if we had. We were invited to dinner. There was corned beef and cabbage, a quiche, bottle of wine, and great new neighbours.
We were home.

*   *   *

The deafening peace and tranquility was broken by a dawn chorus of sparrows. Shane's truck and boat and trailer had already gone by, off fishing. The whining to the left of my sleeping bag, turned into four dirty front paws on the carpet, framing two black dog faces. Scroffie was the one with the white whiskers. Xena was the one with the tail that wouldn't stop banging the deck awake. Both belonged to Rudi the farmer, who would be along any minute. Unlike Rudi, who would only come to visit, and stay the customary several hours for tea on each occasion, Scroffie and Xena would only leave long enough for meals, or to chase an itinerant possum up one of our macrocarpas. Xena would actually climb up into the trees after them.
"They seem to like you." Said Robyn, stretching. Xena's tail picked up speed. *Bang. Bang. Bang.*
I went to make coffee in the kitchen, and noticed how many kinds of tile the previous owners had used in its construction. The dogs came around the front, as the thermonuclear jug reached critical mass. Outside, all over the circular drive, dust bathing their little hearts out, was a grand multitude of portly California quail, top knots quiver-waggling in the sunrise. *Cu-CA-cow, cu-CA-cow, cu-CA-cow.*

547

Rudi's tractor broke the relative silence, arriving with a mattress, and other pieces of furniture, on the back. He stayed for tea and, like the Dutchman he was, became overly generous with the necessary corrections of all the mistaken impressions we had formed of our new home, and life in general. After he left, Robyn and I had a closer look at our white villa and the acreage. We located the passionfruit vines and tamarillos and feijoa trees near where we stumbled upon the clothesline. We figured out how the cement water tanks worked, from where the kiwis would cry at night. We opened the two-car garage, and found the lawnmower that, compared to the acres of lawn I would have to mow, seemed a bit on the small side. Robyn spread her paperwork over the borrowed dining room in the bay window, overlooking the backyard slope.

"We need to go into Kerikeri." She said. Rudi had eaten the last of the leftover quiche. Our red RAV was almost back to the sealed road of State Highway 10, when a loud siren blared up behind us. We pulled onto what passed for a shoulder and, as the dust cleared in our rear view mirror, we could make out the flashing lights of a police cruiser. A big cop got out and slowly waddled over to Robyn's driver door.

"Did you see the stop sign back there?" He asked. She had, because she had made a comment about it being a 'bloody stupid place to put a stop sign.' The cop pulled out his ticket book and began to write. I looked up at him, remembering that Rudi had told us that his son was a policeman, the only one in this entire part of the Far North.

"Are you Rudi's kid?" I asked. He blushed, and lowered the ticket book.

"Are you the new neighbors?" He asked. We introduced ourselves.

"Marco." He said. "Welcome." We invited him over for tea.

The road into Kerikeri passed a large punga tree fern, under which were eight different mailboxes, and over the Kerikeri River beside the Stone Store, the oldest surviving stone building in the country. The first Church Missionary Society station in 1832, it was made of local volcanic rocks, burnt shell mortar, and the Australian sandstone that would be corroded by the iron ties used in its construction. Kerikeri itself, despite its more recent monikers as 'Cradle of the Nation' or North and South magazine's 'New Zealand's Top Small town,' was originally named after either a native stomach ailment, a command to 'keep digging,' or the 'bubbling up' of a chief's half slave baby, who kept rising to the water's surface, despite the tribe's efforts to drown him. There was, and would continue to be, something degenerate about attempts to settle the Far North, including ours.

Nonetheless, there was still something about the vegetative decay in the moist subtropical air that made you want to plant stuff. The plough had seen its first use in New Zealand in Kerikeri, with Reverend Butler in 1820. Robyn and I bought palms and bromeliads, and seven Jacaranda saplings for the mound inside the circular drive.

"Let's call it Jacaranda Hill." I said, imagining a thermonuclear purple explosion of color outside our breakfast nook. We opened a bank account and got library cards, ate an Israeli falafel, bought cracker pepper Merlot and Honey Soy sausages at Churchill's Meats, drove past Serious Bait & Tackle's shark's head mural, rocketing out of water, and along palm-lined Hobson and Kerikeri Roads, searched for permanence. We priced an appliance in Betta Electrical. The salesman must have seen our dejected disbelief. He told us of am elderly woman with a second hand fridge, who we could call. She invited us over to have a look. It cost us more to have it delivered than to buy.

We returned to find Shane on our porch. He had smoked some snapper from the morning and hand-delivered it in person. Shane was a corrections officer at the Ngawha prison. He had told me he wanted to make a difference for 'his people.' We were pleased to be apparently now counted among them, although I was developing a growing concern that, in the inevitable escalation of kindnesses that often accompanies the meeting of different cultures, the side that can't keep up with accelerating indulgences becomes the one held responsible for the dissolution of the relationship, and the peace. We had mentioned to Shane how surprised we were to learn that only Māoris were allowed through a new barricade erected across the road down to the beaches of Takou Bay. The local *iwi* were unhappy about something and the *pākehās* were no longer allowed to visit, even if they offered to pay.

"I'll pick you up tomorrow at nine." Said Shane. The Māori word for the Pacific was Moana-Nui-o-Kiva, the *great ocean of the blue sky*. The local lady manning the checkpoint scrutinized us through Shane's window, but she knew him, and let us through. The road hadn't been maintained at all, and was rough and gutted and potholed all the way down its steep overgrown track. We could smell the big surf before it crashed into view, on big black rocks along one of the most magnificent beaches in the Southern Sea. Gigantic red flowering pohutakawas sprouted on a slant to the coastal chaos. Robyn made straight for the water.

"She likes it here, Wink." Said Shane.

"That she does." I said. "I'm not sure anyone could catch her spirit." Shane laughed.

On the third day Robyn and I embarked on our first tiki tour. For my own piece of mind, I needed to meet the people we bought the place from, to measure our relative pain. We had already dropped into Joanne's real estate office in Waipapa to thank her, and get the measure of her pleasure. It was on high beam, and I knew we had paid more than market. But anything you buy is worth what its worth to you, and that's where it still was with Robyn and I. Joanne made contact with Bev and Mike, and they invited us up to their new 'digs,' in Kaeo.

The road north took us past a rest stop, where a hundred roosters had been abandoned, there for the taking, for anyone with a slow oven and a full set of teeth. We pulled off to the rubbish 'tip,' festooned with every bouquet of plastic flowers that had come through its gate for a decade, a decorated detour of green glass, brown glass, and clear glass. Kaeo was a dozen miles from our villa, and two hundred years from reconciliation. The native tribe had been driven here from the Bay of Islands after killing and eating a French captain and his crew. Except for the BP petrol-station, pharmacy, Pukeko Plaza at the Market Farm and Fuel store, a Bookshop 'N' Kaeo and Beehive crafts in buildings too small to be anything but dunnys, local café and magazine rack, a hairdresser, a bus company, two mechanics, a tyre-shop, a transport company, and a 4-Square shop incorporating a Post Office, there hadn't been much of a change. Just beyond the old Explorer camper truck parked next to the jandal fence, was a beautiful pastel wall mural of tattooed Maori couple, in blues and pinks and browns, with red and white flowers along bottom. We turned up the first of several switchbacks to the big newly planted palms that lined the driveway to Bev and Mike's rambling bungalow. A big light came on half way through the garage cavern, beside the new flash boat and RV. It was on high beam, and I knew we had paid more than market. But anything you buy is worth what its worth to you, and that's where it still was with Robyn and I. Bev was a big lovely Kiwi, no bullshit, and big-hearted, like Robyn's Aunt Nettie used to be. Mike was a classic Kiwi joker- calm, modest, ruggedly rural, fair, good with machines, and able to turn his hand to nearly anything. Mike liked his scotch.

"How d'ya like Na Zillun?" He asked. It was an easy test to pass. I asked him why he thought the All Blacks had been bounced out of the quarter-finals, by the French, no less.

"Not enough mongrel." He said. And we were friends. I told him what a nice place he had, here in Kaeo.

"S'good." He said. "Like yours."

Bev and Mike had been grocers in Auckland, one among many ventures they had embarked upon in their working lives. Most of the time they had lived like every other Kiwi couple, making a virtue out of necessity. Nothing went to waste. Bev used 'everything but the squeal.' There was little reward to compensate for a lifetime of forced frugality- little opportunity, no rich culture, no cheap or easy travel to interesting places. Most of getting ahead was just staying where you were. This reinforced the innate mistrust of intellectual theory that New Zealanders possess. Decisions are made through 'Kiwi ingenuity,' a gift of technical empiricism that requires 'seeing what works.' Robyn is also blessed with this more practical approach to solving problems, and she roundly criticizes my more analytical disposition as 'a useless bunch of pi r squared.' Much better to kick it in the guts and watch what happens.

And so it was that Bev and Mike, for the first time in their lives, had come into money. My money. It wasn't a lot of money, as far as money can go, but it should have been enough to keep them comfortable for the rest of their days. They had moved a 1930's white villa from Mt Eden to Takou Bay, planted olives, and I had been seduced into buying their dream, minus the orange leather lounge suite that Robyn and I had coveted, almost more than the villa. Everyone was set. But we had come on the scene with our eyes half closed, and they had left it with their wallets fully open.

Bev and Mike were Kiwis to the core, and they had channeled their windfall to not only acquire a cavernous garage full of toys, but to become industrious. Bev and Mike were about to open a döner kebab restaurant in downtown Kerikeri. They had a prime location in a small mall beside a liquor outlet, a new fully-equipped kitchen, advertising, and baseball caps. And a big house in Kaeo and a new flash boat and RV. They gave us two baseball caps, and invited us for dinner later in the week.

"Lovely people." Robyn said, on the way out to the red RAV.

"$y = ax^2 + bx + c$." I said.

"What's that?" She asked.

"Equation for a parabola." I said. "Trajectory."

"Pi r squared." She said. "What goes around comes around."
Bev and Mike had built their house above a plain that had
seen destructive flash floods and landslides and road closures
the year we arrived. Cyclone Wilma would KO Kaeo even
worse three years later, but by then the flash boat would be
gone, and Bev and Mike would have already evacuated.

Our tiki tour continued north on State Highway 10, to the
retirement villages of Cable Bay and Cooper's Beach, and on
to the inflection point port town on the Aupouri peninsula
fishtail, that we had flown over, to get this far. Awanui was
known for the dairy conglomerate Fonterra, but not for
another year, that would recall ten thousand tons of infant
formula because of melamine contamination. But it had also
been the epicenter of the Sabritzky flax and cattle and gum
trade and transport dynasty, and Captain Sabritkzy himself
had been involved in the rescue of the *Elingamite* shipwreck in
1902. It was much calmer for Robyn and I. We parked beside
a car with five dogs inside it, and walked around to look at
the murals. There was one of an 'Awanui Tyre' man fixing a
flat on a truck with a 'gone fishing' sign on the side, another
with some beautiful old boats, and an interesting sign on a
nearby ATM. *If this cash machine doesn't work, try the one across the
road, or ask Tim for a loan.*

On the way back to the villa, we stopped into the historic
fishing village of Mangonui, on Doubtless Bay. Captain Cook
had named it in 1769, assured that it was in fact a bay. Kupe,
the Māori discoverer of New Zealand, is said to have made
his initial landfall here, eight hundred years earlier. The lady in
the beautiful Queen Anne information centre under a
magnificent pohutakawa in full-on red flower, directed us to
the Mangonui fish shop, with it's massive red snapper on the
roof, and two tastier facsimiles on the wrap-around deck on
the water, overlooking the sailing yachts. The seagulls had
only a marginally less ecstatic look on their faces than Robyn,
after scoring some of our chips.

"How's the fush?" I asked.

"Mmumph." She said.

We took a tortuous track over the hills to the magic of Waimahana Bay, and lay in the sun. Two little vegemites kicked up the sand around us, racing to be heroes to their father, who was pretending to drown.

"I'll save him." Said the little boy.

"I'll save him first." Said the little girl.

"She should play for the All Blacks." I said, under my kebab cap.

We passed a sign for the Texas Diner and Wild West minigolf, on the final leg home. One day we would make a special effort, to find out why we shouldn't have.

Shane had left another packet of newspaper-wrapped smoked snapper on the deck, and Scroffie and Xena were guarding it, and each other, with their lives.

"What do you get a man who has everything?" I asked.

The days began to feel like our days, at our place, in our time. Robyn rearranged the kitchen and began preparing for the arrival of Nikki and Carl and Millie and Sam, and her other sister's family, coming from Tasmania. Yellow flowers appeared on the dining room table, and potted plants of various descriptions began to fill up the deck.

I was tasked with getting the grounds in order, trimming hedges and mowing lawns and mowing lawns and mowing lawns, and then mowing the steep lawn down into the ravine. I would later find out that it was more reasonable to pay Rudi to do it with his tractor, but I would later find out it was more reasonable to pay for a lot of things. I had already realized that Kiwi ingenuity needed only two tools- WD-40 to make things go, and duct tape to make them stop.

We spent an evening with Bev and Mike on their Pro size pool table, drinking scotch, and getting to know and like them more and more.

Ian and Åsa came up from Kawakawa, *so nice they named it twice*. We hadn't seen them for twenty years, but it only seemed like *yesteryear*. Ian teased me about buying the villa sight unseen, but I had seen it, through his eyes. He stuck out his chest, and we all walked down Takou Bay Road, like it was all meant to be.

A few days later he took us out in his boat on the Bay of Islands. While Ian was down below, diving for scallops, Robyn and I maximized our total allowable quota, topside. This was the bay where Hone Heke, who cut down the flagpole in Russell so many times it started the Flagstaff War, was born. This was where sixty of Chief Te Pahi's people were killed in revenge, wrongly accused of the Boyd massacre. This was where Captain Cook and whalers and missionaries and prostitutes collided in the Hellhole of the Pacific under the second bluest sky in the world, after Rio de Janeiro. This was where the whole country of New Zealand was forged, in the Treaty of Waitangi, 167 years before Ian brought up sixty scallops from the bottom. We had a succulent feast back at their place in the bush beside Åsa's succulent garden, and caught up on two decades of ourselves, late into the evening.

The next day I planted the seven Jacaranda saplings on Jacaranda hill, and hiked down our steep back yard, into the tree fern paradise along the stream at the bottom. Robyn and I had dinner on our back deck, overlooking creation. The stars came out above in the ribbon of dusk, one by one by a thousand. A full moon rose over the ravine. Morepork owls began to hoot in the surrounding hills.

We lay in bed, listening to our own contentment, and for Kiwis near the watertanks. There was a sound from outside our French doors. I got up to pull back the curtain, just a fraction.

Between the matrix of square windows, and the vast expanse of stars and moonlight in the cosmic backdrop, was a wide spasm of *Risus sardonicus*, a white-toothed tetanus Joker grin, smiling as if he had been electrocuted on the spot.

"Shane." I said. "What are you doing here?"

'The ornaments of your house will be the guests who frequent it.'
Anon

*   *   *

'Home is a name, a word, it is a strong one; stronger than magician
ever spoke, or spirit ever answered to, in the strongest conjuration.'
Charles Dickens

"I wanted to show you the moon." He said.
We made out that we believed him, but our doubts had left a hole where that used to be. Shane knew. Polynesians have a highly developed sense of intuition. In a neighborhood where advantage is about knowing who is about to be eaten, it's a survival skill. A neighborhood is a residential area that is changing for the worse. But not before it was going to get as good as it ever was, and maybe ever would be.
The red zodiac careened around Jacaranda Hill behind Carl's white Pajero next morning. Sam and Millie shot out of the back seats, their confinement and tightly wound Waiheke mainsprings finally released. Nikki waved through her window. Behind them came a sedan full of Tasmanians, Debbie and JB, and our other niece and nephew, Kate and Ryan. Scroffie and Xena looked up from between their paws, too slow to avoid their fate. Millie had put them both in a headlock.
Eight new pairs of shoes fell beside them, and the sounds of bottles opening and meat pies dismembering and plots hatching escaped from inside.

The family moved in like they meant to stay. Sam and Millie exploded in spasmodic bursts, exploring every square foot of the olive farm with each new sortie. Scroffie and Xena went into hiding. Ryan helped repair the plumbing, Katie went through a cold turkey detoxification from her social media dependency, and the adults got reacquainted. Millie played 'silly buggers' in the shower, and Sam had elastic bands tied through his hair, they both settled down to Auntie Robbie's ukulele singsong. Refrains of *Pokerekereana* and other mellifluous favorites floated out to the olives and the stars and the moonlight, until the moreporks called time, and Mr. Sandman took the field.

E kore te aroha
e maroke i te rā,
Mākūkū tonu i
aku roimata e.

*My love will never
be dried by the sun,
It will be forever moistened
by my tears.*

The tiki tour that launched next morning, brought us all to an estuary for a swim and a picnic, and a labyrinthine bush walk through the massive Manginangina kauris of Puketi forest. We all joined hands around the girth of the largest one, but barely.

Carl was up at dawn the following day, preparing the zodiac for action.

"Scallops and crays." He said. And we all piled into our vehicles and drove to the kilometer-long white sand beach and crystal clear watered paradise of Matauri Bay. Nikki observed the strangely separate demographic distribution of the foreshore.

"Māoris down one end." She said. "Pākehās down the other."

"And a dead Portuguese photographer in the middle." JB said. Just off the coast, at the Cavalli Islands, was the living reef that had been the *Rainbow Warrior,* before the French blew a hole the size of a garage door in the hull next to the engine room.

"Two cultures divided by a nuclear dispute." I said, trying for a metaphor. A Māori kayaker, wearing a Mexican sombrero, paddled by, and spoiled it.

Carl fired up the zodiac's outboard, and Nikki and Ryan and I piled in, screaming out to where Shane had told us that the crayfish holes and scallop beds would be. Cloth sacks of clinking shells, and black mesh ones full of alien crustacean life forms, would heave over the red rubber sidewalls, before our expedition roared back to land. We were set for the housewarming.

It had been my idea.

"Our new neighbors need to know that we appreciate the welcome they provided." I said. "And that we intend to make a home here, and fit in."

Robyn agreed, and we began to plan for a community convergence, the first event of its kind in a very long while. We invited Shane and Debbie and their daughter, Laurel; Rudi and Greta from the farm next door, Bev and Mike, Joanne the realtor and her boyfriend, also named Mike, and Ian and Åsa, of course.

We introduced ourselves to, and invited the others. Dave and Carrie owned the second hand shop in Kaikohe, and a large property next to the driveway entrance at the turnoff, whose yard looked like a second second hand shop. Across the road were Ruth and her husband, Selwyn, namesake of the first Bishop of New Zealand, and just as pious. Down Takou Bay Road, were Takou River Lodge, owners Ian and Anna, and their young children, Harry and Oliver and Lucy. Rosie and Graham, old friends from when Robyn and I first got together in New Zealand, would drive up from Auckland.

And so, it came to pass, on one afternoon between Christmas and New Years, the neighborhood descended on our white villa like we had descended on it.

Shane's dog, Rex, arrived early. Greta drove in with a sponge cake, and lit up a smoke. Sam and Millie climbed in the back of her wagon, to persecute Scroffie and Xena. Katie and Carl had their cool sunglasses on, and Joanne toted a purse that looked like a leather bodice. Lucy got out of Anna's car wearing a blue gossamer ballgown. As everyone pulled in around Jacaranda Hill, the colony came alive and coalesced and was reborn. Eight bottles of cab-shiraz and four of chardonnay began to lubricate the rust off the parts of the populace that had been frozen by familiarity and isolation.

"I haven't spoken to Carrie for thirteen years.' Said one new neighbour. "Since she shot my horses." Shane grinned at everyone with his beer. Ian grinned back at Shane, with his. Nikki and Debbie and Robyn, reunited, emerged from the kitchen with platters of chicken and Churchill's sausages and salads and garlic bread and *agria* potatoes.

This and twilight collected the congregation closer. The kids played frisbee all over Jacaranda Hill, strategically missing the blazing belly of the outdoor metal fireplace that Carl had just stoked into an inferno, while fresh commitment played among the grownups.

"Are you running from, or looking for?" Asked the cab-shiraz.

"Neither." I said. "I'm only dancing while I can." And I began telling stories from Orion's Cartwheel, as I sometimes do, when the juices flow later into the night.

Eventually the little ones grew tired of running, and ended up in the living room, watching television until the lambent reflection behind their eyes dimmed to black. Outside, the men posed together with muscles flexed, the dogs fell asleep on the deck, and the ladies magically remade the villa back into the nothing that had never happened. Twin beams of light curved around Jacaranda Hill until they didn't, and all was deafening peaceful and tranquil again. Our villa had been vitalized; our house had been warmed.

The next morning we found Sam and Millie lying on the deck, asleep with all three dogs. The Dawn Chorus was subdued, *mezzo piano*. Crayfish tails drooped over the kitchen taps. Colliding calcium clinking sounds of Ryan cleaning scallops landed in buckets off the deck. The grownups stumbled slowly towards the sound of the coffee grinder. We drove to the ninetly-foot Waianiwaniwa Waters of the Rainbow Falls on the Kerikeri River, in stands of young kauri and totara. Off the boardwalk at another reserve we held hands again around the trunk of a large rimu, under cartwheel tree fern fronds that rolled a rippling web across our sky.

We stopped to pick raspberries on the way home. Sam and Millie started with empty baskets, and ended with mouths of jam, and empty baskets, running through rows of olive trees. Back at the villa, Sam and I hiked the late afternoon down into the pungas at the bottom in our gumboots.

> 'Gumboots, they are wonderful, gumboots, they are swell
> 'coz they keep out the water, and they keep in the smell.
> And when you're sittin' round at home, you can always tell
> When one of the Trevs has taken off his gumboots.'

New Years Eve found large crayfish and long skewers of scallops on the barbeque, a study in orange and white. Carl lit the outdoor fireplace, and bubbly was poured all over the night sky on Jacaranda Hill. Shooting stars streaked through the stationary ones until, in the cosmic coalescence that is the Southern Sea firmament, you couldn't make out the difference. Robyn serenaded me with her ukulele and, at midnight, Graham kissed Rosie, Carl kissed Nikki, I kissed Robyn, and Sam and Millie ran circles around the hill, each other, and their innocent young lives.

'There is no place like home.'
Dorothy, *Wizard of Oz*

*　　*　　*

*　　*　　*

They left us in the New Year, and in the last of our dreamtime. The peace and tranquility grew deafening again. The grass hills grew fast and forlorn, the rows of olive trees grew bushy, the gorse grew in between, and the wind blew macrocarpa muck sap spatter onto the clean white paint of the villa.

Robyn drove us up the Karikari Peninsula, *so nice they named it twice*, for a wine tasting at the vineyard, and a beach walk through the white dunes. Character, human and otherwise, is formed in the stormy billows of the world. At the Gumstore Bar, an old pub in Totara North, across from the pointed rock in Whangaroa Harbour, we stumbled across both kinds. The atmosphere began beyond the disintegrating old brick barbeque and *Footrot Flats* lawn bowler weathervane over the entrance. Huge varnished crayfish and snapper and hāpuku and marlin and wild boar heads and harpoons and crosscut saws hung off the pine-paneled walls inside. Up-ended barrels served as tables, and *Export Gold* was served on tap at the hardwood bar. A Māori family played on a pool table with orange vellum.

But the true blue character of the place took his color from all the forms around him. An old codger with a long white beard wore a beaten baseball cap and a blue plaid shirt, almost as worn out as he was. The drink disappeared slowly, in a rhythm that guaranteed a steady state of inebriation. His nose had collapsed inward, possibly from the introspection, but there were other possibilities. Saddle nose is a condition caused by cocaine abuse, leprosy, vasculitis, syphilis, and trauma. My money was on all of them. I ordered us a beer.

"You know about the Boyd?" He asked. Great, I thought. He wants to talk. I assured him I hadn't.

"Right outside the door." He said. "In Whangaroa Harbour." Do tell. He did.

"In the southern spring of December 1809, a four hundred ton brigantine convict ship named the *Boyd* arrived from Australia, to pick up kauri spars. She was under the command of Captain John Thompson and carried about 70 people. One of the chief's sons, Te Ara, had asked to work his passage, but he was flogged for refusing an order. When the ship got back to Whangaroa, Te Ara reported his indignities, his whip marks, and his loss of *mana*. The tribe plotted an *utu* revenge. Three days after the Boyd's arrival, the Māori invited Captain Thompson to follow their canoes, to find suitable kauri trees. Thompson, his chief officer and three others followed the canoes to the entrance of the Kaeo River. When the boats were beyond the Boyd's sight the Māori attacked and killed all the pākehā with clubs and axes. Some stripped the western clothes donned them as disguise, while others carried the victim's bodies to their *pā* village to be eaten.

At dusk the impersonators manned the longboat, and slipped alongside the Boyd. Other Māori canoes waited for their signal. The first to die was the ship's officer who greeted them. The attackers crept around the deck, stealthily killing all the crew. Then the passengers were called to the deck and killed. Five people climbed up the mast among the rigging, where they witnessed the dismembering of their friends below. The Māoris were afraid to climb so high, and couldn't shoot straight enough to hit them.

The next morning the large canoe of Chief Te Pahi from the Bay of Islands entered the harbor, to trade with the Whangaroa Māori. The surviving Europeans in the rigging called out to him for help. Te Pahi collected them from the Boyd, and headed for shore. But two Whangaroa canoes pursued them and, as the survivors fled along the beach, Te

Pahi watched helplessly as all but one were caught and killed by the pursuers.

Five people were spared in the massacre: Ann Morley and her baby, in a cabin; apprentice Thomas Davis, hidden in the hold; two-year-old Betsy Broughton, taken by a local chief who put a feather in her hair and kept her; and the second mate, who was eventually killed and eaten, when his usefulness in making fish-hooks was exhausted.

The Whangaroa Māori towed the Boyd towards their village until it grounded on the mudflats. More interested in the large cache of muskets and gunpowder, they threw the flour, salt pork, and bottled wine overboard. But in their attempt to make the muskets functional, and having smashed the barrels of gunpowder around them, Chief Piopio, *so nice they named him twice*, sparked a massive explosion that killed him and nine other Māoris instantly. The fire that swept the ship ignited its cargo of whale oil, and left the Boyd a burnt-out hull, and *tapu* to the perpetrators. When news of the massacre reached the European settlements, the captain of the *City of Edinburgh*, Alexander Berry, rescued the four survivors, and held the two chiefs responsible for the massacre, until the ship's papers were returned. The piles of human bones he found on the shoreline had showed signs of being feasted upon. Seventy people had been killed and eaten, the highest number of Europeans killed by Māori in a single event, and one of the bloodiest instances of cannibalism on record.

News of the massacre reached Australia and Europe, delayed the first missionary visits to 'that cursed shore,' and caused the number of shipping visits to fall to 'almost nothing.' And there was one more twist to the story."

"What's that?" I asked.

"The ship's chest." He said. "It was made of blackwood, six feet long, three feet deep and four feet wide, with iron bands around it, iron clamped corners, and two ring bolts on either side and at each end. There was treasure."

"And?" I asked.

"It's still out there." He said. "It fell off a Māori canoe, in a mangrove swamp, up Pupuke way. Been looking for it all me life." His arm resumed the rhythm. Sweet fortunes grow sour, crushed between the bitter cannibals and the salty Southern Sea.

Robyn drove us back through nearby Kaeo. I noticed a sign for *Water Cress... Pork Bones*, and another for *Free air*.

The villa felt deserted.

Anna and Ian had invited us to Takou River Lodge for Harry's birthday party next morning. We drove the rolling green hills down Takou Bay Road, tumbling gently towards the wide placid stream, carving its way towards the crescent of beach that Shane had negotiated for us, when we first arrived. Anna met us at the door, beyond a bank of solar hot water tubes angled north, next to the driveway.

The party was well underway. Ian was dressed as a pirate, turning all the young children into his crew. He wasn't a total stranger to the trade, as a petroleum exploration engineer. Anna had been an environmental consultant.

"I made the mess, and she cleaned it up." He said. Between the two of them, they had racked up over forty years in the black gold badlands of Kazakhstan, Georgia, Algeria, Mozambique, Congo, Venezuela, and Papua New Guinea. The irony was that, after so many years in the oil patch, they had bolt-holed to a remote farmstead in the Far North of New Zealand, to build Magic Cottages off the national grid.

They were building a six-bedroom home with cedar weatherboard, a polished 4500 square foot floor of recycled matai from an Auckland community hall and squash court, and a ceiling and main staircase milled on the property from macrocarpa. The external decks would be eucalyptus, also milled on-site. Four 25,000-litre rainwater tanks would supply the house via a small ram-pump and grey water used for native tree irrigation. A huge bank of ten 175-watt photovoltaic panels would charge a 48-volt battery bank though an inverter, providing 220-volt power to the fluorescent ecolights and the motion-sensor system that would turn them off automatically when the kids left a room. They would have wool insulation, LED nightlights under the spiral staircase, dozens of Turkish, Azeri and Turkmen rugs, and an infinity pool disappearing into the distance outside the double-glazed windows. We wished them well and did likewise.

Out on the Purerua Peninsula, Robyn and I made a pilgrimage to one of the rare Southern Sea intersections of missionaries and mercenaries and misfits. In March of 1810, sailors from five whaling ships launched a revenge attack for what happened to the Boyd. Their target was Rangihoua Pā, belonging to Chief Te Pahi, the chief who tried to rescue the Boyd survivors, and then saw them killed. But the whalers had confused his name with that of Te Puhi, one of the Whangaroa architects of the massacre. Between 16 and 60 Māori and one sailor were killed in the assault. Te Pahi, wounded in the neck and chest, realized that he was targeted because of the actions of the Whangaroa Māori. He attacked them with his remaining warriors, and was killed by a spear thrust.

But adjacent to the Rangihoua Pā was the site of the real instrument of revenge for the Boyd. Through a reserve, Robyn and I hiked down through windblown golden tussock, along a beautiful river and waterfall. Hundreds of sheep ran in front of us along the ocean. Above the beach at Oihi, we found ourselves under an immense elaborate stone cross. It marked the landing place where the Reverend Samuel Marsden preached his first sermon to the 400 Māoris he had assembled on Christmas Day, 1814. Marsden was generally well thought of in New Zealand, having introduced Christianity to the heathens. He had come out to Australia by convict ship in 1794, and became the senior Anglican Minister of New South Wales a year later, at the age of thirty. By 1807, he owned three thousand acres of land and two years later, was credited with sending the first shipment of

Antipodean wool to England. Later he introduced sheep to New Zealand.

But in a church without saints, Marsden wasn't going to be the first. He used convicts as farm laborers on his estate. He took an appointment as a judge on the Bench of Magistrates at Parramatta, and became known as the 'Flogging Parson' because, even by the standards of his day, he inflicted severe punishments.

'The unfortunate man had his arms extended round a tree, his two wrists tied with cords, and his breast pressed closely to the tree, so that flinching from the blow was out of the question, for it was impossible for him to stir. Father Harold was ordered to put his hand against the tree by the hands of the prisoner, and two men were appointed to flog, namely, Richard Rice, a left-handed man, and John Johnson, the hangman from Sydney, who was right-handed They stood on each side of Fitzgerald; and I never saw two threshers in a barn move their flails with more regularity than these two man-killers did, unmoved by pity, and rather enjoying their horrid employment than otherwise. The very first blows made the blood spout out from Fitzgerald's shoulders; and I felt so disgusted and horrified, that I turned my face away from the cruel sight. ... I have witnessed many horrible scenes; but this was the most appalling sight I had ever seen. The day was windy, and I protest. that although I was at least fifteen yards to leeward, from the sufferers, the blood, skin, and flesh blew in my face as the executioners shook it off from their cats. Fitzgerald received his whole three hundred lashes...'

'The next prisoner who was tied up was Paddy Galvin, a young lad about twenty years of age; he was also sentenced to receive three hundred lashes. The first hundred were given on his shoulders, and he was cut to the bone between the shoulder-blades, which were both bare. The doctor then directed the next hundred to be inflicted lower down, which reduced his flesh to such a jelly that the doctor ordered him to have the remaining hundred on the calves of his legs. During the whole time Galvin never even whimpered or flinched, if, indeed, it had been possible for him to have done so. He was asked, "where the pikes were hid ?" Galvin answered, that he did not know, and that if he did he would not tell. "You may hang me," said he, "if you like; but shall have no music out of my mouth to others dance upon nothing." He was put the cart and sent to the hospital.'

Two days later Marsden sent orders to the hospital that 'Gavin is to be sent immediately to work at the cyane pepper mill.' In 1822, eight years after bringing the love of Jesus to the Māoris, Marsden was dismissed for exceeding his jurisdiction. The gift of Christianity may have avenged the cannibalized members of the Boyd, but Marsden's cleverness would be repaid by one of his new flock. We avenge intellect when we dupe a fool. Marsden brought a young Ngapuhi warrior back to Australia. Hongi Hika considered Marsden's creed as 'a religion fit only for slaves,' and when he was returned to the Bay of Islands, he brought a large number of flintlocks, and rampaged across a large area of the North Island during the Musket Wars. He traded the smoked heads of captured enemy warriors to Europeans, for more guns and ammunition.

Samuel Marsden further undistinguished himself by blocking a fellow missionary's attempt to publish a Māori grammar book, out of spite. He died in 1838, having 'succumbed to an incipient chill.'

For all his faults, in 1819, Marsden had introduced winegrowing to New Zealand, and planted over a hundred different varieties of vine in Kerikeri. The offerings that Robyn and I tasted, at Cottle Hill and the Fat Pig Vineyard, on our way home, would partially vindicate some of his other accomplishments.

The deafening days of peace and tranquility began to count themselves down. One was set aside for Rudi to drag us mercilessly through the stream and bush at the bottom of our farm, and back up the other side. He knew every footstep, and tormented us by racing through the gorse and slippery rocks, to pose with a victory cigarette at the top of the rise, as we emerged lacerated and breathless, from having fallen behind.

We escaped next morning in one last circle tiki tour, north to Kaitaia. Its name meant 'ample food,' but the portions at the tea and sandwich shop on the other side of the *Please remove your grubby footware* sign, didn't quite live up to its appellation, although they were selling watercress and hand-knitted magi dolls, and a side of mutton could be had for forty-nine dollars. Near the old BNZ bank building were the red bromeliads and red ironwork palms of the nursery, and a mural of five *kahawai* fish, blowing bubbles.

Three miles east of Kaikohe, and five north of Cocky's Corner Bar at the Ohaeawai Hotel Crossroads, were the wooden-sided mud-bottomed hot sulfurous pools of Ngawha Springs. Four dollars bought us ultimate basic rusticity, no showers, no frills. *All persons use pools at own risk.* Patrons had to bring their own towels but we didn't know this, and the owner graciously lent us two of hers.

The springs were the source of the steam used at the nearby geothermal power station. Shane drove to work at the Ngawha Prison next door, to make a difference for his people. The hot springs used to be an old mercury mine.

In 1974, a geologist at the University of Tasmania discovered that cinnabar, the compound mercury sulfide, was produced when the pH of the springs dropped below a certain level, oxidizing the elemental mercury in the pools. And that happened every time it rained.

The hot pools each had their own descriptive names, depending on their temperature and other physical and atmospheric properties- *Bull Dog, Baby, Tanemahuta, Doctor, Solomon, Favorite, Tekotahitanga, Waikato,* and *Tranquility.*

Like the White Villa Blues to come, mercury poisoning was slow and insidious, and would cause a plethora of symptoms and signs, including high blood pressure, sweating, weakness, mood swings, insomnia, and hearing loss.

As it began to rain, Robyn and I dug our toes into the mud bottom of *Tranquility.* The peace was deafening.

'And yet a man who could sit under the shade of his own vines with
his wife and the clusters hanging within their reach, in such a climate
as this and not feel the highest enjoyment is incapable of happiness
and does not know what the word means.'

James Busby, New Zealand's first winemaker 1850

*　　*　　*

'Climb to tranquility, finding it's real worth, conceiving the heavens
flourishing on earth.'

Moody Blues, *Higher and Higher*

We didn't really want to leave, but it was time. I had to get
back to work, and Robyn had to come with me. Renovations
to the villa would have to begin on the other side of the
Southern Sea, in the duvet-covered sleep of our cold dark
winter nights. I took photos of each of the empty rooms,
after returning Shane's furniture and Rudi's bed. I cleaned the
garage and locked in our kitchenware and tools. We invited
over people who we thought might be able to look after
important details, while we were away.

Marco arrived in his police car, to talk about mowing our
lawns. I handed him a beer.

"Won't do it for anything less than twenty dollars an hour."
He said. Police officers were clearly underpaid. Marco would
do the top, and Rudi would use his tractor to take care of the
steep slope.

Bev and Mike had put us onto an olive contractor named
Lloyd, but he wasn't exactly enthusiastic about the offer of
the fruit in exchange for a few bottles of oil and the
responsibility of pruning the trees.

"There are three kinds of olives." He said. "You can get green
ones, you can get black ones, or you can get stuffed." We
decided to let them go feral, for the few months we would be
away.

Country Villa for Rent 3 bedrooms 2 bathrooms 15 minutes north of Kerkeri. Yard Maintenance required. No pets. No smoking. $310 per week. Immediate occupancy available. 407 7084 evenings.

Our ad in the supermarket hadn't generated any phone calls, so we recruited a local real estate rental agent to find us tenants. Becky arrived with more than enough tattoos to not have a critical mass of local prospects.

Scroffie and Xena's heads hung lower between their paws, like they knew.

Meanwhile, Shane had begun behaving badly. It started with his stereo blaring CCR out over the ravine. *Someone told me long ago, There's a calm before the storm, I know, It's been coming for some time.* The prophetic parts went up to full volume. *I see the bad moon arising. I see trouble on the way. I see earthquakes and lightning. I see bad times today.*

He began cutting our hedges and trees, and occupying more of our land, for storage and parking, and turning his boat around. He built burn fires into bonfires, on our property. *Doo, doo, doo, looking out my back door.* Shane was moody, and reclusive, like he was punishing us for leaving.

"Is this some kind of Polynesian thing?" I asked Robyn. She shrugged.

He and Rudi didn't come over the day we left, but Mike and Selwyn did, and we drove twice around Jacaranda Hill, before leaving our circular drive, and innocence. No one tried to catch our spirits.

We made three stops on the way south from the Far North, before our flight back to the Real Far North. The first was to spend a night with Ian and Åsa in Kawakawa. We stopped briefly at the wavy lined irregular ceramic tile and colored glass, and interior live tree and sculptures of the Hundertwasser toilets on the main street, built by a thematically-challenged Austrian resident artist before he died, likely of embarrassment. A sunscreen machine dispensed a dollop of solar shielding for two bucks a pop, and a local butcher sold muttonbirds and 'cheerios,' little red sausages the color of mercurochrome. We met Ian in his office and fêted him and Åsa in a seaside restaurant until late.

Robyn and I drove across to the Coromandel Peninsula to Whitianga, to visit Uncle Bill and Aunt Shona, and cousins David and Lynn and Julie. Buffalo Beach was also a historical repository. Here was Māori explorer Kupe's tribal landing, Captain Cook's Transit of Mercury in 1769, and the destructive frenzy of logging and flax milling and gold mining and gum digging down thirteen feet, that had turned giant kauri forests into sand dunes and scrub and swamp. We took the family for a swim to Alan Hopping's hand-made tropical *Lost Spring* paradise. A former dairy farmer, in 1980 Alan bought a nine-acre camping ground and spent the next quarter century drilling for a lost thermal spring that had been rumored to have once flowed here. He found it almost half a mile down, and we found it rejuvenating.

One morning, David drove us north onto the Kuaotunu Peninsula, and the scenic coastline on the other side of Black Jack Hill. It was spectacular. He still remembers the look of wonderment in Robyn's eyes, and the dread in mine.

Back on Waiheke, we had another fish and chips and champagne reunion on the beach with Nikki and Carl and Sam and Millie, and a final night in the shack under the moonlight and cabbage trees, before boarding our Air New Zealand flight late next afternoon.

The message over the metal measuring rack, that promised carryon conformity on our way out, would also foreshadow far less favorable fortune on our way back in. Before we returned to New Zealand, the blues would descend over the Far North white villa, Shane would go over to an even darker side, Joanne would be exposed as a Black Tip shark, and Bas, the architect who had let us sleep in his scenic olive shed, and warned us about the gritty end of the country, would die of the inkiest Antipodean curse of all. Melanoma.

All the emotional baggage you want, as long as it fits here.

'We prepared to go ashore to publish for the first time in New Zealand the glad tidings of the gospel.'

Samuel Marsden

*   *   *

'Borrow trouble for yourself, if that's your nature, but don't lend it to your neighbours.'

Rudyard Kipling

A neighborhood is where, when you leave it, you get beaten up. But not usually by the one you left.

Back in Canada, the news from Takou Bay was intermittent, the signal weak. Becky had found tenants for the villa, a 'nice Māori family', who had turned the deck into an infinite clothesline, the yard maintenance into an intention, and Shane into a local chieftain. Bev and Mike, who had graciously offered to keep an eye on the place, began calling about bizarre incidents. Marco had mowed over the jacarandas.

The hard short winter days had started to seasonally affect Robyn, beyond what any artificial light could soften.

One particularly frosted evening I caught her again, on the Kiwi Real Estate pages. She had ticked off the 'Waterfront' box. My retirement plan jumped the clock forward another decade.

"Just looking." She said. "It doesn't hurt to look." But it would.

"You already have your deafening yesteryear peace and tranquility." I said.

"But it's not on the ocean." She said.

"But it's not far." I said.

573

"But I need a Māori chaperone to get there." She said. And I began to have misgivings, and they began to have puppies. Several nights later, a howl came off the desktop upstairs.

"Come look at this." She said. I went to look.

"Isn't this the same beach that David took us to?" She asked. It was. I looked at the listing price. It said 'Negotiation.'

"What does that mean?" Asked Robyn.

"It means we can't afford it." I said. But nothing can help the man with the wrong mental attitude, and I was destined to be either solvent and miserable, or destitute and happy.

"Ask them how much they want." I said. They wanted a lot. Negotiation goes better for those who care less. Destiny brought me destitution. The happiness would have to wait until we sold the villa.

And that was another problem. How would we find the courage to tell Bev and Mike, whose formidable years were spent creating the olive farm, that the people they had entrusted to 'take it to the next level' were selling out and leaving for the Coromandel? How would we explain our actions to the neighbors, to whom we expressed our eternal loyalty and dedication at the barbeque that we had not a few months earlier? What would Rudi and Greta think? How would Shane handle it?

Poorly. Poorly would be the right answer. There was trouble in paradise.

The tenants hadn't worked out well, and left with their rent in arrears, and their unwanted possessions in the garage. They left Becky without any purpose, and Shane without any boundaries. Which also left us without any boundaries, as he had chain-sawed the fronds off the Phoenix palms on the other side of our common driveway, uprooted an entire tree on our perimeter, and was producing enough smoke on a regular basis that we wouldn't have been able to see the property line if we had been there. Creedence Clearwater thundered across the valley.

I wrote him from France, in an attempt to placate the sound and fury. I enclosed a copy of his own Correction department's Code of Ethics. But he was fighting some serious spirits, and there was no way he was going to allow us to remain neutral non-combatants. We had to put up a barrier, to prevent further incursions. *Didn't expect to find any fences around here.*

No one would buy the villa under these circumstances, and Robyn and I worked our way through the local realty food chain, trying to find someone with an idea of how to sell the place. We drove up, in between Christmas on Easter Island, and the brief few New Years days we needed to check out our new place in the Coromandel.

Every beloved object is the center point of a paradise. The villa looked sad and abandoned, and it had been. On the veranda where Scroffie and Xena used to sleep was a dead possum. I felt awful. What had started as an Antipodean dream of olive oil and salt water had become a yesteryear of bitter tapenade and salt tears. The silence was deafening.

We spent a couple of days, pruning back the overgrowth and scrubbing back the decay. The sounds of moreporks and kiwis echoed through the empty house at night, and the California quail top knots quiver-waggled in the sunrise. *Cu-CA-cow, cu-CA-cow, cu-CA-cow.*

We drove twice around the stubble stumps of Jacaranda Hill, before driving away for what would be the last time. Robyn refused to look back, in empathy with Lot's wife, who had turned into a pillar of salt upon the sight of God descending down to rain destruction upon Sodom and Gomorrah. That was about right. The only cardinal sin was impatience. *Because of impatience we were driven out of Paradise; because of impatience we could never return.*

Back in the cold Canadian winter, the blues got progressively funkier, fading to black. Selwyn wrote to defend himself against accusations he had been pilfering olives from our trees. We told him not to worry. Bev and Mike came into hard times with the kebab business. The adjacent liquor storeowner had refused to let them have any parking. They sold up in Kaeo and moved back into the old villa, until they could find a place to live.

And Shane? Well, Shane dropped the bombshell he had been saving since the *Boyd* dropped anchor in Whangaroa Bay. It turned out that the 'common driveway' between the two properties, which Robyn and I thought was communally owned, had actually been sold to Shane on his bill of sale. But I had been sold a bill of goods. The entire time I had been pruning his hedges, he never let on they were on his property. He called in his chips, and locked out our access. Bev and Mike found themselves unable to get down the driveway to the villa, to the property adjacent to the one they had originally sold Shane. Robyn and I had to pay to put in a new approach, over a new culvert, raising a new question. Why didn't Joanne inform us about the fact that we didn't own any part of the road access to the villa? But Joanne had absconded to Australia, perhaps on a convict ship.

Sweet fortunes grow sour, crushed between the bitter cannibals and the salty Southern Sea.

*   *   *

'It is better to have your head in the clouds, and know where you are... than to breathe the clearer atmosphere below them, and think that you are in paradise.'

Henry David Thoreau

Robyn and I did finally sell the olive farm, or maybe we gave it away. The purchaser was an airline pilot, who got off his sailboat with his wife one day in Kerikeri, and the next day made us a 'take it or leave it' offer. That part of me, that didn't want to tell him to stick it where the Far North sun

576

didn't shine, accepted his offer. And the other part didn't feel all bad, and held out an olive branch. He would breathe the clearer atmosphere below the clouds soon enough. How thin the veil that lies between the pain of Hell and Heaven.

There is music now, in the air on the Coromandel coast, where Robyn and I finally found our Southern Sea paradise, and in the blind game we had played to discover it. We run down our beach to the sacred jumping off point at the large old pohutakawa tree. And when we launch, you can catch our spirit.

'The only paradise is paradise lost.'
Marcel Proust

*   *   *

*Cover ~ Special thanks to Claire Elliot for her beautiful painting.
(Sorry that David shot your pig.)*

*   *   *

Other Works by Lawrence Winkler

Westwood Lake Chronicles

Orion Cartwheels Quadrilogy
Orions Cartwheel
Between the Cartwheels
Hind Cartwheel
The Final Cartwheel

Wagon Days
Samurai Road
Stout Men

*   *   *